KU-195-537

THE ROUTLEDGE COMPANION
TO CHILDREN'S LITERATURE

Edited by
David Rudd

Routledge
Taylor & Francis Group

LONDON AND NEW YORK

First published 2010
by Routledge
2 Park Square, Milton Park, Abingdon, Oxon OX14 4RN

Simultaneously published in the USA and Canada
by Routledge
270 Madison Avenue, New York, NY 10016

Routledge is an imprint of the Taylor & Francis Group, an informa business

© 2010 David Rudd for selection and editorial matter; individual
contributors for their contributions

Typeset in Times New Roman by Book Now Ltd, London
Printed and bound in Great Britain by TJ International Ltd, Padstow, Cornwall

All rights reserved. No part of this book may be reprinted or reproduced or utilised in any
form or by any electronic, mechanical, or other means, now known or hereafter invented,
including photocopying and recording, or in any information storage or retrieval system,
without permission in writing from the publishers.

British Library Cataloguing in Publication Data
A catalogue record for this book is available from the British Library

Library of Congress Cataloging in Publication Data
The Routledge companion to children's literature / edited by David Rudd.
p. cm.
Includes bibliographical references and index.
1. Children's literature—History and criticism—Handbooks, manuals, etc.
2. Children—Books and reading—Handbooks, manuals etc.
I. Rudd, David, 1950—
PN1009.AIR68 2010
809'89282—dc22
2009045445

ISBN10: 0–415–47270–9 (hbk)
ISBN10: 0–415–47271–7 (pbk)
ISBN10: 0–203–88985–1 (ebk)

ISBN13: 978–0–415–47270–8 (hbk)
ISBN13: 978–0–415–47271–5 (pbk)
ISBN13: 978–0–203–88985–5 (ebk)

CONTENTS

v

CONTRIBUTORS

Part I – Chapter authors

Evelyn Arizpe is a lecturer at the Faculty of Education, University of Glasgow. She has published widely in the areas of literacy, reader response to picture-books and children's literature. She is co-author, with Morag Styles, of *Children Reading Pictures: Interpreting Visual Texts* (2003) and *Reading Lessons from the Eighteenth Century: Mothers, Children and Texts* (2006); and co-editor of *Acts of Reading: Teachers, Texts and Childhood* (2009).

Clare Bradford is Professor of Literary Studies at Deakin University, Melbourne, Australia. She has published six books and over 60 essays on children's literature, focusing on the interplay between children's texts and the cultural discourses which inform them. Her book *Reading Race* (2001) won the IRSCL Award and the ChLA Book Award, and her *Unsettling Narratives* (2007) was the ChLA Honor Book.

Karen Coats is Professor of English at Illinois State University. She is author of *Looking Glasses and Neverlands: Lacan, Desire, and Subjectivity in Children's Literature* (2004); and co-editor of *The Gothic in Children's Literature: Haunting the Borders* (2007) and *The Handbook of Research in Children's and Young Adult Literature* (2010).

Rachel Falconer is Professor of Modern and *Contemporary* Literature at the University of Sheffield, where she teaches crossover literature at undergraduate and MA level. Her book *The Crossover Novel: Contemporary Children's Fiction and Its Adult Readership* was published in 2009. She has also published more widely on a range of contemporary writers and theorists.

Victoria Flanagan is a lecturer in children's literature at Macquarie University in Sydney, Australia. Her research focuses on gender representation in children's literature and film, with a particular focus on transgressive and non-normative gender expression. Her first book, *Into the Closet: Cross-Dressing and the Gendered Body in Children's Literature and Film*, was published in 2007.

Mel Gibson, PhD, is a UK National Teaching Fellow and senior lecturer at the University of Northumbria, where her teaching, research and publishing focuses on visual literacies. She has explored texts, issues and audiences around comics, manga, anime, picture books and graphic novels since 1993, both in academic contexts and through supporting the work of libraries, schools and other organizations in understanding and promoting these media.

Roderick McGillis teaches in the English Department at the University of Calgary. Recent publications include *He Was Some Kind of a Man: Masculinities in the B Western* (2009) and the novel *Les pieds devant* (2007). He recently participated in the MLA radio programme *What's the Word* (Children's Poetry, 2009).

Margaret Mackey is a professor in the School of Library and Information Studies at the University of Alberta. Her most recent books are *Mapping Recreational Literacies* (2007) and a new edition of *Literacies across Media* (2007). She has published widely in the area of young people and their varied literacies and literatures.

Lucy Pearson recently completed a PhD at Newcastle University on the publishing of literature for children and teenagers in the 1960s and 1970s. Her research interests include publishing, new media and culture, and fandom studies.

Kimberley Reynolds is Professor of Children's Literature in the School of English Literature, Language and Linguistics at Newcastle University. She was President of the International Research Society for Children's Literature (2003–7). Recent publications include her monograph *Radical Children's Literature: Future Visions and Aesthetic Transformations in Juvenile Fiction* (2007) and the co-edited *Children's Literature Studies: A Handbook to Research* (forthcoming).

Abigail Rokison began her career as a professional actor, subsequently undertaking a PhD in the English Faculty at Cambridge University. She now lectures in English and Drama in the Education Faculty there. Her monograph *Shakespearean Verse Speaking* was published in 2009. She is currently Chair of the British Shakespeare Association.

David Rudd is Professor of Children's Literature at the University of Bolton, where he runs an MA on Children's Literature and Culture. He has published two monographs on children's literature, both mixing reader response with theory – *A Communication Studies Approach to Children's Literature* (1992) on Roald Dahl, and *Enid Blyton and the Mystery of Children's Literature* (2000) – and some 100 articles.

John Stephens is Emeritus Professor in English at Macquarie University, Sydney, Australia. He is author of *Language and Ideology in Children's Fiction*

(1992); co-author of *Retelling Stories, Framing Culture* (1998) and *New World Orders in Contemporary Children's Literature*; and editor of *Ways of Being Male*, besides authoring about 100 articles and two other books. He is a former IRSCL president and editor of *International Research in Children's Literature*. In 2007 he received the International Brothers Grimm Award.

Morag Styles is Reader in Children's Literature at Cambridge University and Fellow of Homerton College. She lectures internationally on children's literature, poetry, the history of reading and visual literacy. She is author of *From the Garden to the Street: An Introduction to 300 Years of Poetry for Children* (1998); co-author of *Children Reading Pictures: Interpreting Visual Texts* (2003); and *Reading Lessons from the Eighteenth Century: Mothers, Children and Texts* (2006); and co-editor of *Acts of Reading: Teachers, Texts and Childhood* (2009).

Part II – Names and terms

Anne-Marie Bird [AMB]

Clare Bradford [CB]

Karen Coats [KC]

Nolan Dalrymple [ND]

Victoria de Rijke [VdR]

Rachel Falconer [RF]

Victoria Flanagan [VF]

Peter Hunt [PH]

Andrea L. Immel [ALI]

Maria Lassén-Seger [MLS]

Roderick McGillis [RM]

Kate McInally [KMc]

Kerry Mallan [KM]

Karen Sands O'Connor [KSO]

Lucy Pearson [LP]

Pat Pinsent [PP]

Mavis Reimer [MR]

Kimberley Reynolds [KR]

David Rudd [DR]

Lisa Sainsbury [LS]

John Stephens [JS]

Lee Allen Talley [LAT]

Laureen Tedesco [LT]

ACKNOWLEDGEMENTS

There are many people who helped make this book possible. My especial thanks to David Avital at Routledge, who initiated the project, and to Katherine Ong (initially Aimee Foy), for her continual, meticulous support. Thanks, too, to the University of Bolton for supporting this project through their Research Investment Fund grants and to colleagues in the School of Arts Media and Education for their encouragement – especially Sam Johnson, for helping ensure my sanity – but library and IT staff, cleaners and caretakers also played their part, as have my BA and MA students, past and present. Children's Literature colleagues have been there from the outset, too, both in person and on the Rutgers and UK online discussion lists. It seems divisive to name some only, but Michael Joseph, Phil Nel and Lissa Paul deserve a name-check, as do my *Children's Literature in Education* buddies, Victoria de Rijke and Geoff Fox. Also, without the close support of Anne-Marie (Kathryn and Hannah, too) this book would never have come to fruition – I owe you so much. Obviously I am indebted too to all the contributors to this volume, for being so enthusiastic and responsive, but I'm going to single out Kim Reynolds and John Stephens, the latter for bailing me out so admirably on 'Names and terms'. Thanks, too, to the three anonymous readers and their helpful and supportive feedback. My family – Sheena, Duncan and Vanessa, and Sophie and Phil – have been inspirational, as ever.

All, however, will understand that this book must be dedicated to Erin Rudd: may you make the most of that childhood 'thing' and whatever it is that follows!

EDITOR'S INTRODUCTION

Children's Literature Studies has seen remarkable progress since the 1980s, when it was very much a minority interest. A lecturer in higher education might indulge his or her passion for *Little Women* in a course about women's writing, or slip Tolkien into a course on fantasy, but generally such occurrences were few, and they were certainly not labelled 'children's literature'. Other writers who escaped this labelling – Lewis Carroll, Mark Twain and Rudyard Kipling, for instance – did so precisely because, it was argued, they were not really children's writers.

In the past 20 years, this situation has changed dramatically. Children's Literature Studies has reinvented itself, in some places to the extent of casting off its literary moorings and 'going solo' as 'Childhood' or 'Child' Studies. Such courses extend their remit, not only to an examination of other children's artefacts (toys, films, TV, games), but even further afield, looking more widely at the child's position in the world, domestically, politically and economically. However, many of these courses seem to founder because they fail to consider what lies at the heart of their project: the child itself. This 'being' can be reduced to a psychological profile or even to its biological and anatomical features, but such depictions fail to capture the fact that children exist only within particular sociocultural contexts, and these might envisage children as innocent and god-like, or as innately evil, or simply as pint-sized adults. The artefacts produced for such children will vary accordingly. Moreover, children, in being part of this sociocultural world, will themselves manipulate and refashion it (its artefacts and language) – as collectors of children's lore and language have found.

This particular volume, however, keeps children's books central, although the wider issues raised above will surface where relevant. But it certainly does not see *the book* as exclusive; children's literature's links with other media are explored (Chapters 9 and 10), as are questions about the relative neglect of certain literary forms, such as poetry and drama, and of children's own cultural productions (Chapter 11). It should also be noted that this volume approaches the children's book from a literary and cultural studies perspective, so it omits many of the debates more central to those in education or librarianship (e.g. Thwaite, 1972; **Meek** *et al.*, 1977). Thus, there is little on literacy, or on how actual child **readers respond** to texts; or, indeed, on the publishing industry or the history of book production. In short, this book reflects the relocation of courses on children's literature predominantly within higher education departments of literature and cultural studies and addresses students in these areas accordingly, whether on undergraduate programmes or at Masters level. This said, much of its content will still be of interest to those studying children's literature in other contexts or those who are simply interested in knowing more about its current status and remit.

The book is organized to orient the newcomer to this increasingly complex field, though it has also been planned so that each chapter stands on its own, for anyone wishing to pursue a particular topic. It begins by tackling the big questions alluded to above: how have we come to be where we are in studying children's literature as a discipline? What, indeed, is the nature of 'the child' that writers try to address, and how has this addressee changed over time? This opening chapter then leads logically into the second, which considers the various theoretical approaches used to explore the texts of children's literature. As in other areas of literary studies, the student of children's books needs to become familiar with a range of ways of approaching texts. The notion that children's books somehow stand apart in this regard, being 'just for kids', clearly makes little sense when one examines the institutional infrastructure of publishing, bookselling and, indeed, at the adult authorship of the works being studied. As with other texts, those 'for children' are fashioned out of the same materials: from a language that we share, using a way of structuring narratives and using a set of characters that carry the traditional markers of gender, class, **ethnicity**, colour and (dis)ability. Children's books are, perhaps, more likely to emphasize age but, this aside, any theories that address the following issues will have relevance: those around the person (our status as embodied beings not only with ideas but also with emotional and psychological states), those around society (including considerations of gender, ethnicity, nationality and sociality) and those around the environment and our relationship to it. So, whether a book is about a young child coming to terms with his or her anger (Maurice Sendak's *Where the Wild Things Are*, 1963; Mo Willems' *Don't Let the Pigeon Drive the Bus*, 2003) or about an adolescent seeking to understand her or his sexual orientation (e.g. Sara Ryan's *Empress of the World*, 2001), the *Routledge Companion* provides the conceptual apparatus to articulate such concerns. Lastly, given that these various topics must be conveyed to readers either in words or pictures (or a mix), theories about **signification** – the process by which signs construct and represent meaning – will be central.

Such issues are unpacked over the rest of the book. Chapter 3 examines questions of gender and sexuality, and Chapter 4 considers issues of ethnicity and the way that, beneath this seemingly neutral term, a history of **colonialism** and race continues to have its effects. Chapter 5 more explicitly addresses how stories are put together and related and how we, as readers, are expected to respond from particular vantage points, thereby finding ourselves **ideologically** positioned. Leading on from this, Chapters 6 and 7 look at the two prevailing modes of telling stories: realistically or fantastically, though there are many degrees of variation between these two poles.

The remaining chapters concentrate on particular types of text. Chapter 8 examines young adult fiction and the **crossover** novel, which is often seen to blur the division between adult- and childhood. Comics and graphic novels also do this, somewhat contentiously, as explored in Chapter 9, which looks at these two forms alongside the picturebook, a form that has always been seen as more exclusively for children. (Unfortunately, there are no illustrations in this chapter. Although limited quoting of written text is permitted to the scholar, no such 'fair dealing' exists for pictures; consequently, unless artists control their own intellectual property and are willing to grant rights of reproduction – as the current British Children's Laureate, Anthony Browne, frequently does – the process becomes not only time-consuming but often prohibitively expensive.) In Chapter 10 we examine other types of media (plays and films) which regularly have crossover audiences, alongside more child-targeted forms (toys), and, finally, in Chapter 11, some neglected areas of children's literature are explored (poetry and drama, most obviously), which once again raise the question of why children's literature is the way it is. And this brings us back to where we started, making the point that the child reader is only one element in this complex field, and a historically variable element at that.

With this in mind, one can see how the *Companion* might have been organized very differently, with chapters structured around, for example, **genre** (science fiction, animal stories, **school stories** and so on) or period, or, indeed, around different theoretical approaches. However, each of these organizational principles was rejected for being too divisive and limiting. The approach taken here has allowed writers to range across time, genre and theory in order to make their points. And this approach has been facilitated by three other features of the *Routledge Companion*. First, there is the quite extensive 'Timeline' (Part III), which should help give readers a more chronological perspective on the area's development. Second, there is the 'Names and terms' section (Part II), which allows readers to pursue in more detail information about any particular critic, theorist or concept (it was decided to exclude children's authors from this section, unless they qualified as critics, too). These 120 or so mini essays go beyond the definitions of a standard dictionary to contextualize the use of a particular thinker or concept specifically within the field of children's literature, providing concrete examples. Some of the entries deal with established names and terms, but others are newer, pointing towards future directions in children's literature criticism; others, yet again, expand on areas that could not easily be encompassed within particular chapters (e.g. school stories). And third, both the chapter essays and the 'Names and terms' entries recommend further reading on subjects, with the essays giving brief annotations about each chosen title.

HOW TO USE THIS VOLUME

To help you get the most out of this book, all the key terms and names used in the book are picked out in bold type on their first appearance in any particular essay, or 'Names and terms' entry. So, if in your reading you come across a term that is new to you – the **abject**, say – the bold type should lead you to find an explanation of it in Part II, which is organized alphabetically. This applies not only to the actual term but also to its cognates; thus, the words **abjection** and **abjected** are also highlighted in this way. Moreover, when reading an explanation of the concept (the abject, in this case), you will find related words highlighted, helping you see how terms interlink and how they are connected to particular thinkers. In this case you would find that this term is Julia **Kristeva**'s, and you could then find out more about this particular thinker; however, you would also discover that the word **abjection** is often juxtaposed with **agency**, thus deepening your understanding of the concept and how it is deployed.

This linking is not just one way, either. As you read through the entries in Part II you will also find, at the end of most of them, an indication of which chapters deal most thoroughly with particular names and concepts. These links will, therefore, enable you to see the word used in context and should help you develop your own facility in using it. Finally, of course, each occurrence of a particular name or term is to be found in the index where, once again, bold type has been used to key you in to the explanatory entry on the word.

Part III, 'Timeline', should help you understand how the whole area of children's literature has developed in the West since the Middle Ages, giving the dates of key publications. Lastly, Part IV, 'Resources', provides a brief guide to the key journals, organizations and online discussion lists in the area.

Part I

ESSAYS ON CHILDREN'S LITERATURE

1

THE DEVELOPMENT OF
CHILDREN'S LITERATURE

DAVID RUDD

INTRODUCTION

'Before there could be children's books, there had to be children', wrote John Rowe **Townsend** (1990, p. 3) at the very beginning of what was, for many years, the standard popular history of English children's literature. It is a key statement, but one that also encodes the heart of the area's problems. 'Haven't there always been children?' is an obvious response. Townsend elaborates by saying that, while children there were, they weren't recognized in the same way, being seen rather as 'miniature men and women' (Townsend, 1990, p. 3). This, though, doesn't necessarily take the issue much further, for the next question is, how, then, did children come to be recognized? And the answer, of course, is that this could occur only by these miniature beings having increased representation in society's key discourses (e.g. church, education, family), through cultural forms like paintings and literary works, and in various non-discursive ways, too, such as by being given separate spaces (in schools, bedrooms, nurseries), distinctive clothing and other artefacts. With the Industrial Revolution and the growth of capitalism, the child would become a niche market with its own products, including books, illustrations, toys and games. But we then come to a decisive phrase in Townsend's work, one that separates him and other **humanists** from poststructuralist thinkers. He states that these specialized books were to serve the child's 'own particular needs and interests' (Townsend, 1990, p. 3), whereas later critics would ask, 'In what sense were these "needs" the child's own?' Surely it is predominantly *adult* depictions that we have of what children require and, not unsurprisingly, these have changed over time (from a need to be saved and instructed to being amused and educated). So, returning to Townsend's opening statement, we might now suggest that it could be reversed, to claim that children's texts helped produce the very beings that we now recognize as children (beings seen as innocent, natural, helpless, pure and so on).

This revision might seem to complicate considerations of the development of children's literature, but it is a necessary one if we are to avoid being seduced by tabloid notions of 'real' children (frequently white, middle-class, male constructions) and what they 'really' like. This chapter, then, is pluralist throughout: it will look at different versions of the development of children's literature, and of the various types of child that are thereby presupposed, and, in passing, at the different ways that criticism has been informed by conceptions of the child and its literature. This should prepare the reader for the next chapter, which looks more explicitly at various theoretical approaches to the subject, although later chapters will also show how theory has informed particular issues (e.g. in the case of gender studies: feminism).

HISTORIES OF CHILDREN'S LITERATURE

Townsend's standard history has already been mentioned, and the premise of its narrative questioned (children first, texts second). But, beyond this, we might note the whole narrative trajectory of his book, in which a 'proper' children's literature is seen to come to fruition in Victoria's reign with Lewis Carroll's *Alice*. Such a conceptualization can itself be traced back to Harvey **Darton**'s (1932) history, which sees in Carroll's *Alice* 'the coming to the surface, powerfully and permanently, the first unapologetic appearance in print, for readers who sorely needed it, of liberty of thought in children's books' (Darton, 1982, p. 260). There is a notion here of child readers finally being given what they genuinely 'need', which ever since ('permanently') has been recognized. This version of events, then, where the imagination is liberated from a dull instructional past, is a common one, often celebrated in the titles of works such as *From Primer to Pleasure in Reading* (Thwaite, 1972) and *From Instruction to Delight* (Demers, 2009).

But the above story itself has a history – *histoire*, of course, being the French word for 'story' – which more readily fits our **postmodern** suspicion of grand narratives and our preference for versions only. Thus, when we look more carefully at this shift from instruction to delight, we note that there has always existed more frivolous and bawdy material (such as *The Friar and the Boy* [*c.*1512] with its celebration of farting [Cunningham, 2006, p. 58], or nursery rhymes such as 'Piss a Bed / Piss a Bed / Barley Butt – / Your Bum Is So Heavy / You Can't Get Up', which appeared in *Tommy Thumb's Pretty Song Book* [1744; Delamar, 1987, p. 5]. However, not only is such work less likely to be seen as appropriate for the newly fashioned, middle-class child but, because of its coarser nature, it is also less likely to have survived, which is itself linked to the fact that much of this material – in line with jokes and anecdotes – is more frequently transmitted orally. Likewise, we might query later moments in this grand narrative, like the fact that, alongside the liberatory Carroll, others like Hesba Stratton (dubbed 'Ministering Angels' – Cutt, 1979) were writing works more centrally in the instructive vein. Even in our own century the publishing of morally uplifting, religiously informed children's books remains strong (e.g. the 11 million plus sales of the Christian 'Left Behind' series [see Jenkins and LaHaye, 1995] or, from the Islamic tradition, an equally vibrant range of texts [see Islamic Bookstore, 2009]).

Furthermore, there is a tendency to write these histories in a tidy past tense, as though we, in the present, somehow stand outside our own history. Maria **Nikolajeva**'s book *Children's Literature Comes of Age* (1996), which argues for the universality of this instruction-to-delight model of development, is indicative, her title itself suggesting a sense of arrival. Such a 'presentist' stance, though, can ride roughshod over historical differences. 'In one staple **metanarrative**,' as Mitzi **Myers** (1999b, p. 49) wittily puts it, 'the juvenile historian ransacks a vast body of writing for imperialist or racist quotes that earn the collective authors a critical spanking.' This is not to dispute that over the years we have gained far more knowledge about earlier children's literature, merely to be suspicious of the way that accounts of this material have themselves been narratively shaped.

The American literary movement known as **new historicism** tries to address this issue, seeking to situate texts within their context, while recognizing that what we call 'context' is, itself, just another set of texts. It thus works hard to avoid privileging any particular work (either for its 'literary' or 'historical' status), but it does so in the recognition that all writing is a form of power (what Michel **Foucault** [1980], termed the 'power–knowledge' coupling), so that there will always be *attempts* to privilege certain texts, to see them as superior, **canonical**, or whatever, while marginalizing **others** (like the scatological material, above); most famously, it is now recognized as commonplace that most history has been *his*-story rather than *hers*. Certainly, accounts of canonical Golden Age children's literature (e.g. Carpenter, 1985) follow this trend (for a more contentious canon, see **Nodelman**, 1985–9; Lundin, 2004). Cultural materialism, which is often coupled with new historicism as its British equivalent, should be mentioned in this light, for not only does it try to account for a particular text's form and reception but also seeks to show how it could have been otherwise. In short, however 'monologic', or authoritatively controlled, a text is, it always contains 'faultlines' exposing competing discourses (Sinfield, 1992; Brannigan, 1998). To take one, famous example, Heinrich Hoffmann's *Der Struwwelpeter* (1845) has been read as both outrageously **didactic** (a boy having his thumbs cut off because he will not stop sucking them) and as so excessive in its cautionary-ness as to be **parodic**, undermining the whole didactic tradition (Freeman, 1977; Metcalf, 1996).

A particularly rich example of new historicist criticism can be found in Mitzi Myers' work. She has pointed out the extent to which the narrative about the emergence of delight from instruction was predicated on the male, **Romantic** child as the norm, that is, on a child seen to stand outside society: an innocent, natural being. However, this norm was itself established only as a result of a struggle in which many of the female writers of the time were made figures of fun by the male establishment, with Charles Lamb famously dismissing them as 'that cursed Barbauld crew' (see Clarke, 1997). Thus, as Mitzi Myers (1992, p. 135) puts it, 'the Romantic lens we habitually look through is a culturally conditioned **ideology**, a tissue of assumptions, preferences, and perspectives, and not a transhistorical, universal body of truth about childhood'. She has undertaken some alternative readings of these female writers' work, and of Maria Edgeworth especially, in the process helping us rethink what the very terms childhood, Romanticism and didacticism mean.

Taking the latter term, for example, although I earlier alluded to the still thriving religious presses to illustrate the instructional side of children's literature,

I could as easily have turned to the work of Melvin Burgess. For despite his claim that a book like *Bloodtide* has 'no educational value of any sort whatsoever' (2004, p. 294), we surely learn from it that power corrupts, that there is a difference between male and female power, that blood is thicker than water and that the future is a dystopian place where women are still regarded as property. As Wayne C. Booth (1988, pp. 151–2) tersely expresses it, 'all narratives are "didactic"' – from high art to the low, tasteless joke.

This is to say little more than that we should read all texts carefully and closely, in order to note that the conceptual apparatus we use itself has a history, often arising out of conflicting interests, rather than having some transhistorical warrant. Thus, to designate a certain text 'didactic' and another 'subversive' carries certain consequences, each label throwing up different facets. Roald Dahl, for example, is regularly described in terms of the latter; however, he can also be seen as remarkably didactic in, for instance, his disapproval of television (Mike Teavee and the Wormwood parents) and of badly behaved children in general (e.g. all those in *Charlie and the Chocolate Factory* except Charlie himself). Theoretical approaches are no different, of course, in the way they either foreground or marginalize particular issues; it goes without saying (sometimes regrettably) that all histories of children's literature have their agendas. Thus, Robert Leeson (1985) and Andrew O'Malley (2003) – following Darton (1982) – are quite explicit in arguing that the development of children's literature is linked to an emergent middle class; Leeson's work uses a Marxist perspective, whereas O'Malley's is more Foucauldian. Even where critics abjure theory – as for instance Brian **Alderson** does, calling it 'floss' (1995, p. 17; see also Grenby, 2004) and setting it against his own bibliographical approach – theory abides, for example, in Alderson's case as a form of 'abstracted empiricism' (Mills, 1959). Moreover, as with Townsend, a liberal humanist conception of the child as pre-existing and relatively unchanging prevails.

New historicism certainly queries this idea, although it does not explicitly advocate any one theoretical alternative. As a result it is more tentative, recognizing that all readings are not only provisional and partial but also produce their own 'truth-effects'; that is, evidence seems to follow the adoption of a particular explanatory framework, or paradigm – as we saw above with the supposed move from instruction to delight (which is why, as noted earlier, knowledge is always linked to power for Foucault). Another example would be the way that the **fairy tale** is commonly seen to have been developed by Charles Perrault and the Brothers Grimm out of simple tales told by country folk – a history that effaces a rich written tradition to which many female contemporaries of Perrault also contributed (Harries, 2001).

In short, a healthy scepticism is essential when reading any study of children's literature. Why is it conceived the way it is? Why have some **genres** (like the fairy tale or the animal story) come to be seen as prototypically childish? Why does the study of children's literature tend to ignore non-fictional material? Why doesn't it include children's own literary productions? Why is certain material central to the discipline whereas other work is deemed peripheral, often hived off as the concern of others? Storytelling and nursery rhyme thus tend to be seen as the province of folklorists, psychologists and educationalists. Moreover, unless a novel is involved (*Peter Pan*, for instance), children's drama is rarely considered; this applies to children's comics too, whereas children's films have been readily accommodated, albeit with most alacrity when book adaptations are involved (see Chapters 9–11 for more detail).

There are no straightforward answers to these questions; it is simply the way the discipline has developed. It is, therefore, now seen as quite natural for departments of literature to run courses in children's literature, though this was laughable 50 years ago, when education and librarianship were regarded as more suitable homes. And, of course, each of these disciplines produced its own version of what the area's proper concerns should be, generating their particular truth effects. In librarianship, for example, an emphasis on historical, bibliographical work was clearly in order (Alderson, 1995), resulting in the label 'book' people; by contrast, with educationalists, tagged the 'child' people, a developmental approach was preferred, often linked to reading competence – although all remained committed '[t]o give each child the right book at the right time', as the pioneer American librarian Anne Carroll Moore put it (quoted in Lundin, 2004, p. 27). In this regard, the work of Jean **Piaget**, Erik Erikson and others found wide favour (see **Tucker**, 1981).

National histories of children's literature are perhaps the area where truth effects are most readily discernible, but where they are also most prone to challenge as a result of competing interests, often based on cultural differences. To take just one example, Canadian children's literature has the problem of the relationship between its English and French sides, let alone coming to terms with its Aboriginal pre-history, which has its own, distinct, oral tradition. Finally, such attempts to forge a discrete national literature have to contend with the pressure of foreign markets that increasingly want a more 'international' or 'homogeneous' product (Reimer, 2004, p. 1018; also Pouliot, 2004; on Ireland, see Keenan, 2007; and more generally, see **Meek**, 2001).

But in spite of national differences, in an age of increasing specialization children's literature has always prided itself on being more cosmopolitan, with many critics readily crossing national boundaries (e.g. Hürlimann, 1967; Nikolajeva, 1996). While this is commendable, there is always the worry that local differences are forsaken in attempts to generalize and, indeed, that different manifestations of the child are themselves lost in hazy terms like Paul Hazard's (1944, p. 147) 'universal republic of childhood'. In short, it is high time that this 'child' was more carefully considered.

THE CHILD IN CHILDREN'S LITERATURE

Although common sense would suggest that children needed to be recognized in their own right before there could be a literature specifically *for* them, it was suggested above that this 'right' never was children's own; indeed, the category 'child' has no intrinsic referent, only that which different societies have determined – and societies' notions have differed substantially: from seeing children as spawn of the devil to holy innocents, with equally huge differences in childhood's provenance. But though it is hard to dispute that childhood is a socially constructed state, there are still competing notions about what constructionism itself involves. There is not the space here for an in-depth analysis, so I shall simply point to some of the key theorists and some of the problems involved.

The starting point for most discussions is Philippe **Ariès**' seminal *Centuries of Childhood* (1960), which has itself generated a sub-industry of criticism (e.g. Archard, 1993; Cunningham, 1995; Gittins, 1998). Its most famous sentence, 'in medieval society the idea of childhood did not exist' (Ariès, 1973, p. 125), has subsequently proved to be overstated, although many are agreed that childhood was a far less separate sphere at this time. It was only with the emergence of the nuclear family and the development of schooling that a more modern conception of childhood emerged in the seventeenth century. Neil **Postman** (1982) developed a related thesis, linking childhood to the rise of print culture; this, he argues, resulted in children being forced into a position of inferiority to a 'master', until they had learned to decode the **symbolic** system of language. Children's books, of course, can be seen as complicit in this process.

Arising from the notion of childhood being socially constructed, Jacqueline **Rose** (1984, p. 1) provocatively argued that 'children's fiction . . . hangs on an impossibility', in that it is adults who write, publish and criticize it. Karín **Lesnik-Oberstein** (1994, pp. 158–9) took this argument one stage further, claiming that Rose's work not only 'closes down the field of children's fiction' but also, 'by implication, children's literature criticism'. What such apocalyptic pronouncements really showed, however, was just how tenacious a Romantic conception of the child was, such that, if forsaken, the whole field was seen to collapse when, in fact, it has expanded considerably with, ironically, further contributions from those predicting its demise (Lesnik-Oberstein, 2004). In retrospect, we can see these contributions as part of a widening interest in what is now known as 'Childhood Studies', and especially in the theoretical shift towards poststructuralist analyses (e.g. James and Prout, 1990; Kincaid, 1992; Steedman, 1995).

What some theorists also recognized was that if the child is socially constructed then it, too, must also be a construct*ive* being (Stainton Rogers and Stainton Rogers, 1992, p. 84). To claim this prerogative for adults only is already to have set these categories (adult/child) in place and to conceptualize the child as somehow standing outside society. So when Rose (1984, p. 2) claims that '[c]hildren's fiction sets up the child as an outsider to its own process, and then aims, unashamedly, to take the child *in*', one wants to ask what this child's prior 'own process' could possibly be. Clearly we are all beings that exist in language, outside of which some more 'genuine' being is hard to conceptualize.

However, as others have noted, although we can theorize the world through discourse only, this is not to deny that we are embodied beings located in a non-discursive reality (Soper, 1995; Burkitt, 1999; Hacking, 1999). Children's bodies, especially, being relatively smaller and weaker than adults', are particularly likely to have an influence on children's discursive positioning. Otherwise, as Allison James and Alan Prout (1990, p. 26) note, we have merely switched from biological reductionism to 'cultural determinism'. In short, children's literature is a cultural fact that requires attention from all parties: its producers, its audience, and interested others (critics, parents, educationalists, etc.). We are all products of culture (socially constructed), but we occupy different positions in terms of power – which, unsurprisingly, features centrally in what we call 'children's' literature.

THE CHILD'S BOOK

Attempts to define what a child is will no doubt continue, as will related attempts to characterize a children's book. There have been many attempts to deduce the latter from empirical studies of readers' opinions. However, although these should be taken seriously, they have limited provenance and, therefore, generalizability (for instance, what children of today like differs greatly from Victorian times, otherwise we'd have many more nineteenth-century books still in print); likewise, we need to be wary of adults' reflections on what they remember about their childhood reading. This said, neither approach should be summarily rejected, for each has its uses.

An alternative approach is to move away from the reader and try to discern what qualities the books themselves possess. Some of these latter studies look at form and style, for example, arguing that children's books are generally shorter (but then along comes Harry Potter book five, at 800-plus pages) or that they follow a common pattern: home–away–home (Nodelman and Reimer, 2003). Others have attended more to the style of narration. Barbara **Wall**, for example, takes the oral interaction of adult and child as her model. If we overheard someone speaking in an adjacent room, she claims, we would know whether or not it was a child being addressed from 'the kinds of information and explanations being given'; indeed, even without the words, she maintains, we could tell by 'adjustments in pitch and tone' (Wall, 1991, p. 3). Clearly, vocabulary and other matters are still involved, but Wall's emphasis is on 'the relationship of narrator to narratee' (p. 234), from which she discerns three possible forms of address.

The first two emerge developmentally, as adults gradually learn how to write for children without self-consciousness, that is, to use a 'single' address, avoiding asides to their peers. 'Double' address, in contrast, common in the nineteenth century, involves precisely this: talking over the children's heads. It is difficult to know why Wall thinks adults should have experienced initial embarrassment in addressing children, though, especially as it was not seen as a problem in oral communication or, indeed, in earlier didactic writings, like those of Edgeworth (1991, pp. 40, 42). But leaving aside these problems, by the twentieth century 'single' address had become the norm (children's literature had 'come of age' again), with writers able to focus exclusively on the child narratee. Apart from lauded practitioners like Arthur Ransome, Wall unusually defends writers like C. S. Lewis and Enid Blyton, often accused of 'talking down' to children. As

Wall puts it, adults 'must, in fact, write down', this being 'the essence of writing for children' (p. 15).

What is notable about Wall's model is that the child is a constant to which authors, over time, had to adapt; there is no notion of the child itself being constructed differently. Thus, before she begins her analysis, Wall already has a template of what the child is – and it is very much a Romantic creation, allowing her (in the standard manner) to reject early children's books as 'merely . . . vehicles of instruction' (1991, p. 42). Interestingly, such writers are also free of the self-consciousness she sees appearing later – as, too, are fairy and **folktale** writers. The latter have a dispensation for two reasons: because their tales are orally based and 'belonged originally to a wide popular audience' (p. 49). This is a strange move, however, allowing the *genre*, for once, to define the *child* (and liberate the teller). It is also strange that Wall brackets folktales within her final mode of address, 'dual', as they do not seem to fit her description of it elsewhere, in terms of a moral and aesthetic seriousness. With 'dual' address the child is no longer central, as a '[c]oncern for something other than purely children's interests dominates' (p. 35) – although this still has to be converted into 'language, concepts and tone' that are accessible to the child 'without loss of meaning, significance, or dignity' (p. 18). At this point, Wall's concept of the child seems most elastic and woolly, as, indeed, does her use of the term 'adult' ('adult' is bolstered by the qualifier 'educated', but 'child' is not [p. 15]). I leave readers to decide whether Wall's exemplary passage, from T. H. White's *Mistress Masham's Repose*, shows 'child and adult narratees' being addressed 'genuinely in the same voice':

> Now in spite of the homicides or other torts which she might have committed as a pirate, who was partial to the Plank, Maria was not the kind of person who bore malice for injuries, and she was certainly not the kind of kidnapper who habitually stole babies from their heartbroken mothers, for the mere cynical pleasure of hearing them scream.
>
> (Wall, 1991, p. 34)

Crossover fiction is a term that overlaps with 'dual' address, although it seems more open to a two-way exchange of influence, involving 'a **dialogic** mix of older and younger voices' (Myers and **Knoepflmacher**, p. vii). In other words, it does not legislate that the adult must do all the adjusting – as works that have crossed over in the opposite direction indicate (*Black Beauty*, for instance). This said, some critics, like Julia Eccleshare (2004, p. 213), are more critical, arguing that '"crossover" books run the risk of riding roughshod over the absolute essence of the children's book', such that we 'end up with no children's books that are aimed solely at children'. For her, then, a 'dual' audience is always a compromise rather than a triumph.

Peter **Hollindale** also considers children's books special, being one of the relatively few areas to explore 'the meaning and nature of childhood' imaginatively (1997, p. 12). He uses the neglected word **childness** for this quality, to avoid the derogatory connotations of 'childish'. While the former term might seem to free us from the biological baggage of words like 'childhood', in that it can involve adults too, Hollindale keeps its provenance relatively discrete: '"Childness" . . . is the quality of being a child' (p. 47), a child being defined almost redundantly as 'someone who believes on good grounds that his or her condition of childhood is not yet over' (p. 30), and these 'good grounds' are, let us be clear, biological rather than experiential (p. 10). Although, when he does flesh out a child's characteristic behaviours – 'dynamic, imaginative, experimental, interactive and unstable' (p. 4) – they turn out once again to be not only stereotypically Romantic but also gendered (his exemplary model is, notably, of a father and son playing). One might also want to ask why the above attributes do not apply equally to adults, perhaps especially to laddish 'men behaving badly'. However, Hollindale has already excluded adults on developmental grounds: the adult can share childness only retrospectively, 'as a participant observer' (p. 47). But adults, just like the early ethnographers (to sustain Hollindale's anthropological allusion), are not simply observers. Adults have already colonized this space, classifying and codifying its inhabitants accordingly (though never finally).

On the face of it Peter **Hunt**'s (1984a,b) **childist criticism** sounds more radical, presuming that the adult critic might divest himself (in Hunt's case, anyway) of all adult preconceptions in order to read as a child. Childhood is here seen as a conceptual state which one can recreate. But more cynically one might suggest that, rather than phenomenologically capturing childhood *per se*, one would simply be perpetuating adult preconceptions of that state. More than that, Hunt's model, in common with those discussed earlier, presumes that there is some essence of childhood that we can uncover, just as there is, in Eccleshare's previously quoted words, 'an absolute essence of the children's book'.

In contrast I have suggested that these notions are wrong on two counts. First, in presuming that children's literature 'came of age' in some definitive way, in other words suggesting that for much of its history it did not speak properly to the child. I would prefer to say that it spoke to the child differently – indeed to a child audience that was itself differently configured. This leads to the second, related point, which is to recognize the hugely powerful heritage of the Romantic child, such that even some social constructionists cannot envisage children's literature without it. But to try to generalize about such a variegated range of people under the label 'child' has always been doomed, especially when the resulting qualities are then set against those at the other end of this binary: adults. (It is always salutary to try replacing statements about the child with the word 'adult', to confirm the meaninglessness of such generalizations; thus, adults like . . . what? – gritty realism? romance? pornography?) Children are, of course, equally rich and varied in their tastes.

CONCLUSION

Bringing these elements together, then, I would suggest that any critics of children's literature who pin their case on some essential child are doomed.

11

I have stressed that childhood needs to be recognized as having been constructed differently at different times and for different groups within any particular period. At an even more local level there are the responses of individual readers, which can result in a book's status changing (e.g. *The Pilgrim's Progress*, or *Black Beauty*). As I have suggested elsewhere, any book that has a protagonist who is initially weaker – an underdog or victim – has more potential to be attractive to a younger audience (Rudd, 2004b). Central to all these transactions, of course, is language, which we all use but which no one controls. To paraphrase Mikhail **Bakhtin**, the **signs** one utters are half the recipient's, so a reader is likely to respond from a very different social location to an author. A society's discourses are, therefore, continually being redefined and contested, especially about what should be children's.

As for childhood itself, it came into prominence with print technology, since which time it has become more and more the focus of consumer interest. However, although these factors initially generated what was seen as the golden age of childhood (1850–1950, according to Postman), they have also contributed to the current crisis over childhood. Children are now targeted more directly by advertisers and the entertainment industry, such that there is often conflict with parental and educational authorities. Newer technologies have abetted this, allowing a child audience to bypass adult gatekeepers, especially through the Internet, and thus to question their very status as children (which is Postman's complaint, though it is premised in his theory). However, in the way that our postmodern world has generally thrown notions of a stable identity into doubt (our image can readily be changed), there has been more pressure to hold on to something solid and enduring – and childhood is regularly seen to provide such an anchor, if not an Eden (as Rose argued).

In short, the crisis over childhood – whether it is concerns over the child's disappearance and adultification, or the adult's infantilization and **kiddulthood** (or paedophilia, even) – is part of a wider shift in society in which the child has been scapegoated, with increasingly desperate attempts to turn back the clock via stricter controls, 'brat camps' and returns to old-fashioned schooling and values. Not surprisingly, this tension is reflected in the literature, and perhaps most obviously in the cross-generational phenomenon of 'Harry Potter'. Rowling's work not only harks back to the more carefree and traditional childhoods of Malory Towers **school stories**, of Jennings and Ramona, but also has a foot in the problem-novel genre (e.g. Judy Blume, Anne Fine and Morris Gleitzman) and the darker fantasies of writers like Neil Gaiman and Lemony Snicket. It is not that childhood is disappearing so much as shifting its purview, with a far more knowing version replacing the Romantic innocent (Higonnet, 1998). This is territory where many book critics are hesitant to venture, wishing to hold on to their islands of 'childness'. But this area, where pre-teens and 30-somethings often hang-out together unselfconsciously, is one we increasingly need to recognize, as those working in the related areas of film, comics and computer games have already realized.

FURTHER READING

Higonnet, Anne (1998) *Pictures of Innocence: The History and Crisis of Ideal Childhood*, London: Thames & Hudson.
Building on the work of Kincaid and others, Higonnet looks at visual representations of the child, to argue that the Romantic stereotype has much to answer for, creating a double-edged image of innocence. She persuasively argues for society's more healthy recognition of a 'knowing child'.

Nodelman, Perry (2008) *The Hidden Adult: Defining Children's Literature*, Baltimore, MA: Johns Hopkins University Press.
A weighty book that examines many of the issues raised in this chapter. He argues that children's literature is a genre; he not only accepts that the child is indeed a constructed being but also recognizes the child's constructive abilities.

O'Malley, Andrew (2003) *The Making of the Modern Child: Children's Literature and Childhood in the Late Eighteenth Century*, London: Routledge.
The author examines the shifts in representations of childhood in this period, with the middle class busy promulgating its ideology through everything from religious practices to book publication, assimilating older, and more fantastic, chapbook elements.

Rose, Jacqueline (1984) *The Case of Peter Pan, or the Impossibility of Children's Fiction*, Basingstoke: Macmillan.
Not an easy read, but one that remains central to debates about childhood and the status of children's fiction.

Wall, Barbara (1991) *The Narrator's Voice: The Dilemma of Children's Fiction*, Basingstoke: Macmillan.
One of the most thorough attempts to define children's books through their use of narrative voice. Though flawed, Wall's work provides excellent close readings of a wide range of children's texts, and makes us think carefully about how children are addressed.

2

'CRITICISM IS THE THEORY OF LITERATURE': THEORY IS THE CRITICISM OF LITERATURE

RODERICK MCGILLIS

> Criticism will always have two aspects, one turned toward the structure of literature and one turned toward the other cultural phenomena that form the social environment of literature.
>
> (Frye, 1973, p. 25)

We have reached a point from which we can look retrospectively on what I'll call theory's moment. A general consensus suggests that the period of intense foregrounding of theory in literary studies is behind us. We have books and articles with titles such as *What's Left of Theory?* (**Butler** *et al.*, 2000), *After Theory* (Eagleton, 2003), *Life.after.theory* (Payne and Schad, 2003), 'Looking Back at "Literary Theory"' (Rorty, 2006) and 'Theory Is Dead – Like a Zombie' (Boyd, 2006). Theory's moment was the last quarter of the twentieth century when no self-respecting academic in Humanities or Social Sciences could function without some knowledge of a range of theoretical voices, many of which came from France and Germany. This period of theory's ascendancy followed half a century and more of comfort with the study of literary works as the expression of the best that had been thought and written in our various countries. Our various countries usually meant England, the United States, France and Germany, and the best that had been thought and written rarely meant books written and marketed for children. The arrival of theory in a concentrated way was something of a fall from innocence. Theory asked that the academic study of literature be fully conscious, that critics understand and come to terms with the position they take when they begin to interpret literature. In other words, the fall from innocence was the realization that no critical or interpretive activity can take place without some prior assumptions concerning what criticism is or what focus an interpretive investigation ought to take.

Children's literature is not hermetically sealed from either other literature or from the field of cultural production generally. The possibilities for interpretation of this literature are as varied as they are for any literature. This is an important lesson because many books for the young are disarming in their ostensible simplicity. Theory has taught us that what appears simple does so because we have not looked closely enough at that simple thing. Theory involves looking over a subject. From this perspective the notion that we are 'after theory' means

14

not so much that theory's moment has passed than it means we are still chasing theory. It is possible to look back at theory, but it is not possible to look past it. If we are looking back at theory, then what's left of it? This question – what's left of theory? – cues the political agenda some see as theory's objective. In a political sense, theorists are often leftists. This notion derives as much from theory's rise from the activist era of the late 1960s and early 1970s as it does from any actual reality. It may be true that theory's turn to rights-related issues (feminist theory, Marxist theory, queer theory, ecological theory [or ecocriticism]) signals a left-of-centre ideology, but as we should expect, theory attracts voices from the full political spectrum. Children's literature is especially important here because of the ongoing debates over a literature (and a pedagogy) that subverts orthodox thinking or a literature that conserves traditional values and the status quo. Both types of criticism levelled at the 'Harry Potter' series, one that applauds the work's liberatory values and the other that chides the work for its deeply conservative ideology. Thus, whether the critics are left or right in their politics, the 'Harry Potter' series allows room for much to be left of theory.

The moment of high theory, however, appears to be behind us. The foregrounding of theory in literary discussions is a thing of the past. Is, then, theory dead? Or is it dead only like a zombie? Have we somehow come through this fall from innocence that theory initiated none the worse for wear? Can we return to the days of close reading? Can we just enjoy literature for its own sake? Can we get beyond formalism? Or is theory shambling after us with hunger in its eyes? Theory had the force of disruption; it did away with easy certainties and raised ambiguity above the 'seven types' William Empson identified way back in the 1930s. Theory also went with the times and moved us beyond the closed field of literary studies by leading us to see literary studies as a field within the larger field of cultural studies. Theory's moment, then, gave us a variety of ways of approaching texts, and an enlarged sense of the field in which we played. Sometimes the complexity and possibility for meaning that theory offered resulted in a perceived radical relativity in the interpretive process. Theory in its poststructuralist forms considered texts as open, not closed. The New Critical dictum that 'a poem should not mean but be' (MacLeish) means not just one thing, but many things, some of which are contradictory. Because language itself defers meaning while an interpreter traces possible meanings along a chain of **signifiers**, vainly seeking the one great **signified**, all linguistic constructs likewise defer meaning. Theory delighted in the game of elusive and endless possibility. Another effect of theory was the opening of the **canon** to include forgotten writers (many of them women), ignored **genres** (such as fantasy and science fiction), books from former colonial countries and popular formula fiction (such as the 'Goosebumps' or 'Animorphs' series). Children's literature benefited from this expansion of the canon. Indeed, the whole notion of a literary canon became of central interest to children's literature in the 1980s (**Nodelman**, 1985–9; **McGillis**, 2003b).

Then we faced an unsettling *fin de siècle* exceeded quickly by the traumas of 9/11, and theory retreated. Perhaps a better way of expressing what happened is to note that theory confronted its political implications. For quite some time, voices had spoken of theory's apparent leftist bias (e.g. Kimball, 1990; Lehman, 1991). Now theory hesitated and conservative voices found a firmer place among the speakers of high theory. Carl Schmitt, Charles Taylor and Leo Strauss, for instance, found renewed currency in the work of Alain Badiou, Slavoj Žižek and Giorgio Agamben. Paul Virilio (2003) is another thinker who asks us to reconsider the direction of a **postmodern** aesthetics. Large issues have come to the fore: fear, ethical dilemmas and the responsibilities of public and private life. Theory retreated, but it did not die. Theory continues to haunt us and call us to be spectators to large issues. The thing is we are now more apt to seek the security of clear meaning than the insecurity of manifold meaning. We are, perhaps, willing to acknowledge that the act of criticism cannot take place without the infrastructure of theory and that the practising of theory is itself a critical act. Theory is criticism, and, vice versa, criticism is theory.

The survey that follows is less a listing of various types of theory than it is a gathering of theoretical issues. Some theoretical approaches are discussed elsewhere in this volume, including feminism, **postcolonialism**, psychoanalytic criticism, narratology, **new historicism**, close reading and so on, which inevitably arise when we discuss certain texts or certain aspects of what we call children's literature. As theory developed through its various *isms* (Marxism, formalism, feminism, structuralism, poststructuralism, postcolonialism), it bumped against a few non-isms: psychoanalytic theory, disability theory and queer theory being the most prominent. These non-isms register the full complexity of theory by virtue of the tendency of theory to embrace all possibilities and all situations. Theory demands a willingness to consider the field in its full complexity and in its relationship to other fields. Psychoanalytic theory has always taken risk as part of its concern; it is risky business to embrace neuroses and psychoses as well as the stable mind. As for disability theory and queer theory, these by definition contemplate what is outside what the majority consider normalcy. In looking over a field, then, theory manifests both a concern for clarity and stability, for a preservation of traditional value, and also for a freedom from received wisdom. The theoretical mind is a creative mind. In a manner of speaking, theory is exploratory and adventurous, and, by virtue of its adventurousness, it is akin to the playful world we associate with childhood.

The question might be: does theory change when children's literature is in its gaze? Not in any essential way. The various theories mentioned in the previous paragraph might all apply to children's literature, although their focus will inevitably be on the theoretical implications of a literature that describes and, therefore, constructs children, and ultimately seeks an audience of children. For instance, queer theory takes a look at the way sexuality develops among young people, and it interrogates the manner in which heteronormativity gains acceptance over other forms of sexual expression. We might chart changing attitudes to various sexual identities in children's books published over the past two decades. Theory as it relates to children's literature is interested in how society situates children at any time in the past or present, what subjects engage children at any time in the past or present and how adults and children communicate through the literature meant for children. How does children's literature draw the child reader in, and just what is it that this literature sets out to deliver to the young? Not only do we want to understand what this literature teaches but also why it teaches what it teaches. Answers to such questions are both theoretical and practical.

I take the first part of my title and my epigraph from Northrop **Frye**. For Frye, the scholar does not and cannot think for him or herself; he or she cannot think randomly. Rather, the scholar 'can only expand an organic body of thought' (Frye, 1973, p. 24). In other words, the scholar or the student of literature participates in an ongoing public conversation regarding a body of documents we have come to call texts. This conversation cannot take place unless the participants in it have some idea of what it is they are talking about. For example, questions such as what is literature? Why do we read literature? How does literature relate to the other arts and to cultural production generally? Where does literature come from in terms of the creative imagination? How socially important is literature? How does literature reflect history? What is the difference, if any, between literary and non-literary language? What is the truth value of literature? How do texts mean? How do we read a poem or a novel or a short story? Answers to these questions depend on assumptions we have about language and literature, and these assumptions are either conscious or unconscious when we address others in the ongoing conversation that constitutes literature study in an academic context. When these assumptions are unconscious, we are most likely practising criticism in the sense of making statements and perhaps even judgements relating to specific texts or to a body of specific texts. When the assumptions are conscious, we are most likely engaging in theoretical discourse. Theoretical discourse is quite simply looking at a subject conscious of what we are doing and why we are doing it. We are conscious of looking at the subject from a specific vantage point, the stalls or the first balcony or the pit.

What I have just written implies that each of us has both a conscious and an **unconscious** area of our minds, an assumption that gained general acceptance in the twentieth century. Now, however, cognitive science questions this easy assumption. Whether we do or do not have the areas of the mind identified by **Freud** is not what is important here. What is important is that assumptions are always being re-approached and reconsidered by theory. What theory asks us to do is to be clear in stating our theoretical position in any critical activity we undertake and to exhume the implications of why we interpret the way we do. With respect to children's literature, the critic might well set out his or her assumptions regarding the child and the book. We can see such setting out in Karín **Lesnik-Oberstein**'s 'Introduction' to *Children's Literature: New Approaches*. She makes it clear that the intent of the chapters in this book is 'not to stabilize, to end, meaning' and not to affix the idea of the child or childhood to some imagined material reality (2004, p. 20). Ostensibly, at least, Lesnik-Oberstein adopts a postmodernist position towards children's literature. She is candid about her belief that the child and childhood are not essential; rather they are constructs.

This belief leads her to call for a reading of children's literature that sees it as autonomous; for her, children's literature speaks for and about itself. The 'new approaches', focusing on 'authors and authorship, . . . ideas of "history" . . . reading . . . the child, family, and "ideology" . . . and national identity', though, take me back to the similarly named **New Criticism** of the 1920s and 1930s. When she asserts that the chapters in *Children's Literature: New Approaches* will argue that the analysis of narrative 'in and of itself can contribute better to thinking through one's own actions and meanings' (pp. 19–20), she is in the theoretical territory of the *Scrutiny* group with its attention to close reading for purposes of strengthening the moral fibre of the close reader as well as those who read the close reader.

Theory is something of a prison house, but a minimum-security facility. It may seem intimidating at first, but we can find comforts there. We inhabit theory as we inhabit language. Just as language is our means of understanding the world and communicating this understanding for ourselves and for others, so theory is our means of understanding what things are and the way they work in the world – what literature is and the way it works in the world – for ourselves and others. To escape from theory is to escape from understanding, to retreat into muteness before the things we encounter. Whenever we resist the desire to retreat, we must look with eyes that gaze over a field before us. I use the word 'field' here in the way the French cultural critic Pierre **Bourdieu** uses it, as a particular placing of human action (Bourdieu, 1993; also Nodelman, 2008, pp. 117–27). The spatial metaphor suggests an area of activity, but, unlike a playing field or pitch, this field is not separate from other fields. For example, public education may constitute a field, but we can easily see that this field is not absolutely separate from other fields such as politics or economics or the arts. With theory as a field of activity, we can see that it cannot exist in isolation from other fields; theory requires another field to look at or to contemplate. Theory contemplates a subject outside theory and theorizes this subject. We can trace the idea of 'looking' through the etymology of theory: the Greek word for spectacle and spectator – hence the word 'theatre'. Theory is, in effect, an act of seeing. In this sense, theory sees its subject and takes it in the way a spectator takes in a performance. In the very conception of a 'theory' as a seeing, as spectatorship, we have the connection with criticism and its two aspects. The spectator inevitably interprets what he or she sees and attends to both the structure of the play and its cultural implications.

Applying Frye's 'two aspects' of criticism to literary theory, we can locate one way of looking at literature, of theorizing it, in a direct gaze, and another way of looking at it in an indirect gaze. Years ago, these two ways of looking at literature were dubbed intrinsic and extrinsic (Wellek and Warren, 1956). Simply put, we can say that direct or intrinsic ways of looking at literature, of theorizing it, focus as exclusively as possible on the literature itself. From this perspective literature is like nature, a body of organic material capable of sustaining close reading or close scrutiny. From the first quarter of the twentieth century through to the 1960s close scrutiny of literature was the most influential form of criticism. In fact, in 1932 the British journal *Scrutiny*, edited by F. R. Leavis, began publishing. This journal and Leavis-influenced criticism combined close reading with a sense of the moral function of literature. In North America, *The Kenyon Review*, edited by John Crowe Ransom, began publishing in 1939. The American brand of close reading, New Criticism (mentioned earlier), was less openly evaluative than its British counterpart. In the relatively brief history of children's literature as a serious object of study, we have a British Leavisite study by Fred Inglis (1981) and an American-style New Critical study by Rebecca Lukens (2006 [orig.*1976]). In other words, the study of children's literature reflects the study of mainstream or adult literature. Both Inglis and Lukens are clear on this. Literary theory concentrated on the work of literature as a self-contained object of both study and veneration; the poem or novel was a 'verbal icon' distinguished in its language by irony and ambiguity, the work being simultaneously concrete and universal (Wimsatt, 1970). A literary work was a beautiful object rich in significance and clear in meaning (Hirsch, 1967). Just as the criticism of children's literature reflected the methods of reading set out by the various practitioners of close reading, so too did it reflect the mainstream impetus to form a canon of great works, the best that had been thought and written in Anglo-American literature (Leavis and Brooks). In the 1980s, the Children's Literature Association in the United States similarly compiled a list of the great works of children's literature (Nodelman, 1985).

Yet even as the study of literature was concentrating on its subject as separate from other areas of study, even as literature was taken to be a distinct field, a separate discipline, the influence of other fields was apparent. The late nineteenth-century study of **myth** manifested itself in literary studies in the work of Sir James Frazer and Maud Bodkin and, later, Frye. A psychological variant of such criticism appears in the work of C. G. **Jung** and his followers. Psychoanalysis and its most famous practitioner, Freud, began to appear in the work of critics such as Lionel Trilling and Kenneth Burke. Even the close scrutiny of the parts of a literary text – plot, character, setting – foreshadowed a type of criticism that had its impetus in anthropology and linguistics, namely structuralism. As early as 1910, the Finnish folklorist Antti Aarne indexed motifs in **folktales**; Aarne's work was to be extended by the American Stith Thompson in 1928. Even more influential was *Morphology of the Folk Tale* (1928), by the Russian folklorist Vladimir **Propp**. His structuralist reading of folktales derives from the formalism of the time, but it also breaks with or deviates from the incipient 'new' criticism; Propp organized a taxonomy of the folktale by setting out the component parts of a body of stories. He began the process of describing the grammar of the folktale. As structural methods developed they often, but not always, took the form of binary oppositions such as old/young, east/west, sun/moon and country/city. Such a breakdown was easily applied to children's books where we have the binaries child/adult, experience/innocence, independent/dependent, capable/less capable and so on. A recent example of this kind of theory at work in the study of children's literature is Nodelman's *The Hidden Adult* (2008).

Another manifestation of structuralism appears in the study of narrative or narratology. The breakdown of narrative into various parts such as narrator/narratee, time and space, linear and non-linear plots and so on seeks to understand how narrative works as a language with its own grammar or conventions. The work of Mikhail **Bakhtin**, Gérard Genette, Mieke Bal, Gerald Prince and others established the groundwork, and children's literature scholars such as Barbara Wall, John **Stephens** and Maria **Nikolajeva** have applied narratology to children's books.

The advent of structuralism in the 1960s quickly produced a reaction in the form of what came to be known as poststructuralism and, in a more specifically literary variant, deconstruction, challenging the closed systems that structuralism sought to establish. Both the structuralists and the poststructuralists derived their methods from the work of the Swiss linguist Ferdinand de Saussure. On the one hand, his method of categorizing language into a set of binaries proved useful to later structuralists and semioticians interested in the system of signs that language gives us. On the other hand, Saussure's particular binary, signifier/signified, and the arbitrary nature of their connection that he posited, proved fertile to those who looked for a more open sense of textuality. Not only are signifier and signified arbitrarily connected, but they are also fluid in the sense that a particular signifier inevitably suggests more than one signified. We can trace a chain of signifieds leading from one signifier. What this did for interpreters of literature was to open up possibilities; texts became sites of endless and even contradictory meaning. Indeed, for poststructuralists, the word 'text' replaced 'work' precisely because of the idea of texture and its connection with weaving or folding. At the same time, 'text' came to signify other forms of cultural production such as film or graphic art, and Jacques **Derrida** went so far as to see text everywhere. He argues that a text is 'no longer a finished corpus of writing, some content enclosed in a book or its margins, but a differential network' (Derrida, 1979, p. 84). Instead of the unified work of the New Criticism, 'untying the text' (Young, 1981) became the name of the game. The term 'text' implied connections not only between one text and another – **intertextuality** – but also between one type of text and another, between books and films or between books and paintings and so on. Once the intricacies of intertextuality became apparent two other things followed. First, the connections between the production of texts, and the web of influences that texts can have, became clear. A recent example is the appearance of Charles Kingsley's nineteenth-century children's book, *The Water-Babies* (1863), in Margaret Atwood's study (2008), which explores the concept of debt in a theoretical manner. A study related more directly to children's literature is Juliet Dusinberre's *Alice to the Lighthouse* (1987). Children's literature as a type of literature now took its place in the web of connections within the literary system and within the larger system of textuality (see Shavit, 1986). Second, intertextuality draws attention to literature as a system of communication with ties to other systems of communication. Once we realize this, we begin to see that, like all communication systems, literature communicates for a reason. Communication is not some willy-nilly way of passing the time. Of course, children's literature has from its beginnings (wherever we locate these) been defined by its purpose: it sets out to instruct and delight. Theory brought a new dimension to the observation of children's literature's purpose, a new dimension perhaps best stated in Fredric **Jameson**'s *The Political Unconscious*, a book that presupposes that 'the political perspective' is 'the absolute horizon of all reading and all interpretation' (Jameson, 1981, p. 17).

The turn to the political dimensions of literature resulted in many studies of literature from a leftist perspective. Theorists such as Jameson and Eagleton, along with Louis Althusser, Pierre Macherey, Raymond Williams and Žižek, foreground Marx in their discussions. In children's literature, the work of Jack **Zipes** (1979, 1983) and Julia Mickenberg (2006) is cognizant of material reality and the dialectic of history. Much of the political interest in literature manifests itself in the study of ideology and the way ideology is transmitted from text to reader, as explored by Peter **Hollindale** (1988) and John Stephens (1992a) in children's literature studies. The political interests of literary theorists dovetail with postmodernism's challenge to essentialism, especially as it applies to definitions of identity and **subjectivity**. Jacqueline **Rose**'s *The Case of Peter Pan, or The Impossibility of Children's Fiction* (1984) is the most influential study of the construction of childhood. Rose has no truck with the essential child, polymorphously perverse or otherwise. The shaping of subjectivity partly accomplished by story is the subject of Karen Coats's *Looking Glasses and Neverlands* (2004), an intricate analysis of **Lacanian** theory put to the test of literature for young people.

The political impetus in theory has, then, prompted close attention to questions of subjectivity and identity rights. In turn, this close attention has manifested itself in certain other approaches: queer, disability, critical race and postcolonial theories. Critical race theory and postcolonial theory both concentrate on understanding **otherness**. Theorists who are interested in these perspectives go beyond traditional canons of literature to look for marginalized writers and texts that confront history and its lacunae. They focus on the excluded, those assumed to be not normal (Davis, 1995; Keith, 2001). In children's literature the works of Donnarae McCann, Katherine Capshaw Smith and Diane Johnson focus on matters of race. Postcolonialism easily turns to history, as a book such as Daphne Kutzer's *Empire's Children* (2000) illustrates. Current discussions of race and racism, **multiculturalism**, diasporic experience, globalization and aboriginality participate in the ongoing conversation about rights and identity, place and property, and history and memory (e.g. **Bradford**, 2001b, 2007a). Because of the sensitive issues raised in such conversations, considerations of trauma sometimes surface. Trauma derives from any number of sources, but one that has gained consistent recognition is the Holocaust (see Bosmajian, 1979; Kertzer, 2001). Much of the work I cover here is work of recovery, the recovery of texts long forgotten, or the recovery of voices previously silenced or ignored, or the surfacing of abuse. Because recovery's method involves delving into history, the re-exploring of history often forms part of the work of postcolonialism or critical race theory. We can see just how impure theoretical approaches more often than not are. Here we have new historical methods combined with a recovery of native or minority voices. Both new historicism and postcolonialism may share a political agenda with disability theory in that all three are concerned with the rights of individuals and groups, with 'righting' past failures or past injustices.

Postcolonialism takes an interest in the construction of otherness, and it may turn to psychoanalytic theories for clarification. Psychoanalysis has proven useful for theories having to do with identity and subjectivity. Feminist theory, gender theory, queer theory and disability theory all benefit from the work of Freud and his followers. These theories have proven useful to scholars of children's literature because of this literature's inevitable interest in questions of gender construction. Disability too comes in for consideration when the subject is identity and community. Just how are communities formed and who finds inclusion and exclusion? All these theories dealing with identity involve considerations of class and economics. In addition, **performance** theory comes into play precisely because of the performative nature of language as well as a person's adoption of social roles. Once we happen upon this notion of performance, we are also dealing with the existential question of whether we have an essence prior to being or whether we fashion being after finding ourselves in the here and now. The moral of this story is twofold: first, theory is well nigh unavoidable, and second, theory is seldom pure. When we discuss texts, we do so perhaps with a particular theoretical position in mind, but once we get going theory has a way of gathering in a range of conceptual positions. Perhaps Gilles **Deleuze** and Félix Guattari's (2004 [orig.*1980]) notion of the 'rhizome', a stem that radiates in several directions, captures theory's variety best. When we interpret, we bring into play a range of theories branching from a central theoretical assumption about literature or about the reader or the writer. A variant of 'rhizomatic' criticism is what the anthropologist Clifford Geertz, borrowing from Gilbert Ryle, termed 'thick description' (Geertz, 1973). Thick description of literature examines not only the work itself but also its contexts. New historicism is a method that attempts to place a work of literature in as complete a context as possible.

Much of what I am setting out here implicitly refers to the interpretation of a text, assuming the text is the central focus of the interpretive act. This placing of the text in the centre of critical activity is probably what happens more often than not. However, we do have theories that look elsewhere for their focus. Reader-oriented theories may either take a formalist direction and seek the ways a text implies a reader and the type of reader a text implies (**Iser**, 1978) or take a psychoanalytic direction and seek the ways various readers respond to texts and why (Holland, 1968). Reader-oriented studies related to children's literature notably include those by Louise Rosenblatt (1978) and Michael Steig (1989). Phenomenological readings will take into account the circle that encompasses both reader and text; such an approach will try to understand the reader in the text and the text in the reader. The appeal of such approaches to children's literature is obvious: children's literature by definition includes a specific (if amorphous and difficult to generalize about) readership. Because of this specific readership, some critics have attempted to locate a specific approach to this literature based on assumptions about readership, such as Peter **Hunt**'s **childist** method of reading children's literature. Hunt's model finds support in feminist readings, that is, readings of texts from a feminine or female perspective. The difficulty with this approach is the adult reader's questionable ability to enter a child's perspective with any degree of certainty. Finally, we have author-centred theory that can either look to an author's life for clues about his or her writing, or seek to question the very notion of 'author' (**Foucault**, 1977). Theory embraces all three components of a literary text: text itself, author and reader. And the theoretical process is enriched by the placing of each of these components in an exploratory field: new historicism, gender studies, class structure and so on.

In the wake of the range of theories that have political implications, we have seen in the recent past some new theoretical directions for the study of children's literature. Most prominent among these are eco-theory, cognitive theory and Darwinian theory. In children's literature criticism, the attention to our environment is clear, especially so because of the recurring interest in pastoral that children's literature takes. Some books for the young explicitly foreground environmental themes, and **ecocriticism** locates such themes in a range of texts (Dobrin and Kidd, 2004). As for cognitive theory, this turns up in the recent works of both Zipes (2006a) and Nodelman (2008). Both cognitive theory and Darwinian theory focus on the biological human-animal. Their interest is in what motivates human action and human relationships: procreation, the necessity of forming human communities for survival and the nurturing and educative relationship of child and parent, especially the mother. These approaches to literature offer a critique of psychoanalytic approaches that rest on unproven hypotheses such as the castration or **Oedipal complex**. Darwinian theory, taking its name from Charles Darwin and his theory of biological evolution, focuses on the development of character in social situations; it is interested particularly in a scientific approach to plot and character rather than the intuitive approach familiar to literary studies since the nineteenth century (see Carroll, 1995; Dutton, 2004). The central focus is on biology, the human animal reflecting the laws of nature. As Joseph Carroll (1999, p. 166) remarks,

> Among human beings, the sense of individual persons is the conscious correlative for the biological concept of the organism, and this concept is an essential precondition for the organization of behavior in goal-directed ways and for the interaction of individuals in social groups. In literary structures, the idea of an individual self is indispensable to the organization of literary meaning. Characters in poems, plays, and stories are individuals, and authors necessarily present their stories from some distinct point of view. All emotion and cognition is organized within the individual mind, and the response of audiences to literary works is thus necessarily lodged in individuals, even when the response is collectively experienced, as in the audience of a play. For these reasons, the study of individual psychology is integral both to the Darwinian conception of human beings and to literary analysis.

As these newer trends indicate, theory is not hard-edged; it changes and locates new areas to investigate. Theory is, essentially, a looking and a re-looking at a subject from a particular perspective.

Theories, then, are a dime a dozen and can be grouped in different ways – into those that focus only on the text (e.g. formalism, New Criticism, structuralism, deconstruction and so on) or as part of a larger historical and sociological context (e.g. new historicism, gender studies, Marxism, performance theory). We also have theories that focus only on the text or take a larger view depending on the theorists' interests (e.g. psychoanalysis, postcolonialism, phenomenology). Some theories have generated others; for example, postcolonialism has encouraged writers to consider theories of travel (Pratt, 1992) and psychoanalysis has prompted some to consider the theoretical implications of self-writing or autobiography (Berryman, 1999). Any of these theories is applicable to children's literature, although some have proven more fruitful (so far) than others. For example, a couple of decades on, both the New Criticism and archetypal/myth criticism are less in evidence than they once were, whereas theories dealing with gender, history, identity construction and formal features of textuality remain central, as do sociological approaches, with literature as commodity, literature as one aspect of cultural production, literature creating or encouraging consumerism (Steinberg and Kincheloe, 1998; Latham, 2002). Theory, then, informs critical practice, and much critical practice is pluralistic (Coats, 2001). The critic/theorist uses whatever is available from the rag-tag material he or she is able to beg, borrow or steal. The critic/theorist is a ragman who refuses in the end to close an ongoing conversation, both theoretical and practical, which constitutes the study of literature. Unlike the *bricoleur*, a person adept at fashioning something from a range of disparate materials (Lévi-Strauss, 1966), the ragman does not necessarily fashion anything from that which he collects; he recycles, hoping for profit. Ragman and *bricoleur*, collector, purveyor, inventor, the critic/theorist engages in ritualistic behaviour to fashion something new from something old. This ritualistic behaviour amounts to a sort of 'rigmarole'. Ultimately we are left with a mystery, and this is as it should be since mystery initiates exploration and discovery. I might use another metaphor, that of the *flâneur*, that wanderer of city streets who observes the outsides of buildings and people, who has glimpses of the insides, who speculates on what she sees, but who remains always removed and tentative, always attuned to the mystery of things. The nice thing about literature is that it remains silent, still, mysterious, queer. Only the critic and theorist talk, meander, uncover and domesticate. In short, the relationship between scholarship, theory and critical practice is inextricable, yet mysterious.

FURTHER READING

Barry, Peter (2009) *Beginning Theory: An Introduction to Literary and Critical Theory*, 3rd edn, Manchester: Manchester University Press.

A clear review of the main theoretical approaches to literature beginning with liberal **humanism** and then covering the challenges mounted by structuralism and poststructuralism.

Brewton, Vince (2006) 'Literary Theory', *The Internet Encyclopedia of Philosophy*, http://www.iep.utm.edu/l/literary.htm.
A readable and recent review of various approaches to literary theory from a philosophical perspective.

Culler, Jonathan (1997) *Literary Theory: A Very Short Introduction*, Oxford: Oxford University Press.
This book discusses issues and approaches rather than schools or specific methods. Its topics include rhetoric, identity, performance and cultural studies – all theoretical issues particularly important today.

Eagleton, Terry (1996) *Literary Theory: An Introduction*, 2nd edn, Oxford: Blackwell.
This book offers a useful account of the development of literary theory in the twentieth century, especially its ideological import.

Hunt, Peter (1991) *Criticism, Theory and Children's Literature*, Oxford: Blackwell.
Covers a range of theoretical topics such as the definition of children's literature, stylistics, narratology and ideology.

McGillis, Roderick (1996) *The Nimble Reader: Literary Theory and Children's Literature*, New York: Twayne.
A useful overview of theoretical approaches from formalism and New Criticism through to poststructuralism, whose relevance is demonstrated in relation to children's literature texts.

Nodelman, Perry and Reimer, Mavis (2003) *The Pleasures of Children's Literature*, 3rd edn, Boston and New York: Allyn and Bacon.
An unusual textbook that takes the reader through the variety of theoretical approaches to literature, always keeping a focus on the pleasures of critical reading.

Rudd, David (2004) 'Theorizing and Theories: The Conditions of Possibility of Children's Literature', in Peter Hunt (ed.) *International Companion Encyclopedia of Children's Literature*, 2nd edn, Vol. 1, London: Routledge, 29–43.
Argues that children's literature studies are 'messy and complex' precisely because of the 'constructed' and 'constructive' definitions of the child.

3

GENDER STUDIES

VICTORIA FLANAGAN

Gender, as distinct from the biological category of sex, is the social production and reproduction of male and female identities and behaviours. It is a cultural phenomenon rather than a biological one and is thus variable and highly relational (in the sense that each of the binarized genders is defined primarily by its relation to the **other**). The representation of gendered bodies and behaviours in literature produced for children and **adolescents** is an issue that is highly significant – not only because the literature itself so frequently addresses the subject but also because of the enculturating function generally ascribed to children's writing and the critical attention that this writing has received during the latter part of the twentieth century. The project of deconstructing **patriarchal** gender stereotypes and revealing the categories of gender as socially produced, rather than 'natural', is very much an ongoing one. Writers for children and adolescents have embraced feminist principles in their desire to promote feminine **agency** and interrogate normative constructs of gender and sexuality – a process that has also facilitated the representation of gay and lesbian **subjectivities** and other transgressive gender or sexual identities. This chapter will chart the way in which the major areas of contemporary gender studies – such as feminism, gay and lesbian studies, queer theory, transgender studies and masculinity studies – have influenced representations of gender in children's fiction and film.

Understanding the subtleties and implications of gender representations in children's texts, for the purposes of deconstructing patriarchal gender schemata and promoting harmonious gender relations, requires more than just an examination of the different roles performed by male and female characters. The concept of gender, argues John **Stephens**, 'is not simply an attribute of content or reflection of a cultural formation to be identified within texts. Rather, it exists in more complex ways' (1996, p. 17). Evidence of an **ideological** agenda that explicitly seeks to critique normative categories of gender does not automatically guarantee success. This is because there is 'a tendency for major **genre**s in children's literature to be endemically gendered in their character functions, events and outcomes' (Stephens, 1996, p. 17). The process of 'undoing' the textual construction of masculinity and femininity as inherently oppositional concepts requires more than simply altering the schemata of behavioural attributes typically associated with each category of gender. In many respects, this type of change – such as the alteration of character archetypes or story outcomes – maintains the ideological construction of femininity and masculinity as inherently oppositional, binary concepts.

FEMINISM

Feminism has had a substantial impact on children's literature since the 1970s, indicated by the broad range of children's texts that reflect a feminist agenda in their desire to expose the social structures through which patriarchal practices have sought to regulate women's bodies and behaviours. From retellings of popular **fairy tales** that redress the conventional marginalization and passivity of feminine characters by portraying active, self-determining heroines, to works of historical fiction for younger readers that re-imagine various historical periods from a feminine viewpoint, writing for children and adolescents has enjoyed, and continues to enjoy, a longstanding engagement with feminist ideals and agendas.

One of the most significant tasks that has been undertaken by feminist writers for children is the retelling or revision of traditional fairy tales. With their rigidly defined gender roles (which typically ensured the subordination of women and girls) and overtly socializing function, fairy tales offered an ideal space within which to contest patriarchal notions of gender and power. In the introduction to *Don't Bet on the Prince*, a collection of retellings by esteemed authors such as Margaret Atwood, Jane Yolen, Angela Carter and Tanith Lee, Jack **Zipes** (1986, p. 14) suggests that feminist revisions of traditional fairy tale texts 'emanate from a basic impulse for change within society'. The writers of these tales, according to Zipes, therefore 'share the same purpose of questioning socialization . . . and have been stimulated by feminist criticism to rethink both fairy tales as aesthetic compositions and the role they play in conditioning themselves and children' (p. 14). Common to the retellings featured in this anthology are heroines who are autonomous, assured and self-determining. These women challenge the passivity associated with female characters in conventional fairy tales, the equation of beauty with goodness, the limited and stereotypical representation of female roles (princess, evil stepmother or witch) and also, significantly, the paradigms of fairy tale closure which establish a young girl's happiness as wholly dependent upon her ability to secure a prince or husband.

The explicitly feminist agendas of the stories included in Zipes' collection are also evident in books produced for much younger readers. The work of Babette Cole is notable in this regard, particularly her picturebooks *Princess Smartypants* (1986) and *Prince Cinders* (1987), both of which revise archetypal fairy tale motifs and are symptomatic of the way in which alterations to character stereotypes and the rearrangement of narrative patterns – the most common changes made to original tales when they are retold – do not necessarily remedy the endemic gendering of such narratives. *Princess Smartypants*, for example, interrogates the conventional construction of young girls as potential brides in fairy tales with its opening declaration: 'Princess Smartypants did not want to get married. She enjoyed being a Ms.' The narrative employs a typical quest pattern: Smartypants sets her suitors a series of impossible tasks, which they of course fail. One suitor manages to succeed, but after receiving a 'magic kiss' from Smartypants, he is turned into a toad. He and the other suitors then decide that they no longer wish to marry Smartypants – and she lives happily ever after. The narrative is thus not particularly successful in interrogating gender roles (masculinity and femininity remain oppositional constructs). Although Princess Smartypants stays contentedly single, this is because she has positioned herself as 'unmarriageable'. *Prince Cinders*, a retelling of the Cinderella story, substitutes a male character for the subordinated protagonist and then proceeds to **parody** normative constructions of masculinity. Nevertheless, the story closes in a predictable manner with the marriage of the hero to his princess, thereby affirming romantic, heterosexual union as a desirable narrative outcome.

In addressing feminist concerns, children's literature tends to engage with second-wave feminism in the way that it seeks to amend or rework masculine and feminine stereotypes and roles. Roberta Seelinger **Trites**' (1997) survey of feminist children's literature encompasses a broad range of genres – from high fantasy to realism – which provide revisions to the traditional passivity of female characters in literature for children and adolescents. As with feminist fairy tale retellings, however, the endemic gendering of narrative discourse is no less difficult for feminist writers to redress when employing conventions associated with genres other than fairy tale. Gene Kemp's *The Turbulent Term of Tyke Tiler* (1977), Louis Sachar's *Marvin Redpost: Is He a Girl?* (1993) and Anne Fine's *Bill's New Frock* (1989), all junior school stories, are instructive examples of this. *The Turbulent Term of Tyke Tiler* ends with the surprise revelation that its protagonist (whose gender has not been properly identified until this point) is actually female. Kemp's story is hugely successful at revealing masculinity as a social construct: in the absence of specific direction and in the context of Tyke's behaviour and social relationships, readers simply assume that she is male. The narrative, therefore, foregrounds the way in which patriarchal ideology acts to erase feminine subjectivity but does little in the way of proposing more positive and fluid models of femininity and masculinity.

Louis Sachar's *Marvin Redpost: Is He a Girl?* and Anne Fine's *Bill's New Frock* similarly contain feminist themes but ultimately present femininity as an undesirable subject position. Each story revolves around the 'education' of a male protagonist who must learn more about femininity for the purpose of promoting intersubjective gender relations, and each text actively strives to construct a feminist subject position for its readers. Bill and Marvin, the eponymous heroes, temporarily occupy feminine subject positions due to a magical transformation. They experience what it means to be feminine at first hand, but the concept of femininity they are exposed to is inherently patriarchal in construction. For Bill, being a girl means having to occupy a subordinate and marginalized position within the classroom and schoolyard. For Marvin, feminine subjectivity is primarily equated with physical beauty and passivity. The thematic objective of each text is pro-feminist in the way that it encourages readers to think critically about gender, but the successful communication of this theme is compromised by a construction of femininity that is grounded in conventional stereotypes (Flanagan, 2007, p. 159). The story closure of each text, therefore, affirms masculinity as the preferable subject position (if only through each protagonist's relief at returning to it). *Marvin Redpost* and *Bill's New Frock* thus demonstrate that even an explicitly feminist ideological agenda can be compromised by the instantiation of patriarchal gender schemata which maintain the construction of masculinity and femininity as oppositional concepts.

Feminism has also had a profound influence on historical fiction written for children and adolescents, prompting many children's authors to re-imagine significant historical moments from a feminine perspective. *Lyddie* (1991) by Katherine Paterson; *Catherine, Called Birdy* (1994) by Karen Cushman; and *I, Coriander* (2004) by Sally Gardner are examples of this: told from the viewpoint of female protagonists (and often using strategies such as first-person narration to make femininity central), these novels explore the previously untold experiences of women in history. However, much of the resultant history available in this kind of historical fiction ends up distinctly 'ahistorical'. As Anne Scott McLeod puts it, such revisionism involves 'stepping around large slabs of known reality to tell pleasant but historically doubtful stories. Even highly respected authors snip away the less attractive pieces of the past to make their narratives meet current social and political preferences' (1998, p. 34). Female characters thus generally resist the patriarchal social and political discourses which construct them as repressed, passive subjects, despite such resistance being historically dubious.

Aside from second-wave feminism, *écriture féminine* has also had some impact on children's literature criticism. It is concerned with 'the inscription of the feminine body and female difference in language and text' (Showalter, 1986, p. 249) or, as Deborah Thacker (2001, p. 4) puts it, 'a feminine approach to discourse'. Stylistically, such discourse prioritizes feelings and experience, the use of non-linear narrative structures and unconventional syntax, with an emphasis on fluidity and ambiguity. Thacker contends that writers such as George MacDonald and Maurice Sendak exemplify *écriture féminine* in the way that they directly address the issue of power in the discourse of children's literature, challenging the hegemony of controlling ideologies. A particularly effective example can be found in *The Tricksters* (1986), by Margaret Mahy. The open structure, rhythm and self-reflexive nature of this novel are characteristic of *écriture féminine*, as is its theme – which focuses on the transformation of the protagonist's feminine subjectivity through the process of her own writing (see also Wilkie-Stibbs, 2002).

The significance of feminism in relation to modern children's literature (and also in the context of the criticism this literature generates) has been far-reaching in terms of the way that an incredibly diverse range of literature produced for children in the last half-century has actively sought to redress patriarchal discursive practices through the concept of 'equal opportunity' and the reassessment of masculine superiority – objectives which clearly coincide with the goals of second-wave feminism. More recently, however, writing for children has incipiently started to engage with third-wave feminism, which recognizes identity as plural (rejecting essentialist notions of feminine identity) and conceptualizes masculinity and femininity as relational, rather than oppositional. For example, *The Rose and the Beast* (2000), a collection of retold fairy tales by Francesca Lia Block, contains a version of 'Snow White' ('Snow') in which the heroine is lovingly raised by seven deformed brothers, each of whom teaches her to care for and respect the natural world. The story makes direct reference to eco-feminism in the way that it emphasizes the symbiotic interrelationship between human beings and nature, as well as promoting harmonious gender relations via the heroine's decision to forego a romantic union in favour of a peaceful, altruistic life with the brothers. Likewise, Robin McKinley's second novel-length retelling of 'Beauty and the Beast', *Rose Daughter* (1997), uses the characters of Beauty and her sisters to represent femininity as multiple and fluid.

Third-wave feminism's diversified agenda is also reflected in two emerging topics in current children's literature: posthumanism, a critical philosophy which examines how science and technology can affect the human condition, and body modification, the alteration of the human body through practices such as cosmetic surgery. There is an obvious intersection between posthuman ideology and contemporary feminist discourses, as each endeavours to destabilize conventional concepts of subjectivity. Children's texts which engage with posthuman and feminist themes in their representation of individual subjectivity include *Noah and Saskia* (2004), a television series co-produced in Australia and the United Kingdom; *Return of the Perfect Girls* (2001), by Marilyn Kaye; *Star Split* (2001), by Kathryn Lasky; and *ttyl* (i.e. Talk to You Later), by Lauren Myracle (2005).

The controversial topic of body modification, specifically as it relates to cultural constructions of beauty, has also been tentatively addressed in writing for adolescent readers. *Rhino* (1993), by Sheila Solomon Klass, is both unusual and ethically problematic in that it endorses the viability of cosmetic surgery for adolescent girls. *The Fold* (2008), by Korean-American author An Na, is told from the perspective of an Asian-American female protagonist and uses the issues surrounding cosmetic eye surgery to explore beauty myths. (*The Fold* is also noteworthy because it raises questions about the intersection of ethnicity and gender. Irini Savvides' *Sky Legs* [2003] and Matt Zurbo's *Idiot Pride* [1997] similarly explore the relationship between race and gender in the production of identity.) Interestingly, the issue of body modification is specifically connected to posthuman societies in Scott Westerfeld's 'Uglies' trilogy (*Uglies*, 2005; *Pretties*, 2005; and *Specials*, 2006), about a futuristic society in which all inhabitants undergo a surgical procedure at age 16 to erase physical difference and make them 'universally' attractive, and M. T. Anderson's *Feed* (2002), which envisions a future world where individuals have an Internet–television composite implanted directly into their brains.

Gay and Lesbian Studies

Gay and lesbian characters first started appearing in young adult (YA) fiction in the late 1960s and 1970s as a result of the social upheaval which characterized this historical period, in the form of the sexual revolution and gay liberation movement. Since then, the thematic exploration of homosexuality in literature for adolescent readers has undergone a series of radical changes – from early representations of gay and lesbian characters that warned of the dire social consequences of homosexuality to more recent and progressive novels which attribute subjective agency to gay and lesbian subjects, portraying homosexuality as just another aspect of individual identity. It is pertinent to point out at this juncture that there are probably more differences than similarities in fictional representations of gay and lesbian experience. Gay and lesbian subject positions are alike in that both are constructed out of a resistance to heterosexual discourse, but the histories of gay men and lesbians – and hence the discourses surrounding each group – are radically different.

John Donovan's groundbreaking *I'll Get There. It Better Be Worth the Trip* (1969); Isabel Holland's *The Man Without a Face* (1972); Larry Hulse's *Just the Right Amount of Wrong* (1982); and Ron Koertge's *The Arizona Kid* (1988) are generally recognized as some of the first examples of YA fiction to address the subject of gay identity. Many of these early novels set out to provide their readers with a compassionate depiction of gay characters, yet their constructions of homosexuality are problematic because they reinforce the 'otherness' of such subject positions: gay characters are the product of dysfunctional family environments (suggesting a link between environment and sexuality) and their transgressive sexual identities have dire social consequences, often resulting in exile or death. Further, Trites (2000) argues that gay sex is either invisible in most YA fiction or associated with physical pain rather than pleasure – another strategy used to marginalize gay identity and experience. *Dance on My Grave* (1982), by Aidan **Chambers**, ends with the death of one of its gay characters, but this novel is regarded as pioneering because of its sensitive depiction of gay identity and the way in which it challenges the emerging paradigm of gay representation by depicting homosexual sex as genuinely pleasurable. Subsequent novels about gay identity, such as Graeme Aitken's comic and poignant *50 Ways of Saying Fabulous* (1995) or Perry Moore's *Hero* (2007), a fantasy novel about a gay super hero, provide positive and agentic representations of gay subjectivity that redress this history of marginalization.

A similar pattern emerges in YA fiction featuring lesbian characters: the earliest YA novels to address lesbianism focus on the harsh social punishments that expressions of non-normative sexual identities can invite. Sandra Scoppetone's *Happy Endings Are All Alike* (1978) and Nancy Garden's *Annie on My Mind*

(1982) both depict happy lesbian romances, but they also warn readers of the negative consequences of being lesbian in societies hostile to homosexuality. *Happy Endings Are All Alike* is particularly extreme in this respect, as one of the female protagonists is brutally raped after being publicly outed as lesbian. Alternatively, some YA fiction attempts to 'normalize' lesbian identity by erasing its difference. M. E. Kerr's *Deliver Us from Evie* (1994) falls into this category, as does Jenny Pausacker's *What Are Ya?* (1987), which uses two female narrators: one heterosexual, and one lesbian.

YA fictions about gay or lesbian characters have tended to take the form of 'problem' novels, where homosexuality is always represented as the most important aspect of an individual's subjectivity. More recently, however, titles such as Block's *Baby Be-Bop* (1995), Sara Ryan's *Empress of the World* (2001), Alex Sanchez's *Rainbow Boys* (2001) and David Levithan's *Boy Meets Boy* (2003) have begun to examine the construction of an individual's subjectivity in a wider social context. These novels use **postmodern** narrative strategies such as multiple **focalizing** characters, parody, **metafiction** and **intertextuality** to represent lesbian and gay subjectivity as **dialogically** constructed by a variety of social and political discourses.

In addition to YA fiction, gay and lesbian characters have also appeared in a number of picturebooks since the early 1980s. Susanne Bösche's *Jenny Lives with Eric and Martin* (1983) – originally published in Denmark in 1981 – is generally considered to be the first English-language picturebook to address homosexuality. This work and others like it, such as Lesléa Newman's *Heather Has Two Mommies* (1989) and Michael Willhoite's *Daddy's Roommate* (1990), seek to validate gay and lesbian parenting. The verbal and visual texts of these picturebooks revolve around daily chores and activities, reinforcing the idea that gay and lesbian families are no different from heterosexual ones. *Mummy Never Told Me* (2003), by Babette Cole, takes a very different approach in that it addresses homosexuality indirectly. Told from the perspective of a young child, it comprises a list of things that 'mummy never told me', including why some women love women. Cole should be commended for innovatively introducing such concepts to very young children, but because lesbianism is included on a long list of mysterious or inexplicable phenomena, it still retains its cultural status as 'other'.

GENDER PERFORMATIVITY

The concept of gender **performativity** is most closely associated with the work of Judith **Butler** (1990a), who argues that rather than being natural or innate, gender is actually a series of stylized acts and behaviours that are repeated until they give the illusion of authenticity. The conceptualization of gender as a performance is particularly relevant to the long-established history of female-to-male cross-dressing in children's literature. Female cross-dressing appears in a range of genres, including retellings of the story of Joan of Arc (Nancy Garden's *Dove and Sword*, 1995; Michael Morpurgo's *Joan of Arc*, 1998); Disney films like

Mulan (1998) and a retelling of Shakespeare's *Twelfth Night* – Andy Fickman's *She's the Man* (2006); and fantasy fiction about girls who disguise themselves as men to escape repressive social environments (Tamora Pierce's *Alanna*, 1983; Terry Pratchett's *Monstrous Regiment*, 2003). Cross-dressing is used strategically to make the socially constructed nature of gender apparent. In other words, if the cross-dressed woman or girl can successfully imitate the behaviour and gestures that are deemed to be masculine, her performance demonstrates that gender, as argued by Butler (1990b, p. 270), is an 'identity tenuously constituted in time, instituted in an exterior space through a stylized repetition of acts'.

Contemporary YA fiction also reflects the influence of Butler's theory of gender performativity in the political construction of queer and transgender discourses. Unlike gay and lesbian studies, which generally emphasize the political importance of gay and lesbian identity, the concept of performativity problematizes the very notion of identity, making it an ideological precursor to queer theory and transgender discourse, both of which seek to disrupt and destabilize conventional modes of gender and sexual identity formation. YA novels such as *Touch Me* (2000) by James Moloney and *Sky Legs* (2003) by Irini Savvides feature cross-dressing characters who interrogate gender norms through their ability to give a convincing gender performance that disturbs the presumed sex–gender relationship.

QUEER THEORY

A product of both feminism and gay and lesbian studies, queer theory emerged in the 1990s and sought to expose the 'incoherencies in the allegedly stable relations between chromosomal sex, gender and sexual **desire**' (Jagose, 1996b). Queer theory questioned the very notion of previously stable categories of identity, such as man/woman or gay/straight, marking a fundamental shift towards more fluid concepts of sexuality and subjectivity. Eve Kosofsky **Sedgwick** (1985) is considered to have laid the groundwork for the development of queer theory as a discipline, describing 'queer' as 'the open mesh of possibilities, gaps, overlaps, dissonances and resonances, lapses and excesses of meaning when the constituent elements of anyone's gender, of anyone's sexuality are not made (or cannot be made) to **signify** monolithically' (Sedgwick, 1993, p. 8). Annamarie Jagose (1996a, p. 131) further emphasizes the ambiguity of queer, arguing that it resists classification; it 'is less an identity than a critique of identity', and is, therefore, always a category in a state of becoming. Although queer theory is often conflated with gay and lesbian studies, the three discourses are **ideologically** distinct in the way they relate gender to sexuality:

> Very broadly defined, gay studies examines sexual difference as it is applicable to the male gender, lesbian studies examines sexual difference as it is applicable to the female gender, while queer studies examines sexual difference as separate from gender altogether.
>
> (Kaczorowski, 2004, n.p.)

33

While the queer project is indeed radical, its influence is perceptible in representations of characters who refuse to conform to normative categories of gender and sexual identity. (Representations of queer subjectivity are rare in children's literature, generally being confined to YA fiction, as sexual desire is an integral aspect of queer theory.) *Funny Boy* (1994) by Shyam Selvadurai and *Boy Overboard* (1997) by Peter Wells are examples of YA fiction which represent queered subjectivities that are resistant to categorization. Both novels can also be classified as gay coming-of-age stories, but a **carnival**ized form of cross-dressing is used in each to destabilize binary concepts such as man/woman and gay/straight. In *Funny Boy*, the outraged reaction to seven-year-old Arjie's cross-dressing illuminates the rigid gender dualism of his society (Sri Lanka in the 1980s) and prompts him to question and ultimately reject the cultural and ideological values of his environment. He defiantly prioritizes desire, pleasure and sexual freedom – and his quest for subjective agency functions as a powerful critique of heteronormativity (Pennell and Stephens, 2002, p. 176). Jamie, the central character of *Boy Overboard*, occupies a similarly queer subject position. When cross-dressed as Cleopatra, Jamie experiences an intense feeling of pleasure, as well as perceiving himself as simultaneously masculine and feminine. In keeping with the queer project's critique of identity, both novels use such narrative strategies as a reflexive style of first-person narration, stream of consciousness prose and a fragmented narrative structure (which parallels the fragmentary nature of subjectivity) to subvert dominant, heterosexist assumptions about gender and sexuality.

Norma Klein's *My Life as a Body* (1987) is perhaps less successful in sustaining a queer representation of subjectivity but is nevertheless remarkable because it engages with a queer ideological framework despite its early publication date. The novel explores adolescent sexual desire through the depiction of a sexual relationship between its 17-year-old female narrator and a disabled boy. This relationship, combined with the inclusion of secondary gay and lesbian characters, serves to problematize sexual desire. The connection between queer theory and disability studies is an established one, as issues of embodiment and desire are central to both, premised as they are on the idea that the division of the world into the binary distinctions of heterosexual/homosexual (for queer theory) and able-bodied/disabled (for disability studies) is a division that is historical and contingent. Each, therefore, seeks to determine how power is attained and contested around that binary opposition. The representation of a sexual relationship involving a disabled body challenges heteronormative conceptions of masculinity, femininity and sexuality. However, despite an explicit ideological agenda that seeks to interrogate normative assumptions about sexuality and desire, the narrative closure of *My Life as a Body* implicitly reinscribes compulsory heterosexuality: the narrator ends her relationship with Sam, the disabled boy, and begins a new romance with an able-bodied man.

The subversive and destabilizing nature of queer theory makes it difficult to apply to much children's literature, for the simple reason that children's texts predominantly endorse a liberal **humanist** conception of the subject and, therefore, actively reject the queer project's critique of identity politics. However, an increasing amount of fiction for adolescents has begun to interrogate gender and sexual norms by offering representations of characters whose gender or sexual behaviour transgresses conventional categories of identity. Not all of these representations fall into the category of queer, but the way in which they challenge hegemonic assumptions about the relationship between gender and desire demonstrates an engagement with a queer agenda.

TRANSGENDER STUDIES

Transgender is an 'umbrella term that refers to all identities or practices that cross-over, cut across, move between, or otherwise queer socially constructed sex/gender boundaries' (Stryker, 2005, n.p.). Susan Stryker also emphasizes the political aspect of the term, arguing that

> perhaps the most significant aspect of the recent and rapid development of transgender is the role the term has played in giving voice to a wide range of people whose experiences and understandings of gender, embodiment, and sexuality previously had not entered into broader discussions and decision-making processes.
>
> (Stryker, 2005, n.p.)

It is pertinent to note that 'transgender' is a complex and often contested term and can be used for a range of overlapping groups, including transvestites, transsexuals, drag queens, drag kings, intersexed individuals and androgynes.

Transgender representations are not common in children's texts, but this is not to say that they do not occur at all. 'The Mouse, The Thing and The Wand' (Husain, 1995, pp. 117–44) is a Middle Eastern **folktale** that functions as a transsexual fantasy. Raised as a boy, despite her female biology, the central character falls in love with a princess. Outed on their wedding night as a woman, she is then set a series of impossible tasks designed to kill her. Upon completing them she encounters an ogress, who casts a spell and turns her female body into a male one. Rahat thus acquires the only thing missing from her otherwise perfect performance of masculine identity: a phallus. The obvious problem with such a conclusion, however, is that it reinscribes the causal relationship between sex and gender.

Transgendered characters are more plentiful in YA fiction, although the representational strategies currently being used to explore transgender subjectivity still act to marginalize transgender experience – or at least avoid addressing the destabilizing and disruptive potential of the child or adolescent cross-dresser. Nevertheless, representations of transgender subjectivity are an emerging trend in children's literature and film, constituting an area which should be watched closely in the future. Two recent examples include *Luna* (2004), a much-awarded novel by Julie Ann Peters, and *Debbie Harry Sings in French* (2008), by Meagan Brothers. *Luna* is about an adolescent male-to-female transsexual, Liam/Luna, who wishes to live and be accepted as a woman. The story is focalized by Luna's sister, thus suggesting that transgender subjectivity is mediated through a heteronormative perspective. *Debbie Harry Sings in French* focuses on transvestite identity in its tale of Johnny and his obsession with Debbie Harry. Johnny's candid, first-person narration is a sensitive portrayal of his struggle to come to terms with his desire to wear women's clothing. (The narrative's interrogative and queer potential is somewhat compromised by Johnny's constant denial that he is gay and by his heterosexual romance with Maria, which strategically undercuts the blurring of identity categories.)

Contemporary cinema has been particularly successful at providing viewers with compassionate representations of child/adolescent transgender subjectivity and a disquieting picture of the manner in which heterosexual ideology can discriminate against and repress such individuals. *Ma vie en rose* (1997), *Boys Don't Cry* (1999) and *XXY* (2007), the story of a 15-year-old intersex character, all portray transgendered subjects struggling for social acceptance.

MASCULINITY STUDIES

While there have been periodical explorations of masculinity in studies of childhood (as with the concept of **boyology**), the application of gender studies to children's texts has focused predominantly on issues of female representation until recently, when John Stephens' (2002b) groundbreaking collection of criticism, *Ways of Being Male*, examined how patriarchal culture regulates male bodies and behaviour. The work draws extensively on the concept of '**hegemonic masculinity**' made popular by sociologist R. W. Connell, who argues that it 'can be defined as the configuration of gender practice which embodies the currently accepted answer to the problem of the legitimacy of patriarchy, which guarantees (or is taken to guarantee) the dominant position of men and the subordination of women' (1995, p. 77).

Children's literature and film that take issue with patriarchal discourses of masculinity generally do so by depicting 'new' masculinities emerging in opposition to hegemonic masculinity. These narratives recuperate subjective agency for characters who fail to conform to the prescriptive requirements of hegemonic masculinity, which stipulates that boys and men should look and behave in certain ways. Picturebooks such as Anthony Browne's *Willy the Wimp* (1984) and Babette Cole's aforementioned *Prince Cinders* (1987) focus on the male body, replacing the heroic, muscular physique with bodies represented as small and weak. Libby Gleeson's *Where's Mum?* (1992) offers its readers a portrayal of sensitive and domesticated masculinity, while the very humorous and ironically titled *Tough Boris* (Mem Fox, 1994) cleverly disrupts the schematic construction of male pirates as 'tough' by adding new (and traditionally feminine) values to the schema, such as the ability to express emotion openly (which Boris does when he cries for his dead parrot).

Masculine subject formation has similarly become a visible theme in contemporary YA fiction. Narratives which thematize masculinity often do so by instantiating what Stephens calls a 'sensitive new man schema'. This alternative model challenges the values schematically associated with hegemonic masculinity: the 'sensitive' boy characteristically

> reads for pleasure and may aspire to become a writer himself, and this endows him with a mastery over discourse which is germane to subjective agency; his relationships with his peers are other-regarding . . . he tends to lack physical prowess and physical courage, though his moral courage and other-regardingness will prompt him to act courageously.
>
> (Stephens, 2002b, p. 44)

Tim Wynne-Jones' *The Maestro* (1995) is an instructive example of this sensitive new man schema; it is a YA novel about a young man trying to define himself in relation to his abusive father and the reclusive, mysterious composer he befriends while hiding in the woods. The narrative makes intertextual references to Hitchcock films, Andrew Lang's *The Red Fairy Book* (1890) and the Bible, suggesting that masculinity (and individual subjectivity) is constructed in dialogue with multiple cultural discourses. The construction of masculinity as dialogical is also relevant to Australian YA novels such as *Deadly, Unna?* by Philip Gwynne (filmed as *Australian Rules*, Paul Goldman, 2002) and *Idiot Pride* by Matt Zurbo, both of which examine the intersection of race and gender in the development of adolescent subjectivity.

The sensitive new man schema has also been embraced by contemporary teen films. The incredibly successful and quietly subversive *American Pie* (2000), and, more recently, *Superbad* (2007), offer representations of masculinity which are unexpectedly rich in the way they interrogate hegemonic masculine paradigms and offer alternative forms of subjective development for young male characters.

CONCLUSION

Gender is one of the issues most frequently addressed in children's texts. Over the past quarter of a century, many changes have occurred in the way that children's literature and culture address the subject of gender. The application of gender studies to children's texts, however, is still very much a work in progress. While significant inroads have been made, particularly in relation to feminism and the representation of female bodies and behaviours, there is still much to be done in order to achieve and promote harmonious gender relations. If we are to encourage children to see masculinity and femininity not as inherently binaristic and oppositional, but as relational and fluid, then writers, readers and critics need to be aware of how particular genres are gendered, of how narrative discourse can be used to privilege particular models of gender and how texts endorse or interrogate dominant cultural constructions of gender.

FURTHER READING

Clark, Beverly, Lyon and Higonnet, Margaret R. (1999) *Girls, Boys, Books, Toys: Gender in Children's Literature and Culture*, Baltimore, MD: Johns Hopkins University Press.
A selection of critical essays that explore the extent to which children's culture engages with feminist theory, ranging from discussions of traditional fairy tales and dollhouse literature to the gendered representation of dinosaurs and the construction of feminist reading positions. See, especially, essays by Kuznets, Stephens and McCallum, and Meyers. Interestingly, all but one of the essays in this collection associate 'gender' with women and girls.

Stephens, John (ed.) (2002b) *Ways of Being Male: Representing Masculinities in Children's Literature and Film*, New York: Routledge.
One of the first collections of children's literary criticism to address the topic of masculinity. The essays featured in this book discuss the various ways in which patriarchal ideology affects the representation of male bodies and masculine behaviour in books and films produced for younger readers. See, especially, chapters by Pennell, McCallum, and Stephens and Romøren.

Trites, Roberta Seelinger (1997) *Waking Sleeping Beauty: Feminist Voices in Children's Novels*, Iowa City: University of Iowa Press.
This book constructs an accessible and engaging argument about the impact of feminism on children's literature (focusing on texts produced from the late 1960s to the early 1990s), as well as explaining how feminist theory can be used to better understand these texts. Of particular note is Chapter 4, in which Trites discusses the literary strategies used to redress the cultural silencing of women and enable female characters to reclaim their voices.

Wilkie-Stibbs, Christine (2002) *The Feminine Subject in Children's Literature*, New York: Routledge.
Applying the psychoanalytic theories of écriture féminine writers such as Cixous, Irigaray and **Kristeva** to a selection of texts by authors Margaret Mahy and Gillian Cross, Wilkie-Stibbs constructs a persuasive argument about the role of language in the production of subjectivity. This book provides a useful discussion of the ways in which feminist psychoanalytic theory can be used to examine gender constructions in children's literature.

4

RACE, ETHNICITY AND COLONIALISM

CLARE BRADFORD

INTRODUCTION

Just as the development of publishing for children in Europe coincided with the heyday of European imperialism, so contemporary English-language children's literature is produced in nations marked by their histories as imperial powers or former colonies. Moreover, the political instabilities of the post-Cold War period have given rise to mass migrations of refugee populations fleeing conflict, poverty and oppression. Given that children's texts both reflect and promote cultural values and practices, it is inevitable that they disclose conceptions of and attitudes to race, **ethnicity**, **colonialism** and **postcolonialism**, responding to the discourses and practices of the societies where they are produced.

It is not, however, the case that when colonial regimes come to an end, or when ethnic conflicts are resolved, children's texts are necessarily free of the **ideological** freight of those earlier times. Roald Dahl's representation of the Oompa-Loompas in *Charlie and the Chocolate Factory* (1964), for instance, accords with colonial discourses informed by oppositions between civilized and savage. Whereas Willy Wonka is knowing, resourceful and powerful, the Oompa-Loompas are childlike and dependent, relying on Willy Wonka's benevolence when they are transported from their homeland to work for cacao beans in his chocolate factory (Bradford, 2001a). At the time Dahl's novel was published, immigration was a highly contested social issue in Britain: the 'Notting Hill riots' had occurred in 1958, and in 1962 the Conservative government passed the Commonwealth Immigration Act, which sought to limit the number of immigrants to Britain from the West Indies and the Indian subcontinent. Dahl's portrayal of the Oompa-Loompas is oblivious to the wider implications of its representation of a group of immigrant workers exploited by a factory owner. As anyone knows who lives in a postcolonial society or in a culture formerly marked by racialized inequality, habits of thought and valuing persist over many generations, even when they have been superseded by political and cultural change.

A commonly expressed fallacy in children's literature criticism is that older texts, many of which accept that the value of human beings is determined by their racial origins, are merely works of their time, as though the authors of these texts were no more than conduits of prevailing cultural norms. As the historian Inga Clendinnen notes, 'the "men of their time" fiction is always a fiction' (1999, p. 86). For despite the potency of what Michel **Foucault** refers to as a 'régime of truth', the 'system of ordered procedures for the production, regula-tion, distribution, circulation and operation of statements' (Foucault, 1980, pp. 131, 133) whereby societies control and order what is deemed to be true, it is also the case that individuals and groups are not bound by dominant discourses as by a straitjacket but are capable of scepticism or resistance. For this reason, texts sharing a common provenance are liable to differ widely in relation to the thematics, representational modes and discursive features which characterize their treatment of race. Moreover, texts frequently manifest tensions between discursive regimes; for instance, discourses of Christianity which propounded the doctrine of the fatherhood of God were often at odds with colonial discourses which emphasized the inferiority of black races. Such tensions, which manifest themselves in textual contradictions, are indicative of anxieties which disturb the appearance of imperial certainty.

RACE AND CHILDREN'S LITERATURE

The concept of race – the classification of humans into distinct types ordered by physical appearance and genetics – emerged during the later Middle Ages and developed alongside the rise of European imperialism. Like 'race', 'racism' is a slippery and contested term. Graham Huggan (2007, p. 14) describes the connections between the two as follows:

> race is a phantom *theory*, founded on the imagined existence of genetically 'deficient' human descent groupings; racism, by contrast, is an empirically verifiable *practice*, based on an attribution of ineradicable differences that justifies the exploitation, exclusions, or elimination of the people assigned to these 'inferior' groups.

As European powers established colonies in the New World, they sought to dis-tinguish themselves from the various indigenous peoples who occupied territory appropriated to serve the various purposes of the imperial project. Discourses of race were also used to justify the institutionalization of slavery in the late six-teenth century as pseudo-scientific arguments were marshalled to demonstrate that there existed a 'natural' hierarchy of worth which held true across European powers and their colonies. By the nineteenth century it was generally accepted that this hierarchy comprised three major races: white, yellow and black, with white at the apex. After Darwin's *The Origin of Species* was published in 1859, the concept of a hierarchy of races was complicated by the application of prin-ciples of natural selection, which implied that superior, white races might be contaminated through contact with black people or, conversely, that the inferi-ority of black races might be 'bred out' through intermarriage with white people. Another strand of race theory argued that 'primitive' races such as Australian Aborigines were doomed to extinction, being unable to compete with the 'civilized' white race.

Colonial texts for children are informed by these concepts and disclose the tensions which surround them. Emilia Marryat's *Jack Stanley; or, The Young Adventurers* (1882) relies on a storyline featuring a young Englishman who sails for New Zealand in search of the man who reduced his family to poverty. The novel's representation of Maori characters in New Zealand is shaped by unease about natives who adopt European practices:

It seemed strange to [Jack Stanley] every now and then to meet face to face with a native New Zealander mixing with the English settlers. Some of these Maoris were dressed in their native mat, and looked picturesque though filthy; whilst others had quite destroyed all interest in their appearance by adopting European dress, in which they looked awkward and ridiculous.

(Marryat, 1882, pp. 68–9)

Jack's preference for 'picturesque' Maori who maintain their traditional practices ('dressed in their native mat') over those who adopt European clothing is based on a sense of the rightness of hierarchies of race, which are destabilized when, in Homi **Bhabha**'s terms, the colonial subject is 'almost the same, but not quite' (1994, p. 86), as the colonizer. When Maori seek to become like white people, they disclose their inferiority, looking 'awkward and ridiculous'. A key property of civilized white society is that its members are capable of progressing toward prosperity and well-being; indeed, the novel's narrative is structured by such a progression as Jack experiences a transition from poverty to wealth. Like other native populations, the Maori of *Jack Stanley* are incapable of a similar shift, since they are consigned to the lower reaches of the hierarchy of races, condemned to remain forever in a position of inferiority.

Within the category of black races as imagined in *Jack Stanley*, there exist degrees of blackness and hence of value. In this novel, as in many colonial texts, Australian Aborigines are regarded as only just human. Jack is told that Aborigines are quite different from Maori, being 'little removed from the lower animals – utterly mindless' (Marryat, 1882, p. 255), whereas Maori are said to exhibit similarities to white people in 'the formation of the skull; in other words, they show likeness to the Caucasians' (p. 256). The inconsistency of the text's treatment of natives is striking: on the one hand, those Maori who attempt to adopt European practices are exposed as inauthentic; on the other hand, Maori are more like Europeans than other black races according to the principles of phrenology. By projecting its unease onto the Maori and their 'awkward and ridiculous' appearance, the text covers over the epistemic awkwardness of its representation of 'native New Zealanders' who are like white people but who must not look like them.

Contemporary texts are not immune from a tendency to fall back on the racialized hierarchies they ostensibly contest. Malorie Blackman's 'Noughts & Crosses' sequence, which commenced with *Noughts & Crosses* (2001), thematizes race relationships through its depiction of a dystopian, near-future Britain in which the dominant race, the Crosses, are black while the noughts, formerly slaves of the Crosses and now subsisting as an underclass excluded from economic and educational opportunities, are white (the distinction between upper case for Crosses and lower for noughts denotes the value attributed to the former). The storyline of *Noughts & Crosses* is organized around a romantic relationship involving the novel's two first-person narrators: Sephy, a Cross girl who is the daughter of a prominent politician, and Callum, a nought boy.

In the world of *Noughts & Crosses* the colour divide between Crosses and noughts effects a reversal in which blacks are oppressors and whites are powerless. Characters who negotiate between the two groups, such as the mixed-race teacher Mr Jason, and Callum's older sister Lynette (who had a romantic relationship with a Cross and was beaten by nought men), are tortured, self-hating figures. By mapping the power relationships of Crosses and noughts onto practices and histories which have privileged Europeans over their non-white **others**, the novel reinstalls those relationships and normalizes them. In a further echo of colonial discourses Sephy and Callum are treated as exceptional figures, starkly different from their families and friends in their refusal to accede to cultural norms, and in this way they echo the exceptional figures who crop up in colonial texts: black characters who function as loyal servants and devoted protectors of their white employers or owners; white characters who 'go native', aligning themselves with their racialized others; and (importantly for this novel) characters involved in interracial relationships proscribed by dominant (white) cultures. The effect of the representation of Sephy and Callum as exceptional figures is to accentuate the normalcy of racist practices and attitudes and the fixity of cultural formations.

Although the narration alternates between the perspectives of Sephy and Callum, this strategy does not enable dialogue between cultures, histories or identities because such factors are subordinated to the novel's focus on the romantic relationship between the two and on their status as 'star-crossed lovers'. The broadly drawn contrasts between the two characters and their families are metonymic of the divided society which comprises the novel's setting. Thus, Callum and his family – his embittered parents, radicalized brother and traumatized sister – are set against Sephy's wealthy and materialistic family, where her father is unfaithful to her alcoholic mother and Sephy and her sister bicker incessantly. When Callum's father and brother join a terrorist group known as the Liberation Militia, their actions are attributed to their experience of oppression and hopelessness; on the other hand, most of the Crosses in the novel – in particular Sephy's parents and sister – are mere ciphers, their racist attitudes and practices entrenched within a fixed, immutable system. In its focus on a tragic relationship which crosses racial boundaries, *Noughts & Crosses* recapitulates innumerable stories of doomed interracial romances, but the absolutism of its contrast between black and white is not far removed from that of *Jack Stanley*; and its strategy of reversal does nothing to address this contrast.

Canonical texts produced during the colonial period or informed by racist discourses often present a dilemma for publishers and other gatekeepers when they are republished for contemporary audiences. Many such texts – including Helen Bannerman's *Little Black Sambo* (1899), Mary Grant Bruce's 'Billabong' books (1910–42) and Mark Twain's *Adventures of Huckleberry Finn* (1884) – have been subjected to revisions which typically involve the removal of offensive descriptions of colonized or enslaved groups and individuals. What tends to be overlooked in such revisions, however, is that colonial and racist ideologies are commonly encoded in structural, semantic and narrative features which are not ameliorated merely through the removal of words or phrases.

Hugh Lofting's 'Doctor Dolittle' novels, published from 1920, involve episodes during which Doctor Dolittle travels to Africa and other countries in order to act as an animal doctor (he is skilled at communicating with animals and has a vast global network of animal contacts). When Dell reissued the novels in 1988, references to characters' skin colour were removed, so that in the revised version of *The Story of Doctor Dolittle* (Lofting, 1998 [rev. 1988]) Doctor Dolittle is no longer described as a white man, or the King of Golliginki as a black man. Explicit references to skin colour are, however, superfluous in the novel's narrative, in which Doctor Dolittle travels to Africa to cure the monkeys who are dying of a terrible disease; that is, knowledge and expertise are located in the figure of Doctor Dolittle, while Africans are oblivious to the monkeys' plight. The comically threatening figure of the King of Golliginki, too, accords with colonial descriptions of black kings and potentates who must be brought into line by their colonial rulers. The original text (Lofting, 1920) includes an episode in which Prince Bumpo, the son of the King of Golliginki, is tricked into believing that Doctor Dolittle can grant him his greatest wish: that he should be a white prince rather than a black one. The Dell version omits this story element but, instead, incorporates a sequence in which Polynesia the parrot hypnotizes Bumpo into releasing Doctor Dolittle from the dungeon where the king has imprisoned him. What is unaffected by this change is that power lies with Doctor Dolittle, who benefits from an act of trickery of which Bumpo is the dupe. When publishers sanitize older texts in this way through the removal of surface features – words such as 'black' and 'nigger' – they leave intact hierarchies of race and maintain narrative outcomes which promote the superiority of European culture.

POSTCOLONIALISM AND ORIENTALISM

The field of postcolonial studies developed as 'a way of addressing the cultural production of those societies affected by the historical phenomenon of colonialism' (Ashcroft, 2001, p. 7). Despite the fact that children's texts are both implicated in colonial processes and frequently engage with ideas and values about colonialism and its consequences in modernity, they are rarely included in discussions of postcolonial textuality, and postcolonial theory is itself relatively new to children's literature studies (Bradford, 2008, pp. 6–8).

Cultural production for children in colonial settings generally promoted the virtues of progress and modernity, representing indigenous characters according to the stereotypes which held sway in different cultural contexts. The figure of the noble savage was, for instance, frequently invoked in descriptions of Native Americans, notably in James Fenimore Cooper's *The Last of the Mohicans* (1826). Australian Aborigines, on the other hand, were more often represented as cannibals and savages. The pathetic figure of 'the last of' various indigenous groups (the Mohicans in North America, the Beothuk in Newfoundland, the Tasmanians in Australia) was marshalled to demonstrate that black races were destined to fade away, incapable of keeping up with the drive to modernity exemplified by European colonists.

Across colonial settings, ethnographers and folklorists collected the narratives of indigenous peoples, altering them to accord with European narrative practices and publishing them as children's stories; often they were styled as the last remnants of traditional stories saved from extinction by their assiduous collectors. Detached from the cultures from which they originated, such stories were incorporated into Western frames of reference. Indeed, such stories continue to appear as 'West Indian', 'Native American' or 'African' stories in anthologies, where readers can have little or no understanding of how these stories are woven into the values and beliefs of the cultures from which they derive.

While many children's texts deal directly with questions of colonialism, others do so indirectly. Jean de Brunhoff's 'Babar' series is, for instance, riddled with assumptions about the superiority of European culture over the primitive world into which Babar is born in 'the Great Forest'. When his mother is shot by a hunter in *The Story of Babar the Little Elephant* (1934), Babar runs away to a town where he is rescued by 'a very rich old lady who understood little elephants, and knew at once that he was longing for a smart suit' (1955, n.p.). The anthropomorphized figure of Babar functions as a metaphor for the colonized 'other', and his **desire** to wear the smart clothes of the bourgeoisie demonstrates his subjection to the charms of civilization. When he returns to his childhood home, he gains status from the **signifiers** of wealth and European culture which surround him, and, on the sudden death of the king of the elephants, he is offered the throne. The subjection of the elephants is as complete as that of Babar himself, since their argument for making him king is based solely on his acquisition of European knowledge and the signs of wealth.

In *Babar the King* (1936), Babar himself becomes a colonizer, recruiting his fellow elephants as labourers and craftsmen by offering them rewards which evoke the beads and baubles distributed to indigenous peoples: 'My friends, in these trunks and bales and cases I have presents for all of you – dresses, hats, silks, paint-boxes, drums, tins of peaches, feathers, racquets, and many other things' (Brunhoff, 1953, p. 8). The town of Celesteville – named after Celeste, Babar's queen – is built by the elephants, who (like Dahl's Oompa-Loompas) delight in their subjection and work assiduously. Like the colonized others of innumerable missions, reserves and reservations, they are consigned to dwellings constructed on European models but differentiated from the large, important homes of their superiors, which occupy a position offering a panoptic view of the elephants as they perform their duties as docile subjects.

An important component of postcolonial studies is discourse analysis, a strategy which examines how colonial discourse maintains power and determines what counts as knowledge. Edward Said's celebrated study *Orientalism* (1978), which examines the processes whereby the 'Orient' was, and continues to be, constructed by European thought, is the foundational text in this field. While Said's examples of **Orientalist** discourse drew upon the many European scholars who studied Eastern languages, history and cultures, he viewed Orientalism in broader terms as an epistemological and institutional system which served to distinguish the Orient from the Occident and to exercise power over the Orient.

Orientalist discourses inform a variety of children's texts, including retellings and reworkings of *Arabian Nights* stories, collections of **folktales**, colonial fiction and contemporary fiction either set in Asian cultures or tracing the experience of young protagonists who move from Asian countries to resettle in countries such as Britain, the United States, Canada and Australia (**Stephens** and McCallum, 1998, p. 229). In line with the neo-Orientalist doctrines which have dominated political and popular discourses over the past two decades (Tuastad, 2003), contemporary texts dealing with Middle Eastern settings or characters are apt to lump together all such societies under the sign of Islam. Suzanne Fisher Staples' novels *Shabanu: Daughter of the Wind* (1989), *Haveli* (1993) and *Under the Persimmon Tree* (2005) accord with the tenets of neo-Orientalism in their representations of a homogenized Muslim culture characterized by barbarism, the oppression of women and girls and sociopolitical systems based on tribalism rather than loyalty to the nation-state (Bradford, 2007). The protagonists of these novels are exceptional Muslim girls whose aspirations and values are readily aligned with those of their implied Western readers.

As colonized peoples have struggled for recognition, human rights and restitution of land, cultural production by indigenous authors and artists has increased markedly since the 1960s. Children's texts have been a high priority for indigenous publishing houses, which seek to offer indigenous children experiences of narrative **subjectivity** while enabling non-indigenous children to engage with cultural difference. It would be unsound to argue that indigenous texts produce 'better' representations of indigeneity than non-indigenous texts, or that they are more 'authentic', a term which generally implies adherence to an originary cultural identity. Indigenous identities are multifarious, inflected by factors including gender, class, sexuality and access to education, so that no text can speak for or about all indigenous people. Nevertheless, it is the case that non-indigenous texts are much more likely than indigenous texts to recycle the assumptions of dominant cultures.

Since indigenous texts proceed from narrative practices different from those of European cultures, they require different kinds of reading. For instance, Australian Aboriginal stories are produced within regimes of custodianship which determine the territory from which they come, the clans and individuals to whom they belong and the audiences which are entitled to receive them (Bradford, 2001b). Thus they are always presented by Aboriginal – and increasingly, mainstream – publishers in relation to particular places and cultures, through the provision of **paratextual** material such as maps, glossaries and information about storytellers. Such information is crucial to an understanding of the locatedness of these stories. It is common for European readers to experience a sense of apprehending only part of indigenous stories; this is because they are cultural outsiders to texts which are highly selective about what they include and omit. In addition, ancient modes of storytelling inform contemporary texts; thus, Australian Aboriginal stories rarely incorporate the openings and closures which European readers are accustomed to, since most such stories relate to complex narrative systems rather than existing as individual works. Similarly, many Maori stories include genealogical information about characters in sequences which may, to European readers, appear to interrupt or slow down the progress of stories, but which are included because of the high importance placed on ancestry in Maori culture. Again, many Native American stories are organized around a sequence of four events, characters or places, whereas sequences based on the number three are more usual in European narratives (Bradford, 2008).

Sherman Alexie's *The Absolutely True Diary of a Part-Time Indian* (2007) follows a narrative trope common in contemporary Native American children's literature: the process whereby a child or teenager who has lived on a reservation ('the rez') is introduced to mainstream schooling and the practices and values of the majority culture. As the novel's title suggests, Alexie plays with notions of the hybrid 'part-time Indian' subject: at home the protagonist is known as 'Junior', in common with many of the men and some of the women on the reservation; at his new school he is known by his full name, Arthur Spirit Jr. However, the novel resists casting Junior/Arthur as a tragic figure caught between cultures, the flip-side of notions of **hybridity**. Rather, the narrative tracks his formation as an Indian subject who expresses his identity in unconventional ways, going against the norms of the rez where poverty and hopelessness engender a deep pessimism about the future ('Indian', a term reappropriated by many indigenous Americans, is used throughout this novel). The first-person narration addresses white readers, providing explanations of Indian humour, cultural practices and values to a narratee who knows little of Indian culture. For instance, before his first fistfight at his new school Arthur outlines 'The Unofficial and Unwritten (but you better follow them or you're going to get beaten twice as hard) Spokane Indian Rules of Fisticuffs' (Alexie, 2007, pp. 61–2) as the prelude to his account of a fight in which his adversary Roger, a much larger boy, adheres to none of these rules but relies on racial taunts rather than physical action. By foregrounding Arthur's perplexity at the fact that different rules operate in the two cultures, the narrative positions readers as observers of white culture from the 'other' side. The reflexivity of the novel powerfully conveys a sense of the complexity of intersubjective negotiations across cultures through its focus on Arthur's relationships with Rowdy, his childhood friend from the rez, and with Gordy, a white boy from his new school. As a postcolonial text *The Absolutely True Diary* addresses the effects of colonial history on Native Americans even as it interrogates the assumptions which shape relations between Indians and whites in the novel.

ETHNICITY, MULTICULTURALISM, WHITENESS

Deeply invested in processes and ideologies of nation-building, children's books both respond to, and are constitutive of, the cultural and political shifts which attend relationships between ethnic groups in modern nation states. Since the 1960s the term 'ethnicity' has been used as an alternative to the discredited genetically organized hierarchies of 'race', to describe populations distinguished by ancestry, traditions, religious affiliations, values and norms. However, it is also the case that concepts of ethnicity and the discourses of tolerance which conventionally surround them have been marshalled for racist purposes. Etienne Balibar (1991, p. 21) suggests that the dominant theme of the new racism

> is not biological heredity but the insurmountability of cultural differences, a racism which, at first sight, does not postulate the superiority of certain groups or peoples in relation to others but 'only' the harmfulness of abolishing frontiers, the incompatibility of life-styles and traditions.

Staples' novels *Shabanu* and *Haveli* promote this version of ethnicity in the way they represent Muslim men as almost universally cruel and barbaric in their treatment of girls and women. In *Haveli*, only one male character stands out for his adherence to progressive attitudes towards women: Omar, the nephew of Shabanu's elderly husband. The novel's explanation for his different attitude is that he has been educated in the United States. Nevertheless, when Omar sets aside his romantic attachment to Shabanu to serve the interests of his family and conduct a violent attack on its enemies, the implication is that familial (tribal) loyalties are incompatible with Western values such as civil rights and democratic processes. Readers are thus positioned as members of a superior society from which they observe barbarism at work.

Concepts of ethnicity are closely associated with formulations of **multiculturalism** and discussions of 'multicultural children's literature'. Although multiculturalism is often treated as a feature of individual nations – and is conceptualized differently across national settings – it is, in David Bennett's words, an 'epiphenomenon of globalization', the word itself 'entering and inflecting numerous national debates about the politics of cultural difference, the "limits of tolerance", and the future of the nation-state' (1998, p. 2). It follows that, while children's books circulate within a global market, their treatment of ethnicity and multiculturalism engages with national and local politics, addressing the questions of belonging and exclusion, nationhood and history, which have dominated debates in Western nations since the end of the Cold War (Bradford *et al.*, 2007).

In the novel *Falling* (1997), by the Belgian author Anne Provoost, the young protagonist Lucas engages in the painful, complicated process of uncovering the story of his dead grandfather, a Nazi sympathizer who was responsible for the death or incarceration of Jewish children concealed in a local convent. These past events intersect with the contemporary setting of the novel, where 'Arab' immigrants are subjected to negative stereotyping: they are said to be dishonest, dirty and privileged over local people whose jobs they take. In a somewhat similar way, the Australian novel *Secrets of Walden Rising* (1996), by Allan Baillie, involves the recuperation of history, presented through the perspective of Brendan, a British migrant who discovers that the history of the remote town of Jacks Marsh is riddled with incidents of racism and xenophobia which bear upon his own experience as an outsider to the social life of the town. Novels such as these take a critical approach to concepts of multiculturalism, exposing the faultlines which threaten national **mythologies** of tolerance and equality and offering a corrective to the too-ready acceptance of these mythologies as givens.

Cultural theorists working in the field of **whiteness** studies have developed concepts and strategies which offer another approach to critical work in children's literature. An important early text in this area is Toni Morrison's *Playing in the Dark: Whiteness and the Literary Imagination* (1992), which analyses constructions of Americanness in the work of early writers such as Edgar Allen Poe and Willa Cather. Morrison points out that ideas of Americanness habitually depends on the (implied) presence of the racialized other and that 'American means white' (Morrison, 1992, p. 51). The effect of both the absence and the presence of the other is similar: blackness is defined in relation to whiteness, which is assumed to be a normal, natural state.

Enid Blyton's 'Noddy' books offer a clear example of the textual operations of whiteness. In *Noddy and His Car* (1951), Noddy decides to become a taxi driver. The toy cat carelessly leaves her tail hanging out of the car, whereupon it is caught in the car's wheel and comes off. Next, the teddy bear loses his hat when Noddy brakes suddenly, and, finally, the golden-haired doll loses her bag, which has been balancing on the back of the car. In all three cases these characters refuse to pay their fares and in addition demand more money as financial recompense. What drives the story, then, is the fact that rich, white and powerful figures (the cat, the teddy, the doll) exercise power by withholding capital. When Noddy and Big-Ears go in search of the lost items they find that they have been appropriated by a trio of minor villains: a golliwog, a clockwork mouse and Sally Sly, a 'naughty little doll' (1951, p. 45), who are marked as not-white, in the golliwog's case; as not white enough (the mouse); and as working-class trash (in the case of Sally Sly). Noddy returns the tail, the hat and the bag to their owners and is endowed not only with the fare but with extra money as well. In the world Blyton constructs, whiteness is invisible as a racial position for, as Richard Dyer puts it in his seminal work *White*, 'Other people are raced, we are just people' (1997, p. 1). If Noddy is a good little white boy aspiring to be ever whiter (i.e. richer and more attractive to those with power and money), the golliwog is far behind him in the whiteness stakes; he can **perform** whiteness, but he cannot take centre stage with Noddy and Big-Ears. Nevertheless, the smiling face which is his default expression confirms the rightness and normalcy of a world where whiteness is identified with success, prosperity and good order. In this way Blyton's golliwogs (and other non-white and working-class figures) function as markers or **signs** of the legitimacy of a natural order where whiteness is preferred and rewarded.

Conclusion

Many of the lists of 'multicultural children's literature' which feature on websites and in pedagogical material should be regarded with scepticism. Narratives which incorporate characters of various ethnicities do not necessarily engage with cultural difference, and it is important to consider not merely how many characters come from diverse ethnic backgrounds but how such characters and cultures are represented. Children's books commonly trace the identity formation of protagonists and the development of such qualities as empathy and good judgement. Characters from minority cultures are often incorporated into such narrative trajectories. Sometimes children from mainstream culture who encounter cultural difference are shown to benefit from an enhanced understanding of others; sometimes the psychological or material progress of children from minority cultures is defined in terms of their access to mainstream culture. In both cases minority cultures are defined and valued according to a frame of reference in which white, middle-class culture is normative.

Although publishers seek to meet market demands for books featuring minority cultures, it remains the case that mainstream publishing houses cater principally to readers from the dominant culture. Texts by indigenous and minority authors, especially those produced by specialist publishing houses, must compete with the products of multinational publishers, distributed and promoted globally. When books by minority authors find white audiences, this is generally because they are not *too* different. Thus, *The Absolutely True Diary of a Part-Time Indian* deals with a conventional topic, the identity formation of its **adolescent** protagonist, and is set in part in a mainstream location.

Questions of race, ethnicity and colonialism are addressed most overtly in realist texts for children and adolescents. Many such texts locate their narratives in the past, thus distancing readers from contemporary concerns refracted in historical events. Works of fantasy, too, engage with cultural difference: in science fiction narratives and in fiction dealing with posthuman subjects as well as in more traditional varieties of fantasy, protagonists are represented in relation to their affiliations and their experiences of exclusion. From the colonialist novels of the age of empire to contemporary works pointing to the faultlines which threaten to destabilize multicultural societies, children's literature engages with and intervenes in the politics of race.

FURTHER READING

Ashcroft, Bill, Griffiths, Gareth and Tiffin, Helen (1989) *The Empire Writes Back: Theory and Practice in Post-Colonial Literatures*, London: Routledge.
This is an excellent introduction to postcolonial theory and its implications for textual analysis (historical and contemporary material), addressing topics such as canon formation and indigenous literatures.

Bennett, David (ed.) (1998) *Multicultural States: Rethinking Difference and Identity*, London: Routledge.
A selection of contributions by key theorists on multiculturalism in various settings including India, the United States, South Africa and Britain. Particularly useful on relationships between multiculturalism and globalization.

Bhabha, Homi (1994) *The Location of Culture*, London: Routledge.
This collection of essays by Bhabha gathers his most important writings up to 1994, including discussions of hybridity, colonial stereotypes, ambivalence and the instability of colonial constructions of 'home'.

Bradford, Clare (2008) *Unsettling Narratives: Postcolonial Readings of Children's Literature*, Waterloo, ON: Wilfrid Laurier University Press.
This is the first comparative study of children's literature from former British settler nations (Australia, Canada, the United States and New Zealand). It considers indigenous textuality and how indigenous peoples are represented by non-indigenous authors.

Dyer, Richard (1997) *White*, New York: Routledge.
This is one of the foundational texts of whiteness studies. Focusing principally on films, Dyer outlines three ways in which whiteness maintains its power: the shifting discourses of colour, the treatment of white/black skin and the symbolism of whiteness.

Foucault, Michel (1980) *Power/Knowledge: Selected Interviews and Other Writings, 1972–1977*, Brighton: Harvester Wheatsheaf.
In this collection of essays and interviews, Foucault outlines his theories about how power is exercised and how it is constituted as knowledge. An accessible introduction to key concepts including discourse and its normalizing effects in human societies.

Hall, Stuart and du Gay, Paul (eds) (1996) *Questions of Cultural Identity*, London: Sage.
This collection includes a stimulating introduction by Stuart Hall, leading into essays by renowned authors including Zygmunt Bauman, Homi Bhabha and Lawrence Grossberg, on questions of multiculturalism, identity and hybridity.

5

NARRATOLOGY

JOHN STEPHENS

Children's literature mostly consists of narratives – novels and picturebook fictions. Literary scholarship that addresses this body of texts seeks to define what constitutes a story, and hence is concerned with structures and strategies, with the interactions of teller, tale and audience, and with how a particular text relates to the known world that it seeks to represent or to which it refers. When what is now referred to as 'classical' narratology emerged in the 1970s, and within a decade or so became established in English criticism with the availability of major texts by, among others, Seymour Chatman (1978), Gerald Prince (1982), A. J. Greimas (1983) and Mieke Bal (1985), analysis of texts focused on form and technique and paid little attention to context, meaning and reception. In formalist terms, narratology brought much to the understanding of how narrative works, and its insights are still widely employed, as we will see in the following. However, as Jerome Bruner (1991, p. 5) points out, the failure of narratology to include social and literary contexts or audiences in its ambit was quickly perceived as a limitation, and new narratologies emerged even as classical narratology was becoming established. As Monika Fludernik (1996, p. 268) puts it, 'These approaches attempt to combine **ideological** frameworks (of feminism, of power, of the economy of discourse) with the more formal concerns of narratology.' The emphasis in such newer approaches on personal, textual and sociohistorical contexts is of great potential interest to scholars in children's literature. Bal (1987), for example, developed a feminist narratology alongside her more formalist study, while Susan Lanser (1986) and Robyn Warhol (1989) also proposed feminist narratologies. Fludernik (1996), extending the principle that narratology seeks to account for narrative diversity (what makes narratives different), poses the question of whether **postcolonial** narratives work differently from **colonial** or non-colonial narratives, something that Prince (2005) has addressed in his proposal for a postcolonial narratology. Finally, proponents of 'cognitive narratology', such as David Herman or Lisa Zunshine, have shifted the attention of narratology onto readers' mental models in the reception process or, as Herman puts it, 'the process by which interpreters reconstruct the storyworlds encoded in narratives' (2002, p. 5). Significantly, we must understand interpreters' reconstructions as entailing elements both of reproduction and of refashioning on the basis of their own storyworlds.

Despite the predominance of narrative in children's literature, narratology has remained relatively peripheral in a critical tradition dominated by historicist and reader response approaches and a content- and theme-based methodology. John

Stephens (1992a) incorporated narratology into an investigation of the ideology of text and mental models in children's literature, and many of the concepts deployed there – story and discourse, narrative point of view, **focalization**, narrative voice, speech and thought representation, closure and so on – have since become commonplace in critical methodologies. More recently, Clare **Bradford** (2007a) has drawn on narratological concepts in a postcolonial approach to children's literature. These works demonstrate some important possibilities for how critical method might incorporate narratology within thematic or cultural studies approaches. Further, the interdisciplinary approach to narrative in Herman's *Story Logic* offers enormous potential for scholars of children's literature searching for a way to bring new life to **reader response criticism**, although Herman's account of text–reader relationships goes well beyond that and enables us to extrapolate an answer to the question of what readers understand when they lack the concepts to articulate thematic understanding of a text (not a question Herman himself addresses). On the one hand, readers construct a mental model from the narrative depiction of space and time, from participants' interactions, and from the overall configuration of the storyworld (Herman, 2002, p. 331) – in other words, from the narratological elements of the text. On the other hand, readers also inhabit a context of interpretation, and thence draw upon analogous models based in the world they themselves inhabit and know. 'Meaning' lies in the interchange.

Recent theorists demonstrate that the classical narratological frameworks need to be extended to include readers and contexts of interpretation, and thence to consider the relation between how consciousness is structured in stories and how stories represent subjectivities and cultures, but these moves do not entail an abandonment of such key concepts as the distinction between story, discourse and meaning; narrative point of view and narrative voice; focalization; and structure and organization. These concepts are essential for analysing children's texts and will be the focus of this chapter. Space does not permit a discussion here of all the areas that fall within the domain of narratology – **genre** and the representation of speech and thought, for example, are other important issues.

Perhaps the most significant distinction narratology derived from structuralism is the distinction between *story*, or what we might roughly think of as 'what certain characters do with or to each other in a certain place at a certain time', and *discourse*, the complex process of encoding that story which involves choices of vocabulary, of syntax, the presentation of time and space, the order of presentation, how the narrating voice is to be oriented towards what is narrated and towards the implied audience and how character point of view is constructed. The discourse is the 'how' of a narrative. It might be thought of as the words on the page, whereas the story is the characters, the setting and the sequence of events that we infer from those words. The story is an abstraction from the text; it is not directly available to readers but is (re)constructed from a reading and understanding of the text, which usually entails reconstructing the 'actual' chronological sequence of events and temporal order across parallel story strands. It is thus the product of a reader's engagement with that text.

At this point classical narratology introduces a third element, the story's logical and causal structure, which is generally referred to as *plot* (Rimmon-Kenan, 1983). Most narratives depend on cause–effect relationships to differing degrees, and it is arguable that, for any temporal order of events to be a narrative, there must be some connections indicative of causality. In some narratives, every action is causally related to a previous action, a lack or a **desire**; in others, causal coherence is less apparent. When, at the beginning of Philippa Pearce's *Tom's Midnight Garden* (1958), Tom reluctantly departs with his uncle, causality is overt: '[Tom] knew he was being rude, but he made excuses for himself: he did not much like Uncle Alan, and he did not want to like him at all' (Pearce, 1976, p. 9). Tom's attitude and behaviour are brought into the foreground as the product of a state of lack, and, as Tom eventually recognizes, its cause – the absence of 'someone to play with and somewhere to play' (p. 215) – becomes the catalyst for the time-slipping into the garden of the past. In contrast, in Chapter 4 of Neil Gaiman's *Stardust*, the protagonist, Tristran, at the beginning of his quest, meets the same 'little hairy personage' his father had briefly met 18 years earlier, which is narrated in Chapter 1. Readers can consider this a coincidence because the causal coherence of the two encounters is not immediately obvious. It is only towards the end of the novel that readers find an answer to the basic plot structure question, 'Why does this happen?' (The character is part of an obscure fellowship planning to overthrow the society's fratricidal custom for determining royal succession.) This obscure causality contradicts reader expectation that a **fairy tale** will be linearly and tightly plotted – an expectation more directly met in the 2007 film of *Stardust*, which reshapes plot in terms of very overt causality and thus produces a more conventional fairy tale structure.

As already remarked, a weakness of classical narratology was its propensity to privilege form over meaning. To overcome this weakness, a fourth element is added, that of *significance*. When readers ask the question, 'What is this text about?', they are referring to two things: first, to the *story*, which is determined by reading the text for its obvious 'sense', and second, to the unstated *significance*, that is, what the text 'means' in a thematic, ethical or moral sense, or what it implies about the meaning of human life, or, sometimes, what it has to say about literature itself. Readers usually manage to agree about what the *story* is, though even here attempts to retell it will vary in emphasis and selected detail. Consensus seems possible, though, because of common human experiences which render specific characters and situations recognizable, and because some uses of language are unproblematic. Differences among readers enter mainly with the secondary level, that of inferred significance, which is an extrapolation from discourse, story and plot. The four components of narrative interact as in Figure 5.1.

Why these distinctions are useful to the process of reading can be seen from the following simple example from Jay Williams's modern fairy tale, 'Stupid Marco', in which is described the first encounter between a prince on a quest and a helper figure who will turn out to be the proper objective of the quest:

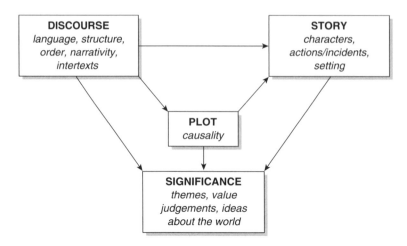

Figure 5.1 The four components of narrative.

In the centre of the city was an elegant castle. In the downstairs window of one of its towers a maiden sat with her chin on her hand, staring into space. Her smooth brown hair hung in long braids tied with golden bows, and her eyes were the colour of forget-me-nots.

Marco took off his hat. 'Good morning!' he said. 'Are you the princess Aurelia?'

The girl yawned. 'Never heard of her,' she said.

(Williams, 1978, p. 21)

Discourse is grounded in language, but meaning also comes from the larger contexts of culture and genre of which the text is part. Within the text, small segments (what can be called micro utterances) acquire purpose and significance as they are combined into larger structures. Here, for example, the set, 'an elegant castle . . . one of its towers . . . a maiden sat', enables readers to infer a story genre in which the young woman is a princess, just as the set, 'smooth brown hair . . . long braids . . . golden bows . . . [and] forget-me-nots', indicates that she is beautiful, although this is also not stated. Her yawn introduces a plot element in that its implied cause is her boredom with a princess's life and may be a catalyst for future action; her demotic, unprincess-like speech reinforces this possibility. In even such a small stretch of text, then, discourse clearly points to story and plot and anticipates significance in its incipient breaching of a genre's gender conventions. To be aware of this enables readers to read self-reflexively. Other aspects of discourse that might be considered here are type of narrator, the implied reader who is constructed by the text, and point of view; that is, it charts what readers do as they read.

In 'Stupid Marco' Williams is playing with his audience's familiarity with a kind of discourse–story relationship. This assumption connects with another good reason for distinguishing story and discourse – the 'same' story can be retold using a different discourse. Robert Browning's narrative poem 'The Pied Piper of Hamelin', for example, has been retold as a picturebook (many times), as a historical novel, as a live-action film, as an **animated** film and so on. The 'story' – that is, the setting, characters, events and actions – remains roughly the same. Minor variations might occur in the story elements that are included or excluded, but there is usually enough similarity between different texts to say that they are versions of the same story. This type of literature, where stories are retold in different forms, is very common in literature for children. A considerable proportion of books produced for children are retellings – retellings of fairy tales, **folktales**, traditional stories of various kinds and so on. Novels as diverse as Terry Pratchett's *The Amazing Maurice and His Educated Rodents* (2001) and Andy Griffiths's *The Day My Bum Went Psycho* (2001) are retold stories, namely 'fractured fairy tales' – a sub-genre which children take great delight in.

A very important implication of the distinction between story and discourse has to do with the production of meaning in texts. The meaning of any one 'story' – such as 'The Pied Piper of Hamelin' – will vary every time the story is retold because of the different discourses that are used to tell it and because of the different contexts in which it is retold. First, the type of language used, the order of events, the viewpoint from which it is told and so on will alter the meaning that a particular story has. Second, the construction of meaning is subject to certain constraints because readers bring with them expectations based on their knowledge of other versions of the same story. Third, any act of narration, or of storytelling, implies a position for its listeners or readers and a relationship between the text and its readers, and this relationship can also affect meaning. In this way, meaning is the product of the interaction between the story and the discourse and the particular context in which a story is told.

In order to address key discoursal elements of narrative fiction, narratology concerns itself with such questions as the following:

How are narration and focalization handled?

How is the narrative structured and organized (space, time, order, causality)?

How does the narrative begin and end?

NARRATION AND FOCALIZATION

Any storytelling situation presupposes a narrator, that is, someone who is telling the story. Because a story is narrated from a constructed position which is not identifiable as that of the author, it is usual to speak of the *narrator* of a story rather than the author. Any story is also going to be told from a particular point of view. Point of view is both perceptual – as it indicates the narrator's physical relation in time and space to the story – and conceptual, as it communicates ideas about and attitudes towards those story elements. Point of view is an extremely important feature to consider in analysing children's texts because it has a crucial role in positioning readers and shaping readers' responses to texts. In narrating a story from a particular point of view, texts offer readers a viewpoint from which to interpret that story. Readers might choose to reject that viewpoint, but children are usually less experienced readers than adults; that is, they are still in the process of developing strategies for reading and interpreting texts.

Point of view may coincide with narrative voice, but the two may be distinct when the point of view that is shaping a narrative is that of a character rather than that of the narrator who is telling the story. Hence point of view emerges through two principal forms: a first-person narrator tells his or her 'own' story, or a third-person narrator presents the story as it impinges on the perceptions of one or more of the characters in it. (Second-person narration is rare, especially so in children's literature.) In first-person narration point of view is usually straightforward: a character in the text tells the story in his or her own words from his or her point of view, which readers assess against the tenets and assumptions of their own storyworld. In third-person narration a narrator who is not a participant in events tells the story. When story events and existents are presented from the point of view of one or more central characters, the technique is referred to as *focalization*, and the perceiving character is known as the *focalizer*. In turn, objects, actions and so on may be described as *focalized*. There can be a lot of switching between narrator focalization and character focalization, and between various characters, though the majority of children's fictions employ only one focalizing character. Multiple focalization (or *polyfocalization*) was widely used in the 1980s and 1990s, however, and was earlier a primary source of the relativism of Robert Cormier's novels. The point of noticing who is the text's focalizer at any moment is tied up with attitude making and the credence we give as readers to what the text offers. Often such an attitudinal judgement is already built into the text itself.

Narration and focalization have been genre characteristics in children's literature, in so far as fantasy and realism have tended to employ different kinds of narrators: first-person narration is unusual in English-language fantasy (although common in Swedish), where it did not appear until 1979 with Diana Wynne Jones's *The Spellcoats*. In recent years it has also become more widespread in picturebooks. Since the 1970s first-person narration has been a majority form in realism because an important strategy in constructing the illusion of realism is to conceal voices or perceptions attributable to an 'author' outside the text. First-person narration enables this by apparently eliding any narrating voice that is not the main character's. Third-person narration, which presents the story from the point of view of a main character, is not much different in effect, however, as it both aligns readers with the perceptions of focalizing characters and has comparable recourse to strategies that undermine the character's narrative authority. A common technique in character focalization is to present perception by means of **free indirect discourse**/thought, which, David Lodge (2002, p. 45) argues, makes it possible to combine 'the realism of assessment that belongs to third-person narration with the realism of presentation that comes from first-person

narration'. Dan Shen (2005, p. 152) makes the important point that narrative techniques are produced and used in sociohistorical contexts, and the preference for
'variable internal focalization' instead of omniscient narration in modern fiction
is a product of the 'more skeptical and more individualized sociohistorical context after the First World War'. It took another World War, and possibly the
Vietnam War, for this tendency to be manifested in children's literature. A further observation made by Shen is that the deployment of such a technique in historical fiction is probably out of place, since it contravenes the narrative
conventions (and hence the ways in which people viewed their world) of earlier
periods.

One of the great exponents of third-person narration techniques that refuse to
allow simplistic reader alignment with character perception is Peter Dickinson.
Here is the opening of *Tulku*:

> Theodore woke in the dark, sucked harshly out of the pit of sleep by a hand
> shaking his shoulder and a voice hissing in his ear. Before he could groan
> a question the hand covered his mouth. He jerked himself free and sat up,
> making the straps of his bed creak with the strain, but by now he had
> recognized the voice, and guessed at the urgency.
>
> 'Fu T'iao! What? Why?' he whispered.
>
> 'Dress. Be quick. Your father says . . .'
>
> No more questions, then. As Theodore reached for his clothes where
> they hung from a peg in the beam above his head he saw Fu T'iao moving
> across the room, and knew by the fact that he could see at all that there was
> more light than there should be, a pinkish flicker of moving flame through
> the window. And there were more noises in the night than the usual faint
> water-rattle from the ravine and wind-hiss from the woods beyond – there
> was a grumbling murmur, which suddenly clacked into recognizably
> human shouts, and now there was Father's voice riding above the racket,
> slow, heavy and confident, with the unmistakable mid-Western honk only
> half-modulated into the tones of the local dialect, Miao.
>
> (Dickinson, 1982, p. 9)

The narrative is in the third person, but it is narrated almost entirely from
Theodore's point of view. Character focalization is indicated by the use of perceptual ('saw') and conceptual ('knew') verbs and implied perception ('a hand
shaking his shoulder and a voice hissing in his ear', and various references to
what is seen or heard). Thus most of Theodore's senses – sight, hearing, touch –
are brought into play, but he has little understanding of what is happening. The
entire narrative remains utterly locked into Theodore's viewpoint, to the point
that he is present on every page. The effect for readers of such heavily character-focalized narration is similar to that of first-person narration in that readers
only perceive as much as the central focalizing (or narrating) character knows and
have very minimal access to any other character's viewpoint, except via dialogue.

It also means that readers are attitudinally aligned with that character – we are offered a position from which to see the world from their point of view – but in this case the protagonist's constant bafflement at the meaning of objects and events he encounters in a world alien to his culture and mentality also positions readers at a distance from him.

Narration and focalization are the aspects of narration in which implicit authorial control of audience reading strategies is probably most powerful. Because the focalizer is the only figure in the text whose thoughts and feelings seem accessible to readers and thus, in effect, he is the only character attributed with a developing **subjectivity**, readers are more apt to engage intersubjectively and align attitudinally and emotionally with that figure. This is a very obvious point. Such alignment, though, may readily yield to the potential in point of view to impose a position from which readers will read. For this reason, an understanding of the principles of narration and focalization is the most important skill young readers of fiction need to cultivate.

NARRATIVE STRUCTURE AND ORGANIZATION

One of the most important things to consider here is that discourse order rarely corresponds completely to story order: story events are normally linear (i.e. chronological) and, therefore, can never precisely correspond with either the order in which happenings are presented or with the representation of more than one story strand (and narratives usually do consist of more than one strand). Readers may reconstruct events of a story according to *linear* (chronological) time, but narrative discourse need not be organized according to the same timeline. There are several possibilities, though the most obvious is that some events situated at an early point in story chronology may be narrated after later events. A narrative will thus frequently change the order in which events are narrated through the use of 'flashbacks' to earlier events and 'flashforwards' to later events.

Some of the functions of ordering narrative like this are to inform readers about 'previous' detail, create suspense, suggest connections or contrasts between 'past' and 'present' and modify retrospectively the meaning of past moments by a shift in emphasis or by offering a new interpretation, that is, enable a naïve reading to be set alongside a more enlightened one or to produce a dialogue between two views of equal status. A notable example of such ordering appears in *Tom's Midnight Garden*, in the way 'Time in the garden had sometimes jumped far ahead, and sometimes gone backwards' (Pearce, 1976, p. 214), so that, most dramatically, one of Tom's early visits to the garden (pp. 55–7) coincides with the last time Hatty, now a grown woman on the eve of her wedding, sees Tom (pp. 211–13) before they meet at the end of the novel in their mutual real time. As Tess Cosslett (2002, p. 250) argues, the effect of such temporal discontinuity is that the characters 'are finally identified with growth, change and forward movement. Their experiences teach them that they cannot remain trapped in the past, they must move on.'

Beginnings and endings

Structure and organization are only fully apparent with reference to the beginning and ending of a narrative, and to the prior question of how textual form relates to empirical reality and the frames of reference – cultural and individual storyworlds – readers call upon to render the world explicable. At the moment at which a story opens readers begin calling upon assumptions about origins, temporality and causality. Readers quickly ascertain at what point of story time the beginning is situated and start to form anticipations and/or hypotheses about whether the story will proceed forward from that point in time or whether it will also involve retrospective movements in order to imbue characters and events with an increased explanatory thickness.

The threshold of a narrative (which may vary in length from a paragraph to several pages) offers a mixture of details, all of which hold potential significance. Readers will attempt to organize the given data by means of such questions as follows: *What* is the story going to be about? *Who* is telling the story? *Where* is it set? *When* does it take place? As readers enter the story proper, they then ask, *what* is happening? and go on to ask, *how* or *why* is it happening? A text may be self-conscious about supplying this information, as in Budge Wilson's short story 'My Cousin Clarette', which begins:

> Toronto, 1984. SCENE, the Dundas station of the Yonge Street subway. Time, about 11.00 A.M. Hanging back as usual, loath to fall onto that track in front of an oncoming train, I leaned against the wall, my arms full of packages and shopping bags. Not so the lady in front of me.
>
> (Wilson, 1990, p. 97)

The details as the text modulates from scene to character compel reader attention and speculation. What is important about this setting? What relationship might emerge between the narrator and the 'lady', shortly identified as the narrator's cousin Clarette? Thematic possibilities quickly emerge, as the text implies rivalry grounded in class, gender **performativity**, and timidity and confidence. Wilson is working well within the conventions of narrative realism here, especially through the combination of overt first-person narratorial voice and 'real-world' existents. From that position, it is relatively easy for a narrative to move chronologically either backwards or forwards in story time, as Wilson's does, bringing the story to a close in which it is Clarette who steps in front of an oncoming train.

Endings may also display self-consciousness, as when Theodore, at the close of *Tulku*, stands in a greenhouse in England, 'Dazed with the mild warmth and the sense of ending' (Dickinson, 1982, p. 285). The formal zeugmatic structure of the clause and the apparent reference to Frank Kermode's *The Sense of an Ending* (1967) have a kind of frame-breaking effect that evokes the narratological distinction between endings and closure (or open and closed endings). The end of a narrative is simply the point at which narration stops, whereas closure is a sense of completion, conclusiveness or finality that a narrative may or may not achieve. The ending of *Tulku* draws attention to a strong sense of thematic closure, while leaving the story open: Theodore, a Christian fundamentalist, will return to his home in America, tell his story, finish his schooling 'and wait God's will' (Dickinson, 1982, pp. 280–1). This kind of structure is also common in series fiction. Novels that achieve a sense of completion in terms of the story, the characters and events, but remain thematically open, are less common in children's fiction, although an increase in the tendency to resist closure is an aspect of modern relativist narrative. An example is M. T. Anderson's *Burger Wuss* (1999), in which an epilogue undoes any thematic certainties suggested by the tying-up of the novel's events: the narrator has not developed after recognizing the foolishness of his actions, and his society is shown to be incapable of transformation. In contrast, David Almond's *The Fire-Eaters* demonstrates a more familiar use of an epilogue. After narrating events set in 1962, the onset of the closing chapter marks a drift towards the present time of reading: 'Now it all seems so long ago, and it's like it happened in some different kind of time . . . ' (Almond, 2003, p. 247). The chapter then summarizes subsequent events that tie up the story elements in a positive outcome and closes by recounting how a lost fawn is returned to its 'family'. The thematic implications of the story of the fawn encapsulate the themes of the novel: reverence for life, faith in deep intersubjectivity in a time of permanent change and the redemptive power of love. *The Fire-Eaters* thus expresses a powerful sense of closure that encompasses both story and theme.

Significance can only be fully attributed to a text from the perspective of the close, so a question readers pose looking back from the point of view of the ending is whether the narrative discourse has constructed and ordered the incidents and characters of the story in order to produce that particular end (meaning both 'conclusion' and 'significance'). A sense of **teleology** (that in retrospect the whole text discloses a purposeful structure) is itself usually an ideological assumption, and it is everywhere informed by what are held to be common cultural assumptions and values. That is, endings reaffirm what society regards as important issues and preferred outcomes.

Conclusion

Jerome Bruner (1991, p. 4) argues that experience and memory of human happenings are organized mainly in the form of narratives – versions of reality whose acceptability is governed by convention rather than by empirical verification. Narrative is thus a form not only of representing but of constituting reality. Narrative fictions are apt to take up more or less directly this interaction between representing and constituting, because they invariably have thematic purpose and function, whether deliberately because they seek to intervene in culture, as feminist narratologies observe, or implicitly because no encoding of a story can be free of societal and/or ideological marking. Broadly speaking, there is conventionally an expectation that readers will always direct attention to textual significance, and the impact within discourse of such elements as social practice, genre and point of view make such a move essential. What any method of analysing narrative must include, then, is a capacity to account for how readers will understand and decode the textual, narrative strategies which enable them to attribute thematic import to particular narrative encodings of a story. But that is only one side of the coin. As scholars of children's literature begin to pay more attention to the concerns of cognitive narratologists such as David Herman with the mental structures that underlie the ability to comprehend narrative, we may move a little closer to explaining how in understanding a story as a narrative structure young readers come to know much more than they can tell.

FURTHER READING

Herman, David (2002) *Story Logic: Problems and Possibilities of Narrative*, Lincoln: University of Nebraska Press.
This substantial monograph is probably the most important book on narratology to appear in the past decade. By taking narratology well beyond its structuralist origins and tying it to a range of disciplines within cognitive science, Herman paves the way for a new approach to narrative fiction.

Herman, David (ed.) (2003) *Narrative Theory and the Cognitive Sciences*, Stanford, CA: CSLI Publications.
A useful collection of essays in the emerging field of cognitive narratology – an approach to the study of narrative fiction that combines concepts and analytical frameworks from narratology with insights from the cognitive sciences. Essays on the study of fictional minds in narrative prose, and on how readers make sense of stories, are significant for children's literature scholarship.

McCallum, Robyn (1999) *Ideologies of Identity in Adolescent Fiction: The Dialogic Construction of Subjectivity*, New York: Garland.
A dedicated study of narratology and children's fiction does not exist, but the field is nevertheless well served by McCallum's thorough examination of novelistic discourse. She carefully introduces numerous narrative concepts and draws them together into an analytical frame that incorporates ideas about subjectivity, multi-vocal and multi-stranded narratives, the representation of time in the novel, maturation and transgression, and **metafiction**. Analysis is tied to perceptive discussion of about 70 novels for young readers.

Martin, Wallace (1986) *Recent Theories of Narrative*, Ithaca, NY: Cornell University Press.
This is an excellent, accessible introduction to the major issues in writing about narrative. Martin surveys the development of criticism on narrative and engages lucidly with specific components of narrative, placing developments within a historical context. For scholars in children's literature, particularly informative are his discussions of the conventions of realism and reader-based theories of narrative.

Nikolajeva, Maria (2002) *The Rhetoric of Character in Children's Literature*, Lanham, MD, and Oxford: Scarecrow Press.
Mixing historical perspectives and structuralist formulations, this is the only study of a single aspect of narrative in children's literature. The focus is particularly important because of the

longstanding emphasis on character and content in the criticism in the field, but the exposition is at times idiosyncratic.

Onega, Susana and Landa, José Ángel García (1996) *Narratology*, London: Longman.
After an introduction presenting a useful survey of historical changes in the conception of narratology, this collection reproduces major essays from classical narratology to the new narratology that emerged in the 1980s under the influence of psychoanalysis, feminism, and film and media studies.

Rimmon-Kenan, Shlomith (1983) *Narrative Fiction: Contemporary Poetics*, London: Methuen.
Rimmon-Kenan clearly and authoritatively introduces a wide range of theories in narratology. Following Genette, she discusses narrative fiction in terms of the distinctions among text, story and narration and, accordingly, offers very helpful accounts of events, characters and characterization, time, focalization, and voice and speech representation. An excellent introductory text.

Stephens, John (1992a) *Language and Ideology in Children's Fiction*, London: Longman.
Bringing together narratology, discourse analysis and ideology critique, this is a foundation study of key concepts such as focalization, reader subject position, **intertextuality** and the **carnivalesque**, and their significance for understanding children's fiction.

6

REALISM

LUCY PEARSON AND KIMBERLEY REYNOLDS

For most of the last century, students of English literature would have had few opportunities to study children's literature but most would have been asked to think about realism as a literary mode. As this chapter will show, the two are linked in important ways, so while realism is no longer a central component in most undergraduate literature degrees, familiarity with debates about realism can be helpful in understanding some of the most significant changes and developments in Anglophone children's literature, past and present.

One of the most influential scholarly studies to deal at length with realism was Catherine Belsey's *Critical Practice* (1980). Based in narratology and paying particular attention to the way texts convey **ideology**, *Critical Practice* rethought realism for the late twentieth century. Belsey identifies three features of what she terms 'classic realist texts', by which she means the mode of writing largely developed in nineteenth-century novels that seeks to draw readers into the world of the book and to accept the fictional world as an analogue of real life. Such books depend, she says, on the orchestration of various voices in the text, including that of a narrator, so that the reader is encouraged to agree with some versions of events and values more than others. This hierarchical structuring of information is embedded in what she calls 'illusionism': the effect, established through a series of narrative conventions to do with conveying the passage of time, describing settings, and characterization, of being in a version of our world created through words. Illusionism is central to most studies of realism, which concentrate on degrees of **mimesis**, or the extent to which the text seems truthfully to reproduce the world in which readers live. By the early twentieth century in the arts generally, 'truthfulness' came to be associated with aspects of style including the use of colloquial language and settings based on the lives of working-class people and the social problems associated with them. As discussed below, children's literature was slow to incorporate the harsher aspects of realism, preferring to reproduce the everyday lives of happy middle-class children. The third element in Belsey's analysis is closure: the moment in the novel when all loose ends are tied up and all questions answered so that readers feel satisfied and disinclined to unpick or challenge what they have read. Closure, she argues, is central to the way classic realist texts seek to efface the fact that they are works of fiction and so **interpellate** readers, drawing them into the world of the book. Through these elements, Belsey maintains, classic realist texts make readers highly prone unconsciously to absorb books' ideological views.

Belsey's focus on the ideological nature of realist fiction was taken up by critics of children's literature such as Peter **Hollindale** (1988) and John **Stephens** (1992a), who pointed out that because for the most part writing for children is concerned with teaching them about the world in which they live and shaping their attitudes, it reveals a great deal about the prevailing ideologies of a given period. Stephens in particular criticized children's writers for their adherence to the kind of realist writing Belsey anatomized on the grounds that 'a mode of reading which locates the reader only within the text is disabling, and leaves readers susceptible to gross forms of intellectual manipulation' (1992a, p. 4). It is certainly the case that from the earliest days of commercial publishing for children, which, it should be noted, predate the nineteenth-century novels Belsey discusses, realist strategies were employed in works that were unapologetically designed to tell their young readers what and how to think and behave. From the accounts of child deaths provided by James Janeway (1671–2) and the rags-to-riches tale of 'Goody Two-Shoes' (1765) through the miscellany of stories written by John Aikin and Anna Laetitia Barbauld for *Evenings at Home* (1792–6), most writers used the modes of classic realism to encourage their young readers to accept the lessons of the texts. They did this by grounding their stories in the everyday settings familiar to middle-class children, populating them with the kinds of figures they regularly encountered – parents, relations, teachers, neighbours, clergymen, servants and playfellows – and basing plots on places or events a child like the reader might expect to experience. There are exceptions, and the extent to which early children's writers turned their backs on **fairy stories** and fantasy has been overstated, but real-life situations conveyed using the conventions Belsey cites undoubtedly dominated. A typical example is Aikin and Barbauld's offering for the Sixteenth Evening, 'On Presence of Mind', in which a mother requires her young daughter to stay and watch while the doctor bleeds her on the grounds that it will develop the qualities necessary to help others at times of crisis or distress. This leads the daughter to ask, 'What is *presence of mind*, mamma?'; the definition is then supported by a series of anecdotes about dramatic events that had happened to family members and friends, each growing out of a remark by the daughter. All stress the importance of staying calm and thinking clearly, whether you are faced with fire, injury or even a tiger.

The purpose of stories such as this is to instruct and acculturate, which makes realist strategies, such as drawing readers in, aligning their views with those of a trustworthy voice and ensuring that no ambiguities complicate the ending, well suited to the task. The emphases on developing the child's reason, fitting the lesson to the child's experience and timing it so that the child (both the child in the story and the one reading the text) is in the right state to learn, reflect ideas about parenting, pedagogy and citizenship in circulation when Aikin and Barbauld were writing. While some of the devices used and conclusions drawn in writing of this sort may seem crude or objectionable to modern eyes, the way they set about creating a world that young readers were prepared to accept as real and enjoy reading about has largely endured. These realist tactics for engaging readers included references to everyday objects and experiences, the use of conversation and action based in such familiar activities as shopping, visiting, excursions and quarrels with siblings. During the nineteenth century, writers such as Thomas Hughes, Charlotte M. Yonge, Louisa May Alcott, Mrs Molesworth and Susan Coolidge developed realistic writing for children in longer, less episodic works. While their fiction too was largely based in homes and schools, in contrast to most earlier writing for children it featured more complex characterization, more elaborate plots, greater interest in character development and more detailed descriptions of place and events, all enhancing the element of illusionism. Writers who used fiction for children to make readers more socially aware and responsible, such as those who produced abolitionist, street arab and temperance stories, were equally dependent on the conventions of literary realism, though the vignettes of life depicted were often far removed from the circumstances of their readers. These books were also striking for their inclusion of seriously flawed (and usually working-class) adult characters – alcoholics, prostitutes, thieves and misers – as opposed to the vigilant and dutiful parents who populate the pages of much early children's fiction. Arguably, the discrepancies between children's lived experiences and those of the children they read about were just as great when fictional children were shown in the kinds of boarding schools invented by Angela Brazil or on the sailing holidays enjoyed by Arthur Ransome's Swallows and Amazons, not to mention the many adventures entered into by Enid Blyton's groups of adventurous children, all of which depend on the modes of realism.

Fiction more closely based in children's everyday experiences and emotions was given new impetus in the twentieth century in response to the educational philosophies of Friedrich Froebel, Jean **Piaget**, Maria Montessori and Rudolf Steiner, which mapped out models of children's physical, cognitive and emotional needs, and the popularization of Sigmund **Freud**'s ideas about the inner world of the child and the importance of childhood experience in the formation of adult identity. For younger readers, books clearly in the tradition of Barbauld and Aikin such as Dorothy Edwards's 'My Naughty Little Sister' stories (1952–74) and those by Beverly Cleary about Ramona Quimby and her family (1968–99) map the everyday vicissitudes of childhood, explaining children to themselves as well as guiding them towards socially acceptable ways of behaving. In these later works, lessons may be more disguised, but they are no less present, and each writer deliberately sets out to draw readers into a fictional world in the way that concerns Stephens. For younger readers texts of this kind have been and remain a staple of children's literature. From the 1960s children went to school or the dentist or had a babysitter with Jean and Gareth Adamson's 'Topsy and Tim'; in the 1970s and 1980s, Shirley Hughes's 'Lucy and Tom' and 'Alfie' were mirroring daily routines and experiences; by the end of the twentieth century, Lauren Child's 'Clarice Bean' had become the image of the typical child in a typical family, but in each case child readers are encouraged to identify with the characters and to accept their worlds as real.

Deliberately trying to impede the extent to which readers are drawn into the text is a practice associated with literary **modernism**, a movement that consciously rejected many of the conventions and tenets of realism and which has incorrectly been identified as antithetical to children's literature, notably by the critic Jacqueline **Rose** (1984), though many educationalists were also critical regarded the ideas behind modernism as too difficult for children who had yet to master the basics of reading and narrative (for counter-arguments, see Boethius, 1998; **Reynolds**, 2007, 2009; Westman, 2007). As modernism was succeeded by **postmodernism** and its accompanying gamut of critical approaches and concerns, realism largely ceased to be a primary area of critical interest in relation to mainstream fiction. In part this was a recognition that the classic realist text is only one of many realisms, not all of which exhibit the elements identified by Belsey; for instance, psychological realism often involves disrupting or distorting illusionism, as in Robert Westall's *The Scarecrows* (1981), in which the powerful emotions of an unhappy **adolescent** apparently cause the scarecrows in the farmland around his stepfather's house to re-enact a murderous love triangle played out in the area some decades earlier. There is also the problem that the modes Belsey identifies as characteristic of realism are identical to those used in other **genres** that are not otherwise considered realistic, the best example being fantasy, which is equally dependent on drawing readers into a fictional world, employing a variety of more and less reliable voices as sources of information and providing a satisfying reading experience by moving towards and through closure.

Although realism is now less studied in most other areas of literary criticism, it continues to be of interest to those working in the area of children's literature studies, whether in relation to historical research, investigations of children as readers, explications of adolescent 'problem novels' or debates about how to represent events such as genocide in fiction for the young. While mapping changing attitudes to realism in writing for children provides useful insights into the development of children's literature, the task is far from straightforward. For instance, one school of thought plots the history of children's literature as one that moves from 'instruction to delight' in the sense that in the eighteenth century the first commercially produced books for children tend to be highly **didactic** and firmly rooted in the everyday, but by the middle of the nineteenth century writing for children became more imaginative and eclectic, embracing modes and genres such as fantasy, nonsense and science fiction that reject the real-life settings central to realism. This model understates the extent to which realism has been a constant aspect of publishing for young people; indeed it dominated children's publishing for much of the last century (see the following). Moreover, because it assumes that 'adult' literature has evolved from forms such as folk and fairy tales, sagas, **myths** and **legends** (all now often regarded as branches of children's literature) to mature, realistic writing, it implies that children's literature, with its emphasis on entertainment, is regressive. This account of literature has its equivalent in models of children's reading such as Aidan Warlow's (1977) notion of a 'hierarchy of veracity' which proposes that because very young children have an undeveloped sense of their 'proper relation to reality', they take pleasure in fantasy and fairy stories; as they mature they increasingly turn to stories about real life.

Warlow was writing in the 1970s, when developmental models such as Piaget's were highly influential among groups involved in bringing children and books together: teachers, librarians, editors, writers and illustrators created a publishing climate that privileged and validated realism in writing for children. This way of thinking was influenced by developments in child psychology; psychologist D. W. Harding (1977), for instance, was among those who argued that the validation of particular **desires** and experiences was an essential part of the reading process. This led to the view that children need books in which they can 'see themselves', giving new impetus to the tradition of realist stories about everyday life. The demand for realist fiction became a key feature of children's literature in America from the 1950s and in the United Kingdom from the 1960s, and was closely connected to the socially progressive values of those groups concerned with children's reading.

Much of the children's fiction published in the first half of the twentieth century was for and about educated, middle-class children; Eve Garnett was one of the first British writers to depict working-class life in *The Family from One End Street* (1937), while in America Betty Smith provided a much more hard-hitting portrayal of industrial poverty in *A Tree Grows in Brooklyn* (1943). High levels of social funding for schools and libraries in the 1950s and 1960s dramatically widened the social demographic of child readers; the demand for books which reflected the lives of these 'ordinary' children created a need for more contemporary realism. Books such as those in Leila Berg's 'Nippers' series (1968–76) simply updated the tradition of Barbauld and Aikin, introducing baked-bean dinners and single-parent families to the range of stories about day-to-day life. The **ethnic** diversity of child readers too began to be reflected in children's books, notably in the work of American writers such as Ezra Jack Keats, whose picturebook *The Snowy Day* (1962), about an African-American boy enjoying an urban snowfall, was awarded the Caldecott Medal. The ideology behind such texts was more overt than in earlier 'everyday' stories like the 'My Naughty Little Sister' series, since they represented a concerted effort to introduce previously neglected voices into children's literature. In many cases these new works were a throw-back to the early days of children's fiction in that they were more didactic than mimetic: the racially tolerant, gender-equal and egalitarian society depicted in books such as Rosemary Stones *et al.*'s *Mother Goose Comes to Cable Street* (1977) and Shirley Hughes's 'Tales from Trotter Street' (1989–91) owed more to ideas of how society *should* be than to the real circumstances in which most children lived.

While the ideological impact of books such as *The Snowy Day* and *Mother Goose Comes to Cable Street* was based upon the way in which they made space for groups and issues that had thus far been absent from children's fiction, from the late 1970s issues such as racism and sexism began to be tackled more directly in children's books. Mildred D. Taylor's *Roll of Thunder, Hear My Cry* (1976) is an unflinching portrayal of Depression-era racism, its consequences and legacies; the book, part one of a saga largely based on her family's history, closes with the attempted lynching and subsequent arrest of 13-year-old T. J., who has been duped into committing a crime by white boys who go unpunished. The problem of racism in contemporary society was addressed in Bernard Ashley's *The Trouble with Donovan Croft* (1974), Jan Needle's *My Mate Shofiq* (1978) and Cynthia Voigt's *Come a Stranger* (1986), among many others. Gene Kemp's *The Turbulent Term of Tyke Tiler* (1977) takes a different approach, cleverly exposing readers' assumptions about gender not by including information, but by omitting it. Books like these challenge the traditional belief that children's literature should offer examples of positive behaviour expressed in standard English, instead of directly depicting the consequences of hatred and bigotry and forcing readers to confront their own prejudices.

The growth in realistic fiction during the 1960s and 1970s was even more apparent in books for older children, which now included adolescents, at whom some of the hardest-hitting examples of realistic fiction were aimed. The boundaries of realism in adult fiction had been radically extended in the 1950s and early 1960s; texts such as James Baldwin's *Go Tell It on the Mountain* (1953) and Alan Sillitoe's *Saturday Night and Sunday Morning* (1958) brought the seamier side of working-class life into mainstream fiction – addressing topics which had previously been taboo, such as illegitimate pregnancy, abortion, inter-racial romance and homosexuality. This trend was gradually reflected in books for children and young people. Hard-hitting realism was a distinctive feature of American literature by writers such as Virginia Hamilton and S. E. Hinton. John Rowe **Townsend**'s *Gumble's Yard* (1961) was one of the first British titles to depict a grittier aspect of real life; the smooth family relationships and comfortable lifestyles which had characterized most twentieth-century children's realism were replaced with more challenging material. One characteristic feature of the realist novels of the 1960s and 1970s was a trend towards less positive adult authority figures; in this respect, as in the return to more overtly ideological works, the books of this period owe a clear debt to the temperance tales of the Victorian era. Child characters, too, became less unambiguously admirable, as in Louise Fitzhugh's *Harriet the Spy* (1964), whose heroine, while certainly engaging, is not altogether *nice*. Such ambiguous characterization reflects a shift in perceptions of childhood which took place during this period: the work of child development experts and psychologists increasingly disrupted the notion of children as innocents in need of protection from the harsher realities of the world, acknowledging the darker and more complex nature of childhood experience.

The once taboo themes of kitchen-sink realism appeared steadily in children's literature during the 1970s and 1980s. The problematic nature of including such material in books for young readers was overridden by a belief in the need for instructive material on controversial issues. The rise of television and new media contributed to a perception that children were already exposed to 'adult' concerns; children's literature was increasingly pressed into service to contextualize and interpret such material. Many of the resultant 'issues' novels were bibliotherapeutic in nature: divorce, puberty, bereavement and bullying were among the host of concerns dealt with by writers such as Judy Blume and Paula Danziger, and, more recently, Jacqueline Wilson. These books, while they continued the tradition of didactic children's literature, were typically less optimistic than those which had gone before, focusing on ways of coping with difficult situations rather than providing outright solutions. Correspondingly, the tone was less overtly didactic: authors assumed the role of sympathetic older siblings rather than wise instructors; Judy Blume's sympathetic treatment of real-life problems in her novels caused many children to write to her with their own confidences. Danziger and Blume extended their sympathetic style to their books for adolescents, but many other books for this age group – which were more likely to feature situations in which young characters were the instigators rather than the victims of undesirable behaviour – were more overtly didactic. *Go Ask Alice* (1971) – marketed as the diary of a real teenager but now widely accepted as fiction – and Kathleen Peyton's *Pennington's Heir* (1973) differ little in essence from the cautionary tales of the Victorian era: although more likely to depict transgressions such as pre-marital sex or drug use rather than impiety or intemperance, taboo behaviours produce the same calamitous results. This strategy legitimized the inclusion of material which might otherwise have been deemed too controversial; it is notable that Judy Blume's *Forever* (1975), which failed to temper its positive depiction of teenage sexuality with an overtly didactic message, attracted far more censure than many more explicit titles (see **censorship**).

A central tension in approaches to realism in children's literature is the question of how much reality children can be expected to bear, or perhaps – as Robert Westall (1979) suggests – how much realism adults can bear to give them. While children's authors up until the twentieth century had no compunction about exposing children to stories of death, torture and disaster, provided that the tales were directed towards edifying and instructing their child readers, children's literature in the twentieth century was dominated by the perception that children have a need for literature which offers a positive resolution. The need for a happy ending has been characterized as a fundamental characteristic of children's literature; in the words of Nicholas **Tucker** (1972, p. 53), 'It is asking too much of a child to expect him [*sic*] to see life in the raw as it actually is'. Nevertheless, the move towards greater verisimilitude in children's fiction during the 1960s admitted the inclusion of situations and emotions which had hitherto been deemed too negative or distressing for children's literature. Depictions of childhood death – prevalent in Victorian moral tales, but largely rejected for most of the twentieth century – made a reappearance in books such as Katherine Paterson's *Bridge to Terabithia* (1977) and Ian Strachan's *The Boy in the Bubble* (1993). Whereas many Victorian writers were primarily concerned with showing the relationship between the kind of life a person had lived and what could be expected in the next life, these stories were essentially aimed at helping children to come to terms with grief and unhappiness. By degrees the insistence on offering a consoling resolution to the problems and traumas depicted in adolescent fiction diminished; writers such as Robert Cormier and Paul Zindel pioneered a darker mode of realism in books for young adults which eschewed clear resolutions in favour of bleaker, more complex outcomes. Such **depressive literature** has become increasingly prevalent in the children's literature of the late twentieth and early twenty-first centuries, extending into books for younger readers as well as those aimed at adolescents. Anne Fine's *The Tulip Touch* (1996) raises hard questions about societal failings, while her novel for teenagers, *The Road of Bones* (2007), explores the effects of violence and totalitarianism on its young protagonist. Similarly, Michael Rosen's *Sad Book* (2004), which deals with the death of his son, Eddie, ends on an image of the grieving father, acknowledging the enduring nature of loss. Depressive literature reflects a move towards a characterization of child readers which privileges their need for truth about the world over their need for protection. This subgenre also frequently employs modernist devices which work to disrupt the process of drawing readers into the text, identified by Stephens as a key ideological tool of realism. Robert Cormier's *I Am the Cheese* (1975) and Australian writer Gary Crew's *Strange Objects* (1991), for example, use layered narratives in which the perceptions of the protagonists are systematically undermined, forcing readers to reconstruct events on successive readings.

The issue of how much realism is too much is brought into sharp focus in Holocaust fiction, where the tension between the desire to document and warn against the horrors of genocide and the impulse to protect children from the worst excesses of human cruelty magnifies the inherent tension surrounding truth-telling in children's fiction. Holocaust narratives might be said to be innately depressive in nature, since there is only so much that writers can do to cushion readers against disturbing material without fundamentally distorting the truth. Consequently, direct accounts of the Holocaust were largely absent from children's literature up until the late 1980s; Roberto Innocenti's picturebook *Rose Blanche* (1986), in which a young girl witnesses the horrors of a concentration camp, stands out for its direct approach to a subject which had typically been addressed more obliquely. Gudrun Pausewang's *The Final Journey* (1996) heralded a more explicit mode for Holocaust narratives in children's fiction, which has continued with books such as John Boyne's *The Boy in the Striped Pyjamas* (2006) and Morris Gleitzman's *Once* (2006), which bring the reader face to face with the murder of their child characters. While critics debate ethical issues raised by Holocaust narratives, the increasing historical distance from the Holocaust is leading writers to experiment with ways of helping young readers understand that the incomprehensible events which comprise it actually took place. This is resulting in challenges to the modes of classic realism, including the use of limited **focalizers**, unreliable points of view, conflicting narratives, texts that shift between words and images, and those that are highly indeterminate. As thinking about the representation of the Holocaust has become more subject to conflicting interpretations, so realistic narratives have become more complex.

The picturebook format of *Rose Blanche* makes it accessible to younger readers, but overall this readership has been provided with simpler stories about everyday life rather than the hard-hitting works typical of realist fiction for older readers. The dominance of dramatic real-life themes in books for the latter group partly derives from the belief that older children demand more complex and exciting plots. Where 'normal' life is the setting in books for readers of, say, ten up, it is often in the form of genre fiction: school, pony, mystery or family stories.

Despite the improbability of their plots and the idealized version of the world they offer, such stories offer scope for the recounting of ordinary day-to-day experiences; **school stories** in particular often focus on the everyday necessities of meals, clothes and washing. Another area where stories of day-to-day life are offered to children beyond the nursery stage is poetry, in which linguistic interest can be used to bring more appeal to stories of ordinary events. Allan Ahlberg and Charles Causley both capture the language and atmosphere of the classroom in their poems, as in Ahlberg's 'Please Mrs Butler' (1983), which takes the form of a conversation between a child and an increasingly exasperated teacher.

The attempt to bring more realism to children's literature has extended to the mode of telling as well as to the range of events depicted. J. D. Salinger's *The Catcher in the Rye* (1951), with its slang-heavy first-person narrative, formed an important model for young adult authors seeking to use a more authentic adolescent voice, and from the 1960s onwards a more informal, less literary mode became an important feature of children's literature. Writers such as Westall argued for the importance of representing children's language faithfully rather than sanitizing it: the pre-pubescent characters of his book *The Machine Gunners* (1975) speak the dialect of their native Tyneside, frequently interspersed with swearing. As mentioned above, some writers have turned to poetry as a way of rendering children's voices more authentically; this strategy can be seen, for instance, not only in the naturalistic dialogue of poems like 'Please Mrs Butler' but also in the work of some prose writers, who have adopted the modes of poetry in order to give voice to their child narrators. Virginia Euwer Wolff's *Make Lemonade* (1993) uses a prose–poem format which – perhaps paradoxically – gives the impression of being less literary and more colloquial and spontaneous than conventional prose as it relates events in the life of its 14-year-old protagonist. For younger readers, Malorie Blackman's *Cloudbusting* (2004), Jacqueline Woodson's *Locomotion* (2003) and Sharon Creech's *Love That Dog* (2001) all use free verse as a means of representing the child's voice in a way that sounds more direct and natural.

The enduring belief in children's need to see their own lives reflected in the books they read has ensured that mimetic realism has retained a central place in children's literature, but the stylistic and generic boundaries of realistic fiction began to become increasingly fluid during the 1970s. The desire to cater for a wider demographic of child readers helped to support the growth of realistic fiction; it also contributed to its encroachment on other genres. Diana Wynne Jones in *The Ogre Downstairs* (1974) and Robert Leeson in *The Third-Class Genie*

(1975) fused fantasy and realism in narratives where magic solves everyday problems. Unlike earlier writers such as E. Nesbit, who used the collision of magical and realistic elements primarily for comic effect, Jones and Leeson place their fantasies firmly in the real world: Leeson's genie is summoned from a beer can discarded in the gutter. Alan Garner fuses the genres even more seamlessly: the three relationships narrated in his young adult novel, *Red Shift* (1973), are not less realistic for the time-slip element which binds them. Garner's novel is also stylistically complex; Maria **Nikolajeva** (1998) classes it as a postmodern narrative, a characteristic it shares with the novels of Garner's contemporary, Aidan **Chambers**. Chambers's 'Dance Sequence' (1978–2005) applies diverse narrative strategies to the task of exploring adolescent life; all six books in the sequence force readers to question the reliability of the narrator, eliminating the coercive effects of interpellation. From the 1970s onwards, then, realism in children's literature has been developing in ways which transcend the boundaries delineated by Belsey.

The didactic impulse behind many of the realist texts published during the 1970s and the 1980s helped to extend the boundaries of realism in children's literature, introducing many topics previously considered too controversial for younger readers. Typically these early books adopted a mimetic style, seeking to portray issues in a recognizable real-world setting and to supply them with a didactic context. Over time, writers have been able to incorporate many hard-hitting elements of realist novels without making them the main focus of the narrative; themes such as family breakdown or homosexuality, for instance, can now form part of the general context. Combined with increased stylistic experimentation in children's literature, this trend has resulted in a more fluid approach to realism. Francesca Lia Block's 'Dangerous Angels' series (1989–2005) deals with themes such as sexuality, AIDS and drug use in a **magic realist** mode which neither seeks to reflect everyday life nor offers a strong didactic message. Melvin Burgess, Kevin Brooks and Ally Kennan all deal with challenging social issues in books which incorporate elements of horror, science fiction and the thriller: Burgess's *Sara's Face* (2006) explores body dysmorphia, plastic surgery and celebrity in a recognizable real-world setting which moves imperceptibly towards the fantastic, while Ally Kennan's *Beast* (2006) takes an entirely realistic approach to the problems of a looked-after child on the cusp of adulthood – except for the central plot motivator, the boy's struggle to deal with his huge and dangerous pet crocodile. While the themes and issues in each of these examples are connected with individuals in the way characteristic of realism, the new hybrid realism is also tackling issues of worldwide concern such as global warming, globalization, pandemics, new technologies and terrorism.

In short, the motivation behind realistic writing may have changed little since the earliest days of children's fiction: it continues to be an essentially didactic mode in that it remains concerned with encouraging young readers to observe and think about the world around them; increasingly, however, it is also doing this in ways that are less obviously one-sided and seductive. Realism in contemporary children's literature is more varied, bold and amorphous than previously; it reaches deeper into the psyche, further into the future and employs a wider stylistic repertoire. This does not mean, however, that realism will necessarily continue to be a dominant force in children's literature. The enlarged range of issues tackled by realistic writers for children in the 1960s and 1970s was a response to the affluence, confidence and educational policies of the postwar years in Britain and the United States, and their optimistic view that children could be prepared to manage the future well. At the start of the new millennium such confidence and optimism are less abundant. The changes in realism – its interactions with other genres and modes – may be symptomatic of a lack of faith in its 'grand narratives' (Lyotard, 1984). Despite the fact that realism has been intensified and enlarged, as a narrative mode it seems inadequate as a way of representing this age of cultural uncertainty.

FURTHER READING

Beaumont, Matthew (ed.) (2007) *Adventures in Realism*, Oxford: Blackwell.
A wide-ranging collection of essays by established critics and philosophers that move beyond literature to consider how realism has developed in different mediums and in response to new technologies.

Booth, Wayne C. (1961) *The Rhetoric of Fiction*, Chicago and London: University of Chicago Press.
Chapter 2 contains an influential discussion of realism as a literary form.

Fisher, Margery (1964) 'Realism and Reality', in *Intent upon Reading: A Critical Appraisal of Modern Fiction for Children*, Aylesbury: Brockhampton Press, 311–45.
Although dated, this survey captures key debates about the place of realism in writing for children in the mid-twentieth century and the extent to which traditional forms and genres were affected by the drive to make them reflect contemporary children's lives.

Hollindale, Peter and Sutherland, Zena (1995) 'Internationalism, Fantasy and Realism 1945–1970', in Peter Hunt (ed.) *Children's Literature: An Illustrated History*, Oxford and New York: Oxford University Press, 257–88.
Embedded in an overview of the development of children's literature in the United Kingdom and United States during the middle years of the last century is a discussion of how it engaged with topical issues such as sexism, racism and classism for readers of different ages.

Hunt, Peter (1994) *An Introduction to Children's Literature*, Oxford: Oxford University Press.
This survey contains a particularly useful discussion of realism in relation to picturebooks and another that deals with 'new realisms', including issue or problem novels, developments in domestic fiction, the impact of political correctness and increased awareness of cultural diversity with reference to developments in the United Kingdom and United States.

Meek, Margaret, Warlow, Aidan and Barton, Griselda (eds) (1977) *The Cool Web: The Pattern of Children's Reading*, London: Bodley Head.
Many of the contributors to this influential collection of essays discuss realism. The contributions bring together experts from several fields including psychologists, educationalists, writers and critics. Over thirty years on there is much to be learned from working through the multiple perspectives it provides. Particular emphasis is given to the changing cognitive and emotional needs of the developing child.

Morris, Pam (2003) *Realism*, London: Routledge.
This volume in the New Critical Idiom series offers a good overview of the development of realism and points to new directions in realist writing, including utopian fiction.

Stephens, John (1992a) *Language and Ideology in Children's Fiction*, London: Longman.
Scattered throughout this study are insights into and examples of the way realism works linguistically: as a metonymic mode, in the construction of character, as a vehicle for ideology and in conversation.

Watts, Ian (2001) *The Rise of the Novel: Studies in Defoe, Richardson and Fielding*, Berkeley and Los Angeles: University of California Press [orig. 1957].
Perhaps one of the most influential books of its day; Chapter 2 of the book focuses specifically on the role and evolving conventions of realism in the development of the novel.

7

FANTASY

KAREN COATS

Kenny Watson, in *The Watsons Go to Birmingham – 1963* (Curtis, 1995), has been warned not to go swimming at Collier's Landing because of a dangerous whirlpool. His grandmother pronounces it 'Wool Pooh' in her accented Alabaman English, and Kenny's usually fearless older brother, Byron, tells him that the Wool Pooh is Winnie's evil twin, eager to suck him under and drown him. Kenny is not about to let a silly fantasy explanation like that stop him from having a cool swim on a hot day, and he enters the seemingly tranquil water only to be grabbed by the Wool Pooh, whose grey fingers he sees and feels clutching his feet and dragging him to his death. He is rescued, but that isn't his last encounter with the Wool Pooh; the second time the monster shows up is at the site of the Birmingham church bombing, moving in and out of the smoke-filled confusion where four teenage girls were killed in a stunning hate crime.

In his perceptive portrayal of a young boy's first encounters with random and violent death, Christopher Paul Curtis personifies Kenny's nemesis as a terrifying monster, a creature of nightmares in an otherwise realistic novel about a family's visit to the American South during the turbulent time of the Civil Rights Movement. Kenny's fantastic encounter with the Wool Pooh is predicated on three things: first, the unexpected sensation of being physically acted on and controlled by a powerful but unseen force; second, the use of unfamiliar language to describe a mysterious phenomenon; and third, an **intertextual** reference to a fantasy story with which he is familiar, but which is twisted in a perverse, **uncanny** way to indicate a dark and repressed underside. These three elements form a definitional matrix for understanding the ways in which fantasy becomes operative for children both in their psychological development and in their literary experience: fantasy begins as a way of understanding and providing **signifiers** for a child's experience of his and other bodies in the world and provides countless metaphors for the vicissitudes of embodiment; fantasy depends for its existence on the innovative use of language to create, develop and sustain worlds, including developing psychic worlds that may or may not have referential ties to actual phenomena; and lastly, fantasy participates in an intertextual web of cross-reference, allusion and literary history for its themes, motifs and structures.

As an ordinary human activity, fantasizing or creating fantasies plays a crucial role in establishing the life-world of a subject; using Martin Heidegger's terminology, we could say that children are thrown into a world that they did not make and yet must make something of, and the tools they have to craft a coherent and meaningful existence consist of their bodies, the language(s) of their social world and a culturally scripted set of narratives and representations that they internalize, test and use innovatively to construct a sense of self. Much of that construction depends not on an unmediated experience of bodies in the world – that is, in the **Real** – but on socially mediated relations fed by the images and words that they are given to think with. For instance, when children are left alone in the dark, their bodies respond by sending signals of fear, isolation and disorientation, but it is stories that populate that dark with monsters. Jacques **Lacan**'s famous formulation of the **mirror stage** asserts that the first recognition of one's own body in a mirror inaugurates the **Imaginary** order and sets the course for all future understandings of the self and others in a fictional direction: the lived experience of the body as fragmented and helpless is eclipsed by a specular image of coherence and control, and that image becomes a fantasized ideal that the subject strives toward. I have argued that stories, as well as the first people that children encounter, function similarly as mirrors that reflect ideals that have little or nothing to do with what we might call 'real' experience and yet populate the **unconscious** with images and signifiers that interact with each other in ways that displace and trump the Real (Coats, 2004). Lacan further specifies the nature of lived reality by introducing a third order which he calls the **Symbolic**, which is a more public realm of language and culture that gives social value to the images children have collected in the Imaginary. Once children become users of language, stories always mediate – that is, stand between, interpret and ascribe value to – phenomena.

A subject's life-world thus consists of Imaginary relations and Symbolic representations that by their very nature are heterogeneous to the three-dimensional status of a body in a world. While their experiences are anchored in their bodies and the material substance of their environment, children must use *words* to narrate and describe these experiences. As the linguistic theories of Ferdinand de **Saussure**, C. S. Pierce and J. L. Austin have taught us, words are at most mere pointers arbitrarily connected to, and thus ultimately constitutive of, the things they purport to describe. This is not to say that language cannot serve a descriptive function: we can and do use language to indicate phenomena with a certain level of precision, but only by virtue of an agreed-upon, conventional acceptance of the meaningfulness of **signs**. It is also not to say that things exist only by virtue of the language we use to describe them. In fact, one of the components of the process whereby children acquire the language of their culture is through a recognition of its independence from the world of phenomena. Once children learn the names for things in their native language, they begin to deploy their most famous question, *why?*, in part seeking to disturb the seeming fixity of the words-to-world connection that they have been given. Simultaneously with their developing knowledge and use of the conventional words for things, they develop their own nomenclature that is often reinforced within the family, and they begin telling themselves stories and engaging in fantasy play that helps them set the elements of their environment into an order over which they exercise some control.

In this project, they often imitate the way they themselves are controlled by the various elements – parents, siblings, caregivers, domestic spaces – in their environment, but they also draw on **mythical** characters, architecture and landscapes from the stories they are told, indicating a relatively sophisticated understanding of the way language can create meaningful worlds that do not reflect the world in which they live. Language begins to become untethered from a fixed one-to-one correspondence of word to object and to develop the abstract and substitutionary character of metaphoric thinking. These stories and fantasy play also take on a defensive character, in the psychoanalytic sense of displacing, condensing or projecting the child's anxieties onto safer targets. Thus, an angry child takes out his aggression on a doll rather than a human sibling, and a fearful one develops her own mythologies surrounding events that are threatening, such as a mother's pregnancy, or a thunderstorm. Like the mythmakers of ancient cultures, children very quickly become accustomed to inventing stories to explain unfamiliar phenomena, finding or fantasizing concrete foci for diffuse emotional states such as love, fear, anger and anxiety. Thus, fantasy becomes functional for children attempting to construct a world that is manageable: small enough for them to acquire a sense of mastery and empowerment and thus mitigate or at least contain their fears and anxieties, yet large enough to facilitate wonder and help them imagine possibilities for things to be other than how they find them.

As a literary mode taken up by writers specifically addressing children and young adults, then, fantasy meets readers on paradoxically familiar ground. Fantasy writers construct worlds in ways homologous to those that children have used to construct their own worlds: they invent family relationships and domestic and outdoor spaces; names for people, places and concepts; and fill in gaps in understanding with storied memories, myths of origin, time shifts and imaginary dangers that insert themselves between the child and what he is not yet ready to encounter or understand. If writers want their fictional worlds to work differently from the world that surrounds them, they invent new words or realign old ones for their concepts – the explanation Mrs Who and Mrs Whatsit offer for 'tessering' as a mode of travel that functions like a wrinkle in the fabric of time being a prime example (Madeleine L'Engle, *A Wrinkle in Time*, 1962). While there are any number of ways in which these worlds might be configured, the ones that seem to hold the most fascination for young world-makers are the bounded ones, the ones J. R. R. Tolkien called Secondary Worlds. This sense of a border is important for children attempting to create a sustainable life-world because part of the anxiety created by living day to day is that one has been set adrift in an infinite universe. For the very young child, as well as for people of any age going through stressful experiences, such as job loss, a change in status or moving from home, this sort of freedom can cause fear rather than exhilaration: the uncertainty of outcomes, the feeling of being without an anchor or guarantee, the anxiety of being in process are all part of the condition of being thrown into the world and having to construct and protect a self from as yet indeterminate dangers. Rosemary Jackson (1981) notes that one of the characteristics of the type of fantasy called the marvellous is that the narrative voice 'has complete knowledge of *completed* events', thus allaying the anxiety of indeterminacy and reinforcing the fantasy of a unified, bounded world. Hence, the created secondary worlds of Middle Earth, Narnia, Neverland, Hogwarts and the Inkworld are filled with compensatory wonders that fill up or cover over the sense of being alone in a world, but, with the exception of Cornelia Funke's Inkworld, they also offer the comforting sense of being in a world where a firm but non-intrusive narrative voice has complete imaginative control. Interestingly, Fenoglio's experience in the **metafictive** Inkworld, where the narrative regularly slips from his control and goes off in unexpected directions, is in fact more analogous to the level of power children actually have over the worlds they construct.

Literary critics and psychoanalytic thinkers address this creative, world-making process in different ways. For Tolkien (1964, p. 50), for instance, 'Fantasy remains a human right: we make in our measure and in our derivative mode, because we are made: and not only made, but made in the image and likeness of a Maker'. David Gooderham (1995) links the need to construct and consume fantasies to Erikson's theory of growth crises, showing how different kinds of fantasy respond to different stages of development. Sigmund **Freud** attributes this kind of creative activity largely to a reaction against the unbearable weight of the reality principle. For Freud, staged measures of development are operative in both individuals and societies; fantasy emerges out of the residue of the infant's belief in her own omnipotence and out of a pre-scientific worldview that sought responses from the gods to prayers, solicitations and sacrifices. As a scientific worldview has displaced a more animistic one, and as an infant realizes the limits of her own power in manipulating her world, human beings must come to terms with the fact that they are not the creator or centre of their own worlds but instead are part of a (signifying) system over which they have little control. Thus, the fantasies produced through the residue of animistic thinking emerge as 'creations with the help of which man, in the unrestricted narcissism of that stage of development, strives to fend off the manifest prohibitions of reality' (Freud, 1955, p. 240).

It is important to remember that Freud was utterly in thrall to a scientific worldview, so that 'manifest prohibitions of reality' were a distinct challenge for him as he studied the more irrational aspects of **desire**, belief and human pathology. Critics such as Maria **Nikolajeva** (2006) and C. W. Sullivan III (1996) point to the growing dominance of the scientific worldview as the condition under which fantasy became a popular mode of literary expression. The increased emphasis on rationality and empiricism during the European Enlightenment denigrated imagination and emotion as ways of knowing; self-appointed guardians of children's literature, such as Anna Laetitia Barbauld, Sarah Trimmer, Mary Wollstonecraft and Maria Edgeworth, followed the **Lockean** injunction to keep children away from fantastic tales of supernatural creatures in order to ensure that their growth in rational judgement would be unperturbed by irrational fears of and wishes for things that didn't exist under a rationalist or empiricist paradigm. They created a literature for children that emphasized the canny, that is, the homelike and familiar. As Dale Townshend (2008) points out, however, at the same time in literary history, the **Gothic** was becoming an enormously popular mode for adult readers. Clearly, what is repressed or ignored does not simply go away; in this case, the increased emphasis on the canny produced a fascination with its opposite – the uncanny – as evidenced by the persistent interest in the more fantastic chapbook stories and the enormous growth in fantasy literature for children beginning with the work of the Grimms, E. T. A. Hoffmann and Hans Christian Andersen.

While the uncanny can summon quite disturbing emotions of estrangement and dis-ease in fantasy literature for adults, the most common form the uncanny takes in children's fantasy has to do with inanimate objects showing signs of life, power and volition. One way of understanding this distinction comes through looking at the needs of the body and the developing **ego**. The human body is vulnerable, hence its fight-or-flight mechanism. Throughout human history, stories have encoded fear and rescue in both natural and supernatural narratives, giving listeners and readers images on which to project and practise their responses to fear, as well as develop the belief that they can survive, conquer or be delivered from whatever threatens them. While Locke and his followers were eager to dismiss the supernatural images as superstition, they could not eradicate the tendency for people to cultivate imaginary creatures and scenarios as the screens on which to project their fears and desires. Nor could they erase the tendency to invest everyday objects with animate properties, either as a help in times of threat or as the source of the threat itself. Things of power – the sword Excalibur, cornucopias, magic cauldrons, Mrs Who's glasses, Harry Potter's wand – link to bodies via their properties as phallic and yonic symbols and in their ability to enhance ordinary physical abilities; they also, as Freud suggested, show the uncanny effect of projecting our unconscious desires onto our environment. Such animistic thinking, while dominant in childhood, never really goes away, as anyone who has ever talked to a computer or car can attest. But it also indicates an internal struggle whereby **id**-generated desires emerge in conflict with limiting realities. Fantasized satisfaction of appetites, the ability to act on our aggression, the desire to transgress our body's limits – these represent powerful wishes; objects empowered to do our bidding without wills of their own become repositories of wish-fulfilment fantasies. On the other hand, however, the reality-attuned **ego** knows that animate objects, like the id-wishes that control them, have the power to be quite frightening and the internalized **superegoic** constraints already operative by the time the child can imagine these scenarios can impose sanctions of their own to render them objects of dread. Countless stories exist to dissuade children from such fantasies, many taking the form of 'The Sorcerer's Apprentice' as visualized in Disney's *Fantasia* (1940), where the novice summons power beyond his ability to control.

But there is more than a desire for personal omnipotence at work in the emergence of fantasy as a prevalent literary mode: a scientific worldview cannot fully account for anomalous events or the irrationality of desire or satisfactorily explain the differences between concepts we can only imagine (such as infinity or a sense of the numinous) and phenomena we can experience and measure (from grazed knees to land speed records). In other words, much lived human experience must be repressed in the service of a scientific worldview. That repressed material finds its way into stories in its various aspects as horror, wish fulfilment or a residual desire for a responsive universe. **Fairy tales**, for instance, which are the wellspring of modern fantasy, often take as their subject a sense of universal responsiveness: personal kindness or goodness results in a supernatural gift of prosperity, whereas greed or callousness results in punishment. In shaping morality as a call and response from an intelligent universe that actually pays attention to human action, folk stories reassert and perpetuate animistic thinking. **Magic realism**, with its intrusion of the fantastic into real-world scenarios, presents an eloquent argument for the reinvigoration of animistic thinking in a world disenchanted by scientific explanations. Each of David Almond's books, for instance, stages an encounter between scientific, technological or simply ordinary realism and a numinous creature; in each case, the creature needs the faith of the protagonists in something beyond what a rationalist, empiricist worldview can provide in order to survive. Kenny Watson's Wool Pooh and Margaret Mahy's ghost stories offer examples of the negative potential of magic realism: aspects of diabolical evil may intrude into a rational world as well as aspects of miraculous wonder.

Despite these calls to reinvigorate an animistic worldview, or at least accommodate it alongside a scientific one, the prohibitions of reality impinge upon the child in multiple ways, the most insistent of which may be upon the body. It grows without our permission, stops growing without our permission and is only partially responsive to non-surgical attempts to change its structure. It can't fly. It is always visible. Flagship fantasies such as those by Lewis Carroll, J. M. Barrie and J. K. Rowling derive much of their fascination from explorations of what might happen if these limitations of embodiment were relaxed or overthrown. Jackson (1981) points out that fantasy treats desire in specific ways: it can tell of desire by giving wishes concrete form, as does Rowling with her creation of a world where children can use magic for personal empowerment and social good; it can seek to expel desire, exposing its likely unpleasant outcomes, as with Carroll in his rather cruel manipulations of Alice's body and her progress; or it can do both, as Barrie does in taking the children to their Neverland and back again. Tracing the body in fantasy literature leads to the identification of instances of jubilant transcendence and competence or horrific expressions of failure and teratology. In each case, embodiment plays a key role in establishing lasting audience appeal: throughout the changing values and circumstances of history, the body persists as a problem of limitations to be imaginatively overcome in the telling of desire or as a warning against trying to transgress those limitations in the expelling of desire.

Whether telling or expelling, what we are really seeking, according to Slavoj **Žižek**, is not a staging of our own desires *per se* but a way of making ourselves visible and desirable for the **Other** and a way of confronting and overcoming the lack we find in both ourselves and the world around us. That is, as we come to terms with the fact that we are merely part of a larger system, we are confronted with the fact that the system is incomplete and flawed and that there is no guarantee of our own importance or desirability in such a system. Thus, we enter into fantasy seeking what Lacan called the *objet a*, 'the secret treasure that guarantees the minimum of fantasmatic consistency of the subject's being . . . that "something in me more than myself" on account of which I perceive myself as worthy of the Other's desire' (Žižek, 1998, p. 194). Messianic children's fantasies operate according to this principle: children are identified as saviours through prophecies or as possessing some special quality that sets them apart from the norm and makes them the only ones who can solve the mystery, pull the sword from the stone, save the world and fix its ills. In other words, these special children are themselves the solution to the problem of lack and desire in the world, and if they perform their task adequately, the world can be made new again. The lessons learned by these heroes, and the readers who identify with them, are not so much that the heroes are in fact special but that they are responsible and must act: they must be ready to take up a position of moral **agency** in the midst of conflict. The recent film *Kung Fu Panda* (2008) illustrates this quite clearly: Po, a lazy panda with an active fantasy life, is surprisingly identified as the Dragon Warrior who, according to prophecy, will save the Valley of Peace from destruction. He completes his training and takes possession of the Dragon Scroll, only to find that the secret of the Dragon Warrior's power is that there is no secret. That is, as Lacan points out, the notion of a secret treasure within is a fantasy; there is no guarantee of desirability for the Other, and the subject must become the source of his or her own consistency and desirability in a system that may or may not recognize him or her.

Lacan calls this recognition 'traversing the fundamental fantasy', a process whereby a subject becomes her own cause. Children begin life as the object of someone else's desire; they are, in effect, caused and protected by this desire. This initially imbues them with feelings of omnipotence and invulnerability, as every utterance of a beloved infant evokes a response and needs are generally met with alacrity. As a child grows, however, she begins to sense that her caregivers have desires other than for her. No longer able to command attention as a birthright, she must seek to become desirable, and when that desirability is not recognized, she compensates with fantasies of empowerment wherein her true worth is recognized or her specialness still affords some protection. At some point, however, she must traverse this fundamental fantasy and become the cause and instigator of her own desire. For instance, while Tom Riddle (aka Voldemort) is forever debilitated by the absence of maternal desire (his mother neither wanted him nor loved him, leaving him to compensate by making power his only love object), Harry is sustained throughout by the narrative Dumbledore gives him of a mother's love strong enough to withstand the most lethal curse. Harry is also challenged by a legacy of extreme competence on the part of both his parents. His desire to be desired by these infinitely desirable parents is first evident when he gazes into the Mirror of Erised, but it reaches its apex in the scene where Harry has travelled back in time and mistakenly thinks that his father is casting the Patronus charm that is protecting him and Sirius from the dementors; at the last possible moment he traverses his fundamental fantasy of parental protection and casts the Patronus himself, effectively becoming his own saviour. Like Po, he has to stop looking for some outside source that will guarantee the consistency and worth of his own being and act without that guarantee.

Becoming the cause of one's own desire doesn't always come about in an epiphanic rush, as is the case with Harry Potter's saving himself, or young Wart pulling the sword from the anvil. Instead, a much more common trigger is boredom, along with the feeling of being cast-off and overlooked. Neil Gaiman's eponymous Coraline, for instance, is bored and feeling neglected by her busy parents, and this is what sends her through the doorway to the realm of the Other Mother and makes Coraline vulnerable to the Other Mother's attentions (see Coats, 2008, for a full analysis). Peter, Susan, Edmund and Lucy are likewise bored, restless and overlooked before their games lead Lucy, and eventually the others, into Narnia. E. Nesbit's 'five children' in *Five Children and It* (1902) would never have discovered 'It' were it not that they had been bored and casting about for something to do. Winnie first encounters the immortal Tucks in Natalie Babbitt's *Tuck Everlasting* (1975) when she is feeling bored, confined and misunderstood by her relatives. The children in Dr Seuss's *The Cat in the Hat* (1957) are bored and abandoned, too, and then the Cat shows up to introduce anarchy and mayhem into their humdrum day. The sense of being neglected and the experience of being bored are related in terms of desire: they both emerge when the child realizes that the Other is no longer taking full charge of his desire. As caregivers turn their attention to other things, children feel abandoned, cast off. Boredom, then, signals the advent of a new phase in a child's psychic life. According to Adam Phillips (1994, p. 69), 'boredom starts as a regular crisis in the child's developing capacity to be alone in the presence of the mother'. It's a developmental achievement when the child realizes that he can, and indeed must, have desires that are his own, rather than directed and controlled by his caregivers. I would argue that boredom is also related to the limitations of the body as discussed above, as well as the limitations imposed by our position within a signifying system; in any instance where we have run up against the demands of the reality principle regarding our embodied circumstances or our position within the Symbolic, our recompense will be to turn to fantasy, to tell and expel, to imagine what might be worth desiring, to test limits by imaginatively transgressing them.

Embarking on this project of developing our own desires is a fraught enterprise, however, as we know from childhood that our desires can be dangerous. This is the premise upon which Bruno **Bettelheim** builds his argument for the 'uses of enchantment'. Fairy tales, claims Bettelheim, 'start where the child really is in his psychological and emotional well-being' (1976, p. 6). That is, fairy tales provide metaphoric outlets for all of the rage, aggression, fear, appetites and yearnings that plague the developing child and help the child own and work through these darker impulses towards more positive social behaviours. Although Bettelheim's methods and his simplistic views of **reader response** have been challenged, there is no doubt that fairy tale narratives become part of the strategy the ego uses to negotiate between the voracious id and the overbearing superego, most often in Jackson's sense of the telling of desire. Nonsense literature, on the other hand, usually proceeds through the expelling of desire, taking a desire to its most vulgar or ridiculous extreme. For instance, Maurice Sendak playfully illustrates the id politics of desire for the mother in the counting poem 'I One My Mother' (Opie and Opie, 1992, pp. 74–5). A baby begins the poem at the mother's breast, consuming more of his mother with each line until she is completely inside him by the line 'I eight [ate] my mother'. The humour that results from the impossibility of the situation enables the child to see the absurdity of the desire itself, and thus to expel it by staging it in fantasy.

Most of these narratives, despite their seeming fondness for anarchy, ultimately result in conservative outcomes; that is to say, they feature protagonists with anti-social drives that threaten the stability of their worlds, but these protagonists then become empowered through mastering these drives, at least until next time. In this sense, the stories demonstrate the function of **Bakhtinian carnival**: rules, hierarchies and social propriety get upended for a time, but when control and order are ultimately restored, they function more smoothly as a result of the release of tension and negative emotions that carnival affords. *Where the Wild Things Are* (1963) is prototypical of this outcome. Max's anti-social behaviour threatens his relationship with his mother, and his threat to eat her up reflects his desire for reunification with the maternal body. When he is sent to his room, he uses fantasy to manage his anger and to assert his own power, but it is only when he becomes to his inner wild things what his mother is to him that he is able to transcend his predicament and face the consequences of his loneliness without her. Given the choice of remaining wild, free and anti-social or of mastering his impulses and going home, he chooses home. The protagonist in Gaiman's *The Wolves in the Walls* (2003) faces a similar situation, where her home is threatened by wolves that she has obviously conjured, like Max, through her drawings. As representations of inner tensions and anti-social tendencies, the wolves are destroying her home, and she realizes that, if she wants it to remain intact, she has to do battle with the things that threaten it. Mo Willems's *Don't Let the Pigeon Drive the Bus* (2003) offers a more participatory version of this for the child reader: instead of passively reading about a child who must master her impulses, these are manifested through a pigeon's desire, and the child reader is put in the position of actively telling the pigeon 'NO!', no matter how frustrated the bird gets. The pigeon's wheedling, cajoling and final temper tantrum will be instantly recognizable as tactics the child herself has employed to get what she wants, but, in this scenario, the child reader is in the more empowered parental position, and she must use it responsibly in order to avert disaster.

This use of fantasy narrative to negotiate between impulse and social propriety continues as a child's life-world becomes more complex, and her body begins to acquire its secondary sexual characteristics. Here again, the demands of the body call forth a need for fantasmatic defences. For instance, the desire for reincorporation into the maternal body (or vice versa) becomes sexualized at **adolescence**, as the body becomes the site of strange and frighteningly strong appetites. Connected to the archaic memories of being inside the mother and feeding off her, it is no wonder that nascent sexual appetites are shot through with guilt: love, sex, violence and consumption are hopelessly entangled in the unconscious. These desires and appetites are linked to social prohibitions as well, specifically prohibitions regarding substances that **Kristeva** identifies as **abject**, such as wayward body fluids that the child has long ago internalized in terms of disgust but are now being transformed into objects of sexual curiosity. Because the adolescent body is changing shape, sprouting hairs and emitting unfamiliar smells, and because hormonal fluctuations result in rapidly shifting moods and strong emotions, the fantasies needed to manage these changes in embodiment and sexual awareness often manifest themselves as Gothic horror. Caught between terror, romance and humour, adolescent fantasy novels play host to an array of abject monsters, giving adolescents a variety of subject positions as they identify with the creatures, or the humans, who fight with and/or love them.

Ideologically speaking, the monsters of fantasy encode our current views about what it means to be human, and how we should respond to those whom we consider other. This kind of ideological work is where Jack **Zipes** locates his version of the uses of enchantment; unlike Bettelheim, who sees the work of fairy tales in terms of a developing inner world, Zipes values fairy tales for helping children see and contest the often unexamined ideologies concerning such things as gender, entitlement and consumerism that are operative in their life-worlds. In terms of the recent flood of vampire literature for teens, for instance, it would be important for an ideological analysis to note that vampires are no longer the sexually rapacious, immoral demons they once were. Rather, a new breed of vampires, spawned by the likes of Joss Whedon (*Buffy the Vampire Slayer*), Scott Westerfeld's *Uglies* (2005), Annette Curtis Klause's *The Silver Kiss* (1990) and Stephenie Meyer's *Twilight* (2005) among others, have emerged, whose destiny is to use their superhuman physical powers to save humanity. These self-controlled vampires are heroes in a culture that encourages full-on consumption and immediate gratification of any real or imagined desire. That they are vampires suggests a belief in teenage voraciousness, the predatory nature of sexual desire and a certain fear of teens as a tribe. However, the fact that they consistently exercise control over their considerable powers for evil in favour of protection and self-restraint reflects the current competing cultural

desire for sustainability over consumption and a strong belief that power, coupled with self-control, is a viable agent for change. The resulting stories exhibit
the continuing tension in literature for young people between an acknowledge-
ment of the demons young people have to fight and the **didactic** impulse to
move the fight in a particular direction. Whereas vampires used to be categori-
cally evil and power could only ever corrupt, new narratives posit the hope that
evil can be redeemed and power can be used for good.

Children's fantasy scripts provide readers with much pleasure, but they also
do important work. They both bring to the surface and disguise fraught emotional and developmental processes in ways that allow readers to stay emotionally engaged in these processes. They connect readers to their bodies such
that young people can manage the horror of change and fragmentation while
maintaining the necessary illusion of coherence and competence. They hold
subjectivities together with a promise of a unified reality when present realities seem in danger of disintegrating. And they challenge those realities in ways
that open new ethical possibilities, even when subjectivities, bodies and histories suggest that violence and consuming desires are the only way of being in
the world. Indeed, without the dynamism of fantasy, readers would be far less
able to meet and conquer their dragons, name and enact their own desires, and
change their world.

FURTHER READING

Armitt, Lucie (2005) *Fantasy Fiction: An Introduction*, New York: Continuum.
A concise and readable introduction to the major themes and issues in fantasy and its literary
criticism. She resists imposing categories on fantasy, focusing instead on theory and the criticism of fantasy, historical developments and **reader response**. She offers close readings of
classic works of fantasy from Lewis Carroll to Harry Potter and posits that utopia is the main
concern of modern fantasy. A useful, annotated reading list of critical work is included.

Gooderham, David (1995) 'Children's Fantasy Literature: Toward an Anatomy', *Children's
Literature in Education*, 26.3: 171–83.
After reviewing the ways in which fantasy categorization schemes have been traditionally
undertaken in criticism, Gooderham identifies five types of fantasy that correspond to the
imaginal themes that connect to Erikson's stages of development. Very useful in thinking
about the connections between form and reader response.

Jackson, Rosemary (1981) *Fantasy: The Literature of Subversion*, New York: Methuen.
Jackson provides a comprehensive review of critical literature on fantasy, and then turns her
focus to psychoanalytic perspectives. Because her emphasis is on works that disturb the psyche and create dis-ease with the status quo, her work is more applicable to young adult fantasy than to children's fantasy, which she rather dismissively relegates to the less interesting
category of the 'marvellous'.

Johansen, K. V. (2005) *Quests and Kingdoms: A Grown-Up's Guide to Children's Fantasy
Literature*, New Brunswick, CA: Sybertooth.
A chronological overview of the history of children's fantasy from the fairy tales of Perrault,
d'Aulnoy and the Grimms to the popular novels of the early twenty-first century. Each chapter begins with a discussion of the major thematic trends of the period covered and concludes

with a summary and analysis of works by major and some minor authors of the period. More than 500 individual works are discussed.

Todorov, Tzvetan (1975) *The Fantastic: A Structural Approach to a Literary Genre*, trans. Richard Howard, Ithaca, NY: Cornell University Press.
This classic work establishes a structural grid of sorts in order to classify fantasy as a genre, and then plays primarily at the boundaries and intersections of these categorical distinctions. Like Jackson's work, it is more useful for studying works for young adults than for children, where the hesitancies and uncertainties that Todorov enjoys pursuing between the psychological and the supernatural are more likely to be shut down with tidy explanations.

Tolkien, J. R. R. (2001) 'On Fairy Stories', in *Tree and Leaf*, London: HarperCollins [orig. 1947].
Oft-quoted source on children's literature in general as well as fantasy in particular, this work lays out Tolkien's perspective on writing in a mode that is often considered non-serious.

8

YOUNG ADULT FICTION AND THE CROSSOVER PHENOMENON

Rachel Falconer

In *The Crossover Novel* (Falconer, 2009) I argued that children's fiction underwent a meteoric rise in popularity and critical esteem among adult readers over the decade 1997–2007. J. K. Rowling's 'Harry Potter' series (1997–2007) is often seen as the catalyst but, although it precipitated more widespread changes in publishing and marketing strategies, which in turn had their impact on readers' choices of consumption, the series was itself successful partly because the social and economic conditions were ripe for such a shift in perspective on children's literature. Thus, it should be viewed as part of a larger cultural change in contemporary Western society which accords greater weight and value to the signifier, the 'child', than in previous decades (whether this translates to more actual power for real children remains open to debate). In Britain, the history of children's literature crossing to adult readers is long and well established. Although published for children, Charles Kingsley's *The Water-Babies* (1863), Lewis Carroll's *Alice's Adventures in Wonderland* (1865) and George MacDonald's *The Princess and the Goblin* (1872) were recognized as 'serious' works by Victorian adult readers. In the twentieth century, the global popularity of J. R. R. Tolkien's *The Lord of the Rings* (1954–5) and Richard Adams's *Watership Down* (1972), not to mention the 'Star Wars' films, gives evidence of 'crossover phenomena' existing *avant la lettre*. But we now have *la lettre*; in other words, the publishing industry, and readers in general, recognize the crossover phenomenon to the degree that it can now be named and acknowledged as legitimate.

Here I wish to focus on the rise to prominence of young adult (YA) fiction among adult readers. For if there have been changes over the millennial decade in the way adult readers engage with children's literature in general, the changes in adults' engagement with YA fiction are, perhaps, even more distinctive and significant. It is important to realize that such changes, like those occurring to children's literature in general, form part of a continuity of historical development and are not simply the result of recent marketing campaigns. In the longer historical view, young adult fiction emerged as a distinct category in the mid-twentieth century, with works such as George Orwell's *Animal Farm* (1945), J. D. Salinger's *The Catcher in the Rye* (1951), William Golding's *Lord of the Flies* (1954) and Harper Lee's *To Kill a Mockingbird* (1960). By pointing out some of the distinct characteristics of millennial YA fiction, I do not wish to lessen the impact of these now classic novels; on the contrary, I would argue that they are more than ever relevant to our times. If the dividing line between youth and adult has been contested by writers from Salinger and Golding to Blume, Cormier and Almond, what seems distinct about the present era is that adult readers are more likely to recognize their continuing investment in concepts like **adolescence**, and the publishing industry has responded by marketing YA fiction for readers on either side of the divide.

But why should adult readers today evince a particular interest in adolescence? Why should questions of youth, beauty and ageing (or its **mythic** opposite, agelessness) dominate contemporary fiction as well as cinema, with film adaptations of *The Picture of Dorian Gray* and any number of teenage vampire stories? In this chapter, I shall, therefore, focus on a few striking and culturally significant aspects of contemporary YA fiction which indicate a broader change in our understanding of human identity, in the context of rapid technological and scientific development and increased globalization. With the notable exception of young writers such as Helen Oyeyemi and Christopher Paolini, most young adult fiction is still being written by adults, so there is a continuous circulation of ideas and values between adult writers, young adult readers and adult readers. Texts about adolescent emergence and ageing have come to the fore recently because these issues concern both writers and readers of different ages. YA fiction, having once been dismissed as an ephemeral and transient **genre**, has, by its very emphasis on transience, become a kind of cultural lightning rod, attracting to its conductive space questions and debates about what it means to be human in the twenty-first century.

One might start with the later 'Harry Potter' books, or with Will and Lyra's transition from innocence to experience at the end of Pullman's *His Dark Materials*, but these examples have been discussed at length elsewhere (e.g. Falconer, 2009), and there are many other novels which deserve our critical attention.

How does one construct an identity in the present age, when the terms 'human' and 'nature' can no longer be taken for granted as essential categories of existence? In a screen-dominated culture, where developments in medicine, biogenetics and nanotechnology are leading us to the threshold of brave new worlds, while at the same time the brave old world of the environment is becoming less sustainable and the prosaic world of everyday life is becoming faster, noisier and more violent (or at least more desensitized to violence), what kind of individual does one choose to become? These are questions that concern social, political and academic leaders today, but they concern young adults even more urgently, since it is their future that is at stake. Young adult fiction has always addressed the existential questions: 'Who am I?', 'Am I by nature good or evil?' and 'Who could I become?' And now it is reformulating these questions in distinctly contemporary terms by asking, for example, 'What gender am I?' (Meg Rosoff, *What I Was*, 2007), 'When am I grown up?' (Jenny Downham, *Before I Die*, 2007), 'When is a machine human?' (David Thorpe, *Hybrids*, 2006), 'Is death the end?' (Stephenie Meyer, *Twilight*, 2006) and 'If there is no God, is there good and evil?' (David Almond, *Clay*, 2005). Because young adult fiction has sought to articulate questions about rapid transitions, identity crises and epiphanies, it is proving to be a ready medium in which to capture the felt, everyday experience of a world on the cusp of fundamental change.

While young adult fiction generally concerns itself at some level with questions of identity, it must be stressed that this broad category of fiction encompasses a vast range of themes, genres and styles. If 'searing' and 'edgy' are adjectives that now commonly appear on YA dust-jackets, it would be wrong to suggest that all young adult fiction concerns itself with extreme or tragic experience. Chick-lit novels such as Louise Rennison's *Angus, Thongs and Perfect Snogging* (1999); lad-lit such as Chris Ryan's 'Alpha Force' series; comic novels such as Frank Cottrell Boyce's *Millions* (2004) and *Framed* (2005); and Pratchettesque science fiction are all young adult genres with substantial crossover readerships. And yet, it is generally recognized that young adult fiction, on the whole, has become more challenging, dark and morally ambivalent than in decades past (Adams, 2008). Granted, William Golding wrote his profoundly dystopic novel, *Lord of the Flies*, more than 50 years ago, but in contemporary YA, violence, death and the apocalypse have become the norm rather than the exception. This is evident across a range of genres from fantasy to realism, and historical novels to futuristic science fiction. Torture and genocide are described in disturbingly exquisite detail in Lian Hearn's **Orientalist** fantasy series, 'Tales of the Otori' (2002–7). And racial violence and terrorism are omnipresent in Malorie Blackman's dystopic 'Noughts & Crosses' trilogy (2001). A long way from sword-slashing fantasy, Markus Zusak's *The Book Thief* (2005) and John Boyne's *The Boy in the Striped Pyjamas* (2006) represent young people's experiences of the Holocaust. Three of Meg Rosoff's novels, *How I Live Now* (2004), *Just in Case* (2006) and *What I Was*, lead the reader into spiritually desolate territory, although always with a Beckettian eye for the humour in bleak situations. As Boyd Tonkin (2005) notes, what is also new and surprising is that, for the first time, adult readers are choosing to 'escape' into these nightmarish adolescences.

Why this dual-aged attraction to the dark side? My answer would be that, in times of fundamental social change, readers evince a heightened appetite for fictions that focus on the edges of identity, the points of transition and rupture, and the places where we might, like microcosms of the greater world, break down and potentially assume new and **hybrid** identities. According to Mikhail **Bakhtin** (1981, pp. 84–5), all literary genres have distinctive **chronotopes**, or representations of time space, which frame and enable their characters to think and act in certain ways. Bakhtin (1981, p. 248) identifies the 'chronotope of the threshold' as being associated with '*crisis* and *break* in life', the moment of 'decision that changes a life (or the indecisiveness that fails to change a life, the fear to step over the threshold)', where time is felt as 'instantaneous . . . as if it had no duration'. Fyodor Dostoevsky was singularly interested in crises, breaks and epiphanies, and in his work, as Bakhtin argues, the threshold and related chronotopes – those of the staircase, the front hall and corridor, as well as the chronotope of street and square that extend those spaces into the open air – are the main places of action . . . places where crisis events occur, the falls, resurrections, renewals, epiphanies, decisions that determine the whole life of a man.

(Bakhtin, 1981, p. 248)

Anyone with a passing knowledge of young adult fiction would be able to cite analogous examples of crises and epiphanies occurring with characters poised on just such literal and metaphorical thresholds, from classic to contemporary novels (the Narnians waiting outside the stable door in C. S. Lewis's *The Last Battle* [1956] and Will Parry cutting his first window into another world in Philip Pullman's *The Subtle Knife* [1997]). Indeed, it is unsurprising that the governing chronotope of much young adult fiction should be that of the threshold, since these time spaces of crisis and transition readily produce fictional characters on the border between childhood and maturity. Once again, what is surprising is that many adult readers of contemporary YA fiction see themselves as belonging to this same time space of life transition, for reasons suggested in what follows.

Not only are the internal chronotopes of young adult fiction dominated by images of the threshold but also young adult fiction is itself a class of fiction (broader, messier and more inclusive than a genre) which exists on a threshold between the markets of children's literature and mainstream, adult literature (**Trites**, 2000, p. 7). Within the individual YA text, too, one finds a tendency to hybridize genres, as if a single generic worldview were not enough to convey the complexity of the adolescent experience. For example, one very popular genre to emerge in recent YA fiction is 'urban faery', which blends the comic *élan* and magic of young children's stories with the higher levels of violence and more darkly ironic perspective of urban realist fiction. Examples include Eoin Colfer's 'Artemis Fowl' series, Melissa Marr's *Wicked Lovely* (2008) and Holly Black's 'modern faerie' novels: *Tithe* (2002), *Valiant* (2005) and *Ironside* (2007). But one can see this hybridizing tendency in a wide range of YA novels, some of which draw on so many existing genres that they appear unclassifiable in any family group. Rosoff's *How I Live Now* includes elements of the childhood idyll, magic adventure story, war novel, mental illness narrative, chick-lit, girl's diary and dystopia. And Mark Haddon's *The Curious Incident of the Dog in the Night-Time* (2003) is at once a boy's diary, disability narrative, comic novel, detective fiction and **postmodern** experimental work.

In all the generic and stylistic variety that constitutes young adult fiction, there are at least one, or possibly two, relatively constant features: the central protagonist, who may also be the text's first-person narrator, is between 11 and 19 years of age, and the text's addressee, or implied reader, is assumed to be of a similar age. Crossover novels, especially those like Haddon's, which was published simultaneously in dual editions, obviously call into question this latter assumption. But the fact that the central protagonist or first-person narrator is adolescent is an important factor in establishing the chronotopic horizons of young adult fiction. The phase of life which we call 'adolescence' itself constitutes a chronotope, one which, like all chronotopes, is historically determined. Characterized early in the twentieth century as a *Sturm und Drang* phase of life, adolescence in the 1950s was understood by Erik Erikson (among others) to be a phase of crisis in the development of an individual, during which received values and worldviews were likely to be questioned and challenged. Contemporary psychologists have challenged the 'storm and stress' model as overly **Romantic** and masculinist, but they generally agree that adolescence is a period of accelerated transition, during which questions of identity formation become paramount: both how to assert oneself as an individual, and how to fit into a socioeconomic context (see Prout, 2005). Adolescence, as a literary time space, bears a close relationship to Bakhtin's 'chronotope of the threshold'. The fact that its fictional worlds are **focalized** through adolescent eyes similarly predisposes YA fiction to represent reality in terms of crises, breaks, rapid transitions and sudden epiphanies.

Julia **Kristeva**'s concept of adolescence provides one persuasive explanation for the tendency of adult readers to empathize with crisis-riven adolescents. In her view, adolescence is an 'open psychic structure' that may be experienced at any stage of life, and not once but repeatedly. In fact, biological adolescence is already a repetition, a collapse and return to a prior infant state, in which the psyche becomes vulnerable and thus 'opens itself to the repressed' (Kristeva, 1990, p. 8). Kristeva argues that reading and writing help prise open the psyche and thus induce feelings of adolescent 'incompleteness' in the reader (p. 139). Karen Coats (2004) persuasively conflates Kristeva's reading of adolescence with her analysis of psychic **abjection** in *Powers of Horror* (1982). In this latter work, Kristeva describes abjection as the sense of revulsion we feel at anything that threatens to disrupt the coherence of the self. 'A wound with blood and pus, or the sickly, acrid smell of sweat, of decay, . . . the corpse, seen without God and outside of science' are all things that show us 'death infecting life' and thus threaten to permeate the boundaries of identity (Kristeva, 1982, p. 4). The abject is always latent; it is that which 'draws me toward the place where meaning collapses' but which 'I permanently thrust aside in order to live' (pp. 2–3). This psychic revolution or return to a primal infancy, where **subjectivity** struggles to assert itself against non-being, is played out 'on the fragile border . . . where identities (subject/object) do not exist or only barely so – double, fuzzy, heterogeneous' (p. 207). As Coats (2004, p. 142) argues, Kristevan adolescence, 'like abjection, breaches and challenges boundaries'. For Coats, this explains why young adult fiction has always had a particular interest in abjection, the doubled sense of horror in which psychic identity is both threatened and reaffirmed. Kristeva's thesis that the dramas of adolescence and abjection are played out on the 'fragile border' of the self returns us to Bakhtin's concept of a particular spatio-temporal configuration in which such a drama could unfold: the chronotope of the threshold.

Kristeva presents her concept of adolescence as a universal truth of the psyche. But one can situate her ideas more precisely in our own historical moment, in which the idea of an 'edge' or 'fragile border' of the self holds a particular fascination. Being on the 'edge' of adulthood in the twenty-first century is a more daunting experience than previously because ageing can flow in both directions: the 'edge' is now double-sided. And this process can unfold not only in either direction but also at varying speeds. Not only are there children zooming to adulthood at an accelerated rate ('tweenagers') but there are also adults tumbling back into childhood (**kiddults**). Teenagers can become arrested in pre-adulthood, failing to secure jobs, mortgages or university degrees or, having taken the first step, may fall back into dependence on their parents ('kippers' and 'boomerangers'). That we need new words for these virtual-age categories suggests that the precarious slipping and sliding between once distinctly marked stages of life has become a recognized social phenomenon in the new millennium.

This fluidity in virtual ageing is probably due to a number of factors, from social and economic to technological and scientific. From the 1980s to 1990s, Western capitalism began to develop an ethics of work as play or self-expression, which in many ways was modelled on the image of a child or young adult. Corporate business began to reward employees who approached their work 'youthfully', focussing on innovation, and moving flexibly between different jobs. In the twenty-first century, argue economists Bogdan Costea *et al.* (2005, p. 148), 'the vectors of self-action have been reversed: adults are encouraged to find and preserve the "inner child", to . . . treat life as continuous play'. At the same time, advances in cosmetic surgery and assisted reproduction have opened up the possibility of a longer adolescence for wealthy adults, and this is only the start of what twenty-first-century medicine may do for its biologically ageing population. Millennial young adult fiction reflects the bewildering flexibility of this new social reality, where adults can pass as children, and children can be treated as adults. In Geraldine McCaughrean's *Peter Pan in Scarlet* (2006), we see adults transmogrifying into children and, in McCaughrean's *The White Darkness* (2005), we see them behaving like spoiled children, while in Rosoff's *How I Live Now*, children are catapulted into premature adulthood.

One can view this new porosity of the border between young and old in both positive and negative terms. On the positive side, the ideas and values of the young are beginning to be heard in the national media, in politics, business and cultural production. As one branch of the latter, crossover fiction has helped to generate public recognition of the child's perspective in the adult, the adult's in the child and both perspectives converging in the adolescent. We are more inclined to see connections and continuities linking this triptych of child, adult and adolescent, given the pivotal role that crossover YA fiction plays between children's and adult fiction markets. Boyce's YA novel *Cosmic* begins with the adolescent narrator remarking, 'everyone lies about their age. Adults pretend to be younger. Teenagers pretend to be older. Children wish they were grown up. Grown ups wish they were children' (Boyce, 2008, p. 3). This exceptionally tall teenager lies about his age, and manages to pass for a qualified astronaut. In this novel, adolescence unfolds within a chronotope where time is future oriented and space is boundlessly open. An adult reader drawn to this adolescent chronotope is recovering a sense of potential future time as unmapped space.

On the negative side, adolescence can be retrospectively constructed as an entirely closed space and time, and one which effaces any sense of potentiality, rather than enhancing it. The image of the human being that emerges from this restrictive chronotope can be compared to Bakhtin's description of the classical body, as opposed to the **grotesque**. The classical body, such as we see in Greek sculpture of the fifth century BC, represents an ideal of perfection. It is essentially ageless, just as certain airbrushed photographs of adolescents are in contemporary fashion magazines. The desire for perfection, or more particularly, to be perfected, was understood by Sigmund **Freud** (1958) to be a form of the death drive which, beyond the pleasure principle, exercises an influence on every living being. In narrative fiction, this death drive manifests itself in the reader's **desire** to get to the end of the story, to finalize at least some of its possible meanings. According to Peter Brooks (1984), reading allows us to satisfy this basic drive and yet survive. When it is translated into narrative fiction, the idealization of an ageless version of adolescence produces a curiously truncated form of novel, a narrative equivalent to arriving at the end too soon, without the deferrals and delays of the pleasure drive which make endings satisfying. In my view, Meyer's bestselling vampire novels *Twilight*, *New Moon* and *Eclipse* fall into this class of truncated fiction. Each is more than 400 pages long, yet there is almost no plot or character development. In *Twilight*, we are introduced almost immediately to the narrator's desire for an impossibly beautiful boy who is set, like a rare stone, in a circle of impossibly beautiful friends. She first sees this group sitting apart and aloof, in a far corner of the school cafeteria:

> They weren't talking, and they weren't eating, though they each had a tray of untouched food in front of them . . . . Of the three boys, one was big – muscled like a serious weight lifter . . . . Another was taller, leaner . . . . The girls were opposites. The tall one was statuesque. She had a beautiful figure, the kind you saw on the cover of the *Sports Illustrated* swimsuit issue, the kind that made every girl around her take a hit on her self-esteem . . . . All their features were straight, perfect, angular . . . . I stared because their faces, so different, so similar, were all devastatingly, inhumanly beautiful. They were faces you never expected to see except perhaps on the airbrushed pages of a fashion magazine.
>
> (Meyer, 2006, pp. 16–17)

This description provides a good illustration of Bakhtin's theory of the classical body, mentioned above, which, with its serene and expressionless face, presents a 'closed, smooth, and impenetrable surface' to the world, refusing all bodily or social interchange. These 'statuesque' and 'inhumanly beautiful' young people are posed, lifeless and sealed off from interaction with ordinary students. Although muscled like athletes, they have no more need to eat than the Discobolus of Myron and sit ignoring the cafeteria food on their dinner trays. Bakhtin (1984b, pp. 317–18) contrasts the closed-off, timeless classical body with the ageing grotesque, whose open orifices suggest a readiness to engage with the material world. The open, laughing mouth of the grotesque 'demolishes fear and piety' in contrast to the classical face which is close-lipped, awe-inspiring and sealed as a tomb (Bakhtin, 1981, p. 23). Given the genre of *Twilight*, we soon guess that these young people are vampires. The narrator's rapt stare (which she indulges for many hundreds of pages) is hypnotic rather than suspenseful. The narrator, far from discovering a potential for evil (or indeed, anything) in herself, merely repeats her longing for this unliving, undead perfection. One might draw an analogy between this hapless narrator and adults who are drawn to adolescence as the chronotope of timeless, perfect youth. This aspect of the crossover phe-nomenon undeniably exists. Ironically there are many who would, given access to all the dizzying new resources of modern medicine and technology, exploit them to pursue a bizarre dream of being trapped at the age of 19 forever.

However, as argued earlier, most crossover YA fiction represents adolescence as a threshold state, which is by definition imperfect, unfinished and radically open to the formation of new and hybrid identities. The adolescent body, subject to rapid, metamorphic change, is often represented in terms of the grotesque, rather than the idealized classical body. This is evident in boys' adventure novels that represent adolescent characters fascinated with the physically freakish, as in Darren Shan's *Cirque Du Freak* (2000), as well as in chick-lit novels, where teenage boys are satirized as freakish by young female protagonists (Meg Cabot's *Tommy Sullivan Is a Freak*, 2008). In the context of YA fiction, being classed as freakish is more often a positive label than a negative one, because it connotes an ability to step outside the system, to create a uniquely individual self or pursue an individual dream. The gigantic narrator of Boyce's *Cosmic* exploits his physical freakery, for example, to pursue a boyhood ambition of flying in outer space. In Haddon's *Curious Incident*, a boy with Asperger's Syndrome uses his extraordi-nary mental facility with numbers and graphs to control the confusion of his emo-tions; for example, to work through his fear of being lost he does maths problems in his head and maps the relationship between time and space. In his study *Freaks, Geeks and Asperger Syndrome: A User Guide to Adolescence*, Luke Jackson (2002) explores a range of types of 'freakish' behaviours associated with young adults. While the extreme mental and physical states which he describes can often disrupt and disturb the normative 'body' of society, like the grotesque, they can also rejuvenate this social body by opening its borders, by provoking interaction and exchange with the feared and excluded **other**.

It is not simply a question of representing the adolescent body as freakish and grotesque, on the one hand, or inhumanly finalized and perfect, on the other. More subtly, Rosoff's *What I Was* explores the same territory as *Twilight*, that is, an adolescent's longing to be or possess someone who appears to embody per-fection. But in Rosoff's novel, this longing is acknowledged from the first to be retrospectively constructed. The epigraph reads, 'I am a century old, an impossible age, and my brain has no anchor in the present. Instead it drifts, nearly always to the same shore. Today, as most days, it is 1962 . . . . I am sixteen years old.' Even the narrator's younger self knows that Finn's perfection is a projection of his own imagination. The novel describes his obsession with Finn, whom he meets living in a hut by the sea, while he himself attends an oppressive boarding school for boys. In pursuing his singular obsession with Finn, he is also working out a set of individual rules by which he wants to live. Unlike the narrator of *Twilight*, then, he is aware of the need to develop a social identity, even while he retreats from social interaction at school. And while the time he spends with Finn is idyllic, the reader is constantly aware of an alternative temporality in which everything continually shifts, distorts and fades. The chronotopic image of this time-bound consciousness is represented by the eroding coast of East Anglia, where the two boys' friendship develops. Amid the taunts of other boys, their relationship intensifies and reaches a crisis-point when the narrator suddenly discovers his beloved is female, not male. In a phrase that calls to mind Kristeva's description of abjection, the narrator relates how 'a wave of something dark flooded the space behind my eyes' (Rosoff, 2007, p. 172). The reader, like the narrator, has then retrospectively to reconstruct the nature of the desire just recounted. The novel ends with the image of a flooded sea coast, and the questions it raises about gender identity continue, as it were, to churn about in that flooded space, inchoate and unresolved: 'The Finn in my head was strong and fearless. Virile. Male. I knew nothing about the real one' (p. 185).

In addition to representing volatile gender identities, crossover young adult fiction explores other 'edges' of being, such as being born and dying. Thus, the protagonist of Jamila Gavin's *The Robber Baron's Daughter* has an exceptionally vivid memory of her infancy: 'she could go back to when everything was above her head' (Gavin, 2008, p. 5). David Almond's *Clay* follows two adolescent boys as they psychologically regress into what seems to be an atavistically primitive state of mind, in order to bring new life into the world and be reborn themselves (Falconer, 2009, pp. 129–52). And, at the other 'edge', as it were, many adolescent protagonists are represented on the brink of dying, or crossing the threshold and magically returning alive. Examples include Garth Nix's 18-year-old Sabriel Abhorsen (*Sabriel*, 1995), J. K. Rowling's 17-year-old Harry Potter (*Deathly Hallow*, 2007) and Philip Pullman's 12-year-old Lyra Belacqua (Pullman, 1999). Tim Bowler's *Bloodchild* begins with an adolescent protagonist discovering himself waking from an unconscious state after an accident at precisely this uncertain border between life and death:

His first impression was of a grey light, the absence of pain, and a certainty that he was dead. A pause; a shift from grey to gold, from the absence of pain to the presence of something else; and with that . . . doubt.
This was not death. Yet nor was it life. It was something he didn't recognize.
(Bowler, 2008, p. 1)

In this novel, adolescence borders on the edge of rational being: the edge between life and death, and the edge between the rational and the irrational.

A different sort of edge appears in young adult novels which explore the complex relation of adolescents to modern technology. In developed countries, technological gadgets have become omnipresent features of everyday life, especially the everyday lives of young people. The protagonist of Sophie McKenzie's *Girl, Missing* (2006) is a typical twenty-first-century adolescent, who sits texting her friend while she conducts a Google search for her family tree on her mother's computer, in preparation for writing an essay on the topic, 'Who am I?' Later she takes a DNA test to confirm the reality of her biological origin, discovered by chance on the Internet. In David Thorpe's novel *Hybrids* (2006), adolescents are prone to a disease in which their electronic gadgets become incorporated into their bodies. Thorpe makes the reader recognize how close to this futuristic fiction we have already come. The back-cover blurb invites us to think literally about our era's intimate dependency on our 'personal' machines: 'are you a slave to your computer? Welded to your mobile phone? Joined at the hip to your iPod? Maybe one day you will be' (Thorpe, 2006). Modern biogenetics and nanotechnology make us conscious of life at the infinitesimally small scale where the human ceases to be distinguishable from the non-human. Thorpe repeatedly draws his reader's eye to this nano-perspective, where human and non-human tissue converges: 'I saw her transition point: the way the flesh changed colour, textures and substances where her hand stopped being a hand' (Thorpe, 2006, p. 11). Read in one way, her medical condition is simply an exaggeration of the metamorphosis the young woman is experiencing at the 'transition point' between child and adulthood. Read in the reverse direction, her adolescence has become a trope for the way technology has permeated our lives to the extent that it is changing the way we think and changing what it means to be human (Hayles, 1999; Greenfield, 2008).

The threshold chronotope also shapes much contemporary thinking about biogenetics and technology, which is one reason why young adult fiction so easily absorbs the image of the human, or posthuman, emerging from new research in these fields. Susan Squier's tellingly entitled study *Liminal Lives* (2004) demonstrates how science fiction explores ways in which stem-cell research and intra- and inter-species organ transplantation are challenging previous definitions of humanness. While her focus is not on YA fiction *per se*, her insights can be applied to many young adult, crossover novels. In Rachel Anderson's YA novel *The Scavenger's Tale* (1998), body parts are harvested from marginalized groups of many kinds: the poor, mentally and physically disabled, and the elderly. If Anderson's novel is focalized through adolescent eyes, Neal Shusterman makes the adolescent the specific target and victim of biogenetic research. In his YA novel *Unwind* (2007), 'surplus' humans can be 'unwound' and their body parts recycled, but this can only be legally done to humans between the ages of 13 and 18. Moreover, unlike Anderson's victims, these teenagers 'do not die, and they do not remain alive' (to paraphrase the last canto of Dante's *Inferno*): they are simply redistributed into other living, human subjects. If the borders of the self – both physical and mental – are so malleable and open to economic exploitation, how then can the work of adolescence, to construct an individual identity, be successfully worked through?

Nanotechnology pushes us to consider even more extreme edges of being. As Colin Milburn (2002, p. 289) writes, experiments at the nano-scale allow us to imagine situations in which

> a wooden chair, subjected to a herd of nanobots, can be transformed into a living fish, . . . a fish can be transformed into a human, . . . [and] a human, subject to a herd of nanobots carrying the data set for another human, can suddenly become someone else.

In fact, though, the breakthrough is not in the ability to *imagine* the possibility of human/non-human hybridization because we have been doing this for a long time. Pieter Brueghel's mid-sixteenth-century painting 'The Fall of the Rebel Angels' shows creatures raining down from the sky, arrested in mid-metamorphosis from human-shaped angels to gaping-mouthed fish and enormous, slit-bellied insects. Our oldest stories reveal the human mind's capacity to imagine genetic hybridization; think of Genesis, in which an old man creates a younger man out of dust, and a young woman out of a piece of bone. What is different about our own situation is that we can not only imagine these genetic mutations but also bring them to life. The **uncanniness** of YA science fiction is that the imagined nightmare is already familiar (and hence, seemingly, already a *fait accompli*) before it takes shape as material reality. As David Morris (1985, p. 307) paraphrases Freud, the *unheimlich* or uncanny 'derives its terror *not* from something externally alien or unknown but – on the contrary – from something strangely *familiar* which defeats our efforts to separate ourselves from it'.

Novels about cloning are in some respects exploring the most vertiginous questions relating to individual identity. What if a sentient individual turns out to be, not a self at all, but a replica of a lost original, or, to draw on Jean Baudrillard, a simulacrum of a replica? The adolescent protagonist of Nancy Farmer's *The House of the Scorpion* (2004) discovers that he is a clone, a product developed in the laboratory to provide a medicine chest of spare organs for his 'original', a powerful Mexican drug baron. Matt turns the tables on 'El Patron' and seizes power for himself, a neat resolution that does nothing to address the existential questions raised by the plot's opening premise. The same situation is handled more deftly in Kazuo Ishiguro's *Never Let Me Go* (2005), where the three adolescent protagonists' agony consists of the slow drip of their accumulating knowledge, so that by the time they arrive at the revelation that they are clones, they have no mental resources to rebel against their fate, since it is a knowledge that they have always, somehow, possessed already.

Ishiguro's novel ends with the image of an edge – a line of fencing stretching across moor land, where years of detritus have gathered: 'all along the fence . . . all sorts of rubbish had caught and tangled'. This bleak fence-line mirrors the narrator's sense of her not-quite human life, drawing mutedly to a close. But to her surprise, it also begins to figure something else, a reversal of her fate, and the possibility of a flesh and blood ending to her inhuman story:

> That was the only time, as I stood there, looking at the strange rubbish, feeling the wind coming across those empty fields, that I started to imagine just a little fantasy thing, because this was Norfolk after all . . . I half-closed my eyes and imagined this was the spot where everything I'd lost since my childhood had washed up, and I was now standing here in front of it, and if I waited long enough, a tiny figure would appear on the horizon across the field, and gradually get larger until I'd see it was Tommy, and he'd wave, maybe even call. The fantasy never got beyond that – I didn't let it.
>
> (Ishiguro, 2005, p. 282)

In her partial identification with a fantasy of redemption based on temporal reversal – going back to childhood, starting again – the narrator of *Never Let Me Go* provides one kind of model for the adult reader of young adult fiction. It is precisely when the horizon ahead begins to look nightmarishly strange, empty but familiar that the adult reader may be tempted to look back at the crises and past decisions that led to this moment and consider how they might have been played out differently. Ishiguro's narrator dismisses her fantasy of an alternative story but, in a sense, this ending falls short of acknowledging the radical openness of possibilities that lie ahead for the reader, whether adolescent or adult. Unlike Ishiguro's clone, we cannot close off the possibility of the fantasy coming true. Readers of every age may well find it a struggle to come to terms with new thresholds of being in the twenty-first century, where the concept of individual identity is increasingly called into question. In relation to the biogenetic, nanotech future that lies not too far ahead, we are all adolescents now.

FURTHER READING

Beckett, Sandra (ed.) (1999) *Transcending Boundaries: Writing for a Dual Audience of Children and Adults*, New York: Garland.
International collection of essays on different aspects of the crossover phenomenon: writers who write for children and adults, and texts which have later been adopted by a mixed-age audience.

Beckett, Sandra (2008) *Crossover Fiction: Its Historical Antecedents and International Dimensions*, New York: Routledge.
Beckett's volume takes a global perspective on crossover literature, covering picturebooks, **fairy tales** and fiction for older children, from around the world.

Falconer, Rachel (2009) *The Crossover Novel: Contemporary Children's Literature and Its Adult Readership*, New York: Routledge.
This volume focuses on the British context of crossover fiction's rise since 1997. There is a broad cultural analysis of shifting attitudes to age and ageing, and six in-depth analyses of prominent crossover texts and their implied and actual readers.

Knoepflmacher, U. C. and **Myers**, Mitzi (eds) (1997) ' "Cross-Writing" and the Reconceptualizing of Children's Literary Studies', *Children's Literature*, 25: special issue.
This volume is a special edition of the journal, devoted to the issue of 'cross-writers'. Little attention is paid to cross-reading, but many other aspects are considered, in what was the first major study of the crossover phenomenon.

9

PICTUREBOOKS, COMICS AND GRAPHIC NOVELS

MEL GIBSON

Picturebooks, comics and graphic novels are rich and complex media, combining image and text in different formats and playing on the interdependence of these signifying systems. This chapter looks at the similarities and differences between these media, which exist largely as separate areas of publishing, although changing patterns of ownership in publishing mean this separation is being eroded. It also explores aspects of the grammar of the media, the challenges they offer the reader and flags up some of the ways in which critics have chosen to approach these visual forms.

These media have been used to create works for readers of all ages, on any subject, whether fiction or non-fiction. They typically employ pictures (predominantly using line and colour) and words (including the use of varied fonts and layouts) to express meaning. Further, they may draw on the grammar of other media; for instance, the notion of the establishing shot from film; thus, in Maurice Sendak's *Outside Over There* (1981) the first double-page spread 'establishes', for the reader, the main figures in a landscape. Comics and picturebooks have also adopted elements from photography and fine art in terms of depicting scenes that might be shown from a particular angle or providing narratives that offer a specific point of view. Thus, in *Outside Over There*, the second double-page spread focuses more specifically on the figures of mother and children, detailing their facial expressions.

As the above suggests, these media are highly **intertextual**, with creators drawing on many sources not just from the arts, like film and painting, but also from popular media and other cultural products. However, while comics tend to refer to other comics, picturebooks refer to their own kind comparatively rarely. Hence *Outside Over There* draws on a **Romantic** tradition of painting, and especially the paintings of Philip Otto Runge, to reflect both the emotional state of the protagonist, Ida, and her family, and the Romantic construction of the child as close to nature. Thus, when Ida discovers the goblins' theft of her sister, the storm we see raging through the window acts as a pathetic fallacy, expressing her fury, while also alluding to the fate of her absent father.

Other works by Sendak show a more eclectic intertextuality. *In the Night Kitchen* (1970), for instance, features more popular intertexts: Winsor McCay's *Little Nemo in Slumberland*, a comic strip (later a film) that debuted in the *New York Herald* (1905); Oliver Hardy's comic persona; and a number of syndicated cooking ingredients, unified by Sendak's distinctive use of line. In addition to borrowing his opening of Mickey in bed directly from the McCay character Nemo, *In the Night Kitchen* also follows the temporal pattern of McCay's strip, suggesting that the adventures are based around a sleeper's dreams. Similarly, Anthony Browne consistently adapts other works, particularly from fine art, most overtly in *Willy's Paintings* (2000), where the diverse works are unified by Browne's style and the appearance of 'Willy' within each image. Such playful intertextuality – particularly in Browne's use of surrealism – makes his work push continually against the bounds of realism, suggesting more **carnivalesque** spaces to be explored, as we also see in *Gorilla* (1983), where the lonely girl, Hannah, enjoys a day out with her idealized father figure.

While both comics and picturebooks show events unfolding in time, each has its own structure, its own distinctive grammar. Graphic novels, to turn to questions of definition for a moment, share the grammar of comics, as they are longer works in comic-strip form, containing a single complete narrative. They may be in the form of a single volume, although the term is also applied to longer series. Moreover, they often address complex and challenging themes, typically for an adult or young adult audience, albeit works for younger readers have also appeared. To offer a very basic and generalized comparison indicating the differences between picturebook and comic/graphic novel, a typical picturebook page will contain a small amount of text alongside a single image or limited number of images. In contrast, a typical comic page will contain a number of boxes, called panels, most commonly between six and nine in number. Within each panel may be found a number of elements, including dialogue in speech balloons or thought bubbles, which can take a number of expressive forms. In relation to depicting time, in the picturebook events unfold from page to page, while in the comic novel, movement from panel to panel on each page, as well as across the whole text, shows temporal shifts. Thierry Groensteen (2007) gives a detailed **semiotic** exploration of this spatio-temporal interplay in comics from across the world, but especially in *bandes dessinée*, or Franco-Belgian comics, which include Hergé's *Tintin* and Goscinny and Uderzo's *Asterix*, looking at the specific placement of panels on the page.

The above media form a contrast with illustrated books, where image and text are not usually interdependent. In the latter, the images may show a key moment described in the narrative but, in contrast to the picturebook and comic, the removal of these images will not result in any difficulty in understanding that moment. Some picturebook theorists have argued that word and image can mirror each other; thus, Maria **Nikolajeva** and Carole Scott (2001, p. 12) use the term 'symmetrical picturebooks' for instances where there are 'two mutually redundant narratives'. However, others, such as David Lewis (2001, p. 39), argue that this symmetry is, in fact, 'illusory, an artefact of word picture interanimation'; in other words, it is only through the words that the reader comes to see a symmetry in the material pictured. At the other extreme from 'symmetry', according to Nikolajeva and Scott, lies 'contradiction'. The dissonance between word and image that the term suggests is an extreme form of 'counterpoint', which can be seen in the work of John Burningham, such as *Come Away from the Water, Shirley* (1977). Both Nikolajeva and Scott (2000) and Bettina Kümmerling-Meibauer (1999) analyse how Burningham juxtaposes coloured images, outlining the titular protagonist's imaginary adventures on a day at the seaside, with less colourful images of her parents engaged in mundane dialogue. For Kümmerling-Meibauer (1999, p. 172), this juxtaposition is an indication of the presence of irony in a book addressing a comparatively young and inexperienced audience.

The contrast between the two worlds, one realistic and another fantastic, is heightened by the fact that Shirley's imaginary adventures are told through image only: there are no words. Further, the images of the parents are framed by a solid line, whereas those of Shirley are not. Line then is indicative of difference. There is a suggestion that children are less confined by language, by what **Lacan** would term the **Symbolic**, and are, therefore, freer to envision alternative worlds. There is also the suggestion of a lack of communication between the generations, which might be imaginatively played out in Shirley's overthrowing of a ship of adult pirates. However, if this is so, the last page, the only one where the colours bleed to the edge, shows the family as a close-knit unit, suggesting some sort of resolution – which a reading of the book between adult and child (the former with the words) would itself enact. In short, the use of two ultimately irreconcilable signifying systems is what allows picturebooks to generate such fascinating and complex interplays.

Of course, there are some picturebooks and comics that almost dispense with one of these systems – the word – entirely. However, even here, the reader's response is guided by a title, as in Raymond Briggs' *The Snowman* (1978) or *Bow-Wow Bugs a Bug* (2008), by Mark Newgarden and Megan Montague Cash. Shaun Tan's graphic novel *The Arrival* (2006) is another example of an almost wordless narrative. Here, apart from the indicative title, there is some text, but it is in an indecipherable font. This underlines one of the book's main themes, about the challenges of being an immigrant. As readers, we are placed in the position of the central character, sharing his experience of trying to understand the customs and language of the fantastic land to which he and others have travelled.

In relation to the academy, while engagement with these media has developed across a number of disciplines, there are large variations as to where and how picturebooks, comics and graphic novels have been considered. There is some common ground in that all can be seen as having been 'Cinderella' media. Scholars interested in these media have, until recently, often begun their analyses with a justification of the appropriateness of studying the medium, with a call for cultural legitimization. This has been more typical in studies of comics, given the ways in which they have historically been seen as a problematic form of popular culture. In contrast, the picturebook has been seen as 'worthy', being linked with developing literacy, but seeing it in this more functional way can bring its own challenges.

What these categorizations of 'worthy' and 'problematic' suggest is that, where these media appear in the same space, views can be polarized. For instance, picturebooks have usually, although not exclusively, been seen in a positive light within the discipline of education. In contrast, comics, graphic novels and, indeed, *manga* (Japanese comics) – which are appearing in the West in increasing numbers – have frequently attracted concern within that same disciplinary space. These texts have been characterized as containing troubling subject matter, under the common assumption (dominant in many countries, especially Britain and the United States) that all comics are for children. Consequently, material that is for adults is seen as problematic and as undermining literacy. It is a clear example of people confusing medium and content. Recently this position has begun to change in that there has been a reawakened interest in the potential of comics for young readers. In the United States and Britain, for instance, comics and *manga* are increasingly being seen as texts which may attract young people to reading (although this does not necessarily signify approval of content because the tendency is to see the medium as a vehicle for the development of literacy rather than an as art form; Gibson, 2008a, pp. 112–13).

Research into picturebooks, comics and graphic novels has typically focused on three main areas, which are emphasized in different ways in different disciplines. First, the form itself is a key area of study. Perry **Nodelman**'s (1988) *Words about Pictures* was one of the first comprehensive studies of how picturebooks work. This approach, as Evelyn Arizpe and Morag Styles (2003, p. 19) explain, focuses on 'the importance of design and the interconnections between word and image'. Studies of the comic also use this type of approach (e.g. McCloud, 1993; Groensteen, 2007). The content of the text is a second key area of research, with commentators looking at each medium across a range of disciplines. In doing so, researchers may work with theoretical tools associated with Literature, Gender, Art History, Media, Film or Cultural Studies. Thus, semiotics, Marxism, psychoanalysis, **dialogism**, narratology, **ecocriticism** and various forms of feminism and queer theory have all been deployed in textual analyses. In addition, many creators, especially those whose work is considered significant in some way, have been the focus of individual studies: artist/writers (e.g. Maurice Sendak, Anthony Browne and Wanda Gág), graphic novelists (e.g. Art Spiegelman and Chris Ware) and comic creators (e.g. Winsor McCay). Of course, the above studies themselves generate further research and, often, disagreement. Nikolajeva and Scott (2001) thus criticize earlier approaches, while their own has been subject to contestation (Lewis, 2001); likewise, in the area of comics, Martin Barker (1989) is critical of many earlier studies, particularly of those that lack any empirical basis. Mention of this brings me to the final key area, that of readership, with studies ranging from those that examine readers' meaning making (e.g. children's understandings, the interpretations of different groups of readers, including different nationalities, and those with contrasting gender or sexual orientation; Arizpe and Styles, 2003) to those that look at practices reaching beyond the mere reading of texts (e.g. fandom, collectors, creators of fanfiction, etc.; Gibson, 2008b).

The emphasis varies, of course, according to the discipline. With the picture-book, one of the most vocal and powerful discourses comes from education, where the value of this medium for literacy development is a key concern. In relation to readership, then, the picturebook is seen as something that can help foster a child's understanding, especially when shared with an adult. Comics, in contrast, are seen as one of the first types of text that a child owns, to be read either alone or shared with friends; they are seen as more a part of children's own culture. Moreover, it is of note that comics are seen as independent reading, whereas picturebooks are usually perused with assistance from an adult, sug-gesting that the former are for those with superior reading skills – although, ironically, comics are often stigmatized.

Another area where these media are on similar ground, although with differ-ent consequences for each, is that they are seen as predominantly associated with childhood, with views about what is 'appropriate' in these texts being refracted through views about what is suitable for children. This connection of specifi-cally visual media with childhood has meant that there can be a resistance to work that challenges such assumptions. Such resistance also occurs with the prose novel, as **crossover** fiction shows, but it is typically less acknowledged within wider culture and the academy that these media produce works for a range of ages. In particular, comics created for adults rather than children have proved problematic in both the United States and Britain in sparking off contro-versies about what the medium should contain, given that visual texts are typi-cally seen as more accessible to, and appropriate for, younger readers. The development of the graphic novel in the 1980s, having associations with notions of maturity in its 'adult' themes, and with the idea of the comic 'growing up', has exacerbated tensions about this medium and its audience. Rather than under-standing comics as a flexible medium that can address any issues for any age, there is a tendency, as McCloud (1993, p. 9) suggests, to see it as a 'corruptor of our Nation's Youth'.

Picturebooks, as Arizpe and Styles (2003, p. 19) state, are seen simultane-ously as 'art objects and the primary literature of childhood'. This not only acknowledges the potential of the form but also indicates its key limitation in the perception of the audience, flagging up tensions between the flexibility of the medium and assumptions about the needs and capabilities of young readers. In both cases, then, cultural constructions of childhood (especially in relation to lit-eracy – for long an ideological battleground) underpin and colour understand-ings of the medium.

A further layer of complexity appears in understanding these media when specific national understandings and articulations are taken into account. This is particularly the case with comics, where pacing, themes and **genres**, for instance, vary, thus creating very different national stereotypes of the medium. Thus, in the United States, superhero comics are commonly seen as the domi-nant genre, with swift pacing and action in each panel being typical, despite the existence of much other work which does not employ either of these elements.

Similarly, the stereotypical British comic is associated with childhood, has humour as a key ingredient and is seen as containing shorter strips (as exemplified in the *Beano* and *Dandy*) rather than longer, ongoing narratives. This stereotype remains dominant despite the impact of British creators internationally, working on longer narratives for adults across a range of genres. In contrast, there is a much broader understanding of comics in much of Europe and in Japan, where such work is more celebrated than castigated, and the notion of a range of texts for different audiences is more generally understood.

The history of each medium also varies depending on where, geographically, the historian is located, with accompanying debates over initiators, influences and other elements. It can be argued overall, nevertheless, that the development of the picturebook is related to changing views of childhood, most often in seeing 'the child' as pupil rather than employee (associated with study rather than paid work), thus linking such texts with changes in education, work legislation, printing technology and shifts in children's position within society. Accounts of the development of picturebooks may, however, focus on other elements, particularly on the texts seen as influential. For instance, in discussing the origin of the picturebook in Britain, Lewis argues that chapbooks from the seventeenth century onwards, together with toys and games from the mid-eighteenth century, influenced how picturebooks developed. He also asserts that cartoonists and illustrators whose work was aimed at adults – artists such as Richard Doyle and John Leech – 'imported into the picturebook a gaiety, liveliness and humour that fitted the emergent form well' and 'began to show how a truly composite text could be created from a combination of words and pictures' (Lewis, 1996, p. 17). Lewis sees this approach being developed by Randolph Caldecott. As it evolved, other creators also shifted from making texts for adults to fashioning them for the new children's medium.

Comics evolved at a similar time and can be seen as being connected to some of the same antecedents. Overall, Swiss teacher Rodolphe Töpffer is credited with initiating the comic strip medium in the 1830s and 1840s. By the end of the nineteenth century, comic strips had come to fruition in Britain in papers like *Ally Sloper's Half Holiday* in the 1880s, which had a predominantly adult audience, demonstrating that the comic was not initially associated with children. However, by the early 1900s titles specifically for children began to appear in Britain, with each era adding titles, such as the *Dandy* and *Beano* in the late 1930s. Similarly in America, newspaper strips opened up a number of potential spaces for the comic strip, including what became the superhero genre, beginning with *Superman* by Jerry Siegel and Joe Shuster in *Action Comics* (1938).

In the Britain of the 1950s gender and age niches developed in the market, partly in response to concerns about American comics with their superhero and crime themes, especially those for adults, and their influence on what was now being seen as the primary audience for comics, the child. This concern, exemplified in America by Fredric Wertham in his book *Seduction of the Innocent* (1954), was adopted in Britain and elsewhere in campaigns that resulted in the medium becoming focused upon narratives and images seen as suitable for the child (and directing boys and girls into specific behaviours). The campaign in Britain, in assuming a blank-slate model of the child, created an early media-effects theory and generated a moral panic, the latter being analysed by Barker (1984). From this point on, then, the comic became seen as a problematic medium internationally. The issue of comics for adults helped to compound the notion of the entire medium being seen as 'rebellious', controversial or subversive. While work for adults continued to appear, the medium was, in effect, forcibly redefined by the comic book campaigns of the 1940s and 1950s. However, by the 1970s the potential of the comic was being explored in picturebooks, as well as in comics themselves, in both Britain and America. As Lewis (1996, p. 19) states, 'picturebook makers of skill and flair began to deploy to their own ends the full range of techniques developed within the comic strip', citing Raymond Briggs as a key example. What is interesting is the way that, at the time of writing, Lewis saw Briggs as a picturebook maker adopting the comic medium, rather than as a creator of comics whose work is labelled a picturebook – another indication that the picturebook medium was the more venerated.

In further exploring these media, particularly in relation to definitions, this chapter will now focus on a small number of specific texts and creators. The texts considered range from comics and graphic novels to picturebooks, but all can be seen as offering challenges to assumptions about these media in relation to content, audience and form. Further, most of these texts refer to other texts, or deploy techniques employed by other media, showing the high degree of **hybridity**, intertextuality and experimentation within each area.

As suggested above, one example of problems of definition around the comic is to be found in the books of Briggs, whose works have been, until fairly recently, seen as picturebooks (although his recent inclusion in the Jonathan Cape 'Classic British Graphic Novel' series suggests a shift in definition that may reflect a reassessment of the graphic novel and comic). *The Snowman* (1978), seen as a 'classic' picturebook that uses the comic strip form, offers a number of challenges to definitions of each medium, as it can simply be seen as a wordless comic. What *The Snowman* illustrates is the power of the comic strip format to express meaning, emotion and narrative, even without supporting text (whether in speech balloons or elsewhere). Briggs' work also indicates that readers need to understand the grammar of the comic. In *The Snowman*, it is a skilled reader, one who knows how panels function, for instance, who will be able to get the most out of the text. In an example located towards the end of the book, a page containing 12 panels shows the boy turning in his sleep over the remainder of the night and then waking up in the morning. This demands that the reader understands that these are not 12 separate images of different boys (as a novice comic reader of whatever age might well assume) but a series of images of the same boy that should be read from left to right, and from top to bottom, unfolding over time. Even without the addition of speech bubbles, such decoding makes many demands upon the reader.

Briggs' work also exemplifies the ability of the comic medium to address a range of audiences. *Ethel & Ernest* (1998) is aimed at adults, in contrast to *The Snowman*, which, despite themes of death and loss, is generally associated with very young readers. The former is considered a graphic novel, rather than a comic, being a longer work. Offering a biography of Briggs' parents and his relationship with them, each chapter covers a decade, showing shifts in education and culture in Britain, engaging with cultural change and political issues in a personal way. One key page shows the moment when Briggs gets a place at a British grammar school and depicts his parents' responses. In particular, the father's comment that he hopes his son will not get 'too posh for us' (1998, p. 58) articulates a great deal about shifting class and educational structures, as does the positioning of the father in that panel and on the page: towards the edge, facing right (and so not looking at what is happening on the page) and with much white space between him and the left-hand side of the panel, thus implying sadness, isolation and, potentially, estrangement. Other pages focus on consumer products, and thus on the growth of consumer capitalism. Even the purchase of the house itself, with its indoor bathroom and large rooms, is seen by Ethel and Ernest with awe, indicating unease about their class position. The adoption of this text in some schools has shown how picturebooks can be used as effective vehicles for conveying complex ideas. Moreover, both texts undermine the stereotype of comics in Britain.

Tan's graphic novel *The Arrival* was influenced by Briggs' *The Snowman*. Both contain wordless journeys about stepping into **other** beings' worlds. However, in creating the world of *The Arrival* Tan draws predominantly on pictorial archives and old family albums, indicated by the use of sepia. The supposed realism of the photograph is, however, juxtaposed with fantasy, as we are presented with other imagined worlds from which the central character and those he meets originate. Offering no guidance as to how one should interpret the text, the reader is constantly working with visual clues and cues as to where they are, what is happening and, even, which character is 'speaking'. However, the shifts to another voice are signalled through subtle changes on the page, both in the images within the panels and in the colour of the page behind the panels. In the latter case, when a character other than the main protagonist tells their story, the colour of the background page changes. One man, for instance, shares a narrative about how he and his partner flee from oppressors depicted as giants with flame-throwers. At this point the page behind the panels turns to black, emphasizing that this is a different narrative. Within the panels, the narratives are indicated largely in changes of tint. In the narrative above, the images take on a yellow tinge, redolent of the flames that have engulfed his community. As his story continues, he and his partner escape into a world of charcoal blacks and abstract shapes (reflecting the use of black on the page behind the panels and suggesting a transitional phase) before escaping by boat to their current location, at which point the images return to sepia. The complex use of tone, tint and colour supports the reader's perception of the characters and their narratives as distinctive, personal voices.

Pacing, in these examples from Tan and Briggs, is linked with the grammar of the comic, with Tan employing a 12-panel page for the majority of this graphic novel. However, double-page spreads are used to emphasize key moments, such as the one showing the huge scale of his journey, where a tiny ship is depicted bottom-left of the verso, the whole being dominated by the clouds above. This is followed by a double-page spread where each page contains 30 panels, each depicting a cloud. The clouds vary tremendously in shape, tone and tint, indicative of both the changing weather conditions and the passage of time.

In looking at Tan and Briggs I have focused on the grammar of visual narrative, emphasizing the complexities of reading what is often seen as a simple 'comic'. The picturebook is similarly versatile, offering great potential for innovation. While the vast majority of creators in these media follow generic, narrative and formal codes that locate their work within the mainstream, there are some creators, like those mentioned earlier, who seek to extend what has been done in both form and content. Once again, innovation can be seen as arising from a number of factors, including developments in technology (especially computer graphics) and in culture (the shift to **postmodernist** ideas and perceptions). Postmodernist ideas seem to have given picturebook artists fresh directions to explore, as Lawrence Sipe and Sylvia Pantaleo's (2008) volume indicates. Lewis (2001) defines postmodernism as being characterized by a number of features, including boundary breaking, excess, indeterminacy, fragmentation and an undermining of notions of **canon**. Lewis, along with Sipe and Pantaleo and others, identifies Jon Scieszka and Lane Smith's *The Stinky Cheese Man and Other Fairly Stupid Tales* (1992) as a significant example.

Thus, Lewis shows how it ironically reworks a number of traditional fairy and **folktales** typically seen as canonical. *The Stinky Cheese Man* **parodies** these narratives, unsettling their canonical status. To appreciate this picturebook fully, therefore, would seem to depend on a 'knowing' reader, drawing on Western notions of 'cultural capital' (**Bourdieu**, 1984). Lewis' comment on this particular book, however, is that he finds it unsettling, suggesting an association of postmodernism with loss of coherence, with 'knowing' and adulthood, constructing a binary opposition with the integrity, coherence and lack of knowledge of childhood (Lewis, 2001, p. 101). In contrast, Pantaleo (2007), exploring young readers' understanding of the same book, finds that its very **metafictive** nature enables readers to develop complex interpretive strategies for understanding the ambiguities of word and image. The children drew on their intertextual knowledge, thus becoming not only 'knowing' readers of this particular text but also more competent readers of narrative and image generally. This is not to dispute Lewis' categories, merely his extrapolations from them. So we certainly find both fragmentation and canonical instability in *The Stinky Cheese Man*; for example, in 'Little Red Running Shorts', the narrator gives a summary of the story which, in being printed, becomes the story itself: a narrative rather too short for the three pages it is allocated. In addition, it is a version very different from

Perrault's or the Grimms' 'Little Red Riding Hood' in that the protagonist triumphs through her talent as a runner. The characters refuse to cooperate in extending the story and so are depicted as white silhouettes, with a trail of footprints crossing the double-page spread from right to left – thus reversing and disrupting the flow of the book for the reader – as they walk out of the story. The page following 'Little Red Running Shorts' is blank as a consequence of the narrator's mistake – something 'Little Red Hen', who should be participating in the following narrative, comments on. In this text, then, the form, as well as the content of the individual narratives, is explored and analysed, even to the extent of questioning non-narrative elements like the title page and ISBN barcode.

In other words, what Lewis terms 'boundary breaking' is prevalent, a quality which points to the constructedness of the text, and removes the reader from an expectation of reading as entering an imaginary world. This text also forces readers to construct a narrative which makes sense to them out of a huge potential range of possibilities, engaging in an act of co-construction, as Pantaleo sees it (2007, p. 291). Thus, the reader is an essential element in the creation of the text's meaning, a large part of which involves the text's visual aspects, including the visual aspects of the text. Lewis suggests that creators of picturebooks feel empowered to envision their child reader as more open and exploratory, which is certainly in line with contemporary notions of postmodernity.

Emily Gravett's work explores other elements of postmodernism, stressing the *bricolage* aspect of the process of composition, especially in *Little Mouse's Big Book of Fears* (2007). Gravett's work builds on the novelty book and the use of multiple narratives and texts within a single story that characterized earlier books, such as the Ahlbergs' *The Jolly Postman or Other People's Letters* (1986), where the contents of the letters, from catalogues to invitations, are included. In *The Jolly Postman*, Janet Ahlberg's distinctive style of drawing was applied to all these inserts, giving the overall work a sense of unity. In contrast, *Little Mouse's Big Book of Fears* employs diverse creative approaches, being presented as a scrapbook, and, therefore, embracing, to an extent, notions of fragmentation.

The scrapbook combines fiction and non-fictional elements, incorporating extracts from catalogues, dictionaries and workbooks (so tying it to genres like the self-help book) alongside nursery rhymes (especially 'Three Blind Mice'), united by a central narrative thread about fear and insecurity. The non-fictional elements offer a series of other texts, each depicting a specific phobia (of spiders, for example, or of being lost), which is named and defined. Below the headings for each phobia are drawings, handwritten segments and other texts, including maps, newspapers, advertisements and postcards. These are sometimes torn, drawn or written upon. The reader is also presented with a workbook, in which each phobia is addressed in a therapeutic yet ironic way. Thus, its form exemplifies aspects of the postmodern picturebook by drawing attention to its status as artefact and also in breaking boundaries. This text, too, can, through these and other elements, be seen as engaging – or at least nurturing – a 'knowing' reader. The materials offer multiple intertextual narratives to the reader, which enrich the central story about the titular character.

However, not only is the book postmodern in form and content but it is also itself part of the postmodern condition, where grand narratives have failed and 'Little Mouse's' (the author's and the reader's) excessive responses and irrational anxieties are exposed. The book's indeterminacy encourages the reader not only to fill in the gaps but also to physically engage with the work and to add to it. This sort of empowering approach to drawing and writing suggests the kinds of creativity associated with Web 2.0, the changing use of web technology and design that has led to web-culture communities such as social networking sites, wikis and blogs, where the emphasis is on collaboration, re-editing, commentary and critique. Further, Gravett's text was created in an act of co-construction with two rats, whose 'modification' of a mock-up with bite-marks and holes is also integrated into the final published work. All of this implies a more fluid conception of self and creativity than has previously been the case in relation to the picturebook medium.

In conclusion, the picturebook, comic and graphic novel are complex and flexible media linked through their shared uses of image and text. Though these media have traditionally been associated with children, it has also been argued that this need not be so and that these forms have had their adult audiences too and, perhaps, with the range of innovation and sophistication currently witnessed, the trend towards crossover works will grow, Tan's *oeuvre* being a key example. Yet there are also countervailing tendencies, as I've indicated, with fears about the young being exposed to inappropriate material – especially in comic form – which connects debates around these media to larger issues concerning the construction of the child. Only the future will reveal how our increasingly pictorial culture will seek to instruct and, indeed, control what is becoming an increasingly visually sophisticated young audience.

FURTHER READING

Arizpe, Evelyn and Styles, Morag (2003) *Children Reading Pictures: Interpreting Visual Texts*, London: RoutledgeFalmer.
This book is based on the findings of a two-year research project on visual literacy ('Reading Pictures') which looked at children's responses to contemporary picturebooks. The authors discuss the sophisticated readings children made of the complex images these texts contain, revealing children's multi-layered understanding of them.

Barker, Martin (1989) *Comics: Ideology, Power and the Critics*, Manchester: Manchester University Press.
Barker looks at a range of work on and responses to comics by various theorists and debates their effectiveness. He analyses work that draws on psychoanalytic theory, semiotics and feminism, among other approaches, offering contrasting interpretations of the meanings and uses of comics.

Gibson, Mel (2009) *Comics Scholarship on the Net: A Brief Annotated Bibliography*, http://www.dr-mel-comics.co.uk/sources/academic.html.

List of sites, ranging from library catalogues to e-journals, which feature academic work on comics. It also offers a number of links to sites which show what primary material is available in library and museum collections.

Groensteen, Thierry (2007) *The System of Comics*, trans. Bart Beaty and Nick Nguyen, Jackson: University of Mississippi Press.
Groensteen's key semiotic analysis of the European comic, focusing predominantly upon BD.

Heer, Jeet and Worcester, Kent (eds) (2009) *A Comic Studies Reader*, Jackson: University of Mississippi Press.
This collection, divided into four sections, considers key writing in relation to historical work on the comic and its grammar, along with explorations of culture, narrative and identity, and provides a section on scholars using a synthesis of theoretical approaches.

McCloud, Scott (1993) *Understanding Comics: The Invisible Art*, New York: HarperCollins.
This very influential work, itself in comic format, shows a range of ways of thinking about the medium. McCloud focuses not on content, but on the grammar of the comic, from the ways that lettering and colour can make meaning through to page layout and to the way that, for instance, time works in the medium.

Nikolajeva, Maria and Scott, Carole (2001) *How Picturebooks Work*, New York: Garland.
A key text exploring the interplay between word and image which undertakes to analyse a range of texts from a number of nations. It offers innovative methodologies, theories and critical tools regarding the medium. It also offers a commentary on work in the field up to the turn of the century.

Nodelman, Perry (1988) *Words about Pictures: The Narrative Art of Children's Picture Books*, Athens, GA: University of Georgia Press.
One of the most influential texts of scholarship about picturebooks. This sophisticated study of the semiotic and narrative aspects of illustration draws on a number of aesthetic and literary sources. Nodelman explores the way in which the interplay of the verbal and visual aspects of picturebooks conveys more than either element could alone.

10

MEDIA ADAPTATIONS

MARGARET MACKEY

Contemporary young people move between media in an eclectic and equable fashion. 'The dispersal of narrative' (Thompson, 2003, p. 74) among different contemporary formats means that they expect to meet their stories in many media guises. They will encounter many adapted texts; they may also expect to produce them. Current adaptation theories must take into account that reception today includes production; many readers now create and publish (often online) their own adapted versions.

Teachers and parents often have a default set of priorities that privileges print. Surprisingly, theories of adaptation tend to operate on the same conservative premises. As Linda Hutcheon (2006, pp. 37–8) tartly observes (her comment is equally true about other forms of adaptation):

> Most of the talk about film adaptation . . . is in negative terms of loss. Sometimes what is meant is simply a reduction of scope: of length, of accretion of detail, of commentary . . . because it usually takes longer to perform an action than to read a written report of it. But at other times the change is perceived as less a question of quantity and more one of quality . . . . In this negative discourse of loss, performance media are said to be incapable of linguistic or narrative subtlety or of representing the psychological or the spiritual.

It is true that the book is generally 'bigger' than its media rivals (though the unabridged audio-book is equally substantial, and a long-running television series can be even larger than a novel in scope). But those who enjoy their fiction multimodally know that different media offer different pleasures and that the secret of being a savvy media-crosser is to appreciate the affordances of each vehicle and to savour the transitions.

Bolter and Grusin talk about 'remediation', which they define as 'the formal logic by which new media refashion prior media forms'. Remediation, they suggest, involves a paradoxical oscillation between *immediacy* and *hypermediacy*. Immediacy is a 'style of visual representation whose goal is to make the viewer forget the presence of the medium (canvas, photographic film, cinema, and so on) and believe that he is in the presence of the objects of representation'. Hypermediacy is a 'style of visual representation whose goal is to remind the viewer of the medium' (Bolter and Grusin, 1999, pp. 272–3).

McFarlane (1996, p. 20), discussing adaptation from novel to film, distinguishes between elements of *narrative* that are transferable from one medium to another and elements of *enunciation* that are specific to a particular medium. Such terms, he suggests, allow for more productive criticism of adaptations than concerns about whether the adapted version is sufficiently faithful to the original. Fidelity questions, he says, rest on 'a notion of the text as having and rendering up to the (intelligent) reader a single, correct "meaning" which the film-maker has either adhered to or in some sense violated or tampered with' (p. 8). The adaptation, he suggests, is more helpfully judged on its own terms as one of a set of interconnected texts.

MULTIPLE INSTANTIATIONS

A multiply told story may be imagined as suspended in an **intertextual** web of incarnations. Such plurality affects all versions, even the originating version that once existed as a singular story. For many young readers, this change of a story's status is perceived as dynamic, introducing a comparative element into their fictional pleasure that they relish and refine.

This intertextual web of different instantiations of a story does not exist in a conceptual or material vacuum. Adaptation is a phenomenon both cultural and industrial, and a material theory of the dissemination of multiple reworkings is an important component of any discussion of children's relation to their stories. Simone Murray suggests that such materialism is almost entirely overlooked in adaptation theory and is scathing about the implications of ignoring the industrial side of proliferating adaptations and risking a sentimental instantiation of what should be a grittier and more grounded concept:

> Dematerialized, immune to commercialism, floating free of any cultural institutions, intellectual property regimes, or industry agents that might have facilitated its creation or indelibly marked its form, the adaptation exists in perfect quarantine from the troubling worlds of commerce, Hollywood, and global corporate media – a formalist textual fetish oblivious to the disciplinary incursions of political economy, book history, or the creative industries.
>
> (Murray, 2008, p. 5)

Jarrod Waetjen and Timothy Gibson (2007, p. 5) suggest that we need to find ways of aligning cultural and material criticism of all our texts, including print: 'what is required is a commitment to taking textual meanings seriously, while at the same time situating such textual openings and closures within a diachronic, material analysis of contemporary media production and distribution'.

Material conditions, of course, affect print and digital texts every bit as much as productions of the 'mass media'. It is important to remember that the book too is a product of commercial interests, and it is equally vital to acknowledge that the limitless world of digital **reader response** is dependent on unequal conditions of access to equipment, know-how and viable online connections. Most contemporary Western children, however, entirely take for granted the plural world being analysed in this chapter, even if their access is variable.

Hutcheon provides a useful way of distinguishing the strengths of different media and offers some insight into why children may enjoy moving between different incarnations of the same story. With *telling*, she says, 'our engagement begins in the realm of imagination, which is simultaneously controlled by the selected directing words of the text and liberated – that is, unconstrained by the limits of the visual or aural'. *Showing* is more concrete: pace is controlled when we view, moving us 'from the imagination to the realm of direct perception'. *Interacting* is physically and kinaesthetically immersive, entailing visceral responses, but pace, to a limited extent, is once more under the control of the interpreter (Hutcheon, 2006, pp. 22–3).

These are useful distinctions but they do not encompass the full range of interpretive possibilities for a contemporary narrative. To explore the implications of adaptation across a broad media range, let us take the example of *The Golden Compass* (published as *Northern Lights* in the United Kingdom) by Philip Pullman (1995), which initially appeared as the first book in a trilogy. This example will allow us to explore print, audio, film, stage play, videogame, toys and fan fiction. What it does not provide is a concrete example of a television version (though a few scenes were dramatized for an interview with Pullman on the UK's ITV arts programme, 'The South Bank Show', 2003). In terms of *The Golden Compass* itself, the long form of the television serial dramatization might provide a good vehicle for telling this complex story in new ways, although such a production does not yet exist. For the purposes of this chapter, however, television is perhaps the most difficult vehicle to discuss for an international audience, given its national provenance and particularities (e.g. the classic serial, so beloved in the United Kingdom, is a much less important feature of children's TV elsewhere). Television provides less border-crossing than other media, though there are obvious blockbuster exceptions. It is also in a state of serious transition. Although it has been a staple of global culture for some decades now, television is mutating under the pressure of the interactive potential of the Internet (Spiegel and Olsson, 2004; Jenkins, 2008). The omission of television from this specific discussion is noted, but the many incarnations of *The Golden Compass* provide much food for thought even without a TV example.

Print

The original novel, the first of the trilogy known as *His Dark Materials*, received glowing reviews and won the Carnegie Medal. (The third book in the trilogy later became the first children's book to win the overall Whitbread Book of the Year prize.) The print story establishes a lively world peopled by varied and exotic beings and develops an exciting adventure in which cruelty is clearly defined and practised, but larger questions of good and evil are more ambiguously delineated and discussed. The narrative voice is authoritative, instructing us how to perceive the heroine, Lyra ('In many ways Lyra was a barbarian . . . . She was a coarse and greedy little savage, for the most part' – Pullman, 1995, pp. 34, 36). The rich panoply of creatures, events and lavish settings is presented with an economy of telling that privileges the drive to the ending. Pullman (1998, p. 51) has elsewhere written about the importance of clearing away distractions and extraneous details that interfere with the need to tell the story: 'you must design the path so that it leads to the destination most surely, and with the maximum effect'.

Even with an author as clearly in control of his story matter as Pullman, readers retain some substantial prerogatives in processing the story. Readers control the pace of the process; they can skip or linger or repeat or race ahead as they choose. Readers also vivify the story with their own imaginations. Christopher Collins (1991, p. 151) describes how readers behave when confronted by the 'nouns situated in a void' that print offers:

> To put it bluntly, when we enter the imaginary space of a text, we don't know where we are. We orient ourselves only in reference to the few landmarks we are given – nouns situated in a void. Those nouns are fashioned into an assumed visuospatial network by prepositions, verbs and adverbs but are displayed to us only in the linear, unidirectional sequence of word order. Not having actually perceived this scene ourselves, we have no peripheral field in which to detect and target an object as our next image.

Faced with this literal and metaphorical surfeit of white space, readers draw on their memories and emotions to bring to imaginative life the abstract black marks that lie before them on the page. It is more than a case of simple visualizing: readers breathe life into the phrases and cadences, and their inner voice merges with the voices on the page; in a very real sense of the word, readers *enliven* – bring to life – the descriptions of emotional responses with their own felt experiences. The production of mental images out of printed words is very much a cooperative affair between author and reader, but the interface of the words on the page remains abstract.

Readers of Pullman's books, therefore, participate in creating some mental version of the North that plays such a strong role in the first novel; they voice the dæmons according to their own inner tones and accents; they feel the strength of the armoured bears in terms of other awe-inspiring experiences in their own lives, and so forth. This cognitive and emotional effort results in the creation of an engrossing world (see Mackey, 2005).

Since the first book of the trilogy was adapted for the cinema, other print reworkings of *The Golden Compass* have appeared (e.g. Harrison, 2007; Woodward, 2007). These creations are hybrids; telling a highly abridged version of the story, they do not rely solely on the abstractions of print but point readers to glossy photographs from the film version, associating the printed words with these specific, concrete images. We know less than we need to know about the psychology of how young children learn to read when so many of their print experiences are explicitly *not* abstract, because they have already seen specific embodiments of the fictional world on television and in movies. These books are not created to explore such interesting questions, however; their material purpose is to supplement revenue from the film release. Children take the flood of repurposed print materials that accompany film adaptation as a standard element of their cultural universe. Books that depend on visual referents to film and television have abounded since the early days of Disney, but the rate of proliferation has expanded in recent times. We need more economic insight into the rate of return and other forms of value of such multiple and attenuated versions of a popular originating story.

Audio

Like the print version of *Northern Lights*, the unabridged audio recording (Pullman, 1999) was hailed as a triumph. With Pullman himself narrating and a full cast of actors playing the characters, the full audio-text lasts nearly 11 hours.

The audio version is in many ways the most intimately similar to the original print story. In an unabridged version, not a word is lost and listeners take on many of the imaginative responsibilities of readers. Nevertheless, the experience is significantly different. Is it useful to think, in Hutcheon's terms, of gains and losses? Or is it more helpful simply to consider differing affordances?

Words are abstract when compared to images and sound effects, but an audio rendition of words communicates some elements of specificity. A voice is not abstract. It conveys information about gender, region and class; it has timbre and cadence. In the case of *Northern Lights*, the voices of Pullman and the actors draw on these indicators to convey a sense of the range and vastness of Pullman's world. A silent reader lifts the words off the page into awareness by dint of his or her own rhythms of breath and speech, even if only at the level of subvocalization. A listener hears, as a substitute, the breath and voice of narrator and actors. One immediate change is that the listener relinquishes control over pacing. The active, dancing eyes lose their power over the story; the imagination is fed instead by the patient ears that cannot skip quickly over less compelling sentences or speed or slow the reception of each word in turn. Proponents of interactivity often refer to paper reading as a linear experience, but listening is actually far more linear and less flexible. Abridgements and adaptations of the original print, though often cheaper to produce and buy, alter the experience once again.

Film

The movie version of *The Golden Compass* (2007) is certainly 'smaller' than the book, and some critics have complained that it is too short even by the standards of a commercial film. Characters and settings are more concretely realized in the movie than in the audio rendition; each actor has a specific appearance, demeanour and affective charge that may or may not match up to a reader's imagined embodiment of a character.

Children absorb the conventions of contemporary film at an early age. They are prepared to accept talking animals as relatively realistic and actively expect witches to fly. Tacitly, they learn to process the limits of the screen (with the presumed extension of the imagined world beyond its borders), to understand camera angle as point of view, to develop awareness of depth conventions and to assemble a sense of continuous flow of information from a series of cuts. Theoretical approaches to children's films, however, pay more attention to the film as text than they do to the children who watch them (see Street, 1983; Wojcik-Andrews, 2000); we must turn to media studies if we want to learn about child viewers (see Bazalgette and Buckingham, 1995; Marsh and Millard, 2000).

In contemporary material culture, films mutate as they move between theatre, television version, and a variety of DVD cuts (basic, extended, director's). Before they turn ten years old, most Western children know the difference between the domesticated screen of television and DVD and the theatrical rituals associated with the cinema screen. The DVD extras frequently offer an education in media literacy, and the movie itself is often subtly altered from the cinema version. Ernest Mathijs suggests that the extended DVD is often marketed for *re*-viewing; purchasers are presumed to be familiar with the story from its theatrical release. When the film is re-edited (to be longer, to restore the director's favourite scenes, to seduce viewers into buying yet another DVD version of the same movie), the effect is textual as well as financial:

> For the extended DVDs, the drive of the story is of less significance. Most people watching these DVDs will already know the story quite well and there is no longer a strong need to provide theatrically graded impulsion . . . . The DVDs function in this sense as exegeses of the theatrical text.
> (Mathijs, 2006, p. 48)

The information provided by the DVD articulates components of the film that viewers often take for granted. One element of film-making ('invisible' in literal as well as metaphorical terms) is the soundtrack. Hutcheon (2006, p. 41) reminds us that the role of the audible is important to movies and is often overlooked:

> First, there are . . . many words spoken in films . . . ; then there are the separate soundtracks that permit elements like voice-overs, music, and noise to intermingle. Soundtracks in movies . . . enhance and direct audience response to characters and action, as they do in videogames, in which music also merges with sound effects both to underscore and to create emotional reactions. Film sound can be used to connect inner and outer states in a less explicit way than do camera associations.

The ongoing nature of our ears' relationship to the world at large is an under-studied element of narrative understanding.

What can be *enunciated* in a film differs significantly from what can be enunciated in a print narrative. For example, Pullman as novelist is able to tell us explicitly how Lyra and Pantalaimon share a joint universe and a tie stronger than anything else in Lyra's life. Film director Chris Weitz (2008) must find ways of demonstrating that tie by showing rather than telling – a challenge made all the more taxing as one of the partners in this relationship is anima-tronically assembled, with computer-enhanced appearance and motion, plus the voice of a human actor. Again we find that audio plays a crucial part: as view-ers we apply our psychological understanding of voice and tone to the computer creation before our eyes. Even so, Weitz does not entirely trust his viewers to make the leap, because the movie opens with a voice-over explaining the nature of the dæmon.

In this example, we can also see issues of *narrative* (Pantalaimon's close rela-tionship to Lyra) and issues of *enunciation* (the need for computer **animation** to express what Pullman could tell us directly in words). It is also not difficult to picture child viewers oscillating between the *immediacy* of Lyra's adventures and the *hypermediacy* of appreciating the effects of the computer graphics that convey Pan's significance to viewers. Those child viewers who have already read the novel may also layer-in other complex oscillations between the world they have previously created in their minds and the one on display on the screen before them.

Pressures of time in the movie mean that the elaborate story of *Northern Lights* is compressed into a fast-moving adventure, with the philosophical underpinnings abridged or eliminated. Such simplification is not necessarily intrinsic to film adaptation, but the radically shorter nature of the movie means that every element has to achieve many ends in order to approach the book's potential for scope and subtlety.

Reviewers of *The Golden Compass* (e.g. French, 2007; Papamichael, 2007; Zacharek, 2007) largely agreed that this particular film did not do justice to the richness of the book; they were particularly dismayed by the omission of the book's complex and dramatic ending. The movie concludes some three chapters before the end of the novel; Weitz's 'decision to end the movie earlier in the narrative had been influenced by the need for a more box office-friendly happy ending to establish the foundation for what he hopes will be a film trilogy' (Collett-White, 2007, n.p.). Pullman seemed content with this decision:

> What a good idea to end the film like that. It's quite the best place to stop. The book is fine as it is, but the opening of the second film would be a much better place for the complex, ambiguous drama of the last chapter; and it was much more likely that the second film would be made if the first one ended on a clear, strong and immediately understandable note.
>
> (Pullman, 2007, n.p.)

The financial framework within which most contemporary films are created is a key material factor in many artistic decisions; budget constraints play a far more constitutive role in film-making than in writing. In the summer of 2008, there were hints that the second film might not be made because of concerns about poor box office returns in the United States (Anon, 2008, n.p.), and by early 2009 there was no sign of a sequel.

The saga of the filmed *Golden Compass* does nothing to challenge the widespread notion that popular films are simpler than other media forms, that **Disneyfication** affects the conventions of movie-making for children in deep and conservative ways and that, of all media, it is most likely to be the film that values safety more than risk.

Stage play

Nicholas Wright (2003) adapted *The Golden Compass* and its sequels into two 3-hour stage plays, first produced at the National Theatre in London in 2003. In terms of Hutcheon's distinctions, a play clearly belongs to the domain of 'showing', but a play does not necessarily work on the realistic conventions of the film that shifts us 'from the imagination to the realm of direct perception' (2006, p. 23). In the film, thanks to editorial and digital manipulations, an animal dæmon can both talk and move realistically; a witch can fly. In a stage production, some of these ingredients must be conveyed partly through conventions of acting and partly through the imaginative work of the audience; they cannot simply be 'shown'. Thus, in the stage version of *His Dark Materials*, the dæmons are presented as handheld puppets, managed by puppeteers who appear on stage dressed in black with black balaclavas. The puppeteer speaks for the dæmon, manages its changes from one form to another and with surprising swiftness merges into the scenery, to be disregarded by playgoers.

In one of this play's great stage moments, Wright and director Nicholas Hytner turn the invisibility of the puppeteer into a *coup de théâtre*. Late in the story, Lyra must confront her own death. An old woman says Lyra's death came into the world when she was born and remains near to her, unseen, all her life; to produce this effect onstage, Pantalaimon's puppeteer stands up, removes his balaclava and, in a bold stroke of imaginative economy, speaks as Lyra's death. This stage non-presence has been near Lyra all along and the audience has been soothed by convention into not seeing him, so his sudden entrance into the world of the plot is startlingly effective.

The stage play resembles the film, however, in its radical abridgement of the story. Even with six hours of playing time, it is impossible for the adaptors to include the entire panoply of Pullman's broad canvas, and major components of the story are omitted. Once again, pace is inexorable, an effect particularly noticeable in the National Theatre production which took place at high speed on a revolving stage.

Game fiction

Although the field of children's literature tends to overlook digital games, the 'dispersal' of such a respected narrative as *The Golden Compass* into a computer game (Sony, 2007) is a phenomenon that calls for attention.

Interactive storytelling operates on principles rather different from those used to communicate story by means of abstract letters or through video and/or audio – though it is important to remember that games also make use of both video and audio affordances.

Interacting involves a key distinction, clarified by Aarseth (1997, p. 1): it is *ergodic*, requiring non-trivial player actions in order for the text to be traversed. In other words, the story itself is shaped by player actions, at least to a limited extent. In the game of *The Golden Compass*, this shaping power of the player comes into contact with a story that is already highly crafted. In a game, players must be able to direct the processing of the story. For example, in the book, Pantalaimon, like the dæmons of all children under the age of puberty, changes shape at will; in the game, this power is given over to the player, and the official game guide describes the result:

> At Lyra's request [actually at the click of the player's mouse], Pan can transform into whichever creature suits her needs.
>
> If she needs a keen eye, Pan can take his ermine form. If Lyra needs to cross a wide gap, the wings of Pan's hawk are just the thing. Similarly, Pan can swing Lyra across large gaps by transforming into a sloth with long nimble arms. Pan's wildcat form allows Lyra to climb certain surfaces like nets and fabric.
>
> (Bueno, 2007, p. 6)

In the book, Pantalaimon has a large range of alternative bodies; the game reduces the option list to four in order to facilitate player decisions about which form is most useful to the challenge of the game-play at any particular time. Although Lyra and Pan make strategic use of his different powers in the book, the utilitarian element is much more strongly emphasized in the game version, and the emotional link between girl and dæmon is correspondingly downplayed. There is no example, for instance, of Pan changing into a particular form just for the sheer comfort of it, though the book abounds with such moments. Games have often been charged with failing to express emotional states successfully, and the strict utility of Pan's dynamism is an example of such rigidity.

Barry Atkins expresses the distinction between telling, showing and interacting in different terms. In traditional narratives, he says, the guiding question is, 'What happens next?' But interactive narratives cannot be understood by waiting for the next event to occur; player **agency** is a crucial part of the story's development and the salient question is, 'What happens next *if I* . . . ?' It is a different kind of orientation towards the future of the story (Atkins, 2006, p. 137).

In the story, the question 'What happens next?' may be answered by Pantalaimon changing into an ermine. The relationship with the narrative alters when the question is, 'What happens next *if I* change Pantalaimon into an ermine?'

In many ways, what the game offers is not so much a story but rather what Henry Jenkins (2004, p. 123) calls an 'evocative space' that offers interpreters the opportunity to play around in a story world that has initially been created elsewhere:

> Increasingly, we inhabit a world of transmedia storytelling, one that depends less on each individual work being self-sufficient than on each work contributing to a larger narrative economy . . . . One can imagine games taking their place within a larger narrative system with story information communicated through books, film, television, comics, and other media, each doing what it does best, each a relatively autonomous experience, but the richest understanding of the story world coming to those who follow the narrative across the various channels. In such a system, what games do best will almost certainly center around their ability to give concrete shape to our memories and imaginings of the storyworld [*sic*], creating an immersive environment we can wander through and interact with.
>
> (p. 124)

Although *The Golden Compass* game is very action oriented, it does also provide players the chance to participate in Lyra's world, with very different cognitive and affective implications from the experience of reading, or of witnessing an acted version.

Toys

It would take a whole other chapter to do justice to the role of toys in the cross-media marketing of successfully adapted children's titles. A quick search of Google reveals hundreds of *Golden Compass* toys and collectibles: action figures, playsets, trading cards, playing cards, collectible miniatures, dolls, stuffed animals and so forth. The commodification of children's literature is a topic that receives mostly negative and pessimistic consideration (see Engelhardt, 1991; **Zipes**, 2001; Hade, 2002). A more even-handed appraisal appears in Mackey (2002), but there is very little scholarly work that takes account of how children themselves respond to literature-based toys and commodities. Do they, for example, perceive a Lyra doll as a source of agency in creating their own responses to the story? As every movie blockbuster leads to a flood of toys and tie-ins, much work remains to be done in this area.

A second issue is the degree to which a story is created and/or accepted for publication or production in the first place because of its capacity to foster toys and spin-offs. Too little is known about the basis on which a story devolves into 'content', being elastic in its ability to be licensed for a variety of commodities.

Fan adaptations

Some fiction readers clearly espouse an absolute right to participate in and change the fictional world. These enthusiasts may create fan fiction or other forms of fan response. It is not hard to see the satisfaction of writing a new and happier ending to *The Golden Compass*, as the work of the fan below demonstrates:

> Lyra knew you were never to touch another's dæmon.
>
> However, Lyra knew what was about to happen to Roger, and under the circumstances, she wasn't about to just wait for. [*sic*] With such strength, that it even left her to tumble into the snow, her boot came into contact with Stelmaria's head. . . .
>
> She simply began to run, grabbing Roger's hand and racing back down the mountain. She *would* learn about Dust. And she *would* get to that other world. And she would have Roger by her side doing it.
>
> (IndigoNight and RayneStorm, 2007, n.p.)

In this version, Lyra's rescue of Roger, through kicking Lord Asriel's dæmon and disrupting the intercision, offers a jaunty alternative to the tragedy of the book and a radical rethinking of the insipid ending of the movie. The happy ending, reasonably based on the kind of resourcefulness Lyra has demonstrated throughout the story, exists, of course, in a kind of palimpsestic relationship to the original. The simplicity of her strategy is effectively funny only when read in the context of the original harsh plot.

Fan adaptations proliferate on the Internet and are currently under-theorized, especially as they relate to literary stories; the narratives of popular culture are somewhat better served (most famously in Jenkins, 1992). Even less clear is the impact of fan power on the experience of reading. We simply do not know enough about how children read when they know they can anticipate the possibility of publishing their own 'improved' version online. Does their stance towards the text change when they have the possibility of 'editing' it to produce something more to their liking? We do not really know if or how the reading experience changes under these circumstances or understand the authority that young readers confer on fan authors. There are many theoretical and research questions to answer.

CONCLUSION

Despite the questions raised above, what is not in doubt is that children have already moved into the complex fictional territory described in this chapter. A new study sponsored by Scholastic (2008, p. 32) revealed that 64 per cent of those children aged 9 to 17 who have access to the Internet 'have participated in at least one activity that extends the reading experience online'. The connection between such online extensions and avid reading of print on paper is clearly established in the study. And we do not need specific research to tell us that the percentage of children who extend their reading experience with film and DVD is even greater.

The children who make sophisticated use of the Internet to enhance their reading experiences will also be at home with adaptations in many other media forms, old as well as new: after all, *Mary Poppins* became a musical; *Where the Wild Things Are* was converted into an opera and is now a movie (with a separate documentary about its creation); *Coraline* became a graphic novel as well as a 3-D stop-action animated film. Thompson suggests that 'tendencies toward adaptations of stories among media, toward sequels, and toward seriality are all part of a general stretching and redefinition of narrative itself' (2003, p. 105). The academic study of children's literature must take account of such developments simply in order to keep abreast of contemporary children. They are the ones who read, enjoy and revisit that literature; they also acknowledge and contribute to its stretching and redefinition. We need to pay attention to the narrative sophistication of both texts and interpreters.

FURTHER READING

Hutcheon, Linda (2006) *A Theory of Adaptation*, New York: Routledge.
As its title suggests, this book is a theoretical exploration of how a fiction alters when it changes medium. Hutcheon draws on familiar questions – What? Who? Why? How? Where? When? – to investigate a deliberately broad range of adaptations. Unlike most other scholars who deal with adaptation, she does not explore particular texts but rather investigates forms, adapters, audiences and contexts.

Jenkins, Henry (2008) *Convergence Culture: Where Old and New Media Collide*, New York: New York University Press.
Jenkins examines the impact of new media on old media experiences: questions of convergence and the ways in which old media experiences change when interpreters are able to 'speak back' in what has been dubbed participatory culture. One chapter specifically addresses these issues in relation to Harry Potter.

McFarlane, Brian (1996) *Novel to Film: An Introduction to the Theory of Adaptation*, Oxford: Clarendon Press.
McFarlane discusses theoretical aspects of adaptation in the context of specific examples, all adult and dating between 1926 and 1991. He addresses the issue of fidelity thoroughly and reaches the conclusion that it is a chimera, that a film can, at best, be faithful only to a particular and singular reading of a book. It is more important, says McFarlane, to consider questions of narrative (the components of a story that are transferable between media because they are not tied to a particular semiotic system) and questions of enunciation (elements that must change because they are so closely allied with one semiotic system that they must be reworked to appear in another).

Reynolds, Kimberley (ed.) (2003) *Children's Literature and Childhood in Performance*, Lichfield: Pied Piper Publishing.
Thirteen essays, plus **Reynolds**' introduction, written by scholars, children's authors and storytellers, explore a broad range of subjects related to the adaptation and performance of literature for and/or about children.

Ridgman, Jeremy and Collins, Fiona M. (eds) (2004) *Turning the Page: Children's Literature in Performance and the Media*, Oxford: Peter Lang.
This collection explores a wide variety of children's titles that have moved from the page to some other kind of presentation. It includes a paper by Reynolds on the stage presentation of *His Dark Materials*, which connects with some of the arguments in this chapter. Relating to the Jenkins chapter listed previously, Andrew Burn explores Harry Potter in book, film and videogame form.

11

SIDELINES

Some neglected dimensions of children's literature and its scholarship

EVELYN ARIZPE AND MORAG STYLES WITH ABIGAIL ROKISON

INTRODUCTION: CHILDREN'S LITERATURE AND THE QUESTION OF GENRE

> Every genre positions those who participate in a text of that kind: as interviewer or interviewee, as listener or storyteller, as a reader or a writer . . .
> as someone to be instructed or as someone who instructs; each of these positionings implies different possibilities for response and for action.
> Each written text provides a 'reading position' for readers, a position constructed by the writer for the 'ideal reader' of the text.
>
> (Kress, 1988, p. 107)

There are many different definitions of **genre**, with some querying whether it can exist at all (Neale, 1995). Jacques **Derrida** (1981, p. 61), however, argues that 'a text cannot belong to no genre, it cannot be without . . . a genre. Every text participates in one or several genres, there is no genreless text'. Children's literature itself is sometimes defined as a literary *genre* although it covers many different classifications of text, most of which have parallel representations in adult literature. New genres are emerging all the time, some of which are hybrid and some of which are slippery to define; as David Buckingham (1993, p. 137) puts it, 'Genre is not . . . simply "given" by the culture: rather, it is in a constant process of negotiation and change'.

Most modern critics would agree with Buckingham, but for children's literature the process of negotiation is complicated by the unequal power relationships (as it is mostly written by adults for children – see **Rose**, 1984). As Tony Thwaites *et al.* (1994, p. 104) suggest, 'in the interaction and conflicts among genres we can see the connections between textuality and power'. The inequality is often manifested in formulaic genres which fit young readers' expectations and which attempt to elicit a particular response from them. Changing expectations on the part of the child, together with the new hybrid texts, however, mean that the 'contract' between writers and readers (**Jameson**, 1975) is constantly being breached as new genres emerge. Some genres have a short life, some become part of the **canon** of 'children's literature', while others remain on the sidelines.

125

NEGLECTED DIMENSIONS OF CHILDREN'S LITERATURE

Children's literature as a field of study is widely marginalized in academic circles, but certain aspects of it are doubly neglected, being less popular, less widely known and less highly regarded than other areas. These disparate, sidelined categories – autobiography, drama, poetry, storytelling, the oral tradition, writings by children and works of domestic literacy – are the focus of this chapter. On the one hand, it could easily be argued that they do not have much in common. On the other hand, most of the texts under consideration share some of the following characteristics: they are short and modest, relatively informal, domestic and sometimes personal, contain an oral dimension, and are generally less visible or by authors of low status. These categories can be considered 'genres' in their own right, as there are enough common characteristics and relationships between the texts that conform to them and also because they fulfil readers' expectations in their own very particular ways, some of which will be explored in what follows. Information texts for children have not been considered, however, partly because there is insufficient space to do so but mainly because the focus of this chapter is predominantly on imaginative works.

Autobiography

Autobiography is not a developed genre within children's literature, not even being given its own entry in recent encyclopaedias on the subject (Watson, 2001; **Hunt**, 2004; **Zipes**, 2006b). However, some popular authors have written about their own lives for a more adult readership (e.g. Hans Christian Andersen, Rosemary Sutcliff); Enid Blyton aimed hers at children; and in the 1980s, Roald Dahl produced two autobiographical works which had strong dual audience appeal: *Boy* (1984) and *Going Solo* (1986). Another autobiography in two parts that pitches its tone and content to young readers' experience is that of Jacqueline Wilson. *Jackie Daydream* (2007) and *My Secret Diary* (2009) are both inventively illustrated by her regular collaborator, Nick Sharratt, and have had huge commercial success. One of the appeals of Wilson's biographical literature is to assume (usually correctly) that her readers are well acquainted with her fiction and to invite them to join in the process of thinking about childhood with reference to her works. There are also diaries written by young people, such as Anne Frank, which were never intended for publication but are now part of the canon of Western literature. More recent examples, such as *Zlata's Diary* (Zlata Filipović, 1994), written during the Bosnian war, and autobiographies such as Jason Gaes' moving work, *My Book for Kids with Cansur [sic]* (1987), also contain harrowing subject matter and raise issues about what publishers consider will be 'of interest' to readers about children's lives.

While biographies of children's authors are not strictly within the purview of this chapter, it is worth noting that many fine authors' lives have never been written, despite the fact that literary biography is described as 'one of the classic genres of children's literature . . . long prized as a tool for inspiring young people' (Stevenson, 2006, p. 163). The entry then goes on to cite James Janeway's gruesome work, *A Token for Children* (1672), and biographies of famous Americans either written specifically for children or available to experienced readers. In the United Kingdom strong examples of the genre include lives of Frances Hodgson Burnett (Thwaite, 1974) A. A. Milne (Thwaite, 1990), Edith Nesbit (Briggs, 1997) and Alan Garner (Philip, 1981). However, where authors are not best known for their children's work, this material tends to be neglected. Frank McLynn's (1994) otherwise excellent biography of Robert Louis Stevenson, for example, devotes little more than a paragraph to his seminal collection, *A Child's Garden of Verses* (1885).

Unlike some of the categories in this chapter, it does seem reasonable that autobiography is fairly small scale within children's literature, because most children are thought to be interested in looking forward in their reading rather than reflecting on mature lives.

Children writing literature

Making up and telling stories, using writing (or 'pretend writing') and even creating handmade books are common activities for children, who attempt to reproduce the literacy practices that occur in their daily interaction with adults. Research shows that from a very early age children are aware of the differences between literary language and everyday speech and that, as soon as they can talk, they begin to make up their own oral stories (Sutton-Smith, 1981; Engel, 1995). When they grasp the connection between language and print, they begin to 'write' their own. Research has shown how even these early texts are influenced by familiar books and popular culture, from its narrative structure and language to its rhythms and sentence length (Fox, 1993; Smith, 1994; Hilton, 1996; Dyson, 1997; Barrs, 2004). This writing can continue through childhood and sometimes beyond, but it usually ends up in the bin, seldom being taken seriously or conserved.

In school, texts will be written within a pedagogic context, and usually the readership will be confined to the teacher, and perhaps peers, though there was a flurry of commercial publishing of children's stories and poetry in the United Kingdom in the 1970s and 1980s, often as the result of national competitions. There was also a phase where primary schools 'published' children's stories for their classmates to read. Sadly, such initiatives are less common today with the primary strategy dominating writing pedagogy in the United Kingdom and greater emphasis on the technicalities of written language since 1998, a trend that seems fairly widespread across the Western world.

Diaries and autobiographies reveal that many famous authors began their writing as young children. Most of the surviving juvenilia seem to be written by girls or young women. The Taylor sisters, Ann and Jane, for example, 'scribbled' verse and prose from the age of 7. Likewise, the Brontë sisters, Charlotte,

Emily and Anne, composed erudite magazines, poems and novels during the 1820s, making the most of their freedom from formal instruction and access to their father's library. Jane Austen, too, was a prolific writer as a teenager, experimenting with plays, epistolary novels and romance. As a final example, Louisa May Alcott wrote poems, stories and non-fiction in her late teens, some of it being published; although other early works, such as her first full-length novel, *The Inheritance*, written at the age of 17, remained unpublished till 1988. We generally know of this work only retrospectively, after the author has achieved fame – as the very term 'juvenilia' suggests (see Juvenilia Press). Daisy Ashford's *The Young Visiters* [*sic*] is a rare exception, being the work of a perceptive 9-year-old who manages to convey, in a fast-paced narrative, the manners and conversation of adults. The details, the language and the misspellings are a source of humour for adult readers and it is this, perhaps, which led to its being published in 1919 (with a preface by James Barrie), when its author was an adult. For example, Chapter 1, titled 'Quite a Young Girl', begins: 'Mr Salteena was an elderly man of 42 and was fond of asking peaple to stay with him . . . . Mr Salteena had dark short hair and mustache and wiskers which were very black and twisty' (Ashford, 1966, p. 15).

But is children's writing a genre in itself? Studies by parent observers (Bissex, 1980; Crago and Crago, 1983; Wolf and Heath, 1992; Lowe, 2007) tend to provide the most comprehensive examples of literary influences on children's storytelling and writing. This is not to deny the **agency** of children, controlling their own output, as Bissex shows in her book about her son learning to write. Although his wider reading had contributed to his developing skills, he acted upon this reading selectively, responding to some influences and experiences but not to others. Whatever the final mix, however, it is certainly the case that children's texts are inextricably embedded in the family context and reflect the literacy practices and culture of home, with such factors as gender, the availability of books and parental modelling and expectations all playing a part.

These observations bring us back to the question about whether children's writing can be considered 'literature', particularly as these texts reflect the same variety of genres as adult writing. There are the questions surrounding the author's age: when does a child writer become an adult writer and does this matter, given the blurring of boundaries between childhood and adulthood? S. E. Hinton began writing *The Outsiders* (1967) at 16 (but didn't publish it until she was 18). In 2005, 10-year-old Michael Dowling (who writes under the name Tobias Druitt) published *Corydon and the Island of Monsters*, the first book of a trilogy, which was long-listed for a children's book prize. In this case, the fact that his mother is an Oxford University lecturer leaves room for speculation about what part she might have played in his work. There is also the question of how we classify books co-authored by a child and an adult, such as *Lionboy* by Zizou Corder (the pseudonym adopted by adult novelist Louisa Young and her teenage daughter Isabel Adomakoh Young). These questions lead us to the central one about children's writing as literature: how much does knowledge, experience and writer's craft count?

The list of published child authors remains quite short, but, both within and without, school children and teenagers are beginning to take advantage of the possibilities that e-publishing offers. Individuals and groups can also set up their own blogs, and many older children are writing fanfiction (see Jenkins, 1992), with some established websites inviting submissions that include use of image and other media (Brown, 1997). The possibility of e-publishing has implications not only for promoting children's writing but also for overcoming the obstacle of access to writing by children. We would, therefore, argue for a definition of children's literature that is inclusive, where writing by children that is of interest to an audience of both young and adult readers is properly valued. However, a serious study of children's writing as literature is still to be written.

The domestic and the ephemeral

In this section we refer to the texts created in the home by adults for children. Although a few stories have ended up as published children's literature, most domestic creations were not intended to last; hence, there are precious few examples extant from before the twentieth century. From the 1900s, the wider availability of books, toys and games, together with changes in family life-styles, meant that handmade versions were less common – at least in the Western world. Even where such ephemeral items have survived, they tend to remain as family souvenirs and do not come to public light.

These types of text have characteristics in common. One is that they have been created with a particular child or children in mind and will, therefore, aim to amuse or instruct (or both) according to individual personalities, likes or dislikes. Because of this, they usually contain references and jokes that are specific to the family in question. Another characteristic is that they will be 'one of a kind', not replicable nor meant to be, because they have been made according to the creator's artistic skills, using materials and odds and ends found in the home (bits of cloth, embroidery, cut-outs from magazines, photographs).

The earliest example of extensive nursery ephemera is the Jane Johnson archive (Arizpe and Styles, with Heath, 2006; Arizpe and Styles, 2009). Jane Johnson (1706–59) lived in London, Olney and Witham in the United Kingdom. She had four children and, as soon as they were old enough, she taught them to read with a series of cards and other handmade materials containing texts that range from the letters of the alphabet to short fables. Most have been decorated with small images from lottery sheets; some are coloured in by hand and framed with Dutch gilt paper. These cut-out images sometimes relate to the text, but at others, tell their own stories, which suggests Johnson used them not only as support for teaching reading but also to encourage discussion and storytelling. Johnson also made two little books which, in the manner of primers of the day, included letters, simple words and short sentences. She incorporated nursery rhymes, oral tales and popular culture as well as selected material from published books, including maxims from Isaac Watts' *The Art of Reading and*

Writing English and fables from John Newbery's *A Little Pretty Pocket-Book* (1744). She included references to the children themselves, to their acquaintances and trades people and to historical and family events.

In 1744, Johnson wrote down a story that she told 'a vast many times' to her children, as she herself writes in the postscript. 'A Very Pretty Story' is ultimately about the consequences of good and bad behaviour; however, the author's understanding of what delights a child audience and her detailed descriptions from a child's perspective bring this charming story to life:

> & the little Angels took a many of the Birds and Birds' nests in their hands, and gave them to the children to play with in the Chariot; and the Birds would sit and sing upon their Hands and shoulders, and then fly out of the Window and fetch fine flowers in their Bills, and lay them in Miss Bab's Lap, and stick them in Master George's Hat and the Button-holes of his coat and lay them on Miss Lucy's Neck and Hair, and divert them with a thousand tunes and pretty tricks all the way they went along.
>
> (Johnson, 2001, p. 34)

The influence of both Puritan stories and **fairy tales** can be seen in this story, but as Brian Alderson (1999, p. 184) has pointed out, it is unusual for its time because not only has Johnson put her own children into the story but it is also a full-length tale that incorporates fantasy into the everyday.

While mothers in the eighteenth century were encouraged by pedagogues such as John **Locke** to create artefacts for teaching their children to read, even earlier writers such as Hugh Platt in the 1500s and Charles Hoole in the 1600s were encouraging the use of printing letters and grammar rules on playing cards. Diaries sometimes include mention of home-made reading material. For example, Mrs Thrale, a confidante of Dr Johnson, writes in her diary that she made her daughter, 'Queenie', 'a little red Book to which I must appeal for her Progress in Improvements' (Hyde, 1977, p. 37). In the late eighteenth and early nineteenth centuries women started publishing texts for children in earnest, with fiction, poetry and reading primers. At this point, what previously might have been regarded as domestic ephemera now became a commercial venture for women, such as Anna Laetitia Barbauld with her *Lessons for Children from Two to Three Years Old* (1778 and 1779) and Ellenor Fenn, who wrote with young family members in mind. Not finding anything 'intellectual' enough for his children, Richard Edgeworth and his eldest daughter, Maria, also set about writing their own stories for the family as well as for cousins and friends.

The new printing technology heralded an improvement in the reproduction of illustration (including coloured images) and in the availability of commercial ephemera. Although this meant that there was less of a need to make reading materials at home, it offered parents the opportunity to use these publications to construct their own texts for children. Home-made picture albums with cut-outs from calendars, picture sheets and silhouettes became common, at least in middle-class households. Hans Andersen, for example, made several albums which included little stories and verses for the amusement of his friends' children. One such 'picturebook' which Andersen helped make for his friend Drewsen's granddaughter in 1859 (Andersen and Drewsen, 1984) contained over 1,000 images, not only from picture sheets but also from theatre advertisements, book-marks, trade prospectuses, menus, fashion-plates, toy-theatres, book illustra-tions, as well as five of Andersen's own paper-cuts. All of these, coupled with the way Andersen and Drewsen juxtaposed the cut-outs and wove in family jokes and allusions to current events, make this book an outstanding example of domestic ephemera.

In most developed countries in the twenty-first century there is so much com-mercially produced written material and sophisticated imagery in digital and other media that one might expect parents and carers to be discouraged from producing domestic texts for the young. Yet caring adults do still make person-alized books by hand, like Marcia Baghban (1984), who, in her longitudinal study of her daughter, Giti, describes how her fascination with labels at the age of 20 months led to the making of a book of logos cut from magazines and news-papers. In some ways, digital technology actually facilitates the making of texts for children, opening up new and more complex forms than in the past. The web-site of Bea Pierce (2006), for instance, shows a fine example of a 'handmade' picturebook. She includes a brief description of the materials used in its making, which was inspired by a comment from her son. There are also simple computer programs which help novices create their own little books (e.g. Realebooks.com, 2009).

But how do these examples of ephemera, produced to please and educate a very specific audience, sit within the realm of children's literature? Does a text only become so-called 'children's' literature when it is available to a wider pub-lic? Most domestic ephemera will certainly lack any general appeal, but it is still of value to the historian of children's literature, and clearly inhabits that liminal region between public and private, where the traffic of influence runs in both directions.

The oral tradition

As mentioned above, some literature that comes out of the oral/folk tradition, such as the fairy tale, is regarded as academically respectable and has proved popular with scholars as well as a young audience. Study of the oral traditions of poetry has also produced excellent scholarship, but as it is thin on the ground the story, once again, is one of neglect. There are many branches of what has come to be considered the poetic oral tradition – that cornucopia of nonsense, riddles, chants to accompany games, songs, ballads, lullabies, jingles, tongue-twisters, counting and finger rhymes of every description – but, for the purposes of this chapter, we will concentrate on two categories that are quite prolific: nursery and playground rhymes.

Robert Graves declared that 'the best of the older ones [nursery rhymes] are nearer to poetry than the greater part of *The Oxford Book of English Verse*' (quoted in Opie and Opie, 1951, p. 2). Iona and Peter Opie, probably the most highly respected scholars of the oral tradition in the United Kingdom, date nursery rhymes to the early nineteenth century in England, citing the popularity of Ann and Jane Taylor's *Rhymes for the Nursery* (1806) as the paradigm, although theirs were actually original poems written for children. Women were energetic in writing nursery rhyme-type poetry in the nineteenth century, though their names are unknown to most, for example 'Old Mother Hubbard' by Sarah Martin (1805), 'The Star' by Jane Taylor (1806), 'Mary's Lamb' by Sara Hale (1830) and 'The Spider and the Fly' by Mary Howitt (1834). In the United States, the term 'Mother Goose rhymes' is more prevalent, probably deriving from the influential *Mother Goose's Melody*, which, besides some rhymes still chanted today, contains some less familiar examples and some extracts or songs from that 'sweet songster of wit and humour, Master William Shakespeare' (*c*.1765). Before that, *Tommy Thumb's Pretty Song-Book* was published in two volumes by Mary Cooper in 1744. It too contains many rhymes still popular plus some delightfully rude ones, no longer anthologized. Another distinguished precursor to the Opies was J. O. Halliwell, who collected *The Nursery Rhymes of England* (1844). It was, however, word of mouth that ensured the survival of these rhymes. Opie (1996, p. 178) tells us that the main characteristics of nursery rhymes

> are their brevity and strongly-marked rhythm; in fact these may be said to be the necessary qualifications for a verse to enter the nursery canon, since they ensure memorability . . . . Another effect of the emphatic syllables is to implant the rhythms of the English language in minds too young to understand all the words . . . .

John Goldthwaite focuses on the memorable characters, lively incidents and playful language that are characteristic of nursery rhymes, containing a mixture of the everyday and the wildly extravagant, but always delivered with musicality. Perhaps privileging Western traditions, Goldthwaite suggests that Mother Goose is

> the only book in the world that everyone in the world, literate and illiterate alike, knows some of by heart . . . . From 'the dish that ran away with the spoon' and so on to Dr Seuss, inspired silliness has been the mainstream of nursery poetics.
>
> (Goldthwaite, 1996, pp. 14–15)

Opie (1996, p. 178) goes on to point out that 'the overwhelming majority of nursery rhymes were not in the first place composed for children. They are for the most part fragments of songs and ballads originally intended for adult delectation.' They are used, however, fairly universally across time and cultures, largely by adults to amuse and pacify the young. Playground rhymes, on the other hand, are part of childhood culture: they are produced by children them-selves and not intended for adult ears. This is an unofficial literature, wonder-fully robust and subversive, that often accompanies games with hand movements, balls and skipping. Because of its scurrilous and childish nature there are few examples in print, so the Opie/Sendak collaboration, *I Saw Esau* (1992), is one to treasure. As the rhymes in *Esau* demonstrate and Kornei Chukovsky (1963, p. viii) asserts, nursery rhymes in some shape or form are a universal part of childhood and 'nonsense serves as a handle to the proportion of logic in an illogical world'. So why the scholarly neglect? The essential orality of the subject matter may be the reason for both the success and failure of this genre; it has stayed alive over time because it is 'memorable speech' (Auden and Garrett, 1935, p. v) but has not, perhaps, been taken so seriously by scholars of the written word.

Poetry for children

In many respects, it is outrageous that as significant a genre as poetry for children should be tucked away in a chapter dealing with Cinderella forms of children's literature. Poetry for children has been innovative and thriving in Britain and North America for over two centuries, with distinguished poets choosing to spend a significant part of their professional lives writing for a young as well as an adult audience (from William Blake in the eighteenth century, to Edward Lear, Christina Rossetti and Robert Louis Stevenson in the nineteenth; and Walter De La Mare, A. A. Milne, Laura Richards, Ogden Nash, Charles Causley, Langston Hughes, Michael Rosen, Shel Silverstein, Roger McGough, Ted Hughes, James Berry and Carol Ann Duffy in the twentieth century). When Ted Hughes was British Poet Laureate (1984–98), he still devoted half his writ-ing time to a young audience. It will be interesting to see what the current British Poet Laureate, Carol Ann Duffy, brings to the post. Many high-profile authors have championed children's poetry and made every effort to raise its profile in the United Kingdom, yet sales (especially single-poet collections) have slumped, and currently there is little critical discussion of poetry. In scholarly publications and international conferences it also tends to be a minority interest. In sum, the relative neglect of children's poetry seems to be fairly universal.

As children's poetry has a shared history and, to some extent, subject matter with children's fiction, sometimes showing itself to be more imaginative or experimental, it is not immediately obvious why this should be the case. Poetry for children, the oral tradition and the work of particular poets are included in major guides (see, for example, Watson, 2001; Hunt, 2004; Zipes, 2006b) and in historical books on children's literature such as Goldthwaite (1996), Styles (1998) and Demers (2009), while poets themselves offer young readers insights into their craft and inspiration in a variety of texts (e.g. Lawson, 2008).

A recent, well-informed UK report on poetry teaching suggests that it is less well taught than other aspects of English; indeed, that 'poetry was underdevel-oped in many of the schools surveyed' (HMI, 2007, p. 3). This was confirmed in a research study carried out with over a 1,000 teachers (Cremin *et al.*, 2008), which found that very few could name six children's poets and that there was a tendency to focus on 'light-hearted' ones or a small number whose poetry might be seen as 'classic'. Very few women poets or black poets received any mention at all. Lastly, it was found that poetry teaching in the United Kingdom was weaker even where other aspects of teaching were strong (Ofsted, 2007). Unfortunately, anxieties about the technicalities of poetry appear to affect teachers and pupils from generation to generation despite the fact that most young children are responsive to musical language and that poetry can readily be linked to a love of nursery and playground rhymes. Part of the reason for this neglect may lie in the apparent unwillingness of publishers to promote poetry collections in a market driven by best sellers and bottom-line commercial success (Holifield, 2008).

Plays for children

David Wood (2009, p. 299) reports that when he began writing plays for children in 1967 he was struck by 'how few proper plays were then written and performed for children'. He laments the fact that, over 40 years on, 'children's theatre is still often perceived as third division theatre; funding for it is less than for its adult counterpart . . . critics generally ignore it; and most theatre folk seem to think it is only for beginners or failures.' Peter **Hollindale** (1996, p. 206) agrees:

> the field is a very narrow one. It begins only in the late nineteenth century, falls into relative inertia in the years between the two World Wars, and gathers momentum only after 1945. Even now, many plays for children achieve only local performance, remain unpublished, and fail to win a regular place in the repertoire.

As if confirming Wood's assertion about the third-class treatment of children's theatre, Samuel French's *Guide to Selecting Plays for Performance*, published every three years, relegates plays for 'Children and Young People' to a separate section from their other full-length and one-act plays. While this may appear a useful division for those selecting plays to be performed by schools or youth groups, in this section the *Guide* does not distinguish plays written for an adult cast from those written to be performed by children and young people.

These are two quite different forms of drama. The former is invariably written for the professional theatre and, for David Wood (2009, p. 300), this is the type of work to which the term 'children's theatre' applies. The latter is more often written for performance in schools or youth theatres, offering writers little chance of public recognition or national press reviews. As a consequence this form of writing for children, invariably viewed as 'amateur', is sidelined to an even greater degree than its professional counterpart.

In the United Kingdom, the most prominent showcase for drama written to be performed by young people is the National Theatre 'Connections' programme, running since 1993. Youth groups, youth theatres and schools are given the opportunity to perform plays written by well-known professional playwrights, such as Timberlake Wertenbaker, at their home venues and participating professional theatres around the country. However, these performances are one-off events, and the plays are no longer than an hour in length – a frequent feature of drama for children and young people. The only full-length play with an all-child cast to have been performed in London's West End is *Bugsy Malone* – Alan Parker's musical adapted from his 1976 film – first performed in 1983 and subsequently in the West End by the National Youth Music Theatre (themselves an amateur company) in 1997. Despite the success of the film, however, the play itself is rarely given an outing, undoubtedly due to child labour regulations and also to the complexities this creates for rehearsal and performance with a cast of minors.

Turning to what David Wood (2009, p. 300) describes as children's theatre – 'theatre produced by adults for children to watch' – of which J. M. Barrie's celebrated play *Peter Pan* provides one of the earliest, and most enduring, examples – one might counter his claim about its low status by citing a list of plays adapted from children's novels performed at some of the country's leading theatres over the past few years. The National Theatre in London, for example, has seen three hugely successful productions based on children's books in the last five years – *His Dark Materials* (2003/4) based on Philip Pullman's successful trilogy, Jamila Gavin's *Coram Boy* (2005) and Michael Morpurgo's *War Horse* (2007/8). However, all of these productions, despite being based on novels regularly enjoyed by pre-teens, were advertised as suitable for 12 years and above only. This adaptation of children's literature into drama for a predominantly adult audience has been undoubtedly influenced by the **crossover** popularity of children's books among adults in recent years.

Elsewhere, adaptations of children's books aimed at younger children have proved extremely successful in the United Kingdom – for example, Julia Donaldson's *The Gruffalo* (Tall Stories Theatre Company). Plays based on popular children's novels are also increasingly seen in place of the traditional pantomime at regional theatres in the United Kingdom. However, while adaptations continue to gain success, original plays aimed at a children's audience are less frequently seen at major venues, being the province rather of theatres whose work is aimed exclusively at children. Theatres such as the Polka Theatre and Unicorn Theatre in London consistently run programmes of children's drama, aimed at a pre-teen audience, much of which is original. However, as French's *Guide* demonstrates, only a limited number of playwrights have consistently written full-length original professional plays for children. Wood is the most productive, but Alan Ayckbourn has written nine original plays for a children's audience, as has Adrian Mitchell, besides adapting children's novels for the theatre. Many other playwrights have only one published play listed, testament perhaps to the fact that writing children's drama is neither a lucrative nor a sustaining profession.

Paul Harman (2005, p. 56) notes that 'much theatre for children in the United Kingdom is made by a locally-based company', rarely attracting public funding, and that those that are publicly funded tend to 'focus on social themes of interest to teachers who book shows for children to watch in school time'. He contrasts this with many other countries where theatre is seen less as an education tool and more as 'an independent, artistic field contributing to children's cultural, emotional and spiritual development'. Harman speaks from his experience of the Association Internationale du Théâtre pour l'Enfance et la Jeunesse (ASSITEJ), an organization with national centres in 78 countries all dedicated to facilitating 'the development of theatre for children and young people on the highest artistic level' (ASSITEJ, 2009). However, despite having been formed in 1965, 'in practice, ASSITEJ has remained a quite small, voluntary body with little influence on policy at an international level' (Harman, 2005, p. 54). Although it has served to encourage contact between children's theatre companies in six continents, in the United Kingdom these have tended to be small organizations rather than the large producing houses such as the National Theatre or Royal Shakespeare Company.

However, while the UK centre for ASSITEJ – TYA UK – is not particularly prolific, other national centres appear far more active in their promotion of theatre for children and young people. The French centre, for example, produces publications, has a programme of events which includes the active promotion of 'the creation of companies and the right of children to the theatre' through 'dialogue with representatives of the State, regional governments, professional associations and those interested in the theatrical practices of children and youth', and has an archive centre of books, articles, posters, photos and other documents relating to theatre for young audiences. It seems that the United Kingdom has suffered more than most countries from lack of funding for children's theatre. Tony Graham (2005, p. 77) quotes Caryl Jenner of the Unicorn Theatre on this: 'It makes me blind with rage when I think that Yugoslavia has 123 state-subsidized children's theatres, the Soviet Union 300.'

In considering why children's drama remains a marginalized area of children's writing in the United Kingdom one might look to cinema for an answer. Films for children, both adaptations of popular books (by writers such as Rowling, Pullman, C. S. Lewis, Frances Hodgson Burnett and Roald Dahl) and original films, are regular cinema fare, generating high figures at the box office and costing much less than a trip to the theatre. Hollindale thus laments that

> our dramatic literature for children, more prolific than ever before . . . is in dire need of serious critical attention and institutional support . . . . Until that happens, drama will remain the Cinderella of children's literature, when it is arguably the most important children's art form of all, the one they are sure to live with, through the media of film and television, all their lives.
>
> (Hollindale, 1996, p. 219)

136

CONCLUSION

The sidelined 'genres' mentioned above invite reappraisal by scholars not only because they challenge the dominant notions of what constitutes children's literature but also because of the value they have for educationalists, librarians and for children themselves. There is no denying the impact that storytelling, poetry and drama have on children or the pride that can arise from a child having a 'personal' story or book created by their parents or by seeing their own early efforts on the printed page. Like main literary genres, those discussed here also 'position' readers, and, as Kress (1988, p. 107) writes, 'each of these positionings implies different possibilities for response and for action'. The more genres, the more possibilities publishers, librarians, parents and teachers have for introducing children to literature and, of course, the more possibilities there are for the child audience to participate in the world of literature.

FURTHER READING

Alexander, Christine and McMaster, Juliet (eds) (2005) *The Child Writer from Austen to Woolf*, Cambridge: Cambridge University Press.
A unique collection of essays on the early writings of major authors such as Jane Austen, Byron, Elizabeth Barrett, Charlotte and Branwell Brontë, Louisa May Alcott, George Eliot, John Ruskin, Lewis Carroll and Virginia Woolf. The volume also includes a useful annotated bibliography of juvenilia.

Arizpe, Evelyn and Styles, Morag (2010) 'Children Reading at Home: An Historical Overview', in Shelby Anne Wolf, Karen Coats, Pat Enciso and C. A. Jenkins (eds) *The Handbook of Research on Children's and Young Adult Literature*, New York: Erlbaum.
A useful overview of the history of domestic literacy as it relates to children as readers, focusing on evidence from the seventeenth century to the present day about children reading in the home context, as well as parents (usually mothers) teaching children to read. It includes the cases of contemporary parents and caregivers who, in shaping children's early engagement with literature, have also defined and redefined the meanings of readers and reading, besides recent research which sheds light on changing notions of reading in the digital age and on the multimodal texts children encounter in the home.

Arizpe, Evelyn and Styles, Morag, with Heath, Shirley Brice (2006) *Reading Lessons from the Eighteenth Century: Mothers, Children and Texts*, Lichfield: Pied Piper Press www.indiana.edu/~liblilly/janejohnson/reading-lessons-fulltext.pdf [27.1.1.]
This book traces the life of Jane Johnson and her family and examines her Nursery Library in depth, as well as other documents in this unique archive, which sheds light on the reading practices of upper-middle-class families in the eighteenth century. It discusses early children's literature through the history of reading and includes a chapter by Shirley Brice Heath on the presence of play and games in Jane Johnson's materials, which prepared the children's transition from the private to the public spheres.

Chapleau, Sebastien (2007) 'Quand l'enfant parle et que l'adulte se met à écouter, ou la littérature enfantine de retour à sa source' ['When the child speaks and the adult listens, or, children's literature returns to its source'], *Canadian Children's Literature/Littérature canadienne pour la jeunesse*, 33.2: 112–26.

This article discusses the place of the child in children's literature studies as represented by texts written by children and asks for more attention to be paid to these texts. Various scholars responded to this essay, both in French and in English, in the Spring issue, engaging with the idea of the child writer.

Opie, Iona and Opie, Peter (eds) (1973) *The Oxford Book of Children's Verse*, Oxford: Clarendon Press.

As W. H. Auden remarked, this 'is a book all parents and lovers of poetry should possess', as it contains the best selection of the most significant children's poetry from the sixteenth to the twentieth centuries (up to T. S. Eliot's famous 'cats' of 1939), as well as informative notes by the editors. But other scholarly books by the Opies are also relevant to this chapter's concerns.

Styles, Morag (1998) *From the Garden to the Street: An Introduction to 300 Years of Poetry for Children*, London: Cassell.

The only full-length history of children's poetry in Britain and the United States, as far as we are aware. It considers poetry written for children in literary historical periods in terms of sub-genres such as humorous, narrative, oral, religious and so on, citing key poets and collections.

Part II

NAMES AND TERMS

ABJECT/ABJECTION From general meanings such as 'the act of bringing down or humbling', 'the state of being rejected or cast out', 'abasement', 'degradation and self-abasement', the term *abjection* has developed in somewhat different ways in psychoanalytic and sociological criticism, both of which are reflected in children's literature. In the former, abjection signifies the place where meaning collapses, that which threatens life and must be radically excluded from the place of the living subject, propelled away from the body and deposited on the other side of an imaginary border which separates the self from that which threatens the self. Julia **Kristeva** develops this conceptualization to argue that the abject threatens the self with something that cannot be categorized in terms of identity/ non-identity, human/non-human. In Kristeva's terms, abjection is a process whereby an infant establishes itself as separate from the mother's body – a necessary, psychological and corporeal rift if the infant is to move to the **mirror stage** and achieve a sense of independent identity. The return of the abject is thus associated with borderline phenomena – the collapse of bodily boundaries (especially through bodily fluids like blood, vomit or faeces), as well as the breakdown of structures of

signification. However, this claim can be seen as a mystification of the maternal body as a universal source of drives under which Kristeva subsumes all **others**.

A contrary view is that the abject assumes different codings and is identified with different marginal zones of social life in different sociohistorical contexts. Sociological criticism perceives abjection as a process by which **subjectivities** that are acceptable and desirable are designated in contrast to zones of social life that are unacceptable, undesirable and uninhabitable. When we are cast into the world of the abject, our imaginary borders disintegrate and the abject becomes a tangible threat because our identity system and conception of order have been disrupted. Hence, in fiction, figures that are in a state of transition or transformation may be aptly considered in terms of abjection.

Ideas of abjection are germane to the theme of growth and maturation in children's literature because the abject is located on the margins of two possibilities: it may resolve by spiralling into death or by forging a new subjectivity. A character lacking **agency** and development may thereby experience some form of social exclusion, including self-exclusion. In *The Graveyard Book* (2008), Neil Gaiman offers a comprehensive (albeit humorous) anatomy of abjection and its overcoming, through the depiction of an orphaned character, renamed Nobody, hidden from his would-be killers in a graveyard, where his only companions and teachers are the dead and his mentor, an undead vampire. Gaiman explores the subversive possibilities of the abject to identify the structures of oppression that produce it and the anxiety of those structures to sustain themselves, while showing, from a position outside the social order, what it is to experience oppression. In contrast, Titus, the principal character of M. T. Anderson's *Feed* (2002), exemplifies a form of abjection that moves, without hope of redemption, inexorably closer to nothingness. In such ways, representations of abjection play a major role in children's literature. [JS]

See also Chapters 7 and 8.

Further reading

Creed (1999), Fletcher and Benjamin (1990), Kristeva (1982), **Stephens** (2002a), Wilkie-Stibbs (2006).

ADOLESCENCE Broadly, adolescence refers to a period of physical and mental human transition that lies between childhood and adulthood – roughly, between the ages of 12 and 20 (but varies from one society to another and between males and females). It is primarily a twentieth-century concept, not widely employed until the period following World War II. It is thus still an evolving concept, as is the literature directed at adolescents, which did not begin to appear in any substantial way until the end of the 1950s. Ideas about adolescence have tended to emphasize development and growth, on the one hand, and conflict with authority, on the other. Psychologist Erik Erikson, for example, who largely established the tenor for discussing the concept, argues that during adolescence the sense of self is in a greater state of flux than at any other life stage, and so the period is characterized by problems or crises. These are prompted by physical changes, the need to make choices from among conflicting possibilities and the development of individual judgement about the social world, which in turn may lead to alienation from a society that fails to instantiate its own ideals. Julia **Kristeva** (1990, p. 8) defined 'adolescence' in a similar manner to Erikson, except that she loosened the term from its chronological moorings, arguing that the 'open psychic structure' of adolescence could recur whenever vulnerability was experienced. Notably, Kristeva suggests that the very process of reading fiction (and writing it) helps open the psyche to the possibility of change. As this process involves challenging the bounds of identity, it is strange that Kristeva did not draw on her own, related concept of **abjection** – a link that Karen Coats (2004, pp. 142–3) productively explores.

A dominant preoccupation of much adolescent fiction is with how notions of identity are formed within specific contexts and shaped by larger social structures and processes. Thus, the school, peer group, family and other cultural institutions frequently have important metonymic functions within adolescent fiction. Within these frames, an adolescent is depicted as facing multiple anxieties: personal concerns over physical appearance, social presentability, emerging sexuality, desire for privacy and personal safety; family concerns relating to intergenerational conflict stemming from differing **ideologies** or aspirations, conflict with siblings and dissolution of the family through parental divorce or death; and interpersonal concerns involving peer groups and wider social interactions, such as conflicts with peer groups and authority figures, and a sense of alienation from contemporary culture and values.

Roberta **Trites** makes the important point that personal and social issues represented in adolescent literature are linked to operations of power: the place of adolescents in the social structure and in relation to the many institutions that shape them (see **Ideological State Apparatuses**) and the need for young people to balance their emerging **desire** for personal power with the power of authority figures. Trites also argues that it is imperative for critical work in the field to draw on contemporary cultural and literary studies to elucidate children's literature. In psychological accounts of adolescence, an emphasis on problems, crises and tasks to be performed to enable maturation is apt to translate into a more superficial content analysis of fiction. But the emergence of the fiction coincides with the belated impact of **modernist** relativism and the rise to dominance of **realism**, first-person narration and a character-focused perspective in children's literature. J. D. Salinger's *The Catcher in the Rye* (1951) is often seen as an *ur*-text for the field in its introduction

of an unstable and alienated adolescent protagonist, narrating a story about everyday acts. Thus, Holden Caulfield's fragmented **subjectivity** prompts him to construct multiple identities as a defence against a meaningless world. In his wake, themes linked with sexuality, violence and death became germane to adolescent fiction. Concomitantly, there arises a critical need to consider the possible subtleties of these themes as they are produced within complex relationships among discourse, narrative structures and ideology. [JS]

See also Chapters 3, 6, 7 and 8.

Further reading

Cart (1996), Erikson (1968), Kristeva (1990), Russell (1988), Trites (2000).

AGENCY Human agency entails the claim that human action can transcend its material context, and hence people as individuals have a capacity to act reflectively and purposively and, through intersubjective relationships, have a capacity for either self-alteration or remaking the world. Such actions are in contrast to society's propensity to represent itself as always already instituted (thereby denying the possibility of creative action to individuals). The importance of agency has been foregrounded by modernity in that the weakening of hegemonic moral codes, the structures of social class and fixed gender roles enable and require individuals to act more self-reflectively in making life choices. Indeed, the concept entered the critical discourse of children's literature from second-wave feminism, when the perception that female agency had been restricted by social codes became extended to the perception that children's agency was similarly restricted.

Agency is always limited, however, and anti-**humanists**, such as Louis Althusser or Michel **Foucault**, emphasized the difficulty or even impossibility of human agency, which was perceived to be in binary opposition to social structures and the alignments of power in society (see **Ideological State Apparatuses**). If **subjectivity** is made possible by social forces, it may have few possibilities of resistance to those forces and hence may only be genuinely agential in a limited way. This position has weakened under the impact of such studies as Paul Smith's *Discerning the Subject* (1988) and Judith **Butler**'s more recent thinking (Magnus, 2006). Largely independent of such movements, children's literature since the middle of the twentieth century has tended to reduce the degree and define the contexts in which the agency of young people is possible. Where agency is reactive, dependent on circumstances that compel an individual to make choices, it is limited by the choices that are available, although there is a common paradox whereby agency entails freely choosing that which one has no choice but to choose. Further, agency is often relative, and because any agential action involves intersubjectivity, the outcomes that flow from a particular act have implications for others. Agency thus has a moral component: moral agency suggests that one person should not gain agency by denying it to another. The notorious transfer of narrative attention from Mary to Colin

in Burnett's *The Secret Garden* (1911) is an example of a relative operation of agency: Mary has fought to gain agency from a subjected position, only to find it diminished when she enables Colin's agency. Agency constitutes a failure of intersubjectivity if it is merely a self-centred search for personal satisfaction or an assertion of one's own idea of oneself. [JS]

See also Chapters 3, 5 and 7.

Further reading

Halliwell and Mousley (2003), McNay (2000), Magnus (2006).

ALDERSON, BRIAN (1930–) One of the pioneers of children's literature studies in Britain, Alderson began as a specialist bookseller before becoming a lecturer on children's books in the Department of Librarianship at the Polytechnic of North London. He is a prolific writer, reviewer, translator, organizer of exhibitions and founding member of the UK Children's Books History Society. In terms of publications he is perhaps best known for updating F. J. Harvey **Darton**'s standard work *Children's Books in England* (1982) and for translating Bettina Hürlimann's *Three Centuries of Children's Books in Europe* (1967). In 2006 he published (with Felix de Marez Oyens) the sumptuously illustrated *Be Merry and Wise: Origins of Children's Book Publishing in England, 1650–1850*. Alderson has always had little time for literary and cultural theory, also provocatively asserting 'the irrelevance of children to the children's book reviewer' (Alderson,

1969). Instead, he champions a more historically attentive understanding of children's books, based on a knowledge of their materiality and on publishing and printing practices; this, he argues, should give the discipline a solid bibliographical foundation. [DR]

See also Chapter 1.

Further reading

Alderson (1969, 1995), Alderson and Oyens (2006), **Hunt** (1995).

ANIMATION This is the process of bringing static drawings (or objects) to life on film. The audience for animated films is frequently children, although the highly innovative Japanese animation industry has major markets among both young adult and adult audiences. While a surreal, philosophical, adult animated film such as Richard Linklater's *Waking Life* (2001) is a rarity in the West, Japanese anime classics such as Katsuhiro's *Akira* (1988) or Mamoru Oshii's *Ghost in the Shell* (1995) target an adult audience and come with an 'R' rating. Western animation was largely dominated by the Disney industry (in feature films; *see* **Disneyfication**) and Warner Bros. (cartoons and television animation), until the arrival of Pixar with the first, totally computer-generated feature film in 1995: *Toy Story* (directed by John Lasseter), which produced some long-overdue competition. After protracted negotiations, Disney acquired Pixar in 2006. Another relative newcomer is Dreamworks, beginning with *The Prince of Egypt* (1998) and making a major impact with the *Shrek* films (2001–).

Animated films originated as cel animation, in which drawn or painted characters or objects are transferred to a clear sheet of plastic called a cel which is then placed over a static background drawing. The cels are photographed frame by frame, and with each frame differing slightly from the one preceding it, the illusion of movement is produced when the frames are projected in rapid succession. Cel animation has been the primary technique of the industry, but has now been supplanted by computer-generated imagery (CGI), in which the animators' drawings are scanned into a computer, where they are coloured and processed. Dreamworks, for example, has only produced CGI animated films since 2004, with its final, traditionally animated film being *Sinbad: Legend of the Seven Seas* (2003).

CGI has transformed film animation. Computers are able to generate moving pictures from a small number of images from a variety of media (hand drawings or paintings, photographs, moving pictures and audio files) and can depict a highly realistic, three-dimensional scene. Apart from *Toy Story*, Studio Ghibli made its first use of CGI in the same year with *Mimi wo Sumaseba* (*Whisper of the Heart*), in which elements animated by traditional means were combined with CGI.

For a brief period (2000–6), Dreamworks had a partnership with Aardman Animations, a stop-motion animation company in England perhaps best known for Nick Park's 'Wallace and Gromit' series (1989–). Films such as *Chicken Run* (2000) combined claymation and CGI. Claymation uses hand-crafted, sculpted plasticine or clay in combination with a stop-motion camera (either motion picture or digital). This is a slow process; however, CGI, supported by a variety of commercially available processing programs, offers possibilities to produce animated films at relatively little cost. [JS]

See also Chapter 10.

Further reading

Johnston and Thomas (1995), Napier (2005), Wells (2002).

ARIÈS, PHILIPPE (1914–84) Renowned in childhood studies for querying the concept of the child, Ariès was one of the first to show how the term's signification had changed over time, suggesting that societies conceptualized childhood differently. Ariès's *Centuries of Childhood* (1960) appeared in English in 1962. The book not only influenced children's literature studies but also led to an extensive sub-discipline in history. As a member of what was termed the 'Annales' school of history, he was interested in everyday life more than great historic events, exploring childhood, the family and, later, death and mourning. The influence of his work can be seen in Michel **Foucault**, though the latter would reject the notion of collective 'mindsets', or *mentalités*, guiding behaviour. Many of Ariès's specific claims about childhood have been challenged, most infamously that, 'in medieval society, the idea of childhood did not exist' (Ariès, 1973, p. 125), a general awareness appearing only in the seventeenth century. Ariès was later to admit his relative ignorance of the period, which

has been thoroughly researched since (see King, 2007). However, it would be a mistake to reject his work outright, as some critics have done. Children certainly existed, but there does not seem to have been the firm polarization between them and adults which occurred later, largely as a result of education (see **Postman**). Ariès thus demonstrated Foucault's point about how discourses increasingly inscribe the subject. There are many variations on Ariès's original thesis, from the constructionist (e.g. **Lesnik-Oberstein**) to the more essentialist, such as Joseph Zornado's contention that there is an underlying child with 'biological and emotional needs' (2001, p. xiv), which has been systematically misconstructed by adults throughout history. [DR]

See also Chapter 1.

Further reading

Ariès (1973), Hutton (2004), King (2007), Zornado (2001).

BAKHTIN, MIKHAIL (1895–1975) A Russian philosopher and cultural theorist who analysed how language signifies in social and historical contexts. He is well known for his theory of the novel, the dialogic nature of linguistic production and key concepts such as heteroglossia, polyphony, the **carnivalesque**, the **grotesque** body and the **chronotope**. In the four essays collected in *The Dialogic Imagination* (1981), Bakhtin revolutionized the study of the novel by arguing that, far from being inferior to poetry (as was then the critical consensus), the novel was the aesthetic form most able to harness the diversifying and emancipating energies of language and to represent the most complex and densely historical images of human beings in literature. Moreover, by arranging characters' voices on the same plane of authority as the author's, or as we would say, the narrator's (an organizational structure Bakhtin termed 'polyphony'), a novelist like Dostoevsky was able to construct characters who appeared to be radically free subjects, masters of their own discourse and destinies (Bakhtin, 1984a). Bakhtin polemically argued that while poetry aimed to harmonize language into monologically closed aesthetic structures, the novel aimed rather to include all the **ideological** voices of its historical era, representing a wide diversity of social discourses – a 'heteroglossia'. The novel (and especially, the realist novels of Dostoevsky) provides Bakhtin with his most developed and complex examples of '**dialogism**', the centrifugal, de-hierarchizing, diversifying force in language that constantly seeks to disrupt and undermine the weighty, serious, centripetal or 'monologic' discourses of church, state, judiciary and other official institutions. Bakhtin's concept of dialogism has been incorporated and extended into many areas of literary theory, from formal narratology to feminist, psychoanalytic and **postcolonial** theory.

In children's literature criticism, Maria **Nikolajeva** has been an outstanding proponent of Bakhtin, introducing concepts such as polyphony (Nikolajeva, 1996) and the chronotope to produce in-depth readings of twentieth-century texts by authors such as Alan Garner. Nikolajeva's work has had significant impact in shifting the focus of children's literary criticism from sociology to aesthetics. She explains Bakhtin's concepts with admirable clarity and precision and suggests formalist applications of these to produce close textual readings (Nikolajeva, 2005). But drawing on Bakhtin's polarization of classical epic versus novelistic discourse, Nikolajeva somewhat sweepingly reduces the development of children's literature to a linear progression from epic to polyphony (Nikolajeva, 1996). Bakhtin's case against epic cannot be unilaterally applied to pre-modern children's literature, and many contemporary children's novels are clearly *not* self-consciously polyphonic or multivoiced. Furthermore, children's epic narrative (whether verse or prose) often stylizes, **parodies** or revises traditional adult epic narrative (Richard Adams's *Watership Down* and the descent into the underworld in Philip Pullman's *The Amber Spyglass* both rewrite Virgil's *Aeneid*, for example), so in its self-conscious **intertextuality** it is already a dialogized form of literature and closer to polyphony than Nikolajeva allows.

Aside from Nikolajeva's work, poststructuralist theories of intersubjective identity are richly indebted to Bakhtin's concept of speech being inflected by the discourse of the **other**. In other words, dialogic discourse is that which recognizes the influence of another's ideas and orients itself to that other's response; hence, it provides an analogy, on the linguistic level, with identities which are socially and relationally, rather than individually, constructed (McCallum, 1999). More generally, Bakhtin's writings invite us to revisit the whole question of the changing relationships between adult and children's cultures, aspects of which mirror his analysis of the conflict between the monologizing discourses of power and the dialogic strategies of the disempowered to survive, to be heard and to transform their erstwhile oppressors (Rudd, 2004b). [RF]

See also Chapter 8.

Further reading

Bakhtin (1981, 1984a), McCallum (1999), **Nikolajeva** (1996).

BARTHES, ROLAND (1915–80) A French cultural theorist who was particularly influential in the development of post-structuralist ideas. One key idea was that texts could be divided into the *readerly* and the *writerly* (Barthes, 1990). The former are seen to impose particular meanings on readers, whereas the *writerly* are more open and playful (related to what **Bakhtin** called **dialogic** texts), allowing readers to formulate their own interpretations. The latter are characterized by having different narrative threads, or narrators, by a lack of tidy plot resolution, and by drawing attention to their own construction (their use of language, illustration and **intertextuality**). However, having made the division, Barthes went on to suggest that all texts could be approached in a writerly manner, made to expose their constructedness and the values they encoded, in such a way that these values could be challenged and the text read differently. Catherine Belsey (1980) makes a similar move when she distinguishes

classic realist from *interrogative* texts (*see* Chapter 6).

Barthes' notion of a writerly text is also explored in his most famous essay, 'The Death of the Author', where he argues that the idea of a God-like author controlling the meanings of 'His' texts is untenable, because texts are precisely that: intertextual weavings of earlier writings, of words and phrases. No one can, therefore, dictate a text's reception; Barthes thus commends the 'birth of the reader'. Given that young children are less aware of the authorial function, it could be argued that they might more readily appropriate texts for their own purposes.

The above division (readerly/writerly) is related to another key idea of Barthes' (1975): between texts which give 'pleasure' as opposed to those that go beyond this, providing what he calls *jouissance*, sometimes translated as 'bliss'. The former deliver the standard pleasures of mastery, satisfaction and completion, whereas the latter involve a loss of control, disrupting the coordinates of one's being and language. Raymond Briggs' *Fungus the Bogeyman* (1977) might be described as a text that revels in excess in this way. Certainly, it is in the discussions of picture books that Barthes' notion of the writerly text has been most productively used, though more literary writers have also been described in these terms (e.g. Aidan **Chambers**).

These ideas represent the poststructuralist side of Barthes' work, but he first came to public attention as a structuralist, seeking to develop a science of **signs**, or semiology, drawing on the work of Ferdinand de Saussure. Out of this came Barthes' brilliant

Mythologies (1957), a collection of articles in which Barthes examines everyday cultural objects and practices, showing the **ideological** dimensions (or **myths**) of what we take to be a natural reality. In an accompanying theoretical essay, 'Myth Today', he elaborates his method of teasing out '*what-goes-without-saying*' in cultural practice (Barthes, 1993, p. 11). For example, in an essay of particular interest to children's studies, 'Toys', Barthes points out how the social order becomes naturalized through children's playthings, such that kings and queens, soldiers and workers, are all seen as having their preordained place. Ahead of his time, Barthes was effectively gesturing towards a more loaded interpretation of 'Toys R Us'!

The essays of *Mythologies* were seminal in opening up ways of talking about popular cultural objects that were not simply dismissive and patronizing, giving them a seriousness that had previously been granted to high culture only. [DR]

Further reading

Barthes (1975, 1977, 1990, 1993).

BETTELHEIM, BRUNO (1903–90) A controversial psychoanalyst who worked extensively with psychologically damaged children, best known for his seminal, psychoanalytical reading of **fairy tales**, *The Uses of Enchantment* (1976). Fittingly, Bettelheim, a fairly orthodox **Freudian** psychoanalyst, was born in Vienna, where Freud was active for most of his life. Following Nazi occupation, Bettelheim was incarcerated in Dachau and Buchenwald (1938–9), fortunately being allowed to emigrate to America before the war. He drew on this experience in later work, when he ran the Orthogenic School for disturbed children at the University of Chicago. However, he became controversial in arguing that autism was a product of 'cold' mothering.

He is most famous, though, in championing the therapeutic value of literature, criticizing standard literacy texts and reading schemes (Bettelheim and Zelan, 1982). Children, he argued, look for stories with emotional and existential resonances. This is where he thought fairy tales excelled. While it is refreshing for scholars in the area to see these stories accorded such significance and attention, Bettelheim's own interpretations are rather slavishly Freudian. Moreover, although he talks about the openness of the texts, his actual readings are quite procrustean. Furthermore, he tends to see the Grimms' versions as definitive – often speaking about the importance of the 'original' tales, as though they had not shifted to fit different historical conditions and audiences and as though they had always had the modern child of the nuclear family in mind (**Zipes**, 1979). However, when it came to many modern works for children, he was often dismissive, famously rejecting Sendak's *Where the Wild Things Are*. As if this wasn't enough, Alan Dundes (1991) convincingly argued that Bettelheim had plagiarized Julius E. Heuscher's work, *A Psychiatric Study of Fairy Tales: Their Origin, Meaning and Usefulness* (1963). Bettelheim, suffering badly from illness, committed suicide in 1990. [DR]

See also Chapter 7.

Further reading

Bettelheim (1976), Dundes (1991), Fisher (2008).

BHABHA, HOMI K. (1949–) One of the most influential theorists of **postcolonialism**, Bhabha was born in Mumbai, India, and educated at Oxford. He now teaches in the United States. He is critical of straightforward Marxist accounts of the colonial enterprise, drawing on poststructuralist writers like **Derrida**, and on psychoanalytical theory (especially via **Lacan**), to explicate the ambivalence of **colonialism** – despite the economic and physical oppression exercised by colonial powers.

In his early work Bhabha explains this ambivalence through the notion of the stereotype. Rather than being simply a crude representation of the **other**, Bhabha argues that the stereotype is far more troublesome. In order for the colonizer to hold on to his own fantasized identity (as a whole and complete being), he disavows any knowledge that might compromise this, making it part of 'the other' instead (e.g. being lazy or animal-like). But the continual need for the colonizer to reassert such gross caricatures shows his lack of self-identity, his dependence on the other.

Bhabha also explores this process in terms of what he calls 'mimicry'. On the one hand the colonizer needs to be a shining example of what the colonized might become. However, if his behaviour can be so easily copied, then this undermines the whole basis of the colonizer's superiority in the first place. He has no innately masterful identity; indeed, it seems to be based on nothing but an ability to learn particular codes of behaviour and deportment. Bhabha is unclear as to whether this is something that the colonized can exploit, mimicking the behaviour of their oppressors, or whether it reflects the colonizers' fears about their own inadequacies – but Bhabha certainly has more to say about the latter. He thus talks about the colonizers wanting their subaltern population to be '*almost the same, but not quite*', that is, for the colonized to continually produce **signs** of their failure, their 'slippage . . . excess' and 'difference' (Bhabha, 1994, p. 86).

A third key term of Bhabha's is **hybridity**, which is related to the above in that he has always sought to show how the separation between binary opposites such as self and other, colonizer and colonized, or East and West, is false (i.e. we are always in a state of becoming, rather than being). For Bhabha, it is along these border zones that cultural activity can be most productive. Nationalities themselves need to recognize this, that the concept of 'nation' is only held in place by the way a people narrates its identity, which, to be productive, must always recognize its various competing elements – hence Bhabha's frontier-challenging term 'DissemiNation'.

Bhabha's writing is difficult – both playful and allusive – and he has been criticized for losing sight of the particularities and atrocities of colonial rule, replacing it with an ahistorical and universal, psychoanalytical answer (Parry, 1994). However, in literary terms his insights have produced some intelligent and sensitive readings of colonial texts (e.g. Moore-Gilbert, 1996). Moreover, a number of writers have drawn attention to the parallels between childhood and colonization (**Rose**, 1984; **Nodelman**, 1992; Rudd, 2004a), pointing out the uneasy relationship between adults and children often figured in texts. [DR]

See also Chapter 4.

Further reading

Bhabha (1994), Huddart (2006), Moore-Gilbert (1996), Parry (1994), Rudd (2004a).

BOTTIGHEIMER, RUTH B. (1939–) Beginning with *Grimms' Bad Girls and Bold Boys* (1987), Bottigheimer's research examines ways that gender and societal values influence literary production and cultural reception of originally orally transmitted tales. Her work moved away from psychological interpretation, popularized by Bruno **Bettelheim**, and towards an understanding of the impact of morality and society in the formation of foundational narratives. Bottigheimer followed her book on the Grimms with research on other European **fairy tale** producers and collectors, particularly Italy's Straparola, whom she posits as the creator of the 'rise tale' (Bottigheimer, 2002). This claim incited considerable debate on the origins of fairy tales. The contribution of societal values to the production of children's literature also formed the basis of her seminal work *The Bible for Children* (1996), covering European and North American Bibles for children in the Judaeo-Christian tradition throughout print history. Her work on

gender and story extends beyond Western children's literature to her collaboration with Indian scholars on the traditional literature of Southern India (Prasad *et al.*, 2007). Bottigheimer's concentration on early children's literature has not precluded her from joining the digital age, however; her extensive online bibliography *Early British Books for Children* (2008) places needed information at all scholars' fingertips and invites participation in extending the bibliography. [KSO]

Further reading

Bottigheimer (1987, 1996, 2002, 2008).

BOURDIEU, PIERRE (1930–2002) He was a French cultural critic, generally referred to as a sociologist, though his areas of interest reach beyond this. His key concepts have influenced not only the arts but also other social sciences such as education. However, because he is so hard to pigeonhole, his impact has been less than obvious. His most well-known concept is 'cultural capital', which is best demonstrated in his empirical study *Distinction* (1984), where he shows how different tastes in cultural products are not just based on individual preferences but are, rather, underpinned by social class differences. While the different classes might celebrate their respective likes and dislikes, it is recognized that some cultural objects, or practices, are distinctive, superior. Bourdieu's point is that these things are not innately better; they are symbolically accepted as being so, with 'symbolic violence' (as he terms it) being visited on the inferior, whereas the superior cultural items are underwritten by institutional supports (e.g. being housed in museums, galleries and libraries; being written and talked about in the media and in books; being taught in educational establishments, etc.; see **Ideological State Apparatuses**). In this way, the rawness of economic capital becomes partially concealed behind more palatable, cultural screens, while the cultural capital of certain items becomes naturalized (or **canonized**), being seen as the way things are. While **postmodernism** might seem to question this, mixing high and low culture (interesting adjectives), the audience's appreciation of these very differences is often being drawn upon.

Other key terms that critics have found useful are 'habitus' and 'field', which go together: habitus is concerned with a disposition to act and behave in certain ways, part of which involves responding to cultural capital in an appropriate manner. But it is far wider than this, for Bourdieu's point is that what we think of as natural is socially informed, so that even our body movements are subject to cultural influence (usually we are aware of this only when it becomes excessive, as in the stereotypical walk of a rapper). One could profitably link this concept with **Foucault**'s notion of the 'capillary' action of power, which Judith **Butler** and others have talked about in terms of gender as **performance**. Allison James *et al.* (1998) draw on Bourdieu's work in order to suggest that childhood has its own habitus. In children's literature, Perry **Nodelman** (2008) has also used the term alongside 'field', the latter designating

any social space where those with similar habitus engage in debate and dispute, which in turn influences their habitus, their way of acting and viewing things. Clearly, the field of children's literature studies is continually doing this, this book itself being part of that process. [DR]

See also Chapter 2.

Further reading

Bourdieu (1984), Pileggi and Patton (2003).

BOYOLOGY This is an American term most closely associated with Henry William Gibson, an author and YMCA leader, who published *Boyology, or Boy Analysis* in 1916. The word, almost a homophone of 'biology', was used at this time to address the nature of boys and how society should deal with them. The YMCA was one such organizational response, and the Boy Scouts another. The term came back into prominence more recently with the publication of Kenneth Kidd's *Making American Boys: Boyology and the Feral Tale* (2004), where he shows the longer ancestry of the word, dating back to the 1860s. However, he also takes boyology forward to the *fin de millennium*, noting the growing crisis over boys and the suggested ways of dealing with it, such as Robert Bly's ideas in *Iron John* (drawing on the Grimms' story of that name): that boys be given more space to explore their feral side, with proper male role models. Kidd details how the feral tale also fed into debates on boyology, with boys being seen as naturally having this wolfish side (Max in Sendak's

Where the Wild Things Are, for example). [DR]

See also Chapter 3.

Further reading

Kidd (2004), Males (1998).

BRADFORD, CLARE (1945–) The work of this New Zealand-born, Australian scholar forms a cornerstone of **postcolonial** children's literature criticism. Her monograph *Reading Race* (2001b) received two major awards for scholarship in children's literature. Another award-winning monograph, *Unsettling Narratives* (2007a), being the first comparative study of contemporary settler society in children's literature, draws on texts from New Zealand, Australia, Canada and the United States. Bradford challenges the traditional postulation that children and indigenous peoples occupy a comparable site of **colonization**. Instead, she attempts to portray postcolonial **subjectivity** as contingent upon the influence of race, politics, language, place and space. Furthermore, she contends that to employ the trope of 'child as colonized' privileges the discourse of **whiteness**, failing to take account of subject positions offered to non-indigenous child readers. By attending to the local and the particular, Bradford's postcolonial readings of children's literature consider texts in relation to the politics of production and reception that inform them, as well as to those features that postcolonial children's texts share with their corresponding national literatures for children.

In addition to her postcolonial studies, other significant publications (Bradford, 1996; Bradford *et al.*, 2008) address how post-Cold War children's literature has engaged with political, social and environmental questions. She is the co-editor of *Papers: Explorations into Children's Literature*, a key Australian journal.

Overall, Bradford's contribution to the field of children's literature has been substantial. She has raised questions about the constitution of identity, challenged the authority of any monolithic, legitimizing discourse and undermined the epistemological privileging of Western thought and aesthetics over other modes, in both indigenous and non-indigenous texts for children. [KM]

See also Chapter 4.

Further reading

Bradford (1996, 2001b, 2007a), Bradford *et al.* (2008).

BUTLER, JUDITH (1956–) An American poststructuralist, feminist and philosopher whose seminal work *Gender Trouble* (1990a) played a central role in destabilizing the presumed relationship between sex and gender. Butler argues that, rather than being natural or innate, gender is a social construction. Individuals perform the physical gestures and behaviours associated with masculinity or femininity, and the continued repetition of these acts produces the illusion that gender is real: 'Gender reality is **performative** which means, quite simply, that it is real only to the extent that it is performed' (1990b, p. 278). Butler has published widely in the areas of feminist theory, sexuality studies, philosophy and literature, but it was her theory of gender performativity which catapulted her onto the international stage and has remained one of the most significant gender theories in the past two decades.

Given that Butler herself famously used drag to illustrate her argument about the socially constructed nature of gender, it is not surprising that her work is particularly germane to representations of female cross-dressing in children's literature, of which there is an established tradition. **Folktales** such as 'What Will Be Will Be' and 'A Riddle for a King' (both of which appear in Shahrukh Husain's collection *Women Who Wear the Breeches*, 1995), sword-and-sorcery fantasy such as Tamora Pierce's *Alanna: The First Adventure* (1983) and the Disney film *Mulan* (1998) all feature female protagonists who demonstrate the illusory nature of gender by successfully performing a masculine identity. Contemporary fiction for young adults has also tentatively begun to explore the production of other categories of identity, such as race, using the concept of performativity. Novels such as *Ten Things I Hate about Me* (Randa Abdel-Fattah, 2006), and *A Step from Heaven* (2001) and *Wait for Me* (2006) by Korean-American writer An Na, feature protagonists who occupy multiple subject positions. These texts address the complexity of racial and gender identity formation by depicting a tension between a character's 'authentic' self and the culturally constructed role that she performs for the benefit of others. [VF]

See also Chapter 3.

Further reading

Butler (1990a, 1990b), Salih (2004).

CANON The notion of compiling lists that contain a culture's most important texts is often traced back to the English poet, cultural critic and inspector of schools Matthew Arnold (1822–88), who, in his *Culture and Anarchy* (1869), speaks of coming to know 'the best which has been thought and said in the world' (p. viii). But this statement simply provokes the question, 'Who says?' The trouble with such lists is that what is proclaimed to be universal usually turns out to be more parochial; in particular, values associated with the ruling class, with those recognized as having 'cultural capital', are passed off as though they were universal. Works by those deemed lesser in some way (children, **ethnic** minorities, women) are, in turn, less likely to be selected. Children's literature has fared particularly badly in this regard, being linked to **didacticism** and popular culture.

But if children's books could not attain the heights of the adult canon, this did not stop those involved in the area from developing their own lists of the best, such as the works celebrated by the American *Horn Book* magazine (1924), which claimed to 'blow the horn for fine books' (Lundin, 2004, p. 32), the Children's Literature Association's *Touchstones* (a touchstone being a stone used to test for the presence of gold; **Nodelman**, 1985–9) or Fred Inglis's 'lesser great tradition', which overtly gestures to F. R. Leavis's 'adult' version.

However, if we go back to the root of the word, in the Greek *kanon*, it originally referred to a rod (maintaining its **phallocentric** links, some might say) used for measuring. Of note, though, is the fact that, in these terms, a canon was a guide only, lacking its later evaluative dimension. The latter meaning seems to have arisen from the use of the word in Christianity to refer to writings that had been divinely sanctioned. Arnold, in the nineteenth century, clearly wanted to hold on to what he saw as the best of culture as a bastion against what he also saw as a growing 'Philistinism' among the middle classes, hence a fear of subsequent anarchy among the masses.

There might be much dispute about what should be canonical, but this simply reinforces the notion that, like it or not, we are canon builders (or list makers, at the least), and our canons are then underwritten by the establishment in such forms as prizes, critical writings, anthologies and syllabuses. [DR]

See also Chapters 1 and 2.

Further reading

Gorak (1991), Lundin (2004), **Nodelman** (1985–9).

CARNIVAL/CARNIVALESQUE A literary critical term derived from Mikhail **Bakhtin**'s studies of late medieval carnivals and their literary counterparts. Bakhtin saw in fiction a great potential to represent a world turned upside down and hence to constitute sites of resistance to authority and to envisage cultural and political change. Carnivalesque texts, then, interrogate the normal subject positions created for children within socially dominant **ideological** frames. Though examples of such texts can be found throughout the history of children's books, it was in the 1960s that they became a significant feature. These texts may be divided into three types. First, those which offer the characters 'time out' from the habitual constraints of society but incorporate a safe return to social normality. This type shares many traits with adventure stories in which adults are not present to intervene in events. The second type strives through gentle mockery to dismantle socially received ideas and replace them with their opposite, privileging weakness over strength, for example. The third type, which is likely to be more recent and more transgressive, consists of books which are endemically subversive of such things as social authority, received paradigms of behaviour and morality and major literary **genres** associated with children's literature. Andy Griffiths' *The Day My Bum Went Psycho* (2001), in which the hero is on a pseudo-Tolkienesque quest to thwart the ambition of the bums of the world to change places with the heads, is a paradigmatic example of Bakhtinian carnivalesque. Likewise, Dav Pilkey's 'Captain Underpants' series (1997–) for younger readers uses its **school** setting to carnivalize the process whereby children are civilized and socialized in order to take their place in adult society. Pivoting on what Bakhtin termed 'the material bodily principle' – the human body and its concerns with food and drink, sexuality and excretion – these books mock and challenge authoritative figures and structures of the adult world (parents, teachers, political and religious institutions), approved social values such as independence and individuality, and the activities of striving, aggression and conquest. A delight in taboo language and moments of *schadenfreude* discourage empathetic alignment of readers with characters or with the ways that characters relate to the storyworld of the text and its events, since what is depicted is an anti-model of the known world. [JS]

See also Chapters 7 and 8.

Further reading

Danow (1995), Stallybrass and White (1986), **Stephens** (1992a).

CENSORSHIP In the abstract, the idea of impeding the circulation of particular texts seems abhorrent to the liberal minded. However, when it comes to children, that view is often qualified, in that the young are seen to need 'protecting' from certain issues. Defining what issues, though – violence, scatology, carnal knowledge, contraception, drugs, Darwinism, Harry Potter – is more problematic, and the list changes across time and cultural context, from Plato onwards. Children, then, present a particular problem because, in the definition of many, children, precisely, are beings who are 'innocent' of certain knowledge (consider just the biblical meaning of the word 'knowledge'); so, by sharing these 'secrets' with children, their formerly pure state is seen to be destroyed. It is difficult, though, to separate this moral dimension of censorship from a more Marxist

notion, where knowledge is linked to power; in other words, it is **ideological**. Censorship thus operates not just at the whim of knowing individuals, but at a more macro level whereby people often connive to defend mistaken beliefs about themselves (e.g. that they are inferior or that children are 'little devils' rather than 'holy innocents'). Under the sway of hegemonic ideas, then, people conform to a type of self-censorship. In Michel **Foucault**'s poststructuralist reading of society, censorship becomes even more amorphous in that knowledge is itself a form of power producing particular truths. According to this account, there are no underlying truths that children are protected from; rather, they are simply subjected to varying 'regimes of truth', dependent on the discursive frameworks operative in that society, whether 'fundamentalist' or 'liberal'.

But whether the approach is Marxist or Foucauldian, it is certainly the case that censorship can be resisted and, for the very reason that works for children are deemed innocent, these very items often become vehicles for expressing what is otherwise prohibited. A number of authors in a special issue of *Para*Doxa* demonstrate this: examples range from the **fairy tale** (see Auerbach and Knoepflmacher, 1992) and Rushdie's *Haroun and the Sea of Stories* to subversion in the lullaby (Nilsen and Bosmajian, 1996). This said, the above critics can speak only of texts that have already made successful inroads. Many publishers, especially those that are part of larger media conglomerates, have the muscle to demand that authors conform in various ways (in their language, their subject matter, their character types). This is particularly the case where publishers distribute books internationally, to countries with differing sensitivities; moreover, controls are also tighter if the material is explicitly for educational purposes or for libraries. Of course, this sort of pressure often results in authors censoring themselves, a pressure that both Lois Lowry and Gillian Rubinstein confess to experiencing (Nilsen and Bosmajian, 1996).

Lastly, though, the countervailing forces of new technologies like the Internet should not be discounted. They make the circulation of material far harder to control such that children often have access to information formerly denied them; also, their own work can be posted on the Web, in however original or derivative a form (e.g. the more raunchy 'fanfiction' versions of 'Harry Potter', 'Buffy' and the like). This would itself help change not just notions of censorship but of childhood itself, in a way that some critics might fear (e.g. **Postman**, 1982) but others might welcome (Higonnet, 1998). [DR]

See also Chapters 1, 10 and 11.

Further reading

Auerbach and Knoepflmacher (1992), Heins (2007), Nilsen and Bosmajian (1996), West (1988).

CHAMBERS, AIDAN (1934–) AND NANCY (1936–) Co-founders of the Thimble Press, publishers of the journal *Signal: Approaches to Children's Books* (1970–2003) and specialist book guides and books. In 1982 they received the Eleanor Farjeon Award in recognition of their outstanding contribution to the world of children's books.

Nancy Chambers (née Lockwood) is the Thimble Press editor. In addition to *Signal* she has edited more than 40 other publications, including the annual new-book surveys *Signal Review* and *Signal Selection* (1982–9), and influential books by Lissa Paul (1998), Jane Doonan and Peter **Hollindale** (1997). Prior to *Signal* she edited *Children's Book News* (1966–8).

Aidan Chambers is a critic, editor and novelist and has been active in the fields of education and librarianship. He is particularly notable for his groundbreaking work on **reader response** theory: his 1977 essay, 'The Reader in the Book', recipient of the first Children's Literature Association award for critical excellence, draws on the theories of Wolfgang Iser in developing an approach to children's literature based on the concept of the implied child reader. His interest in literary theory and experimental narrative is clearly discernible in his novels for young adults, the 'Dance Sequence', begun with *Breaktime* (1978) and completed with *This Is All: The Pillow Book of Cordelia Kenn* (2005). The sequence addresses fundamental issues to do with death, religion and pregnancy, dealing sensitively yet provocatively with gender and sexuality. The fifth book, *Postcards from No Man's Land* (1999), received the Carnegie Medal, and in 2002 Chambers was awarded the Hans Christian Andersen Medal for the totality of his works. [LP]

See also Chapter 6.

Further reading

Chambers (1995), Cocks (2004).

CHILDIST CRITICISM A term devised by Peter **Hunt** (1984a), intended to parallel 'feminist criticism' in the way it seeks to consider and foreground the views and practices of a particular readership, in this case children. However, although Hunt gives many examples of how adults appropriate this area, speaking on the child's behalf and using a critical vocabulary that keeps aesthetic considerations central, there are few practical examples of how to undertake this difficult process of reading as a child, putting aside adult preconceptions (Hunt [1984b] is the most thorough). Like gynocriticism, which sought to develop a particularly female framework for analysing women's literature, based on studies of their experience, childist criticism takes an essentially **humanist** perspective; that is, it assumes that there is such a singular thing as a distinctively *child* perspective which can be objectively caught and rendered in language. Moreover, in Hunt's use of terms like 'anarchic counter-culture' he himself seems to be wedded to a particularly romantic conception of the child, with which critics influenced by poststructuralism have taken issue (**Lesnik-Oberstein**, 1994). [DR]

See also Chapters 1 and 2.

Further reading

Gannon (2001), **Hunt** (1984a).

CHRONOTOPE Mikhail **Bakhtin** uses this term to indicate the matrix of time and space represented in a literary work or, more broadly, in all linguistic acts. The term derives from the Greek *chronos* and *topos*, which translate literally as 'time-space'. Bakhtin develops his theory of the chronotope in 'Forms of Time and of the Chronotope in the Novel'. Here he argues, first, that time and space are inextricably interconnected, and second, that the chronotope can be identified as a unit of analysis for studying language in its relationship to time and space:

> The chronotope is where the knots of narrative are tied and untied … . Time becomes, in effect, palpable and visible; the chronotope makes narrative events concrete, makes them take on flesh, causes blood to flow in their veins … . Thus the chronotope, functioning as the primary means for materializing time in space, emerges as a center for concretizing representation, as a force giving body to the entire novel.
>
> (Bakhtin, 1981, p. 250)

The chronotope, then, indicates the literary work's embeddedness in a particular time and space, which, after Einstein, we have to understand as a construction, rather than a given, of human existence. Bakhtin argues, furthermore, that each literary **genre** has its own specific chronotopic image which, in turn, reveals that genre's particular worldview. Thus, the defining chronotopic image of the adventure novel is the road, because that genre's 'worldview' is of the human being in transit, subject to chance encounters and radical change. Every chronotope, therefore, embodies a particular 'way of knowing', and, in the case of literary works, a narrative filter through which we make sense of reality (see Pickstone, 2001; Harris, 2007). The spatial and temporal configurations of a particular genre structure the ways a character can experience his or her world and (except when rules of genre are being deliberately transgressed) limit the kinds of action he or she may undertake. For example, a realist hero can't slay **mythical** beasts and a questing knight can't philosophize over drinks in a café. In *Harry Potter and the Philosopher's Stone*, the magic staircases of Hogwarts are chronotopic images that represent the open-endedness and flexibility of time and space in Rowling's wizarding world: 'there were . . . wide, sweeping ones; narrow, rickety ones; some led somewhere different on a Friday; some with a vanishing step halfway up that you had to remember to jump' (Rowling, 1997, p. 98).

Recent extensions of Bakhtin's theory have sought to define the chronotopes of new and emergent genres such as chick-lit (Helen Fielding's *Bridget Jones's Diary*, 1996), lad-lit (Nick Hornby's *About a Boy*, 1998), retrospective novels (Michael Frayn's *Spies*, 2002; Martin Amis's *Experience*, 2000), the graphic novel and hypertext fiction. Maria **Nikolajeva** usefully analyses some of the major chronotopes and their genres in children's literature – for example, the idyll (1999). Less persuasively, she argues for an overall shift from mythic time (*kairos*) to linear or measurable time (*kronos*) in the historical development of children's literature. But her argument does demonstrate that chronotopes are not only the bearers of a (diachronically) generic worldview; they are also the (synchronic) embodiment of particular historical circumstances. The coffee house is an important chronotopic image in the novels of Balzac, Bakhtin argues, because this was the 'happening space' in Balzac's day, where you were likely to meet people outside your immediate circle and social class and where change and adventure would likeliest occur. New chronotopic images (or 'kenotypes', as Nikolajeva argues) in children's literature reflect the technological world in which contemporary Western children are growing up. Representations of mobile phones, iPods and PCs embody a way of knowing the world that is about being connected 24/7 to social networks and information channels. Particularly relevant to contemporary children's fiction is Bakhtin's notion that different chronotopes can be brought into conflict within a single work or genre and these clashes can produce **dialogic** 'inter-illuminations' between existing genres. Such 'heterochrony' is the spatio-temporal equivalent of linguistic 'heteroglossia' (diversity of discourses) and is evident in many of the generically hybrid works of children's fiction being produced today. In *His Dark Materials* (2001), Will Parry's 'subtle knife' is arguably a hybridized chronotope derived from the sword of traditional fantasy, requiring not only a heroically masculine sense of purpose but also imaginative empathy from its user, thus indicating the complex blend of realist and fantasy worldviews represented in Pullman's trilogy. [RF]

See also Chapter 8.

Further reading

Bakhtin (1981), Harris (2007), Morson and Emerson (1990), Nikolajeva (1999), Pickstone (2001).

COLONIALISM The term is most profitably contrasted with 'imperialism', which refers to the formation of an empire, a process which has been an abiding aspect of human history. Edward Said (1993, p. 8) refers to imperialism as 'the practice, theory, and the attitudes of a dominating metropolitan centre ruling a distant territory', while colonialism, which results from imperialism, refers to the systematic development of settlements in far-flung locations. The expansion of European society following the Renaissance comprised three phases: the age of discovery during the fifteenth and sixteenth centuries, mercantilism during the seventeenth and eighteenth, and colonialism during the nineteenth. The Europeanization of the globe coincided with the development of capitalism, whose interests were served by colonial appropriation of territories in order to resettle surplus populations, produce goods for consumption in Europe or provide strategic footholds for further expansion. British imperialism dominated the globe from 1815 and was intimately bound up with the Industrial Revolution in that the colonies provided raw materials which were manufactured into goods marketed in Britain and elsewhere. Bill Ashcroft et al. (2000, p. 127) point out, however, that 'it was the power of imperial discourse rather than military or economic might that confirmed the hegemony of imperialism in the late nineteenth century'. European colonialism took two principal forms: settler colonies such as America, Australia and Canada, where colonists (settlers) largely displaced indigenous inhabitants, and colonies of occupation, such as India and Nigeria, where indigenous peoples comprised the majority of the population but were subjected to colonial rule. Other countries, including Ireland, South Africa and Algeria, fall between these two types of colonialism. Colonists in settler colonies commonly experienced a sense of displacement, gradually differentiating themselves from the metropolitan culture which discriminated against them as colonials. At the same time, they derived economic advantage from processes of colonization. They thus occupied an ambiguous position, being both colonizers and colonized. [CB]

See also Chapter 4.

Further reading

Ashcroft *et al.* (2000), Said (1993).

CROSSOVER LITERATURE The term became widely used in the first decade of the twenty-first century to describe books that attracted both child and adult readers. Sometimes published in dual editions for child and adult markets, 'crossover books' generally comprise children's novels that have crossed over to adult readers rather than the other way round. In Britain, three contemporary authors were particularly influential in establishing this trend: J. K. Rowling, Philip Pullman and Mark Haddon. There is ample historical precedent for crossover from child to adult as well as adult to child readerships. Richard Adams, J. M. Barrie, Lewis Carroll, Charles Dickens, Kenneth Grahame,

George Orwell, J. D. Salinger, Robert Louis Stevenson and J. R. R. Tolkien are just some of the pre-contemporary authors whose works are read by children and adults. What differs in our time is the scale of the traffic across literary markets, the pre-eminence of the child-to-adult flow of traffic and the conscious marketing of fiction as 'crossover'. While sceptics dismiss 'crossover literature' as an invention of publishers' marketing departments, it is hard to see how clever marketing alone could create the mass demand for children's fiction that has grown steadily since the turn of the century. Undoubtedly the globalization of children's literature publishing, along with its collaboration with the film industry in producing screen adaptations of best-selling children's texts, has contributed to the growth of adult readerships. But more important than the influence of marketing is the question of whether 'crossover' refers to the characteristics of a set of texts or of a group of readers. In other words, is crossover an emergent literary **genre** with identifiable formal traits (such as mixed mode of address, a young protagonist, a complex style, moral ambivalence, themes of identity formation), or does it suggest the emergence of a new kind of reader (less bound by age categories, looking to be entertained or, conversely, more willing to confront **otherness**)?

Attempts to define crossover novels formally, without reference to their readers, generally fail to account for the huge variety of texts moving across markets. The reception of the early 'Harry Potter' novels encouraged the general view that crossover novels must be works of fantasy, and the crossover success of Eoin Colfer, Anthony Horowitz, Garth Nix, Michelle Paver, Philip Pullman, G. P. Taylor, Lian Hearn and Lemony Snicket all seemed to support this hypothesis. But by the end of the 'Harry Potter' decade, other children's authors, such as David Almond, Malorie Blackman, Mark Haddon, Sonya Hartnett, Geraldine McCaughrean, Meg Rosoff and Louis Sachar, had produced works of realism and hybrid realism which succeeded just as easily in dual markets. Since genre proved not to be the determining factor, many adduced that crossover novels succeeded because they brought 'storytelling' back to the heart of writing fiction. According to Amanda Craig (as well as Philip Pullman and others), adult literary fiction suffered a fall into disabling self-consciousness over the last century, and to recover its power 'to grip and entertain' it had to turn back to its origins, which survive undiminished in children's literature because child readers are unimpressed by literary sophistry. This account of crossover's rise is **Romantic** and specifically Blakean, as innocence (children's literature) is said to lead through experience (twentieth-century adult literary fiction) to backward-looking wisdom (current crossover literature). While obviously inadequate as a description of twentieth-century literary fiction, this Romantic account of the crossover novel's rise is appealing for two reasons. First, it reverses the hierarchy of values in the binary opposition between child and adult fiction, since children's fiction here represents the summit of literary creativity, while adult fiction struggles away on the lower slopes. And second, it reproduces at the level of literary history the plot content of many young adult and crossover novels, which often focus on the psychosexual and moral coming of age of teenage protagonists.

But these two points lead us to consider the cross-*reader* of children's and young adult literature. For socio-economic and cultural reasons, adults today are more likely to engage with such literature than in previous generations because, on the one hand, they place a higher value on 'child's play', flexibility, inventiveness and creativity, and, on the other, they are more likely to identify with the ambivalent 'in-between-ness' of **adolescent** experience. When one considers the reader of crossover literature, it seems necessary to distinguish, at the very least, two types of experience: the reading of fiction for younger children (Colfer, Rowling, Snicket), where many adults are conscious of reading across a temporal and cognitive gap, and the reading of young adult fiction, where adults may lose any sense of an age boundary, and simply engage with the text as if it were written 'for' them (Donnelly, Haddon, Hearn, Rosoff). These two types of cross-reading are quite different, and even when they are experienced in relation to a single work, as in Philip Pullman's *His Dark Materials*, there may be an irresolvable conflict between valuing childlike creativity, on the one hand, and transitional, adolescent **subjectivity** on the other. While the latter blurs the boundary between child- and adulthood, leading us to question assumptions about what constitutes a child or adult, the former (reading young children's fiction)

can lead the adult reader to confront the radical difference and otherness of childhood. Indeed, the power of crossover fiction may lie in its inability to resolve this central conflict of values: looking back, it values the experience of childhood and invites the adult to recover a measure of that experience by reading as if he or she were a child; looking forward, it values adolescence as the potential for metamorphosis in a reader of any age. [RF]

See also Chapter 8.

Further reading

Beckett (2008), Falconer (2004, 2009), **Myers** and Knoepflmacher (1997), **Nikolajeva** (1998).

DARTON, **F**[REDERICK] **J**[OSEPH] **H**ARVEY (1876–1936) He was a scion of a notable publishing family: William Darton was a London bookseller from c.1787 and formed a partnership with Joseph Harvey in 1791. F. J. Harvey Darton worked for Wells, Gardner, Darton (1899–1928), edited *Chatterbox* for a time, and published around 30 books, including *The Life and Times of Mrs Sherwood* (1910). He was a pioneer of children's book history, contributing a chapter on children's books to the *Cambridge History of English Literature* in 1914.

His major work, *Children's Books in England: Five Centuries of Social Life* (1932), was the first serious and extensive history of children's books. Heavily weighted towards early books (he devotes just over 20 pages to the period post-1880), the book laid the groundwork not only for all subsequent bibliographical studies but also, as Matthew Grenby (2004, p. 205) puts it, 'set an astonishingly durable **ideological** agenda', and his categorizations (e.g. between 'godly or imaginative, **fairy tales** or moral tales') have been highly influential. In the revised version by Brian **Alderson** (Darton, 1982), it remains one of the essential texts in children's literature studies. Since 1992, the Children's Books History Society has presented a biennial award in Darton's name, 'for the best book on the history or an aspect of the history of British Children's Literature' (CBHS, 1992, p. 7). [PH]

See also Chapter 1.

Further reading

Darton (1982), Grenby (2004).

DELEUZE, GILLES (1925–95) Deleuze's work was centrally concerned with what it means to think, which for him meant to *create concepts*. Like his contemporaries **Foucault** and **Derrida**, he took an anti-**humanist** stance, but he came to emphasize ontology as primary, seeing all beings as flows in the process of a life which is constantly changing, moving and recreating itself. For Deleuze, thought is part of the *flow of intensities* that is lived experience, not measurable via some kind of higher ideal or being.

Deleuze was particularly interested in ideas about identity and difference. Whereas we normally think of difference as being concerned with what distinguishes one thing from another – a man from a woman, an adult from a child – Deleuze rejected this concept, which both binarizes and essentializes difference, privileging the white, middle-class, heterosexual male as expressing the default identity. He favoured theorizing difference *itself*, seeing us all as expressions of the multiplicity of differences that constitute us. Life (including sexuality, love and **desire**) is thus a series of flows – not fixed, not static – which means that in every encounter, every event that we experience, there is change: we affect others and are affected. We are thus both multiple and connected.

Such connections, or assemblages, are always productive and, particularly through their expression in the arts, enabling 'concepts, or new ways of thinking, percepts, or new ways of seeing and hearing, and affects, or new ways of feeling' (Deleuze, 1995, p. 165). Desire is one of the key forces that impels us to make connections.

Deleuze rejected the psychoanalytic tenet that desire is formed through lack and repression and saw it instead as a productive and positive force, one that is 'revolutionary' in its potential to destabilize the way we currently view relationships. At the same time, desire is carefully managed by state and cultural institutions and re-channelled into hegemonic expressions. Deleuze, along with Félix Guattari, called this an 'arborescent' system; that is, it is treelike, firmly rooted and grounded in established knowledge and beliefs that benefit the dominant group. In contrast, Deleuze advocated a 'rhizomatic' form of thinking, rhizomes being plants that have horizontal and decentred root systems, and burst with life at connected points. Rhizomatic thinking can potentially destabilize established social structures.

Such concepts always refer to the centrality of desire, because thinking, creating concepts and challenging received ideas is not simply a *result* of a flow of desire: it *is* a flow of desire itself. As desire creates us, and desire is a constant flow, we are also always potentially being re-created: rather than 'being', having a fixed identity – or, more pertinently for children, maturing towards one – we can shift our sense of ourselves to be 'becoming'. Thus, to read children's or young adult fiction through Deleuzean theory might not only entail identifying the points at which children's desires are blocked or re-channelled into socially sanctioned expressions but also to identify the points of intensity of desire, which challenge the dominant expressions of how to be and how to live in the world.

Ann Brashares' popular young adult novel *The Sisterhood of the Traveling Pants* (2005) offers an example of the ways in which desire is constantly in flux, or, in Deleuzean terms, territorialized, deterritorialized and reterritorialized. The four protagonists have been best friends from birth and initially reside in a territory of childhood, defined by normative expectations about what kinds of desire are legitimate to express. However, for a time they deterritorialize the dominant rules about desirous expression because they prioritize each other and gain pleasure through bodily and sexual connection, symbolized by a pair of jeans they share. However, on their first summer apart, the girls are forced to learn 'life

lessons'. Each girl's maturation is then achieved by her ability to redirect her desire away from the others and towards male characters. This is effectively a reterritorialization of their desire. Moreover, the story can also be read in terms of **Oedipalization**, as Deleuze and Guattari term it. They note that much fiction reproduces this narrative based on lack; that is, on the repression of what is deemed anti-social or immature behaviour, and the centralization of **patriarchy**. However, Deleuzean theory allows for a more *creative* deconstruction of such narratives, because it allows for a positive reading of often delegitimized (i.e. childish) desire at connective points in a novel, while concurrently calling for an analysis of the hegemonic **ideologies** that structure or code the narrative action.

Deleuze's work remains under-utilized in children's literature scholarship. While it allows, or even insists on, a deconstructive reading, it also calls for recognition of the productivity of reading desire outside the constraints of the narrative. [KMc]

See also Chapter 2.

Further reading

Colebrook (2006), Deleuze and Guattari (1984), McInally (2010).

DEPRESSIVE LITERATURE A term adopted by Nicholas **Tucker** to refer to texts which reject the optimistic tone that characterizes much children's literature in favour of a bleaker, ostensibly more realistic portrayal of events. The term 'depressive' was initially applied to the school of realist teenage fiction which began to emerge in the 1970s, notably in the work of Robert Cormier and Paul Zindel. Cormier's *The Chocolate War* (1974) was a ground-breaking example of the **genre**. These texts – which attracted much criticism at the time of publication – explored some of the darker facets of human interaction and eschewed unambiguously happy endings. In his 2006 essay, Tucker explored the concept of depressive literature for younger children, tracing a line from the melancholy of Hans Christian Andersen to the depictions of issues such as homelessness and suicide in some contemporary picture-books. Tucker cites books such as Maurice Sendak's *We Are All in the Dumps with Jack and Guy* (1983) and Tomi Ungerer's *Le Nuage Bleu* (2000) as examples of depressive literature intended for infants, suggesting that the controversy surrounding such texts is based upon adult discomfort with the *idea* of children experiencing feelings of depression, anxiety and hopelessness, rather than the absence of such feelings in childhood. [LP]

See also Chapter 6.

Further reading

Tucker (1972, 2006).

DERRIDA, JACQUES (1930–2004) An Algerian-born giant of French post-structuralist philosophy, vastly prolific, whose contribution to a number of different fields of study has yet to be gauged. For some academics he was an aberration whose star waned with what is labelled the 'end of theory'; for others he remains one of the most innovative thinkers, who changed our whole way of thinking about Western philosophy. This involves a shift from philosophical systems that have particular organizing principles at their centre (e.g. God, being, truth, the **unconscious**) to a way of thinking that is always attentive to the absence of the organizing principle from the very system that it seeks to explain. To take two well-known examples: God and the unconscious organize very different systems of thought, yet are alike in their own inexplicability, in alluding to something that stands outside the system, something extra-linguistic. These 'outsides' are thus 'transcendental **signified**s', terms that signify nothing in particular, yet attempt to explain all.

However, as Derrida pointed out (following Saussure), no term is fully meaningful in itself; words only mean in relation to other words which, through their contrast, hold meaning in place (male being the opposite of female, adult of child, etc.). What a word means, therefore, always needs supplementing with other words in order to make its meaning clear. And there can only ever be other words for, in Derrida's most quoted line, 'there is nothing outside the text'; for example, it makes no sense to refer to Literature with a capital L, or to Humanity with a capital H, and expect these words to have some overarching **signification**.

A system of thought, then, is held in place by repeated iterations of terms, which seek to prevent language's inherent play, such that meanings slip and slide. Literature, however, exploits this play, as does Derrida with his notion of 'deconstruction', which involves 'the careful teasing out of warring forces of signification within the text' (Johnson, 1981, p. 5). However, Derrida's own work seeks to avoid what he criticizes in others precisely by not allowing 'deconstruction' to become a transcendental signified; it is, therefore, always an operation specific to a particular text.

Deconstruction works by focusing on the *différance* of words, that is, the way that they mean only by being *different* from other words and thus *deferring* their meaning. Deconstruction explores the etymology of words, their homophones and connotations, to show language's innate slipperiness. It particularly looks for points where a text seems to falter, to show signs of contradiction. *Peter Pan* (1904), for example, seems to present us with an eternal, innocent child while simultaneously undercutting this notion, the character also signifying an unnerving knowingness and being associated with death. The terms 'adult' and 'child', therefore, become destabilized in this text, as **Rose** (1984) eloquently demonstrates.

From what was said earlier, a 'Derridean approach' is something of a contradiction in terms, but his influence can be seen in various critical works, especially in the work of the Centre for International Research in Childhood: Literature, Culture, Media (CIRCL) at the University of Reading; Karín **Lesnik-Oberstein** thus explores how the reality of the child (as transcendental signified) is continually used by critics to ground their analyses of children's literature, albeit the child itself seems to stand outside signification, unexplained and untheorized.

Likewise, James Kincaid analyses the term 'innocence', showing how its meaning is inextricably linked to its opposite, 'depravity', thus creating a textual shadow that falls across any character depicted as pure and innocent. Finally, for a specifically literary example, there is Anne-Marie Bird's (2005) Derridean reading of the concept of dust in Philip Pullman's *His Dark Materials*. [DR]

Further reading

Bird (2005), Derrida (1992), Johnson (1981), Royle (2003a).

DESIRE Perhaps the central concept in Lacanian psychoanalysis, desire is the driving force of human experience. Everyday usage of the term equates it with the longing for some thing which, when obtained, will satisfy. In psychoanalytic terms, however, only demands for things like food or immediate attention can be satisfied. Desire is more complexly formulated as an **unconscious** effect of signification, which, with its logic of substitution and deferral, can never offer complete satisfaction; words themselves are always inadequate to expressing what we really want, which is to be unconditionally understood and loved without need of the mediating interference of signifiers ('Subversion of the Subject and the Dialectic of Desire in the **Freudian** Unconscious' – Lacan, 2006). Unconscious desire emerges for the child when he sees that the (m)**other** has desires that his presence cannot satisfy. This realization of the distance between himself and his first love object (which he saw as part of himself) instantiates a sense of lack; that is, there are gaps in the other that cannot be filled within the dual relationship of mother and child. In concert with this is the sense that he is incomplete: if there are people and things in the world that are not a part of him, if there is a gap in his relationship with his mother, if there is difference of any kind, then he and his objects do not encompass the entire world. This situation is at once intolerable and indispensable for his coming into being as a subject. He senses his lack, and desires for it to be filled, and he must learn to express his desire in such a way as to get a response from the world. But expressing desire in language is always a compromised project: we can only express a desire for those things for which there is a signifier, so in some senses we are always already asking for a substitute for what we really want, which is to ameliorate any sense of lack in the unconscious. The most persistent conscious desire is the desire for recognition. We long for our qualities and our identity to be recognized by others. [KC]

Further reading

Bracher (2002), Van Haute (2001).

DIALOGISM This term expresses Mikhail **Bakhtin**'s central idea about the nature of language, identity and historical change and is now widely used in feminist, **postcolonial** and other critical theory. Bakhtin employed the term 'fluidly', sometimes to indicate specific types of discourse and sometimes globally to indicate emancipatory energies operating in and through language. In the most technical sense, dialogism refers to discourse that is

'double-voiced'. In *Problems of Dostoevsky's Poetics*, Bakhtin describes single-voiced or monologic discourse as that which sets itself up as the ultimate semantic authority within a given linguistic context. It is discourse that does not recognize authority beyond its own. By contrast, double-voiced discourse contains within it a conscious reference to someone else's words, inserting 'a new semantic intention into a discourse which already has, and which retains, an intention of its own' (Bakhtin 1984a, p. 189). Bakhtin then discusses four types of double-voiced discourse, ordered from least to greatest degree of dialogism: stylization, **parody**, *skaz* (oral speech, slang) and hidden polemic. Unlike stylization and parody, which adapt the other's words to the speaker's own intentions, hidden polemic internalizes an anticipated hostile response and argues against it, creating an internal, unresolved split in the speaker's own discourse. Thus, in Dostoevsky's *Notes from Underground* (1864), a paranoid narrator anticipates being disbelieved by his reader: 'I am a sick man . . . I am a spiteful man . . . I refuse to consult a doctor from spite. That you probably will not understand.' In a more global sense, however, 'dialogism' is also Bakhtin's term for one of a pair of forces that, throughout the history of language, have been constantly at war (Bakhtin, 1981). The first force is 'monologic', centripetal and unifying; all the normative voices of society – the state, the church, the court and other regulating institutions (whether just or corrupt) – are essentially monologic in Bakhtin's view. The second force is centrifugal and strives continually to evade capture in official discourse. Although there must always be a presence of both forces in society as in language (unlike Marxist dialect, they are never resolved into a third term), dialogism is clearly the privileged force in Bakhtin's analysis. Dialogic discourse represents the force of language in its most democratic, generative and creative aspect.

Dialogism, in both its technical and global aspects, is a key concept in children's literature criticism and theory. At the technical end of the scale, Mark Haddon's *The Curious Incident of the Dog in the Night-Time* (2003) provides an example of double-voiced stylization in the voice of the young narrator. At the same time, the novel is dialogic in the way it destabilizes authority figures such as policemen, parents and counsellors by filtering them through Christopher's detached perspective. A text may also be monologic or dialogic in its relationship to real or implied readers, as Barbara Wall's (1991) analysis of narratorial address (single, double or dual) implies. There may also be a dialogic split of consciousness between a former and present self in both the writer and reader of children's fiction (particularly in an older reader) or between a present and anticipated future self (particularly in a younger reader). The changing shapes of children's dæmons in Philip Pullman's *His Dark Materials* (2001) provide a good visual image of internally divided, dialogic consciousness, whether in a character, a writer or a reader. Jacqueline **Rose** (1984) controversially argued that the child as **other** was almost entirely appropriated by adult authorial discourse and **desire**

and, therefore, could not in any uninflected sense be 'heard' in children's literature. But contrarily one could argue that the implied presence of a child in the discourse of an adult narrator or author (unhelpfully, Bakhtin did not usually distinguish these terms) always introduces a note of inner polemic or dialogization in the adult voice, hence asserting its authority even if absent or suppressed. Likewise a child narrator may internalize, and be dialogized by, an imaginary adult interlocutor, as occurs engagingly in Geraldine McCaughrean's *The White Darkness* (2005). David Rudd (1994, p. 93) has characterized children's culture as fundamentally dialogic, and a similar claim may be made for much children's literature in its ongoing dialogue with adult literature and culture. When **fairy tales** are deployed to subvert authoritarian discourses, they become dialogic (although they may also be used monologically, as Jack **Zipes** [1997] argues); an example of a dialogizing fairy tale is Guillermo Del Toro's *Pan's Labyrinth* (2006), since it is used as a vehicle for telling a story about Spanish fascism from a dissident perspective. Another way in which children's fiction, particularly young adult fiction, may be dialogic in Bakhtin's global sense is that it represents characters whose identities are unfixed, open to otherness and in a process of becoming (rather than being) as argued persuasively by Robyn McCallum (1999). [RF]

Further reading

Bakhtin (1984a, 1984b), McCallum (1999), Rudd (1994).

Didactic/Didacticism To call a children's book 'didactic' is usually seen as a slur. The word means 'instructional' but carries a far stronger, negative connotation – something like 'preachy'. Given that children's books are seen to have developed *From Instruction to Delight* (Demers, 2009), as one title has it, early works are seen to be tainted by their moral platitudes. Good children's literature, famously defined by Harvey **Darton**, is seen to have freed itself from this didactic past. However, this view itself wants questioning, for we are extrapolating contemporary notions of childhood into the past, when much of this instructional literature was very popular. It is also notable that much of it was written by women, often with their own children or charges in mind. Moreover, it has generally been women scholars who have re-examined this literature, finding it far richer than traditional criticisms – often from male writers – allow (**Myers**, 1992; Hilton *et al.*, 1997).

We should also realize that we are talking about a wide range of material under this heading. There is strictly religious material, such as children's Bible stories and catechisms, like Cotton Mather's *The A, B, C. of Religion*; there is devotional literature, deriving not from scripture but from historical sources, which 'strengthens religious identity in political, religious, moral and doctrinal terms'; and there is moral literature, more concerned with 'inculcating values (which may be religious or devotional) that lead to worldly success' (**Bottigheimer**, 2004, p. 299). One might add pedagogical material, which would involve some of the foregoing, but also include alphabet books, books on literacy and textbooks in general, and, lastly, books of manners.

Although what is discussed earlier, that is, religious, moral and pedagogical literature, might be seen as justifiably 'didactic', in its more evaluative sense the term is applied to works where the moralizing becomes intrusive, out of place – for it would be a mistake to think that any work could escape a moral dimension; as Wayne C. Booth (1988, pp. 151–2) has argued, works of high art and low jokes alike are ethically framed. This moralizing is not simply a historical phenomenon either. The 'problem' novel of the 1970s became notorious for its artificial staging and resolution of issues. Finally, it is worth noting that what is seen as didactic at one time may not be seen so at another. *Wall-E* (2008) is a recent example: a film that is relentlessly critical of our future as a consumer society but whose message most find perfectly acceptable and sensible. Related to this, the charge of didacticism is rarely levelled at works that have a sense of humour when making their points. [DR]

See also Chapters 1 and 6.

Further reading

Bottigheimer (2004), Hilton *et al.* (1997), Wilkie-Stibbs (2004a).

Disneyfication A term derived from the surname of Walt Disney (1901–66), who is widely recognized as being the most influential figure in the development of the **animated** cartoon.

His studio made history with landmark films like *Steamboat Willie* (1928), the first animated cartoon with synchronized sound, featuring the (later) iconic Mickey Mouse, and, less than a decade later, *Snow White and the Seven Dwarfs* (1937), arguably the first feature-length animated cartoon. But aside from the studio's continued technical and aesthetic virtuosity, it was the growing power of the Disney empire that many found of concern, as it moved increasingly into merchandising, publishing, setting up theme parks and generally building its sociopolitical muscle. Disney seemed to define not just a style of animation but a way of life, which many found narrow and exclusive, with its predominantly white, middle-class American values and celebration of a rather artificial and sentimental status quo. This bias is particularly apparent where the source material is derived from other cultures, as with *The Lion King* (1994), *Pocahontas* (1995), *Hunchback of Notre Dame* (1996) and *Mulan* (1998), to name a few, fairly recent examples. Accusations of racism, sexism and class bias have been repeatedly made, which, when linked to Disney's market penetration, have given the term 'Disneyfication' its derogatory associations. Even the Disney style of animation – realistic, naturalistic, character and action driven – has been seen to overshadow others, such as the more frenetic and violent, episodic, open-ended, surreal and anarchic work of Warner Bros. on the one hand, or the more leisurely paced, impressionistic and fantastic style of Studio Ghibli's work on the other. [DR]

See also Chapter 10.

Further reading

Ayres (2003), Bell *et al.* (1995), Smoodin (1994).

ECOCRITICISM As an interdisciplinary approach to the study of nature, environment and culture, the concept only emerged in the last quarter of the twentieth century. Although writings about the natural environment, or 'nature writing' more loosely, have been produced in children's literature since at least the time of Charles Kingsley's *The Water-Babies* (1863), it is still a fledgling study in children's literature.

Since Rachel Carson's *Silent Spring* (1962), degradation of the natural environment through human action has become a major theme, but it was only in the 1990s that environmental issues really percolated into public consciousness: global warming, habitat protection and the celebration of wilderness, ecosystem advocacy and conservation, pollution prevention, and resource depletion have all become international concerns. In general, there is a recognition that the continued survival of human beings depends on a harmonic balance between human subjects and natural environments.

Ecocriticism is thus both a critical method and an ethical discourse that focuses on the interconnections between nature and culture as these are expressed in language, literature and the plastic arts. It is concerned with how these interconnections pivot on a negotiation between the human and the nonhuman. Early developments in ecocriticism, especially derived from deep ecology, had perceived an endemic disjuncture between human subjects and natural environments. Humanity's anthropocentric assumptions privilege culture over nature, and this practice was exacerbated both in children's literature and its criticism by the domination of discourses around individual maturation that keep the human subject forever at the centre.

This is where ecofeminism, a more critical branch of ecocriticism, has much to offer children's literature. Arising from a fusion of feminist and ecological thinking, ecofeminism proposes that the social assumptions that underpin the domination and oppression of women are the same assumptions that bring about the abuse of the environment. Ecocriticism aims, therefore, to find ways of understanding both humans and the natural environment that are not male biased and which promote intersubjective relationships with **others**: human others, other creatures, natural environments. **Subjectivity** and sustainable life modes thus emerge from interactions among places, cultural, political or economic processes and the natural world. [JS]

Further reading

Bradford *et al.* (2008), Branch and Slovic (2003), Dobrin and Kidd (2004), Glotfelty and Fromm (1996).

ÉCRITURE FÉMININE, or 'feminine writing', is a term first coined by Hélène Cixous in her 1975 essay, 'The Laugh

of the Medusa' (Cixous, 1976). Cixous cautions against attempting to define *écriture féminine* precisely, since it is a practice which exceeds theorization, enclosure or codification. Nevertheless, certain stylistic features are identified: fluidity of syntactic and narrative structures, a blending of written and oral forms (or what **Bakhtin** terms *skaz*, representations of oral speech) and strong use of rhythm, lyricism and **intertextuality**. Writing in the politicized atmosphere of 1970s France, alongside other theorists such as Luce Irigaray, Julia **Kristeva** and Catherine Clément, Cixous aims to deconstruct the **phallogocentric** hegemony of Western, white, European, ruling-class culture. Resistance persists in the margins, gaps and silences (the **unconscious**, so to speak) of this **patriarchal** economy, which is otherwise dominated by what **Lacan** terms the Law of the Father. These writers' concerns with marginal experience, registered in concepts like *écriture féminine*, the semiotic and *jouissance*, reflect the influence of Lacanian psychoanalysis and **Derridean** deconstruction, which themselves critiqued the Kantian view of man as the 'transcendental **signifier**', the source of all truth and knowledge.

But Cixous and Irigaray oppose the masculine bias of Lacanian psychoanalysis, in which femininity is relegated to the realm of the **Imaginary**. For Lacan, to become a subject in the **symbolic** order (the order of language and patriarchal society), one has to repress one's feminine **otherness**. Rather than rejecting binary opposition altogether (as do materialist feminists such as Simone de Beauvoir), Cixous, Irigaray and Kristeva celebrate the difference (or *différance*, Derrida's term) of feminine discourse. Cixous thus characterizes *écriture féminine* as writing which proceeds from the uniquely female experience of the body and its gendered 'pulsions' or drives. Unlike masculine discourse, which possesses or suppresses otherness, the 'feminine' writer never ceases to hear 'the song' of the mother within herself; uniquely open to otherness, 'she writes in white ink' (p. 881). Likewise, the distinctive intertextuality of *écriture féminine* reflects the experience of female **desire** which is complex and mobile with a 'thousand and one thresholds of ardor' (p. 885). Counterintuitively, *écriture féminine* is not necessarily written by women; indeed most of Cixous's examples are from male writers (e.g. Molly Bloom's monologue in Joyce's *Ulysses*). When a fully fledged, female-authored *écriture féminine* does emerge, Cixous apocalyptically predicts, its impact will be 'volcanically' subversive: 'to shatter the framework of institutions, to blow up the law, to break up the "truth" with laughter' (p. 888).

Although Ann Rosalind Jones and others have objected that *écriture féminine* depends upon essentialist definitions of femininity and ignores the fact that bodily experience is culturally determined, nevertheless a broad spectrum of feminists agree that it provides a necessary critique and strategic response to phallogocentrism. Deborah Thacker and Christine Wilkie-Stibbs, among others, have explored the close links between children's literature and *écriture féminine*. Thacker argues that the imposition of the patriarchal, symbolic order onto the imaginary – a feminine/maternal space – includes the process by which we are constructed as subjects from childhood onwards. She argues that, by employing 'multiple, fluctuating and dream-like' language, the most challenging, imaginative children's literature (her example is again male, George MacDonald) provides resistance to this patriarchal process of socialization (Thacker, 2001, p. 9). Whether such writing 'gives children a voice' is open to question, but like *écriture féminine*, children's literature is often radically innovative in terms of literary form (**Reynolds**, 2007). Cixous, Kristeva and Irigaray draw frequent analogies between the powerlessness of children and that of women in patriarchal cultures. And like Irigaray in *This Sex Which Is Not One* (1977), Cixous alludes to Carroll's *Alice's Adventures in Wonderland* and *Through the Looking-Glass* in defining *écriture féminine*, arguing that both children and women have 'ill-mannered' bodies that fluidly assume different forms until patriarchy 'immures' them 'in the mirror', where they will remain, petrified, until they can learn to claim their bodies and experience as their own (Cixous, 1976, p. 882). [RF]

See also Chapter 3.

Further reading

Cixous (1976), Irigaray (1985), Jones (1981), Wittig (1992).

EGO One of the three **agencies** in **Freud**'s structural model of the psyche. The ego performs the executive function of negotiating between the appetites of the **id**, the demands of the **superego** and the exigencies of the real world. As the seat of consciousness, the ego's job is to minimize tension and protect the psyche as it keeps the id and the superego in balance, working to meet their needs in socially sanctioned ways. Because the ego primarily uses defensive mechanisms in order to perform these negotiations, **Lacan** refers to it as the 'seat of illusions' (Lacan, 1988b, p. 62) and is vehemently opposed to the goals of ego-psychology to strengthen the ego and its ability to adapt to the world. Instead, he holds to Freud's more radical insight that the **unconscious** is at the centre of human functioning and believes that an emphasis on the ego masks this insight and its possibilities for helping people realize their **desires**. [KC]

See also Chapter 7.

Further reading

Freud (1961), Lacan (1988b, 1988c), Rollin and West (1999).

ETHNICITY A term which has increasingly been used since the 1960s in place of the discredited word 'race'. Avoiding the pseudoscientific explanations by which formulations of race constructed hierarchies of worth, 'ethnicity' refers to the combination of cultural practices, language, ancestry and values which characterize groups within and across nation-states. In many countries, however, the term 'ethnic' distinguishes between members of a core (European) culture and groups regarded as marginal to this culture, who may be blamed for the degradation or disintegration of the core culture. Individuals are socialized into ethnic groupings which provide social networks of support and obligation; however, they are, as Christian Karner (2007, p. 72) notes, also 'subject to multiple power structures and their corresponding discursive practices'. Thus, a person's ethnicity is only one of the many influences which shape identity formation. In his essay 'The Local and the Global', Stuart Hall (1997, p. 184) argues that individuals and groups may 'retreat into their own exclusivist and defensive enclaves' in order to preserve ethnic identities as pure or fundamentalist entities, or they may negotiate identities by claiming voices and space for themselves as they engage with the societies in which they live. Diasporic communities which share common national and cultural origins form transnational groupings; for instance, South Asian diasporic communities may be part of familial and friendship networks in Britain, the United States and Canada. For such diasporic groups, formulations of ethnicity incorporate three components: a current location, the homeland from which the group comes and transnational networks which connect people of a shared ethnicity. [CB]

See also Chapter 4.

Further reading

Hall (1997), Karner (2007).

FAIRY TALES A type of story traditionally related in oral form, involving limited character types and magical events, though not necessarily caused by 'fairies'. The word 'fairy' is derived from the Latin *fatum* ('fate'), which literally means 'that which is spoken', and ties the mythical 'old wives' who told them, like Mother Goose, with the three Fates who spun and eventually cut the thread of life (**Warner**, 1994a, pp. 14–16). Some people distinguish traditional, orally circulated fairy tales from the literary fairy tale, written by named authors. Others distinguish the fairy (or 'wonder') tale from the **folktale**, the latter being more about everyday events and lacking a magical component. But the divide between these, and **myths** and **legends**, is often hard to sustain.

The notion that fairy tales came initially from rural folk, later to be written down and collected, is something of a **Romantic** myth. The Brothers Grimm, for example, had some quite educated sources, with tales deriving from earlier written versions. More recently, scholars have traced many of our well-known tales – such as 'Cinderella', 'Snow White', 'Bluebeard', 'Beauty and the Beast', 'Little Red Riding Hood' – back to versions existing in the Ancient World (Anderson, 2000), so it seems that the tales have dipped in and out of print a number of times. They certainly have a long history, existing in some form in most cultures: the Arabic *Thousand and One Nights*, the Indian *Panchatantra* and the Finnish *Kalevala*. It is also of note that the fairy tale was not aimed specifically at children – although critics like Bruno **Bettelheim** (1976, p. 12) speak of how it 'enriches the child's existence' at particular stages of development.

In the West, many fairy stories came to us via Italy, with Straparola's *Le piacevoli notti* (The Pleasant Nights, 1550) and Giambattista Basile's *Lo cunto de li cunti* (The Tale of Tales, better known as *Il Pentamerone*, in 1634–6); thence from France, most famously in Charles Perrault's 1697 collection, *Histoires ou contes du temps passé* (Stories of Olden Times), with the subtitle *Contes de ma Mère l'Oye* (Stories of Mother Goose); and finally Germany, with the Brothers Grimm transforming their original scholarly collection *Kinder- und Hausmärchen* (1812–57) into one more specially for children. Britain itself is conspicuously absent from this history, although translations of the latter two authors were popular when they appeared. Fairy stories certainly existed in England, but from the late eighteenth to the early nineteenth century there was much controversy about tales of fantasy, with more realistic, morally improving tales being preferred – particularly after the cautionary example of France, which had recently undergone a Revolution (1789). Fairy tales' circulation in England, then, was more in oral and ephemeral 'chapbook' form – which probably fuelled fears about their subversiveness – until the 1820s and 1830s, when they came into their own, with many well-known writers penning them (Dickens, Thackeray, Ruskin), besides enthusiastically receiving those of Hans Christian Andersen (1846) and, later, those by Oscar Wilde. America, too, developed its own distinctive voice with writers like Frank Stockton and L. Frank Baum (in his 'Oz' books).

The fairy tale's flexible form has made it the perfect vehicle for expressing a society's concerns and **desires**.

Neither reactionary nor conservative in itself, it has been endlessly adapted over time. Earthy, erotic tales jostle with more moral, cautionary ones (Perrault's 'Little Red Riding Hood' could be said to contain both elements); dreams of a world of plenty rub shoulders with depictions of poverty and hunger; likewise, powerful and dangerous women exist alongside passive and silent ones. When feminists and others decry fairy tales, then, it is usually particular versions that are being targeted; not, for example, early versions of 'Little Red Riding Hood', where a feisty girl escapes a wolf using her own wiles (the Delarue version – **Zipes**, 1993). Unfortunately, the **Disneyfied** versions of many of the tales dominate the popular imagination. This said, more recent retellings – like Roald Dahl's *Revolting Rhymes* (1982) or Babette Cole's *Princess Smartypants* (1986) – have sought to challenge some stereotypes. The tales have also been reappropriated by adults, most famously in Angela Carter's reworkings (see Bacchilega, 1997), and there are now far more collections dedicated to the tales of particular communities (e.g. Virginia Hamilton's *The People Could Fly: American Black Folktales* [1985] or Laurence Yep's *The Rainbow People* [1990], tales of Chinese American immigrants).

Critical work on the fairy tale is almost as wide in range as the tales themselves. Folklorists were initially interested in collecting the tales and noting variant versions, which led to more systematic attempts to classify them, the Arne-Thomson Index being the most comprehensive (Ashliman,

1987). Vladimir **Propp**'s (1968) related analysis draws attention to the limited functions performed by the characters (as heroes, villains, helpers, etc.), and to the way the tales unfold according to set patterns. Structuralists similarly approached the tales as though they had an underlying grammar; they sought binary oppositions like nature versus culture, male versus female, light versus dark. With developments in narratology, such approaches have become more nuanced, taking account of who speaks, who is seen and whose viewpoint we are given (**Stephens**, 1992a).

Psychoanalysis has also been extensively drawn upon, interpreters noting that most of the tales revolve around family relationships – even where characters leave home; thus kings and queens, witches and fairy helpers can be read as projections of nuclear family members or as aspects of the central character. **Freud** himself often drew on fairy tales, although his follower, Bruno Bettelheim, analysed them most fully. A slightly different approach came from Carl **Jung**, who saw fairy tales as both reflecting psychic processes of the 'collective **unconscious**' – using such archetypes as the Wise Old Woman and the Trickster – and as fostering personal development or 'individuation'. Jung had his own expert follower, Marie-Louise von Franz.

Informative as structuralism and psychoanalysis have been, their tendency to make universal claims has meant that more variable features – historical, geographical, literary and **ideological** aspects – have been neglected. Jack Zipes has taken Bettelheim to task for this, seeking to give a more culturally specific reading of the tales. Zipes (1995), in particular, has been prolific in examining the development of the tales, the way that early emancipatory elements were steadily eroded and transformed to meet more utilitarian, capitalist interests, including the whole idea of there being specific 'national' traditions. Related to this, one can see particular societies shaping tales for their own ends, with, for instance, German versions of Grimm making the stories increasingly anti-Semitic up to the Second World War. In terms of **patriarchy**, feminist writers have been particularly sensitive to the way that women were portrayed as increasingly passive (or malevolent) in the tales (e.g. Zipes, 1986; **Bottigheimer**, 1987). While all approaches have contributed insights, the most informed analyses are generally written by those who exhibit a healthy eclecticism (e.g. Warner, 1994a). [DR]

See also Chapters 3 and 7.

Further reading

Anderson (2000), Bacchilega (1997), **Warner** (1994a), Zipes (1995).

FOCALIZATION The term refers to the technique whereby events are narrated from the point of view of a narrator or character within a story as if these events were being physically perceived. The agent of perception is known as the focalizer, while events and non-focalizing characters are said to be focalized. So, while omniscient narration allows us access to the thoughts of characters, because it is narrator-focalized, the viewpoint of the narrator dominates. Limited third-person narration typically shifts between narrator-focalized and character-focalized narration, often doing so gradually, and often cutting to and fro. Some texts are almost entirely character-focalized and hence are much like first-person narration in effect.

Focalization is marked in several ways, usually deployed in combination: first by perceptual verbs indicating a character's visual or sensory perspective ('looked', 'saw', 'heard'); second, by verbs indicating cognitive processes ('thought', 'wondered', 'was surprised'); third, by shifts between narrated direct speech or thought and character-focalized **free indirect** or free direct speech or thought; fourth, by the use of indirect discourse in which vocabulary and syntax are more likely to be associated by readers with a particular character than with the narrator; and finally, by speech reporting tags which mark the relationship in which the focalizer stands to other characters ('Mum said').

Focalization has many important effects, mostly stemming from its capacity to represent both the consciousness of a character and the impact of the world on that consciousness. It thence represents characters as subjects and **agents**, that is, as having **subjectivity**. In general, readers can attribute at most only a limited subjectivity to characters that are not focalizers. Focalization can also be more variable, however, in that some novels use multiple focalization to depict acts of perception by several characters and hence achieve a more **dialogic** effect. In Helen Fox's *Eager* (2003), for example, multiple focalization functions to attribute the robot, Eager, with a subjectivity as fully 'human' as that of other focalizers; hence, posing the question of the human nature of artificial intelligence or, indeed, of the extent to which people's humanness is anything more than a textual construct. This example shows how focalization can point up or formulate thematic concerns. Finally, because readers are apt to align themselves with a focalizing character, the technique is crucial for the positioning of implied readers, as focalization strategies construct an implicit position from which to perceive and interpret the world represented in the text. First-person narration and character-focalized narration are similar in this respect. Only a small minority of narratives written for children are extensively focalized through more than a narrator plus one main character, however, and this restriction of narrative points of view frequently has the effect of restricting the interpretative positions available to implied readers. [JS]

See also Chapter 5.

Further reading

Herman (2002), Rimmon-Kenan (1983), **Stephens** (1992a).

FOLKTALES It is common to find 'folktale' and '**fairy tale**' used as interchangeable terms, despite various attempts to distinguish them; for instance, to see the grounds of folktale in the oral tradition, whereas the fairy tale has a written, literary history, or to argue that fairy tales turn on interventions by supernatural or fantastic elements, whereas any paranormal elements in folktale might rather consist of encounters with talking animals and other non-human creatures. However, scholars of the stature of Stith Thompson have preferred to treat the fairy tale as a sub-set of folktale.

Processes of collection and retelling further blur the boundary, so that a tale that originates as a folktale can become a fairy tale. Thus, the well-known 'Jack and the Beanstalk', described by Neil Philip (Jacobs 1992, p. 1) as 'the quintessential English folktale', is enmeshed in literariness from its earliest recorded versions. This is how it begins in versions by three eminent exponents of folktales:

There was once upon a time a poor widow who had an only son named Jack, and a cow named Milky-white. And all they had to live on was the milk the cow gave every morning, which they carried to the market and sold. But one morning Milky-white gave no milk and they didn't know what to do.

(Joseph Jacobs [1890], 1992, p. 1)

Once upon a time there was a poor widow who lived in a little cottage with her only son Jack. Jack was a giddy, thoughtless boy, but very kind-hearted and affectionate. There had been a hard winter, and after it the poor woman had suffered from fever and ague. Jack did no work as yet, and by degrees they grew dreadfully poor.

(Andrew Lang [1890], in Lang, 1996, p. 133)

Beyond the blue hills and silver-roan forests, far beyond the sheep-runs and string-thin paths, lies a sleepy village . . .

(Kevin Crossley-Holland, 1987, p. 118)

The Jacobs version, a reworking of the tale he remembered hearing as a child 40 years earlier, is usually considered closest to an oral folktale. It has the 'once upon a time' onset, generically identified characters, and immediately introduces the state of lack which is the catalyst for action in a folktale. Its aggregative style (and . . . and . . . but . . . and) clearly replicates the form of oral folktale narrative. Lang's version, derived from Tabart's chapbook (1805/7), has a similar onset, with a structure that is again aggregative, but now without the obvious markers. The lack has here been reformulated as a moral issue, a focus that is extensively developed as the tale unfolds, especially through the character of a wise old woman (a fairy in Tabart) who articulates the tale's moral implications. The tale has become more literary. Both of these versions evidence the minimal setting characteristic of folktale, whereas Crossley-Holland, in contrast, opens with an elaborate setting and self-consciously literary language, overt here in the figurative expression 'string-thin paths'. His retelling goes on to give a name ('Martha') and extended characterization to the widow and to develop an account of her son's worthlessness at considerable length. There is little trace here of the structures of oral narration: the **genre** has now become what might be termed 'literary folktale'.

Oral folktales are built up from patterns, repetitions, formulaic phrases and unspecified settings, and the familiarity of these structures enables both production and reception of the tale. The story unfolds as a straightforward, linear series of events. Characters are types (the indigent widow, the feckless son, the innocent persecuted heroine, the greedy stepmother). Actions occur in a formulaic series, often as a sequence of three, which aggregate suspense or danger, as in Jack's three trips to the ogre's castle at the top of the beanstalk, each entailing more danger of discovery than its predecessor.

Folktales are set in a version of an everyday world, and although they may contain improbabilities such as magic beans that grow overnight until they reach another world in the sky, they have a grounding in social experience, in eras when a poor widow might have starved, and when the great and powerful, as apparently represented by the ogre in 'Jack and the Beanstalk', hoarded wealth and 'devoured' the weak. Social conflict, reflecting basic human **desires** and fears, is thus a common folktale theme. The hero's journey, whether physical or symbolic, is a rite of passage through which the self may evolve. Jack's three trips to the ogre's castle, for example, may be seen as symbolic indications of maturation: on the first, he steals a bag of gold to meet an immediate need; on the second, he steals a sustainable investment, the hen that lays golden eggs; and on the third visit, inspired more by curiosity than need, he steals a cultural artefact, the golden harp. Thus, the plenitude which is the expected outcome of a folktale hero's adventures seems to be shaped as a developmental process.

The suggestion that there are three stages in Jack's encounters with the ogre points to the more general proposition that the meaning of a folktale transcends the basic conditions of life and survival to address aspirations about how life might be lived if societies were organized differently. Eleazar Meletinsky has made the productive suggestion that the structure of a folktale reflects the thought processes of its producing society and hence discloses the tale's aetiology, a suggestion which seems confirmed by the shape and outcome of a folktale such as 'Jack and the Beanstalk'. Meletinsky's insight engages with the two main approaches to folktale study: the assumption that folktales are so many variants of a cognate form, which is reflected in repeated motifs (the 'historic-geographic' method associated with Antti Aarne and Stith Thompson), or the later structuralist approach (associated with Vladimir **Propp**), which concentrates on models and structures rather than origins. [JS]

Further reading

Benson (2003), Meletinsky *et al.* (1974), Thompson (1977).

FOUCAULT, MICHEL (1926–84) More than the other celebrated French post-structuralists Jacques **Derrida** and Jacques **Lacan**, Foucault has had a more widespread impact on various branches of the social sciences and humanities, including literary and cultural studies (although Foucault himself did not write much about literature).

He is one of the main theorists behind **new historicism**; he was also heavily influential in the development of **post-colonial** studies (Edward Said and Homi **Bhabha** especially); and, lastly, he had an impact on gender and queer studies through his work on sex and the body. Foucault is probably best described as a historian of ideas, exploring the development of various institutions and practices and analysing how they have impacted on the way people are defined and treated.

In his early works there is more of a structuralist influence, as he seeks to determine the differing conceptions of such issues as madness over time, leading those so labelled to be treated in distinct ways. In his first major work, *Madness and Civilization* (1967), Foucault found that up to the end of the Middle Ages society was fairly sanguine about the mad, often explaining their behaviour in religious terms. It was in the Age of Reason that there were clear attempts to separate the mad from the sane (folly from reason), incarcerating the former alongside **other** groups considered socially unproductive (the poor and the abnormal). Only towards the nineteenth century does madness become part of a medical discourse, being seen as an illness requiring treatment.

In a later work Foucault similarly looks at the way that regimes of punishment have changed, from an emphasis on the public spectacle of torture to supposedly more humane and private methods (though he questions their humanity). Particularly insidious is the panopticon, a model for an ideal prison system devised by the English political philosopher Jeremy

Bentham, in which prisoners could be observed at any time of day, although the inmates themselves were never sure when they were under surveillance. This system is seen to produce more compliant prisoners because they continually suspect being overseen. In today's society of omnipresent CCTV, such ideas are particularly resonant.

The notion of the panopticon demonstrates one of Foucault's main ideas, that power circulates at all levels of society: it is not simply imposed from above. So the prisoners (or subjects in general) connive in their own policing. This example also shows how non-discursive elements, such as architectural features and the arrangement of bodies, are involved in relationships of power. Third, Foucault notes how power always produces resistance; for example, though the slaves in the United States faced immense brutality, it was the Christianity, forced upon them, which also provided subversive narratives of salvation in spirituals like 'Michael, Row the Boat Ashore' and 'Swing Low, Sweet Chariot'. Moreover, slavery also gave trickster tales an added impact: tales about the lowly Brer Rabbit outwitting the more powerful animals who would hunt and kill him.

Lastly, Foucault argues that all attempts to gain information are linked to power, such that he speaks of 'power-knowledge'. Thus, one might point to seemingly innocent travellers and explorers who, in discovering the customs and habits of various peoples, and the geography of their lands, were gathering information (one thinks of the double meaning of 'intelligence') that would assist future invaders and colonial powers. Closer to home, we might consider the huge amounts of information gathered about children's development, allowing the medical profession to set up norms of growth – usually middle-class ones – from which some children could then be seen to deviate (becoming abnormal), or, in terms of schooling, allowing some children to be seen as 'backward' or 'retarded' and to need 'remedial' education. In this way, Foucault shows how what he calls 'bio-power' flows through us, working with a sort of capillary action.

Foucault is always attentive to how aspects of our behaviour – such as 'madness' or our sexual practices – can be seen otherwise, rejecting notions of an essential human nature. For him, then, the idea that the Victorians repressed sexuality is a nonsense. As he argues, they talked endlessly about how it should *not* be talked about, with extensive manuals and mechanical devices addressing such issues as the dangers of child masturbation.

Foucault's style of analysis thus involves looking at how discourses circulate on a particular topic at a particular time, and he is especially attentive to what he calls 'neglected knowledges', which official history tends to ignore. In studying children's literature, then, it is important to look not just at primary texts but also at such things as legislation, educational practices, child-rearing manuals and so on; moreover, it is equally important to examine neglected areas like commonsense knowledge, superstitions, chapbooks, comics, jokes and rhymes. Lastly, to return to the primary texts, we should also consider critically the very nature of authorship and be careful about how a designated name (e.g. Lewis Carroll, Louisa May Alcott) causes us to group certain texts and distinguish them from others, seeing a writer's development as itself almost organic (the 'mature' Ransome). Such considerations are particularly useful in the area of children's studies, where a writer's work for children is often omitted from what are labelled 'collected' works (e.g. T. S. Eliot's *Collected Poems* [1991] omits *Old Possum's Book of Practical Cats* – despite having sections on 'Minor poems' and 'Occasional verses'). [DR]

See also Chapters 1 and 4.

Further reading

During (1992), O'Malley (2003), Rabinow (1984), **Trites** (2000).

FREE INDIRECT DISCOURSE The representation of speech is central to the **mimetic** effect of narrative, the illusion that in some way readers have access to a version of an actual world. Children's fiction employs the full range of speech types that have developed in fiction since the early nineteenth century, from reported speech to untagged direct speech, although very little critical attention has been paid to how it uses speech forms. The subtlest speech type, and most difficult to interpret, is free indirect discourse (FID), a form which linguistically and mimetically lies between indirect and direct discourse and which has received substantial literary and linguistic attention since the 1980s. In essence, FID is a representation of a character's speech or thought which is neither introduced by a speech reporting tag such as 'she said/thought that' nor reproduces the forms of direct speech. It is an important element of **focalization**, as it brings together or slips between the perceptions of the narrator and a represented character and hence can make point of view hard to determine and ambiguous. In children's fiction, FID is more frequently a mode of thought representation, rather than of speech, since its primary function is to evoke a character's mental processes and the information-processing mechanisms that lead to some understanding of self, others or a situation. It is thus an aspect of how a text establishes a notional **subjectivity**. The move from narration to FID is often linguistically marked by such features as tense shifting and proximal deictics (e.g. the use of *now* and *here* where *then* and *there* might be expected), but more generally FID is identified through the surrounding context. Some examples will make this clearer:

> Then he thought, *Hester!*
> He had promised her he would go back. She would be waiting, down there among the fires. He couldn't let her down. He took a deep breath and leaned on the controls.
> (Philip Reeve, 2001, p. 278)

The sequence begins with tagged direct thought, moves to indirect thought ('had promised [that]') and concludes with clear narration ('He took a deep breath'). The two sentences between are FID, indicated linguistically by the third-person pronoun

179

and past tense of 'He couldn't' and mimetically by the spatial orientation of 'down there'. Dramatically, the sequence enacts the mental process whereby Tom moves from self-regarding despair to taking responsibility for someone else.

> Geoffrey ordered the best meats for the messenger and praised Henry. But why was this news painful? For a reason he could not guess, Geoffrey did not like the idea of Robin being surprised.
>
> (Michael Cadnum, 1998, p. 182)

Here the sudden shift to FID with the second sentence marks Geoffrey's increasing ambivalence about his duty as sheriff to capture Robin Hood. As often, the focus on mental processes in the third sentence confirms the status of the second as FID, although initially there seems to be an ambiguity between the character's free indirect thought and narration.

> When Mary vanished from the hillside and went into the place where the water of the Dig came out, she had several things to look after. The grass rope was the most important: it would not matter if it got wet, but it must not be lost: the reason for coming here was the unicorn, and a grass rope is what you must bring. Another anxiety was the bag of biscuits.
>
> (William Mayne, 1957, p. 150)

This sequence is also framed by narrated segments, but shifts into FID within the second sentence, evident in the proximal deictic ('here') and the subjective perspective of Mary's consciousness ('you must'). As often in Mayne's writing, a mental process is enacted through FID and then subsequently identified in narrative ('anxiety'). The effect is to represent a mind reiterating known details in order to ward off fear of the unknown.

FID has several common functions, although individual examples may have more specific effects. The shifting between the respective voices of narrator and character may not only create an ironic distance from the latter but may also prompt empathy when the voice of the narrator reproduces elements of the character's language. Either way, the text becomes not only semantically denser because of the shifting but also alerts readers to elements of linguistic deviation that can indicate, for example, that a character's perspective is untrustworthy. This latter effect opens up questions about the authority of the text in that, while a represented perspective may be rejected, the origin of any utterance can be called into doubt. Finally, and in contrast, by reproducing the speech features of a character's language, FID can be a medium for representing stream of consciousness (as the Mayne example briefly illustrates) and prompting close reader alignment with character.

FID has been visible in children's fiction for over a century, but there is little doubt that its use increased significantly as the literature engaged with the increasing relativism of the second half of the twentieth century. [JS]

See also Chapter 5.

Further reading

Fludernik (1993), Martin (1986), Rimmon-Kenan (1983).

FREUD, SIGMUND (1856–1939) Freud was the inventor of psychoanalysis, one of the most controversial theories and forms of therapy of the twentieth century. At heart, psychoanalysis posits that we are split beings: we present a conscious self to the world but, beneath this, we are driven – and riven – by **unconscious desires**. His theory is revolutionary in that it challenges the idea that humans are rational, Cartesian beings ('I think, therefore I am'). Freud's discoveries began in Vienna, where he lived most of his life till forced to flee the Nazis in 1938, dying in London in 1939.

He began his professional life as a neurologist, but became more interested in the fact that physiological effects could be produced by the mind, under hypnosis. He also found that many of his women patients ('hysterics') confessed to having been abused by their fathers when young. Freud could not believe the extent of this abuse, though, so he abandoned his 'seduction theory' – to the detriment of science according to some critics (e.g. Masson, 1984) – in favour of an explanation that saw the abuse as a fantasy produced by the patient.

In this we can see the potential importance of Freud for children's literature studies, given that adults create children's narratives. Freud himself liked to draw the parallel, too, that the 'child at play behaves like a creative writer, in that he creates a world of his own, or, rather, re-arranges the things of his world in a new way which pleases him' (Freud [1908] 1959, pp. 143–4). He regularly drew on literary works to explain his concepts, whether **fairy tales** (mentioned in his idea of the 'family romance', the notion that one's real family was more elevated and perfect than the existing one) or fantasy works in a more general sense (his exploration of the **uncanny**, for instance, draws most explicitly on the fantastic tales of E. T. A. Hoffmann).

After rejecting the 'seduction theory', then, childhood becomes central to Freud's theories, with even the 'innocent' baby being regarded as 'polymorphously perverse'; that is, as experiencing sexual or, more generally, sensual pleasures and desires over its entire body. In his key work of 1905, *Three Essays on the Theory of Sexuality* – which heads Karín **Lesnik-Oberstein**'s list of 'significant publications for Children's Literature Criticism and Theory' in the twentieth century (2004, p. xiv) – Freud notes a developmental trajectory from an initial, oral stage (clearly seen in many fairy tales, like 'Hansel and Gretel', and also elsewhere – Sendak's *Where the Wild Things Are*), to an anal, then to a concern with the genitals, before a period of latency, culminating in 'genital' sexuality itself, at puberty. The notion of being 'anal' or 'anally retentive' has become something of a cliché, indicating someone who hoards money, or other possessions, and is in some way emotionally inhibited (Scrooge being a prime example). Whereas Freud sees heterosexual identity as the endpoint of normal development, his theory is open to many variations on this, given our initial polymorphous perversity. Moreover, development in Freud's model is culturally produced, through the child's interaction with significant **others** (chiefly the parents). Freud's controversial **Oedipus complex** is the most famous example of this, through which the child, fearing castration, has to give up his erotic longing for his mother. However, this account only explained boys' development; despite many attempts, Freud could not successfully account for girls', resulting in his despairing question, 'What does Woman want?'

But in presenting development in the above manner there is a danger of losing the dynamic appeal of Freud's writing: a sense of probing mysteries, uncanny happenings, uncovering puns and double meanings, discerning character types and, generally, of undertaking a 'close reading' which, it could be argued, is very much the territory of literary criticism. This is where *The Interpretation of Dreams* (1900) or some of Freud's case histories can prove most illuminating – not, as hinted above, for their outcome, but for exploring the *process* of interpretation. Freud was one of the first to note the overdetermination, or the multiple-meanings, of texts, and, perhaps even more importantly, to note how meaning is responsive to the occasion of telling – something that Jacqueline **Rose** (1984) explores in her 'case history' of *Peter Pan*.

Psychoanalytical ideas have become so much part of our culture that it is often hard to recall their roots, as phrases like 'being anal' attest notions of repression, the unconscious, the **ego**, **id** and **superego**, penis envy, projection and transference are commonplace. But if these ideas are to be used in literary criticism, a certain precision is necessary to avoid what is known as 'vulgar' Freudianism, where anything pointed and upright represents a penis, anything hollow or circular, a vagina (see Crews [1964] for a witty **parody** of such criticism; ironically Crews [1995] himself turned from championing psychoanalysis to being virulently opposed to it). This said, readers' individual ways of responding to texts can themselves be of psychoanalytic interest (Holland, 1975), and certainly, some of the best Freudian criticism explores this text–reader interaction (e.g. Brooks, 1985) rather than trying to psychoanalyse the author through the text (e.g. Grinstein, 1995) or, even, to psychoanalyse the characters (Rollin and West, 1999, pp. 45–52). Regardless of how far-fetched some of Freud's individual notions might seem then, as Pamela Thurschwell (2000, pp. 59–60) notes,

his great discovery was to realise that people's sexuality emerged from the translation of instinctual drives into stories – stories that involved the parents and the young lover's early life, stories that children told to themselves and to each other about where babies come from, fears and anxieties about punishment, and fantasies about love. [DR]

See also Chapter 7.

Further reading

Brooks (1985), De Berg (2003), Gay (1995), Rollin and West (1999), Thurschwell (2000).

FRYE, NORTHROP (1912–91) A Canadian literary critic and theorist whose work was hugely influential during the second half of the twentieth century. Frye's first book, *Fearful Symmetry* (1947), is a landmark in studies of William Blake, and he followed this with perhaps his most enduring work, *Anatomy of Criticism* (1957). This is Frye's ambitious attempt to grasp the literary field in its entirety and to bring the rigour of scientific method to the study of literature. The book offers a generalized focus on the specifics of literary study, on **genre**, modes, symbols and ethics. *Anatomy* spawned a number of smaller books by Frye that take up aspects of the larger study. Perhaps the three most important of his books for scholars of children's literature are *The Educated Imagination* (1963), *The Secular Scripture* (1976) and *On Education* (1988); the chapter 'Charms and Riddles' in *Spiritus Mundi* (1976) is also relevant. *The Educated Imagination* consists of a series of six radio talks which are a distillation of his theory of literature. Here Frye conceives the literary universe as a structure of words independent of the material world in which we live. He views literature as a displacement of **myth**, all literary work stemming from the myth of a quest for the golden city or a return to Eden. In terms of children's literature, Frye's theory offers a focus on literary expression as a search for home and stability within a world of darkness and even despair. Frye examines the familiar pattern – home–departure–wilderness adventure–home again – at length in his study of Romance, *The Secular Scripture*. Romance patterns inform much of what we think of as children's literature, from **fairy tales** to contemporary fantasies. His interest is largely cartographic and spatial with its focus on a hierarchy of characters, plot movements of descent and ascent, specific **chronotopes**, and images that are either demonic or angelic. Much of our understanding of images of the garden, the forest, the wasteland, the hero, the city – in short, the archetypes of literature – we owe to Frye. His work concentrates on formal and structural aspects of literature. In 'Charms and Riddles' he provocatively sorts literary expression into these two categories, the one (riddles) setting the reader at a distance from the text and rousing the mental faculties to act in order to solve the riddle, and the other (charms) drawing the reader in and putting him or her under a spell through the incantatory power of language. Children's literature (the nursery rhyme, for example) clearly exhibits both charm and riddle. Frye is also interested in the place of literature in education, as we see in *On Education* and in the essay 'Elementary Teaching and Elementary Scholarship' (in *The Stubborn Structure*, 1970). In this essay, Frye argues that literature, as the 'grammar of the imagination', should begin as early as elementary school, and he notes that what students learn is not literature but the criticism of literature. Frye's theory and method form the basis of Glenna Sloan's *The Child as Critic* (1991). [RM]

See also Chapter 2.

Further reading

Frye (1963, 1966, 1976, 1988), Hart (1994), Sloan (1991).

GENRE The word derives from the French for 'kind' or 'type' and indicates the division of literature (among other areas) into useful categories. In the modern world the most common divisions are novel, poetry and drama (also known as 'modes'), though other forms are also regularly categorized (e.g. short story, autobiography, soap opera). Each of the main modes is then subdivided, with the novel, for example, being broken into such subgenres as chick-lit, **Gothic** and science fiction. Beyond this, though, *aficionados* make further divisions; thus, science fiction has such subcategories as classical, New Wave and cyberpunk, and new, hybrid creations continually evolve, such as steampunk, which mixes the historical (usually Victorian, in the style of Jules Verne or H. G. Wells) with the posthuman – as in Philip Reeve's *Larklight* (2006). Likewise, novel and poetry have come together in 'verse novels' – such as Sharon Creech's *Love That Dog* – which have had some popularity in children's literature (Alexander, 2005).

There are three main approaches to genre: one stresses formal features, another looks at content and a third concentrates on reception. In terms of form, Vladimir **Propp**'s discussion of the distinctive features of the **folk** or **fairy tale** has been hugely influential, as has Northrop **Frye**'s more inclusive taxonomy of textual features. Formal approaches have certainly featured in discussions of children's literature (e.g. claims that its texts are shorter, with simpler narratives and restricted **focalizing** agents). Other writers have concentrated on content (e.g. child

characters at the centre, happy endings, an absence of sexual material), while others, yet again, have looked to the readership and its expectations, as with the romance (Cherland, 1994) or science fiction (Mendlesohn, 2009). The majority of today's theorists, though, are eclectic, especially given the **postmodern** tendency to mix or **hybridize** genres in varying degrees of **parody** or pastiche.

Questions about children's literature being a genre in its own right, however (e.g. Weinreich, 2000), are controversial. The most expansive defence of this idea has come from Perry **Nodelman** (2008), who sees the area as defined by adult notions of children and childhood, and specifically by a profound ambivalence about these lesser beings against which adults define themselves. Thus, though Nodelman also characterizes this literature in terms of its simplicity, repetitions and utopian hope, he argues that it simultaneously gestures towards the complex – which is where the 'hidden adult' of Nodelman's title lurks. Nodelman further argues, contrary to other theorists, that child readers are at least partially aware of these more complex meanings; however, in buying into the childhood proffered by the text, children pretend otherwise. In reality, Nodelman suggests, few children would accept that they live in such an edenic world with its endless 'happy endings'; rather, children consent to this portrayal merely as the generic convention of a form that ostensibly speaks to and for them. Children's literature is, therefore, profoundly ambivalent in its oscillations around childhood and adulthood, innocence and experience, and so on.

Nodelman's work cleverly steers between the views of some social constructionists, for whom the genre is an impossibility, and essentialists who have fixed ideas about childhood and/or its literature. But as Nodelman (2008, p. 150) himself says, children's literature is a genre in adult terms only: he is concerned with what 'adults have imagined as appropriate' rather than actual 'children's reading'. Innovative and fruitful as Nodelman's approach is, then, it tends to lose the very generic distinctions that readers find productive (as explored, for example, by Gibson [2000], Mendlesohn [2009] and others), sometimes losing focus altogether: 'children's literature . . . might . . . be a specific genre of fiction' (2008, p. 81). [DR]

See also Chapters 5 and 11.

Further reading

Duff (2000), Frow (2005), Nodelman (2008).

GOTHIC Originating in the eighteenth century as a mode (rather than a **genre**) which enabled fiction to focus attention on interior and subjective experience, the Gothic has had a strong influence on various kinds of writing concerned with emotive effects and still flourishes in contemporary popular literature, especially in romance and fantasy. One of the main principles of early Gothic writing was to load the discourse with **signifiers** indicating darkness, silence, eeriness,

fear and a sense of things happening just beyond the threshold of perception, and many of these rhetorical and textual strategies live on in modern Gothic (though sometimes in less obvious forms). Because of what were perceived as its excessive and transgressive properties – its dwelling on terrors, ghosts and vampires, depraved aristocrats, and evil clergy – Gothic writing was long deemed inappropriate for children's literature, but had clearly entered the field with Frances Hodgson Burnett's *The Secret Garden* (1911), where the labyrinthine architecture of Misselthwaite Manor, the eccentric behaviour of the house's aristocratic owner, family secrets, enclosed places and mysterious sounds in the night are obviously elements of a Gothic mode.

Because Gothic is related to medievalism (reconstructions of an imaginary medieval past), it employs textual strategies that purport to evoke the pastness of the past. For example, Roger Lancelyn Green's retelling of the story of King Arthur (1953) imbued the unadorned fifteenth-century prose of his source with distinctively Gothic settings, and the popular genre of Arthurian retellings has subsequently retained this Gothic tinge, both in text and illustration.

In modern children's literature the Gothic mode is extensive, from the Gothic horror of Virginia Andrews' *Flowers in the Attic* (1979) and the various dark narratives of Tanith Lee's **fairy tale** retellings, to comic versions of the mode in Robert D. San Souci and David Catrow's *Cinderella Skeleton* (2000) or in Neil Gaiman's richly **intertextual** *The Graveyard Book* (2008). The latter interrogates many assumptions about the Gothic, **parodying**, for example, the way Gothic narrative constructs a particular kind of controlled character **focalization**; that is, the characters themselves seem to be focalizing objects and events, but the feedback readers receive, of the characters' reactions, comes via the perception of the narrator. Gaiman also plays with the graveyard as a metaphor, both for an evolving, individual consciousness and, relatedly, for a more general, psychoanalytical interpretation of Gothic writing, by inverting the notion of the **uncanny**: in this novel, the *unheimlich* site of the graveyard becomes a *heimlich* site in which the orphaned protagonist is nurtured (by ghosts, a vampire and a werewolf) to become a mature, well-balanced young adult. Gaiman's inversion of the expected reminds us that, from *The Secret Garden* to *The Graveyard Book*, the Gothic mode in children's literature has affirmed that subjective **agency** can be wrested from settings of decay and death, primarily by means of intersubjective relationships. [JS]

See also Chapter 7.

Further reading

Botting (1996), Cavallaro (2002), Jackson *et al.* (2008), Punter (2001).

GROTESQUE The idea that something is grotesque derives from cultural perceptions of what constitutes a normal body: symmetrical, self-contained and proportioned according to the size and shape fashionable in a particular time and place. What deviates from such

perceptions and hence transgresses rather than expresses norms may be deemed grotesque. As children's texts have consistently recognized, grotesqueness is itself the effect of an aesthetic perception, not a property of the thing or person perceived. Two principal understandings of the function and significance of the grotesque equate it either with the **uncanny** or terrifying (following Wolfgang Kayser) or with the **carnivalesque** (following Mikhail **Bakhtin**). The uncanny grotesque is associated with fantastic and **Gothic** modes and has been the main source for the association of evil with the grotesque, so that a grotesque body designates an evil character. This is immediately evident in the evil queens of the early Disney films *Snow White* (1937) or *Sleeping Beauty* (1959). The use of the grotesque as a **sign** of moral lack persists in children's fiction and films, but its use has weakened under the impact of the ludic and satiric emphases of the carnivalesque, as can already be seen, for example, in the comic villain of Roald Dahl's *Matilda*, Miss Trunchbull. *Shrek* (2001) was instrumental in bringing this shift to public attention. As Dieter Petzold concludes, 'When dealing with the grotesque in children's culture, it is tempting to subscribe to the Bakhtinian view; but the disturbing aspect of the grotesque is by no means absent in children's books' (2006, p. 182). *Cinderella Skeleton* (San Souci and Catrow, 2000), for example, deftly locates the grotesque in the liminal space between the Gothic macabre and anarchic **parody**, while Neil Gaiman's *The Graveyard Book* (2008) makes effective use of the grotesque uncanny in its introduction of the medieval *danse macabre*.

An important function of the grotesque is to break the textual nexus between difference and monstrosity: if an appearance is naturalized as monstrous then audience responses to it are also naturalized and seen as unmediated. The grotesque thus has a socially transformative purpose: it is transgressive because it challenges normative forms of representation and behaviour, and it disturbs boundaries by giving the **abject** social recognition. *The Graveyard Book* is again exemplary when it depicts the protagonist's altruistic efforts to embrace socially the ghost of a witch-girl, 'Drownded and burnded and buried here without so much as a stone to mark the spot' (Gaiman, 2008, p. 100). In such ways, the **metanarratives** and customs of official culture are exposed to scrutiny, and normative modes of cultural and political expression are undermined, thereby enabling new possibilities for identity making. [JS]

See also Chapter 8.

Further reading

Bakhtin (1984b), Harpham (1982), Kayser (1981), Petzold (2006).

HEGEMONIC MASCULINITY The concept of hegemonic masculinity was first introduced by sociologist R. W. Connell, who defines it as 'the configuration of gender practice which embodies the currently accepted answer to the problem of the legitimacy of **patriarchy**, which guarantees (or is taken to guarantee) the dominant position of men and the subordination of women' (1995, p. 77). Connell views masculinities as patterns of behaviour, attitudes and physical attributes that are deemed to be masculine in a particular society at a particular time. Hegemonic masculinity is thus the most socially acceptable form of masculinity in a culture at a given moment – although, as the term 'hegemonic' would suggest, it is both variable and relational. Connell's pioneering work on masculinities has constituted a framework for masculinity studies over the past 20 years. Its relevance to the field of children's literature lies primarily in the recognition of multiple types of masculinity and also in the construction of masculinity and femininity as relational, rather than oppositional, concepts. Contemporary writing for children which thematizes masculinity frequently represents the formation of masculine **subjectivity** as a **dialogic** process. Different characters are representative of different types of masculinity, and the central male character typically has to negotiate his own subjectivity against and in relationship to these masculinities. Philip Gwynne's *Deadly, Unna?* (1998); Gayle Friesen's *Men of Stone* (2000); and Scot Gardner's *Burning Eddy* (2003) are useful examples of this type of gender representation, as each depicts the subjectivity of its male protagonist developing in resistance to hegemonic masculinity. [VF]

See also Chapter 3.

Further reading

Buchbinder (1994), Connell (1995), Potter (2007), **Stephens** (2002b).

HOLLINDALE, PETER (1936–) One of the pioneers in introducing children's literature to undergraduate degree courses in the United Kingdom, Hollindale was a lecturer and later Reader in English and Education at the University of York (1965–99). He has published widely since his *Choosing Books for Children* (1974), producing two works of particular significance and influence. In the first of these, an essay on **ideology** originally published in *Signal*, Hollindale urges a move away from simplistic, surface treatments of ideology, to articulate three main dimensions: the explicit beliefs of the individual writer (what Hollindale [1988] terms 'the most conspicuous element in the ideology of children's books' [p. 11]); and *'passive* ideology' (p. 12) in the form of the individual writer's unexamined assumptions; and broader ideological forces rooted in the way that a 'large part of any book is written not by its author but by the world its author lives in' (p. 15). Central to this work is the idea that ideology ought properly to be considered less 'a political policy' than 'a climate of belief' (p. 19). His later *Signs of Childness in Children's Books* is largely concerned with redefining the critical terminology of children's literature criticism; Hollindale suggests the closely associated terms 'childness' and 'childly' as best suited to describing what he terms 'the *event* of children's literature' (Hollindale, 1997, p. 29), enacted through the interaction of both the adult author's and child reader's constructions of what it means to be a child. [ND]

See also Chapter 1.

Further reading

Hollindale (1988, 1991, 1997).

HUMANISM A concept with a broad range of applications but with shared assumptions and concerns about the nature of human beings and their relationships to societies. A core assumption is that selfhood, although it may not be innate, is shaped by choices as to the kind of self a person becomes through engagement with social formations. The production and reception of children's literature has long seemed to be grounded principally in a humanist **ideology**. This is evident in underlying **metanarratives** concerned with tradition and the conserving of culture, cultivation of imagination, valuing altruistically intersubjective social and personal relationships, and privileging organically unified, **teleological** outcomes. The human subject envisaged in Enlightenment and post-Enlightenment humanism was male, who stood at the centre of a world in which he acted as a historically independent agent, not subject to any divine authority for his thoughts or actions. His **subjectivity** inhered in his essential humanity. Some very fine children's literature has been produced within this framework – Richard Jefferies' *Bevis* (1882) and Kenneth Grahame's *The Wind in the Willows* (1908) are outstanding examples – but by the second half of the twentieth century it was challenged by different ways of thinking about the world, especially by a change in attitudes towards race and gender and, by the end of the century, by posthumanism. This shifted the humanist subject away from someone who, at first, was merely male and/or white, to someone – or something – who queried the very interface between the organic and the mechanical (as explored in Spielberg's *A.I.: Artificial Intelligence*).

The humanist subject in general literature and social theory has been directly challenged by some tenets of **postmodern** theory, in particular arguments that human identity is socially constructed, that ideas of a universal 'human nature' lack foundation, that reality is linguistically constructed, that all meaning is contingent and, therefore, truth is another social construct. These tenets have had some impact on young adult fiction: M. T. Anderson's *Feed* (2002) and Jan Mark's *Useful Idiots* (2004) clearly invoke them, but with the implication that such assumptions have played a large role in producing the dystopian worlds of the novels. It is to be inferred, then, that the greatest lack in such imagined societies is a foundation in some form of (neo)humanist values. Such a response is crystallized in the stalkers of Philip Reeve's *Mortal Engines* (2001) and subsequent books in the series. Post-human machines with human components, the stalkers embody what seems most to be feared in the modern world: a capacity for inhumanity and violence, scientific inquiry harnessed to serve imperial power, and the ethical vacuity of those in power. But as the stalker Shrike emerges as one of the heroes of the series, he increasingly evolves a humanistic subjectivity, especially through his emerging **agency** and, finally, creativity: as such, he encapsulates an ideological imperative that underlies this literature.

Children's literature in general has worked with a constantly evolving humanist subject, responsive to social and cultural changes in the world around, and its exponents can perhaps find assurance in the terms in which major thinkers such as Edward Said and Terry Eagleton advocate humanism or humanistic ideas. Said argues that there is clear evidence for the historical impact of human agency, moved by ideals of justice and equality, and for the affiliated notion that humanistic ideals of liberty and learning promote resistance to despotism and tyranny. Eagleton also affirms a need to recognize some absolute truths, such as the evils of racism, the oppression of women and the vulnerability of the natural environment, because such common grounds enable collective political action. The major themes of modern children's literature are reflected here. [JS]

See also Chapters 1 and 2.

Further reading

Davies (1996), Eagleton (2003), Halliwell and Mousley (2003), Said (2004), Soper (1986), **Stephens** and McCallum (1998).

HUNT, PETER (1945–) A critic, lecturer, editor and novelist who became the first children's literature specialist to be appointed Professor of English at a British university. Based at Cardiff University, Hunt came to prominence in the field of children's literature through his essays on **childist criticism** (Hunt, 1984a, 1984b) in which he challenges the relevance of established critical approaches to children's books. In *Criticism, Theory and*

Children's Literature he confronts a number of prominent theorists, uncovering shortcomings in the narrative theories of **Propp** and Rimmon-Kenan, for example (Hunt, 1991, pp. 119–20); this forthright stance is evident throughout his career. He typically establishes his critical position through incisive close reading; when he exposes the lack of 'adjectival imagination' in *The Lion, the Witch and the Wardrobe*, he critiques not only the text but also the theoretical and cultural frameworks shaping it (p. 108). A prolific writer and editor, he has published numerous books and articles on children's literature and been instrumental in developing postgraduate study in children's literature.

As a novelist, he has published two short books for young children and four novels for young adults, including *Backtrack* (1986). The postmodern playfulness of this book suggests that his work as a novelist is intimately tied to his concerns as a critic. In his 'childist' articles he calls for more adventurous children's books that mirror the complexity of techniques utilized in other media and which refuse the 'attitude of mind that says, "This is what can be understood; this is how books shall be"' (Hunt, 1984b, p. 198). The 'tricks' he observes at work in TV and film, 'flashbacks and flashforwards, alternative stories, complex cross-cutting' (p. 199), could equally describe the narrative devices at work in *Backtrack*, which demonstrates his refusal to underestimate young readers; as novelist and critic he seeks to create and identify an active role for the reading child. Professor Emeritus since 2005, he continues to produce

critical and historical resources (e.g. Hunt, 2006) essential to this burgeoning field of academic study. [LS]

Further reading

Hunt (1991, 1994, 2004, 2006).

HYBRIDITY A highly contested term in cultural criticism and **postcolonial** theory which refers to how individuals and groups develop transcultural identities and forms. The main theorist of hybridity is Homi **Bhabha**, who contends that **colonial** settings are characterized by *ambivalence*, a state in which repulsion and attraction coexist, inflecting cross-cultural relationships as well as subject formation. Bhabha usefully identifies the complexity of colonial and postcolonial relationships and argues against simple, black-and-white distinctions between colonized and colonizer. Further, Bhabha develops the concept of a colonial version of *mimicry*, the process whereby colonized subjects imitate (and mock) their colonial rulers, so reducing their power and authority. The concept of hybridity is contentious because it is sometimes treated merely as a form of cultural syncretism in which elements of different cultures mix and match, without reference to how social, economic and political relationships of power affect people's capacity for **agency**. Moreover, people from indigenous and minority groups have often objected to the implication that they exist in a neither/nor state, caught between cultures and criticized for their lack of 'authenticity'. Miscegenation or *métissage* (interracial union) was regarded in many colonial settings as a dangerous and transgressive act, threatening European prestige and leading to moral degeneracy. Robert Young argues that these racially charged attitudes of contempt for the mixed-race subject colour contemporary versions of hybridity. Other theorists point to the potential for hybrid forms of art and literary production to undermine the foundations of colonial discourse and its claims to superiority. [CB]

See also Chapter 4.

Further reading

Bhabha (1994), Brah and Combes (2000), Randall (2000), Young (1995).

ID The most primal of the three **agencies** of the psyche in **Freud**'s structural model (the other two being the **ego** and the **superego**), the id strives for immediate satisfaction of drives and appetites. As the seat of the instincts, the id's contents are **unconscious**; some of them are inborn, while some are acquired through repression. The id has no morals or limits, does not understand temporality and is fundamentally selfish, thus it exerts continual pressure on the ego to fulfil its demands even when those demands go against social mores, ethical interactions between people or long-term somatic benefits. It wants what it wants when it wants it, no matter the consequences. Examples of characters in children's literature who operate solely on id-based principles include the Cat from Dr Seuss's *The Cat in the Hat*, and Templeton from E. B. White's *Charlotte's Web*. [KC]

See also Chapter 7.

Further reading

Freud (1961, 1966), Rollin and West (1999).

IDEOLOGICAL STATE APPARATUSES A term coined by Louis Althusser in his essay 'Ideology and Ideological State Apparatuses', in which he points out that institutions like the church, education and the family are complicit in maintaining the existing order of things; that is, in ensuring that various inequalities in terms of wealth and power are seen as natural, rather than socially sustained. In this, Althusser drew on Gramsci's notion of hegemony, where the latter makes the point that power is not usually sustained by repressive force in modern capitalist societies; rather, it is maintained by the willing compliance of citizens who see society as being naturally and justly organized in a particular way. One can see the power of ISAs in a number of children's literary texts, for example the power of the church in Philip Pullman's *His Dark Materials* trilogy, of whites over **other** groups (blacks in Mildred Taylor's *Roll of Thunder, Hear My Cry*, Pakistanis in Jan Needle's *My Mate Shofiq*; Malorie Blackman adeptly foregrounds the ISAs by reversing the black/white polarity in *Noughts & Crosses*), or of males over females, as in Anne Fine's *Bill's New Frock*. Obviously, children's books are themselves a product of such ISAs as publishing houses, schools and the family and should in no way be seen as neutral in the way they depict 'reality'. [DR]

See also Chapter 6.

Further reading

Althusser (2001), McCallum (1999), Plaistow (2006).

IDEOLOGY This concept refers to the system of beliefs which a society shares and uses to make sense of the world and which, therefore, pervades the texts produced by that society. While the term is often used in the narrow Marxist sense – that is, of a discourse that promotes 'false consciousness' (misleading ideas about the social and political regimes subjects inhabit) – its wider sense is more applicable in children's literature. According to this more open conception, all aspects of textual discourse, from story outcomes to the expressive forms of language, are informed and shaped by ideology. Texts produced for children thus serve to sustain, and sometimes redefine, social values that are assumed to be shared by text and audience, and they perform the cognitive function of supplying a meaningful organization of the social attitudes and relationships which constitute narrative plots. Ideologies can, therefore, be 'good' or 'bad' depending on the consequences of the social practices based on them. In the last quarter of the twentieth century, for example, children's literature was heavily committed to transforming ideologies of race and gender. In part the process aspires to change a subject's ideological assumptions, but many overtly interrogative texts also encourage audiences to think critically about the ideals they advocate because all ideologies are socially and historically contingent.

Such consciousness is important, for if a child is to participate in society and achieve some measure of personal **agency** within its forms or structures, he or she must learn to understand and negotiate the various **signifying** codes society uses to order itself. The principal code is language (both verbal and visual) and then for children's literature the various textual codes of fiction, picturebook, poetry and so on. Because texts are constructed out of language, and ideology is formulated in and through language, an ideology-free text is unthinkable.

Because children's literature is persistently concerned with social issues and values, books may openly advocate attitudes or ideological positions, although advocacy is mostly implicit in narrative forms and outcomes. Since fictive characters and actions are broadly isomorphic with actions in the actual world of readers, however, and characters are generally depicted as developing a changed perception by the narrative close, a text embeds an ideology. Where a text's implicit ideology reflects a writer's unexamined assumptions, it is often the case that these are assumptions taken for granted in the culture that produces and consumes the text.

The ideology implicit in the form of assumed social structures and habits of thought can be a powerful vehicle for affirming that 'this is the way things are'. Closure, in particular, has crucial ideological impact. How a narrative resolves the complications of story, both to arrive at a satisfying ending and to achieve a coherent significance, affirms the social function of ideology to sustain or redefine social attitudes and relationships. The closing dialogue of Robin McKinley's *Rose Daughter*, after Beauty has discovered that the best outcome is for the Beast to retain his bestial form, is a succinct example:

' ... I love my Beast, and I would miss him very much if he went away from me and left me with some handsome stranger.'

'Then everything is exactly as it should be,' said the Beast.

(McKinley, 1997, p. 301)

A highly complex novel thus concludes with a simple affirmation of the value of love between people, grounded in human qualities and an intersubjective relationship rather than appearances. Readers may regard this as an obvious 'truth' and agree with the Beast that the ending is 'exactly' right, but that doesn't elide the fact that it is also a profoundly ideological ending, while neither articulated nor acknowledged as such.

The example also illustrates how language is permeated by ideology. Almost every signifying word in Beauty's utterance has negative or positive connotations interacting within a single semantic field: 'I love . . . Beast . . . miss him . . . if he went away . . . left me . . . handsome stranger.' The ideological subtlety lies in the transfer of 'handsome' from the positive to the negative pole of romance. It is important to bear in mind here that Beauty has made the decision for both of them, and the ending transforms the outcome from a romantic discourse of femininity to a third-wave feminist valorization of inter**subjectivity**.

Rose Daughter demonstrates how a novel can enact resistance to a cultural ideology – in this case, of a form of gendered behaviour. Using a known story, McKinley enables resistance through a negotiation of **intertextual** space wherein the **patriarchal** discourses which position female characters within feminine discourse are questioned and challenged. Such a strategy constructs a narrative in which the **focalizing** female character comes to recognize this positioning process and the nature of its oppressiveness, in order to seek an alternative and more personally empowered subject position for herself. Reader alignment with the point of view of the focalizing character, together with an evaluation of that point of view, constructs a reading position from which the narrative outcomes are affirmed as narratively coherent and socially satisfactory. Insofar as the outcomes conform to a feminist agenda, the implied reading position constitutes a feminist reading position – and a 'preferable' ideology displaces a less preferable one. [JS]

See also Chapters 2–6.

Further reading

Hollindale (1988), McCallum (1999), Roman *et al.* (1988), **Stephens** (1992a).

IMAGINARY In **Lacanian** psychoanalysis, the Imaginary is one of three orders (the other two being the **Real** and the **Symbolic**) that distinguish the various ways human beings process their experience. Though linked both semantically and conceptually with illusion and fantasy, the Imaginary is crucial to the formation of the ego, as it is the realm of images and ideals that allows the child to imagine her or himself as whole, competent and autonomous. Because it is a realm of images, however, these ideations are limited to what can be seen on the surface and are thus deceptively simplistic, as they tend to ignore underlying complexities and depend on reductive binary oppositions. For instance, those people and things that most conform to a child's imaginary ideals are seen as good and/or right, while those things that are farthest from these concepts are bad and/or wrong. The Imaginary is thus the seat of unexplored hate and prejudice as well as love and loyalty. The danger with the Imaginary lies in its power to captivate and immobilize the subject through the power of the specular image, much like Narcissus; it is only through the transformation of images into words that the subject can move beyond identification into a complex critical stance towards his or her own images. The Imaginary comes into being during the **mirror stage**, when a child adopts a mirror image as an illusory representation of the self; fiction also plays a large role in furnishing the images that populate the Imaginary. [KC]

See also Chapter 7.

Further reading

Lacan (1988c, 1993, 2006).

INTERPELLATION This concept is generally derived from Louis Althusser's 'Ideology and **Ideological State Apparatuses**' (1971), where it is defined as the mechanism that underlies the recognition and adoption of an **ideology** and its practices. The practices of powerful social institutions – religion, **patriarchy**, educational institutions, capitalism, corporate power and globalized consumer cultures, socialism and so on – reproduce themselves because individuals, who are born

within the domain of some form of ideology, are 'hailed' (interpellated) to participate in these practices as 'subjects': individuals experience moments of recognition, in which they recognize themselves because they have been hailed in a particular way, and their subjection to the dominant authority is thereby sustained. The impact may seem more powerful because identity is constructed from frames of different kinds: some apparatuses of interpellation are pedagogical (school systems) and others are **performative** (globalized culture). In post-industrial societies, in which production is driven not by need but by producing and satisfying consumer **desires**, individuals are interpellated by performing these manufactured desires. M. T. Anderson's *Feed* (2002) pivots on this principle.

Two implications for children's literature arise here. First, what sources of resistance are available? Second, to what extent are readers interpellated by textual processes? The 'bad' citizen is Althusser's term for subjects who resist interpellation, but while they thus invite punishment, they also create a possibility for social change. Readers may likewise resist the ideology of a text because, as Mikhail **Bakhtin** argued, literary production is a dialogic process that brings together a multiplicity of social discourses, including the practicality that any subject position offered to an implied reader is set against the subject position brought to the text by an actual reader. While some textual strategies will succeed in interpellating a reader as a particular subject – a reader who feels better informed and wiser *in a* *particular way* than the represented characters, say – there will always be elements in the text that open up other possibilities for response. A good example is Babette Cole's *Prince Cinders* (1987), which overtly intervenes in gender assumptions, but its perspective can be destabilized by oppositional ways of reading the ending. [JS]

See also Chapters 5 and 6.

Further reading

McCallum (1999), **Trites** (2000), Vanden Bossche (2005).

INTERTEXTUALITY Reflecting a modern understanding of textuality, intertextuality is the recognition that meaning is not contained simply within any given text, but emerges from the relationships between a text and other texts and/or cultural contexts. A work is not the product of an individual imaginative act but is made out of prior works, in a very wide sense, and becomes a site within which multiple voices, discourses and **subjectivities** intersect. These other texts are generally referred to as intertexts, or, where direct citation or allusion seems evident, pre-texts. Intertextual meaning is thus the meaning that exists *in the space between* a text and its intertexts, and these in turn extend well beyond literary or written texts. Contemporary children may connect a focused text with previously read fictions, including other works by the author concerned; well-known story patterns such as **myths**, nursery rhymes or **fairy stories**; film, illustration and television programmes; popular culture texts such as cartoons, electronic games, comic books, advertisements and songs; and cultural practices of other kinds. One of the most original elements in the 'Harry Potter' series, the game of quidditch, offers a clear example: while the rules of the game are not fully articulated, the game makes sense in relation to other ball games; that is, readers comprehend the game because its rules are intertextual.

A text can relate to other texts or cultural discourses by (1) directly quoting, alluding to or retelling other literary or non-literary works; (2) relating to or modelling itself on a particular **genre**, sharing recognizable literary codes and conventions around such elements as content, structure, character types and patterns of represented behaviour (**school stories** and quest narratives are evident intertexts for the 'Harry Potter' series, for example); (3) seeking to **parody**, pastiche or even overthrow its pre-texts (J. R. R. Tolkien's *The Lord of the Rings* has been parodied in works as diverse as Michael de Larrabeiti's 'Borribles' series [1976–86] and Andy Griffiths' **carnivalesque** *The Day My Bum Went Psycho* [2001]); (4) being interpreted in relation to subsequent texts: the operation of intertextuality may be achronological, especially since young readers are apt to encounter 'after-texts' before pre-texts (the Robinsonade genre – stories that use Defoe's *Robinson Crusoe* as a pre-textual model for imposing culture upon wilderness – affords obvious examples). These relationships draw attention to the processes of making meaning, both by authors and readers, and particularly to the ways readers make sense of how pre-texts and subsequent texts interpret each other. Thus, intertextuality not only responds to what producers of texts are doing, and what readers bring to those texts, but can be a stepping stone to other ways of thinking about children's texts: for example, their tendency to be **metafictive**, their concentration on representations of **subjectivity** and their concern with the relationships between high culture and popular culture in the ways we make sense of the world. [JS]

Further reading

Bloome and Egan-Robertson (1993), Culler (1981), **Stephens** (1992a), Wilkie-Stibbs (2004b).

JAGOSE, ANNAMARIE [RUSTOM] (1965–) The author of both award-winning fiction and gender studies criticism, Jagose garnered international attention upon the publication of *Queer Theory* (1996a), an accessible and comprehensive explanation of queer theory and its cultural impact, which remains one of the most cited sources in the area. She argues that queer theory 'focuses on mismatches between sex, gender and **desire**' and resists classification because it is fundamentally indeterminate. 'Queer,' Jagose contends, 'is an identity without an essence' (pp. 3, 96). Queer theory is closely connected with the gay liberation movement in its desire to denaturalize gender and expose it as an oppressive system of classification. However, Jagose also points out that queer theory takes issue with the identity politics that necessarily characterize gay liberation. The vision of queer theory favoured by Jagose involves a radical deconstruction and

interrogation of identity that is not easily applicable to most children's literature. Nevertheless, Jagose's conceptualization of queer theory has proved apposite to a small, but continually increasing, subset of young adult novels which seek to problematize and disrupt the presumed relationship between sex, gender and desire. *Funny Boy* (Shyam Sevadurai, 1994), *Boy Overboard* (Peter Wells, 1997) and the graphic novel *Fun Home: A Family Tragicomic* (Alison Bechdel, 2006) provide fluid and transgressive representations of **subjectivity** that demonstrate multiple incoherencies in the supposedly stable systems that naturalize heterosexuality. A particularly innovative application of Jagose's central arguments pertaining to queer theory can be found in Roderick **McGillis**'s (2003a) analysis of the **fairy tales** of George MacDonald. [VF]

See also Chapter 3.

Further reading

Flanagan (2007), Jagose (1996a), Pennell and **Stephens** (2002).

JAMESON, FREDRIC (1934–) American cultural critic who has published prolifically on **canonical** and popular literature, on film, and on culture and society more generally. Throughout his writing, though, Marxism remains a guiding compass, despite engagements with poststructuralist and **postmodernist** thinking, and attempts to integrate a psychoanalytical dimension. Jameson's ideas usually reward the effort of reading him, though he is renowned for the exacting nature of his prose. This said, *The Political Unconscious* (1981) opens with a very straightforward instruction: 'Always historicize.' The whole notion of a political **unconscious** is a powerful mixture of Marx and **Freud**. Thus, Jameson argues that underlying the surface manifestations of a culture, in literature and the other arts, its repressed elements (or 'political unconscious') can be discerned, albeit never experienced directly. Jameson's defence and celebration of popular culture (both literature and film) have been particularly influential, pointing to the utopian strand such work incorporates, however reactionary it might otherwise be. Finally, he is one of the most interesting writers on postmodernism, neither celebrating nor berating it, but arguing that, as part of the logic of late capitalism, it cannot be ignored.

Many critics in children's literature, as in other areas, tend to allude to Jameson's perceptions, but there is little that could be labelled 'Jamesonian' in approach. It is his 'political unconscious', though, that has probably had the biggest impact, for example, in Patrick Burger's work on Romance, which includes discussion of Tolkien's *Lord of the Rings*. [DR]

See also Chapter 2.

Further reading

Burger (2001), Jameson (2000), Roberts (2000).

JUNG, CARL GUSTAV (1875–1961) Originally a disciple of **Freud**, the Swiss psychologist was far more optimistic than Freud about the therapeutic properties of art. He believed that literature managed to access the collective **unconscious**, where various archetypal figures and symbols could be drawn upon. It is for this reason that **fairy tales**, like **myths** and dreams, are so powerful with their elemental cast of characters – and why there are so many commonalities in stories across cultures (Campbell, 1968). Throughout life, then, a person seeks 'individuation', but this is not in terms of establishing a self-reliant ego; rather, it means connecting successfully and openly with unconscious processes and accepting the shadowy, darker parts of the self ('the shadow' is one of his archetypes). It also means coming to terms with the oppositely gendered part of the self (for males, the 'anima'; for females, the 'animus').

Jung's terminology and concepts have been taken up and developed by many others – often in quite a selective way, though. Terms like 'synchronicity', 'introversion' and 'extraversion' (with the latter's spelling standardly revised) are well known. Archetypal criticism also developed in its own direction, most famously under the Canadian literary critic Northrop **Frye**. Joseph Campbell's *The Hero with a Thousand Faces* (1968) has influenced many writers too, most celebratedly the work of George Lucas, who explicitly acknowledges structuring his 'Star Wars' movies around Campbell's findings. Work drawing more closely on Jung's ideas is found extensively in fairy tale research (e.g. Marie-Louise von Franz; Stein and Corbett, 1991).

However, after his huge popularity in the counterculture of the 1960s,

Jung fell out of favour in cultural studies. The 'linguistic turn' in philosophy made Freud, who focused far more closely on the written word, a preferable theorist for the new French cultural critics. Moreover, Jung's more universalistic approach, together with what was seen as a tendency to typify people according to gender and age, was less acceptable in a period that became far more concerned with 'difference' and with the relativity of knowledge. More recently, though, some scholars have challenged Jung's universalism, arguing that his ideas even prefigure certain poststructuralist notions (e.g. Sugg, 1993; Rowland, 2008). [DR]

Further reading

Jung (1978), Rowland (2008), Stein and Corbett (1991), Sugg (1993).

Kɪᴅ(ᴅ)ᴜʟᴛ A kiddult (or sometimes 'kidult') is a man or woman who refuses to 'put away childish things', despite advancing age and social convention strongly suggesting she or he should. In the mid-1990s, such 'childish things' included Sony Playstations, scooters, school uniforms, school discos, cartoons, Disney films and, above all, the world of 'Harry Potter'. At its height, the kiddult phenomenon expanded to include many children's (and more rarely, young adult) books and family films, particularly **animated** ones (*Shrek*, *Toy Story*, *Wallace and Gromit*), as well as any adult fashion or music with a childhood-associated, kitsch element (the 'Lolita look', Baby Spice, Mandy Patinkin's *Kidults* [2000]). But for a decade, J. K. Rowling's 'Harry Potter' books were

the *sine qua non*, the badge of honour of any self-respecting kiddult. Fittingly, the first chapter of the first volume sets the 'perfectly normal, thank you very much' Dursley parents against kiddult-like 'weirdos' who dress unsuitably in green and purple cloaks (Rowling, 1997, pp. 7–8).

In an earlier decade, critics and psychologists would have said that these socially immature adults were suffering from 'Peter Pan syndrome' (Kiley, 1983). Indeed, the **myth** of the *puer aeternus* dates back to Roman times (Bacchus is so described in Ovid's *Metamorphoses*). But the kiddult can be seen as the product of our particular historical moment, when a generation of affluent, Western, middle-class, mostly childless adults reached their 30s and 40s with time and money to spend discovering their 'inner child'. The established use of the term is in contrast to its earliest known appearance, where it refers to entertainment likely to appeal to children and young adults, rather than to adults masquerading as children (Martin, 1985). Menhaj Huda's *Kidulthood* (2006) also gives the term a different connotation, using it to describe inner-city London teenagers, mostly black and poor, rather than white and affluent. But such exceptions aside, a kiddult (noun) generally refers to an adult who engages in youth culture (cf. adultescent, babydult, boomeranger, kipper, middlescent, parachute kid, rejuvenile, thresholder). 'Kiddult' and '**crossover**' would appear to be synonymous terms when applied adjectivally to literature, film and other artistic production, but in fact they carry diametrically opposite connotations. The former connotes adults playfully, often self-consciously, transgressing social norms, whereas the latter emphasizes the moral weight and artistic excellence of children's and young adult literature. Unlike 'crossover', 'kiddult' is used either ironically (by those in favour) or as a term of abuse (by those against), and in the latter usage, appears in the context of general invectives against the 'infantilization' of Western culture. [RF]

See also Chapter 8.

Further reading

Barfield (2005), Falconer (2009).

KLEIN, MELANIE (1882–1960) An Austrian psychoanalyst whose ideas have been influential with a number of children's literature critics, perhaps because Klein herself worked so extensively with children, developing 'play analysis' involving toys. She rejected **Freud**'s stress on the **Oedipus complex**, which had always made girls' development problematic. Instead, she concentrated on the pre-Oedipal period, especially the child's relationship with the mother's body. She sees fantasy as a central component in coming to terms with reality. Thus, she speaks about the child dealing with 'objects' rather than actual people (hence the term 'object-relations theory' for her approach). One of the first objects encountered is the mother's breast, which the child splits into two parts: the good breast, giving milk, and the bad breast, withholding it. The child develops by processes of projection and introjection; that is, by separating out wanted from unwanted

aspects of objects, taking on board what it wants and rejecting what it fears. Subsequent writers have found Klein's exploration of the pre-Oedipal particularly powerful, suggesting non-**patriarchal** models of development, and of mother–daughter relationships.

In children's literature, Steven Daniels (1990) has explored *The Velveteen Rabbit* from this perspective and Margaret and Michael Rustin have a whole book of criticism which draws on Kleinian insights, significantly entitled *Narratives of Love and Loss* (1987). The latter looks at the way that children in many classic children's books develop through splitting the world into good and bad parts (as do many **fairy tales**), projecting their fears and anxieties accordingly; the Rustins also examine the way that objects in the stories function as 'symbolic containers' for the protagonists, such as the plastic Indian for Omri, the boy protagonist of Lynne Reid Banks's *The Indian in the Cupboard* (1981). [DR]

See also Chapter 7.

Further reading

Daniels (1990), Klein (1986), Rustin and Rustin (1987).

KRISTEVA, JULIA (1941–) A very influential Bulgarian born, French-based poststructuralist thinker, who brings together psychoanalytical, philosophical and linguistic insights in her richly varied work, which also includes a number of novels. Her intellectual roots are varied, but the influence of Mikhail **Bakhtin** and Jacques **Lacan** is particularly evident. Her concept of intertextuality can, therefore, be seen to grow out of dialogism: the notion that later texts not only allude to earlier ones but also engage in a dialogue with them. As a consequence, no text is a closed book: it is always open to revision, to reader intervention. This can occur in a general, generic sense, or on a more specific basis – as, for example, with Jan Needle's *Wild Wood* (1981), which doesn't just make reference to Kenneth Grahame's *The Wind in the Willows* (1908) but also actively criticizes its middle-class bias. In *Revolution in Poetic Language* (1974), Kristeva takes issue with Lacan's notion of the Symbolic as initiating language. She argues that there is an earlier, pre-Oedipal form of language, the Semiotic, which arises from the child's relationship to its mother: in the sound of her voice, its timbre, melody and rhythm, and, beyond that, in the mother's body, her rocking and jiggling, the rise and fall of breath, her pulse. This is a very different form of language from that based on precise signification, on grammatical placing. Clearly, nonsense verse, such as Spike Milligan's 'On the Ning Nang Nong' or much of Edward Lear's work, celebrates the Semiotic. But Kristeva's point is that one form does not supersede the other; rather, they continue alongside, the one animating the other.

A related juxtaposition of terms occurs in Kristeva's distinction between men's time (linear, chronological) and 'woman's time', which is cyclical and rhythmic. One can often find these different conceptions in children's books, like *Tom's Midnight Garden* (1958), where the logical and ordered time of Tom's Uncle Alan is set against the more mythical time of Hetty. In *Powers of Horror* (1982), Kristeva introduces probably her most influential concept, the abject, which is clearly linked to the Semiotic. For despite the Semiotic's appeal, a child has to establish its identity as a separate being, becoming a subject by expelling that which seems to connect it to the mother, while simultaneously realizing that the abject is always part of us. In a later work, *Strangers to Ourselves* (1991), she pursues this line of thought in a more political vein, reflecting her own experience as an émigré.

Kristeva's abject has been particularly taken up by critics of adolescent fiction and film, with links drawn between this concept and her discussion of the adolescent novel as an 'open psychic structure' (e.g. Coats, 2004). Adolescence, in other words, is seen as a time when the boundaries of one's identity are once more fluid and open, and one can refashion oneself. The popularity of horror and Gothic motifs in adolescent literature can thus be seen as invoking this simultaneous attraction to, and repulsion at, the abject: 'how gross is that?', as one might say. Kristeva's investigation of depression in *Black Sun* (1989) has also made her work attractive to those investigating the darker side of adolescent fiction, sometimes termed depressive literature (Westwater, 2000). [DR]

See also Chapters 7 and 8.

Further reading

Kristeva (1982, 1986, 1990), Westwater (2000).

LACAN, JACQUES (1901–81) Along with **Derrida** and **Foucault**, Lacan is one of the key poststructuralist thinkers, giving a distinctly linguistic emphasis to **Freudian** psychoanalytic theory and practice. Some of his key ideas, though, date back to the 1930s, particularly his notion of the **mirror stage**, where the child first sees itself as an entity. But as Lacan noted, this **Imaginary** identification (i.e. identification with an image) involves the child misrecognizing itself. In other words, a child does not have the seeming completeness that it is presented with; furthermore, the image is separate from the child itself. This tendency to identify with idealizations continues throughout life, whether it is to partners, film stars or other things (cars and other consumer goods). But if the Imaginary presents the subject as standing outside itself in a mirror image, the **Symbolic** (the second order of being) makes alienation more a central condition of existence. The Symbolic, essentially, is language. Lacan argues that, as we learn words, we lose the things themselves: empty **signifiers** replace them; 'MUM' is not the being we cleave to and experience tactilely, oflactorily and so on. Here Lacan reworks Freud's notion of the **Oedipus complex**. Instead of a fear of actual castration, Lacan argues that it is language that severs us from actuality, and from the mother especially. And what causes this split is the father, representative of the Phallus, the Law. More plainly, society demands that we relinquish the mother and take up a subject position in the world that ties us to certain signifiers (a name, a gender, etc.).

With this move into the world of signifiers, Lacan argues, our **unconscious** is born. Words, forming chains in sentences, are always unsatisfactory, never capturing the fullness of being we think we once experienced. In a state of lack, therefore, we always **desire** that former state and are always driven – through identifications, through the sentences we speak – to regain that earlier sense of plenitude. The unconscious is thus an effect of language and is, therefore, structured by it (through puns, metaphorical and metonymic links, etc.). Lacan's third order is the **Real**, which is what stands outside symbolization: the brute materiality of things.

Lacan's influence on cultural studies has been profound, despite his notoriously difficult writing. A number of feminists explored the notion that we are all castrated by language, hence no one possesses the phallus – although men might think they do; thus women, being seen as **other** in the **patriarchal** symbolic order, saw ways to challenge their positioning. Lacan's theories have also helped link **ideology** to notions of identity (one becomes **interpellated** by language); in film studies, the whole cinematic apparatus has been interpreted in Lacanian terms, with Laura Mulvey drawing out the patriarchal implications of the camera replicating the mirror phase of identification, except that the camera's gaze is always male and voyeuristic, privileging men's pleasure. In literary studies, too, drawing on Lacan's own studies (famously, his reading of Poe's 'The Purloined Letter'), there has been much significant work, Jacqueline **Rose**'s study of children's fiction being seminal. Despite criticisms that his work lacks empirical proof, that his terms are inconsistent, that his algebraic symbols, and, indeed, much of his prose, are unintelligible, his ideas continue to attract attention, especially as much of his work is only now beginning to be published, let alone translated. In many countries, and Latin America in particular, Lacanian psycho-analysis has become the orthodox therapy. Moreover, prolific writers like Slavoj **Žižek** have given his ideas new life. [DR]

See also Chapter 7.

Further reading

Coats (2004), Fink (1995), Homer (2005), Lacan (2006), Rudd (2006b).

LEGEND A folk narrative form distinct from **folktale** and **myth**, the legend is a traditional historical tale attributed with truth-value, but at most containing a mixture of fact and fiction. One of the best-known examples in English is the legend of King Arthur, which, although scholars have shown it to have a shadowy historical basis in the period at the close of the Roman occupation of Britain, accreted a vast amount of unhistorical material through the Middle Ages. Thus, popular knowledge of pivotal events in the legend – the sword in the stone, the affair between Lancelot and Guenevere, the evil of Mordred – are romance additions. As this example shows, while a legend is popularly believed to be historical, it characteristically consists of folk beliefs that are considered to be unofficial knowledge: what everyone knows.

A gerundive of the Latin verb *legere*, 'to read', signifying 'what should be read', and hence suggesting a story productive of moral edification, the term 'legend' was long associated with the lives of the saints as recorded in Christian tradition in the Western world. The best-known example is the compilation by Jacobus de Voragine, the *Legenda Aurea* or *Golden Legend*, in which Jacobus constructed numerous saints' lives from their commemoration in the church liturgy and from more popular hagiographical sources. In 1969 the Roman Catholic Church decreed that a large number of these 'saints' were indeed legendary and acknowledged that the narratives associated with them were derived from misunderstandings (as in the case of the popular Saint Christopher, protector of travellers, derived from a misinterpretation of *Christopher*, 'Christ bearer'), appropriations of pagan deities (as with Ireland's St Bridget) and so on. Such stories had survived because they were thought to have an historical foundation.

In its most basic form, the legend (equivalent to the German term *Sage*) is a simple structure, consisting of a single narrative motif. The legend of the Pied Piper of Hamelin, for example, has been retold at various times as historical fiction, but generally as an elaboration of the single motif of a town's breaching of a contract and the subsequent revenge exacted upon it.

As a folk narrative form, legends flourish in contemporary society and are accepted as believable because they contain a blend of fact and fiction. Factual events involving, for example, notorious killers are apt to precipitate an increase in legend-telling. The mid-twentieth-century urban legend of 'The Hook' – a story about a couple who flee after being disturbed while making-out in a car and who then find a prosthesis jammed in the door – proliferated in response to stories of an actual atrocity, but were also influenced by the horror film **genre**. Such stories circulated widely among school children, and hence are useful material for children's writers, especially in comic genres. At a more literary level, David Almond's *Clay* establishes a dialogue among thematically related, well-known legends from diverse traditions: the classical Greek legend of Prometheus, the Jewish legend of the golem and modern 'Frankenstein' legends stemming from James Whale's 1931 film of Mary Shelley's novel. Like 'The Hook', which extends geographically from England to the United States and Australia, *Clay* is an excellent, albeit literary, example of how a legend may not be merely local and historical but a story which moves in space and across cultures. [JS]

Further reading

Bennett *et al.* (1987), Dégh (2001), Wilson (1998).

LESNIK-OBERSTEIN, KARÍN (1965–) Director of the Centre for International Research in Childhood: Literature, Culture, Media (CIRCL), where she followed Tony Watkins in running what was the first MA in Children's Literature in the United Kingdom. She came to prominence after the publication of *Children's Literature: Criticism and the Fictional Child* (1994), where, pursuing Jacqueline **Rose**'s argument

about the 'impossibility of children's fiction', she extended Rose's case to suggest that the criticism of children's literature was also impossible in that it needs 'to find the good book for the child' (Lesnik-Oberstein, 1994, p. 3). In other words, children's literature criticism is premised on already knowing the child (its wants and needs) and hence on knowing which books will be appropriate for it. Whereas some might see this as applying to **didactic** work only, Lesnik-Oberstein argues that, at root, this material is no different from supposedly 'amusing' or escapist literature. Just as all literature for children seeks to define the child in some way (Rose's claim), so critics in this area respond by indicating the extent to which texts have indeed produced what such (constructed) children will really like. The 'real child' is, therefore, not only a *sine qua non* of their criticism but is also something that stands outside that criticism, beyond words. Following poststructuralist thinkers like Jacques **Derrida**, for Lesnik-Oberstein there can never be any extra-textual child, and attempts to ground arguments by referring to 'real children' are merely rhetorical flourishes, such children being themselves constructed through particular discourses (of law, education, the family, etc.).

In this, her one monograph to date, Lesnik-Oberstein opposes children's literature to psychotherapy which, she argues, in its attention to the individual child, and in its recognition of the dynamic and constructed nature of that relationship, can perhaps allow the child voice some authenticity. However, in using the vocabulary of 'therapist' and 'patient' (Lesnik-Oberstein, 1994,

p. 185), Lesnik-Oberstein invokes the standard criticism of those feminists who reconfigured the therapist as 'the rapist'; that is, the **Foucauldian** (and **Lacanian**) notion of normalization in therapy that, at heart, involves issues of power, with the psychoanalyst being the one presumed to know. It is hard to see why this professional relationship is regarded as more valid than that of a mother/parent and child engaged in conversation or, indeed, in storytelling.

Lesnik-Oberstein has also been criticized for smuggling in essentialist notions of the child in her insistence on its lack of voice and, conversely, in overrating the **agency** of the adult. The child is thus positioned as ineluctably different from an adult, almost in **Romantic** terms, rather than as a subject also caught up in particular relationships of power and discourse.

Despite these criticisms, Lesnik-Oberstein and her colleagues at Reading have produced an impressive body of work that holds fast to its premises (albeit the psychoanalytical slant has not reappeared). This said, after proclaiming that 'children's literature criticism is disposed of' (1994, p. 167), a later collection entitled *Children's Literature: New Approaches* (2004) was something of a surprise, seeming rather to suggest its opposite; in Mark Twain's terms, that news of children's literature criticism's death had been exaggerated. At the time of writing there seems to be something of a stand-off between these supposedly 'new' and 'old' approaches, despite Perry **Nodelman**'s (2007) public call for more open dialogue. [DR]

See also Chapters 1 and 2.

Further reading

Lesnik-Oberstein (1994, 2004), Nodelman (2007), Rudd (2004b).

LOCKE, JOHN (1632–1704) A key thinker in modern formulations of the child, which are detailed in his very influential *Some Thoughts Concerning Education* (1693), regularly reprinted throughout the eighteenth century. Rather than see the infant as innately sinful, or, indeed, as innately rational, Locke argued that the child comes into the world as a *tabula rasa*, or 'blank slate' (he did use other metaphors, but this one has stuck), and learns by experience; corporal punishment should, therefore, be avoided as much as possible.

The child should be encouraged to follow its own interests, though guided by adults, and explore the outside world. In gaining knowledge of the world, books could play a key role, especially if illustrated (the pictures would help explain things). However, at the time there were few books around that Locke felt he could recommend, especially as he thought the frivolous and frightening should be avoided. He does suggest Aesop's *Fables* and *Reynard the Fox*, though (two of the earliest printed books in England). Locke always emphasizes, however, that reading be made amusing, recommending a number of instructional aids (such as dice) to make learning to read more engaging (he, therefore, warns against using the Bible as early reading material, though he is in favour of religious education). It is thought that Locke's ideas had a powerful influence on how the children's book industry was to develop in England, especially on the pioneer publisher John Newbery, who championed the idea of instruction through amusement. [DR]

Further reading

Pickering (1982).

MᴄGɪʟʟɪs, Rᴏᴅᴇʀɪᴄᴋ (1945–) A highly respected and prolific Canadian critic of children's literature. Roderick McGillis seeks to address how an adult, and an academic, might orient himself (in this case) towards a literature that is multifarious, often amorphous, and where, notoriously, the target audience produces neither the creative texts nor the critical and analytic discourses that comment on those texts and, at times, contribute to their shaping. He has done this not only as a critic but also through his contribution to the field as an editor of collections of essays and of journals, and, in particular, for various editorial roles for the *Children's Literature Association Quarterly* (1986–2001) and on the editorial board of ten other journals. He is an engaging storyteller, too, often taking this art into schools.

In a more complex way, McGillis contributes to the scholarly understanding of children's literature through the flexibility and fluidity of his theoretical and critical stance. Around the midpoint of his career, he wrote the book for which he is best known, *The Nimble Reader*. There he declares himself 'fundamentally a formalist' (1996, p. vii), although in practice that positioning only points to a principle evident throughout his career: that analysis is most successfully communicative when close attention is paid to the text but is also grounded self-consciously in an awareness that a piece of writing can be read in many ways and through many entry points. Thus, a concern with **reader response** is a consistent strand in his work, and his deft analysis (McGillis, 1985) of how a child's apparent misreading of a story reveals the way in which narrative form evokes creative, thematically nuanced (but not articulated) responses from children remains exemplary. His later critical writings are always apt to swerve and incorporate examples from actual readers.

The Nimble Reader encapsulates the state of children's literature criticism in the first half of the 1990s, as it tentatively considered where the criticism was coming from and where it might go to. The book was praised for its scope in exploring the relevance to children's literature of a considerable range of contemporary social and literary theories. It offers, for example, probably the first lucid account of the possible applications of some of **Lacan**'s theories. On the other hand, its conception of feminism was already inadequate, and it omits all **postcolonial** literature and criticism, perhaps because its focus primary texts are written by white (mainly American) males. These areas are indeed expounded in his monograph about *A Little Princess*, also 1996. McGillis subsequently extended discussion of postcolonial literatures, especially in *Voices of the Other* (2000). He also has many informative things to say about voices from popular culture, as in his study of the *Captain Underpants* series, for example, which incorporates a broad range of cultural theories.

One of the mainstays of McGillis's work, and one of its major contributions, is his interest in nineteenth- and early twentieth-century children's literature. He writes about Frances Hodgson Burnett and Lewis Carroll, but is above all an authority in George MacDonald studies, both the works themselves and their formative role in the English fantasy tradition. [JS]

Further reading

McGillis (1985, 1996, 2002a).

MAGIC(AL) REALISM A term depicting the intermixing of two modes of representation, realism and fantasy, where the emphasis continues to lie with the former. Though the term dates back to the 1920s, it was used in a slightly different way to its later popular usage. The latter gained currency in the 1960s, being applied to Latin American novelists like Gabriel García Márquez, who introduced fantastic elements into what was otherwise a realistic world. One could say that Franz Kafka's story 'Metamorphosis' is the archetype, matter-of-factly describing how the main character wakes up one morning to find that he's been transformed into a giant insect, but, apart from this one impossible event, the story otherwise resists any move into a fantasy world.

In children's literature, David Almond and Sonya Hartnett are probably the most well-known exponents of this form of writing. In the former's *Skellig* (1998), for example, a boy encounters a strange being in his garage, who is a mixture of tramp and angelic, winged being. But apart from this magical intrusion, the story otherwise maintains its realistic footing. In Almond's case, he troubles materialistic conceptions of the world, suggesting, like William Blake, that there are mysteries and wonders lurking within the everyday. And in picking up Blake's criticism of the Enlightenment project, which Blake jokingly referred to as 'Newton's sleep', we can see how magic realism is linked to terms like the **uncanny** where, similarly, what is strange and disturbing is found among that which is presumed familiar. Moreover, we can also discern magic realism's political roots, as the term was initially used by writers from former colonies, where the rule-bound, rationalistic world of the **colonial** powers was shown to conceal alternative worldviews.

Some writers on magic realism (e.g. Bowers, 2004) have argued that children's literature itself has a long tradition of this mode, to be found, for instance, in the Edwardian E. Nesbit's parochial fantasies (e.g. *Five Children and It*, 1902). However, if we follow this line, we seem to lose precisely the hesitation and uncertainty around reality and fantasy that magic realism enacts. The related term 'fantastic realism' might be more applicable for Nesbit and others, where the protagonists continue to marvel at the events occurring (Waller, 2008). [DR]

See also Chapter 7.

Further reading

Bowers (2004), Faris (2004).

MEEK (SPENCER), MARGARET (1925–)
The Grande Dame of literacy, reading
and the 'real books' movement, whose
influence is felt from every British
primary classroom and library to panels of judges for book awards and
World Congresses on reading. From
her first collaboratively edited book,
The Cool Web (1977), to her most
recent, *Coming of Age in Children's
Literature* (2005), Meek has consistently broadened our understanding of
children and of how educationalists
might approach literacy through literature, with her characteristic blend
of philosophically and theoretically
underpinned yet accessible child-based
observations.

Meek joined the Department of
English in the University of London's
Institute of Education in 1968 and
retired in 1990, remaining Emeritus
Reader in Education. During that time
huge developments in the understanding of children's language and thought
took place as theoreticians such as Lev
Vygotsky and Jerome Bruner, together
with researchers like Shirley Brice
Heath, radically influenced educational
thinking. Writing on this subject since
the 1970s, Meek has uniquely been
involved in teaching, researching and
commenting across a bewildering array
of shifts and swings in educational
trends following political intervention
into the teaching of literacy in British
schools. From the child-centred experiential 1970s to the English National
Curriculum stranglehold of the 1980s,
and thence to its much-tampered-with
form in the present, Meek (citing
philosopher Richard Rorty) has
strongly critiqued pupil testing and
teacher accountability: 'Reading and

literacy are crammed with the final
vocabulary of military metaphors:
"strategies", "word-attack skills" and
the like' (Meek, 1992, p. 233). A champion of discursive, imaginative child
readers and teachers of reading through
these troubled and turbulent times,
Meek's has been the voice of reason.

Meek has also invariably been a
collaborator and co-researcher, producing monographs in the 1960s on
Geoffrey Trease and Rosemary
Sutcliff, but soon turning to co-edited
works such as *The Cool Web* (1977), a
formidable anthology of writings on
the form and functions of narrative
with contributions from writers of
children's literature, educationalists
and other theorists. For many teachers
this would have been the first time real
writers such as Maurice Sendak discussed their work for child readers in
aesthetic terms. The picturebook as
critical art form was born. The gauntlet had been thrown down: reading
scheme books were seen to be impov-
erished, whereas literature was celebrated as joyous, surprising and
endlessly rich in its rewards. This has
been Meek's lifelong project.

Meek's research work is grounded
in the real: real contexts, children,
readers, real books. As she puts it in
New Readings, her 'most important
dialogues about reading have been
with children' (Meek, 1992, p. 233).
How Texts Teach (1987), a 'workshop'
publication on emergent readers and
picturebooks, is still probably the most
read book for teachers of early literacy
in England today.

In the context of world literature for
children, reading for Meek is both about
belonging and difference. Literature

addresses the complex relationships of individual and social life, with books constructing identity positions for children, negotiating the wide range of Englishes described in *Children's Literature and National Identity* (2001). Meek believes in literary classics, as her introduction to a new edition of Russell Hoban's *The Mouse and His Child* (1993) and her chapters in *Coming of Age* (2005) prove. But she has always been ahead of the game, writing and lecturing since the 1990s about the need to be more open about what constitutes reading, to 'redescribe' it, given that multi-literacies are an everyday part of twenty-first-century life. Above all else, Meek's work reminds us of the need to question everything; in her own memorable words: 'What if it is otherwise?' [VdR]

Further reading

Meek (1987, 1992, 2001), Meek and Watson (2005).

METAFICTION Generally attributed to William Gass, the term was coined in the 1970s to describe fiction that is self-conscious, that takes fiction itself as its topic. Although originally used to describe recent literary works and often associated with postmodern practices of fiction, metafictional devices can be seen in texts as old as Cervantes' *Don Quixote* (1605/15) and Laurence Sterne's *Tristram Shandy* (1759–67). Hence, it is useful to take Mark Currie's (1995, p. 2) definition of metafiction as a starting point: 'a borderline discourse, . . . a kind of writing which places itself on the border between fiction and criticism, and which takes that border as its subject.' Metafictional texts are, therefore, highly self-reflexive and deliberately seek to disrupt the suspension of disbelief in the reader. This might be achieved through frequent direct address and the use of innovative typographical devices, as in *Tristram Shandy*. Again, it is useful to note that such devices are not exclusive to overtly metafictional texts. As Patricia Waugh argues, metafiction is perhaps best understood as 'a tendency or function inherent in *all* novels' (1984, p. 5).

Many picturebooks have metafictive characteristics. For example, John Scieszka and Lane Smith's *The Stinky Cheese Man and Other Fairly Stupid Tales* (1992) rewrites nine traditional **fairy tales** in a **parodic** manner. This book makes explicit the constructedness of stories by foregrounding and interrogating both artistic and publishing conventions. For instance, the contents page is not conventionally where it should be, and the narrative begins before the title page. Moreover, the boundaries between author, narrator and reader are effectively breached, thus disrupting the expectations of readers and challenging their notions of a unified, coherent text. Another highly metafictive text relying on overt parodic **intertextuality** is Lauren Child's *Who's Afraid of the Big Bad Book?* (2003). In this text, the main character, Herb, falls asleep and finds himself inside a version of the book he has just been reading. Once 'inside' he meets familiar characters from traditional fairy tales. Unfortunately, he had already 'personalized' this book, drawing on it, cutting out things, thus changing the traditional fairy tale narratives. In addition, he had managed to stick some of the pages together with sticky-tape and, in one instance, had repaired the book with one page inverted. Readers, therefore, have to do more than simply turn the page to continue the narrative: they must turn the book upside-down in order to read the dialogue. Moreover, the dialogue itself occasionally needs to be read from the bottom of the page upwards, and sometimes, to be read diagonally. Herb eventually escapes this doctored book-within-a-book by cutting a hole in the page and climbing up onto the text, gripping hold of letters and sentences, eventually returning to the fictional reality 'outside' the big bad book. Metafictive texts such as these, therefore, demand a more writerly engagement from the reader, opening up meaning as opposed to shutting it down. [AMB]

Further reading

Currie (1995), Lyotard (1984), Sipe and Pantaleo (2008), Waugh (1984).

METANARRATIVE Also referred to as *grand narrative* and *master narrative*, it can be understood as both an aspect of literary texts and an aspect of critical understanding, although the two often overlap. Readers will recognize a particular story as, loosely, a variant of an already known story, not so much in its specific plot details as in its overarching shape; for example, a young man goes out into the world equipped with nothing but his own good nature and inherent creativity

and, usually because the social order is beneficent towards such traits, achieves a desirable position in the world. This is not merely a common story pattern, but a pattern of behaviour which affirms some kinds of action, proscribes undesirable behaviour and embodies a version of the culture's **ideologies**. Underlying most children's texts are predetermined horizons of expectation about processes and outcomes, including the values and ideas about the world that may become visible as **teleological** by the end of the narrative. These horizons of expectation are metanarratives, that is, the implicit and usually invisible ideologies, systems and assumptions which operate globally in a society to order knowledge and experience and which take on narrative form in literature. Thus, the notion that truth and justice will – or morally should – prevail is a metanarrative: when a text replicates the metanarratival shape the outcome is socially and emotionally satisfying; if the shape is not replicated, the outcome is recognized as 'tragic'. In this way, metanarratives furnish both the structure for individual narratives and the criteria for perception and appreciation by which sense is made of that structure. Ideas about the social world can thereby seem self-evident, especially since narrative is a form not only of representing but also of constituting reality.

Although, notoriously, Jean-François Lyotard argued that a condition of postmodernity was the emergence of local narratives in place of monolithic metanarratives, the latter continue to hold sway at the level of nation and beyond. It seems reasonable to propose that the following statements have metanarrative force throughout European and English-language children's literature: 'knowledge is important for its own sake'; 'knowledge is a pathway to emancipation and personal growth'; 'when individuals improve their lives, society is a better place'. Such assumptions may appear to be self-evident, and critics may readily find them unobjectionable, to the extent that they function as metanarratives to underpin arguments that knit events, actions and characters into a meaningful and desirable social picture. Feminist criticism, on the other hand, has done much to dismantle **patriarchal** gender metanarratives, and literature has followed. Other kinds of questioning may also occur – for example, towards the end of the twentieth century, youth literature began expressing unease about surveillance technologies in everyday life (Jan Mark's *Useful Idiots* [2004] is a good example). In contrast, a common plot motif in TV detective dramas whereby CCTV or DNA registers are used to solve crimes, and justice is obstructed if these tools are unavailable, implies acceptance of, or blindness to, an emerging metanarrative that pulls together surveillance, personal safety, terrorism and a voluntary abandoning of some human freedoms. Because metanarrative is, in short, the consensual scheme of things on a large scale, such an example illustrates how social practices feared by one generation may be incorporated into a subsequent generation's uninterrogated metanarratives. [JS]

See also Chapter 5.

Further reading

Klein (1995), Lyotard (1984), **Stephens** and McCallum (1998).

MIMESIS A Greek word usually translated in English as 'mime' or 'imitate', which, in literary criticism, refers to the way texts represent reality. Plato uses the term to distinguish between reality and artistic representations of it, concluding that mimesis is an illusion and, therefore, untruthful. Aristotle was less interested in the philosophical dimensions of mimesis than in the technicalities of how it is achieved and the social value of realistic representations of others' lives and possible ways of behaving. It is from Aristotle's *Poetics* that current usage derives, particularly as developed by Eric Auerbach (2003), whose *Mimesis: The Representation of Reality in Western Literature* (1946) is the definitive study of the mode. Auerbach examines and compares how writers have represented everyday life, making it feel true to lived experience, from classical and early Christian writers to Virginia Woolf. Arguably in an age of reality television, webcams, high-fidelity film and graphics, and cyberspace, there is a need to reappraise the term. [KR]

See also Chapter 6.

Further reading

Auerbach (2003), Nightingale (2006), Potolsky (2006).

MIRROR STAGE A concept formulated by Jacques **Lacan**, the mirror stage is the event that inaugurates the infant into subjecthood. At some point between 6 and 18 months of age, a baby recognizes her own image in a mirror. Though this moment is one of jubilation for the infant, it is one of alienation, nevertheless, because from this point forward, the child's experience of her body is replaced by an image to which she must connect through identification. The differences between her embodied experience and her apprehended image are profound: while her body is here, its image is over there; her body is three dimensional, the image is flat; her body feels fragmented, the image is coherent; her body is unsure of its boundaries, the image is self-contained. Hence, the image is both self and **other** for the child, and by identifying with it she begins a process whereby she will come into being as a subject deeply invested in the Other. By taking the image as a representation of herself, the child enters into a new way of conceiving reality through a process of projection and introjection of herself onto various images and representations that ultimately constitute her sense of self. For instance, she might identify with the princess in a **fairy tale**, and thus include the princess's qualities (beauty, kindness, passivity) and potential (heterosexual marriage, a castle, servants) as aspects or ideals for her to aspire to in her – or, equally, to exchange pronouns, in his – own life. [KC]

See also Chapter 7.

Further reading

Coats (2004), Lacan (2006), Nobus (1998).

MODERNISM The term refers to a range of experimental cultural movements in Western society in the late nineteenth and early twentieth centuries which rebelled against traditional forms of art. In adult literature, modernism was a tendency rather than a clearly discernible movement. Though the impact of modernism on children's literature was, and remained, slight (though see **Reynolds** [2007] for an overview), after the middle of the century, it was evident in some of its most significant writers, especially William Mayne, Alan Garner and Jill Paton Walsh. Modernists have a preference for a kind of narrative which differs from the nineteenth-century realist novel without necessarily abandoning realist probability in representing characters and events. In novels which remain among the greatest works in children's literature – Mayne's *A Grass Rope* (1957) and *The Jersey Shore* (1973), Walsh's *Goldengrove* (1972), Garner's *Red Shift* (1973) and *The Stone Book Quartet* (1979) – interpretation of the world is provisional, fragmentary and unaccepting of the **teleological** descriptions and explanations of the world characteristic of traditional realism. There emerges a preoccupation with the perceiving subject, a subject in crisis, absorbed by and sometimes confused by the sensations that impact upon him or her.

The aesthetic function of the text thus leads primarily to a perceptual process which focuses on *models* of knowledge and action rather than on particular knowledge and action. Hence, these mid-twentieth-century children's writers employ crucial modernist strategies: a restricted narratorial presence, combined with an emphasized but limited point of view; representation of objects and incidents as they impact upon a focalizing **subjectivity** and hence a sense that the meaning of something resides in its presence to a perceiving mind; shifts between character **focalization** and stream of consciousness (usually as **free indirect** thought or free direct thought); a tendency to move away from the shape of the well-made traditional plot in order to proliferate micronarratives within the frame of the overarching, chronological narrative; a pervasive use of figurative language to invest narrative events and existents with significance; and the foregrounding of narrative discourse. Many of these strategies were subsequently also identified as elements of **postmodernism**. [JS]

See also Chapter 6.

Further reading

Dusinberre (1987), Reynolds (2007), **Stephens** (1992b).

MULTICULTURALISM In the 1960s and 1970s, multiculturalism emerged as a diversified manifestation of the politics of recognition, with a common core grounded in concepts of social justice, with particular reference to inequality, discrimination and oppression. The idea of multiculturalism first appeared in Western societies with **colonial** histories, whether as an imperial power (Britain) or a settler society with a continuing history of migration (United States, Canada, Australia). While these societies overtly included distinct cultural groups, they had been premised on a single national culture into which all citizens assimilate. Multiculturalism comes into being when it is acknowledged that non-assimilating groups have a right to define their own cultural identity on their own terms. In its widest definition, multiculturalism embraces all issues of cultural diversity: nationality, **ethnicity**, regionalism, class, gender, sexual orientation, religion, disability and all other identity-related differences. While there are some inclinations in children's literature to maintain this width of reference, the term is most commonly applied to communal diversity evident in the existence of long-established, ethnically distinct communities with a distinctive way of life which they wish to perpetuate. Even within this narrower sense, multiculturalism is understood and applied in diverse ways. In countries such as the United States or France, where citizenship structures social and political belief, implicitly assimilationist tendencies are apt to be stronger. An obvious characteristic of multicultural children's literature in the United States is that colour is more significant than ethnicity; the critical literature is dominated by the drive to define a multicultural curriculum and implement a corresponding educational practice, and so a syllabus consists of books depicting minority cultures: African American, Asian American, Latina/Latino. Selection of such books is in turn determined by notions of authenticity, but as Weimin Mo and Wenju Shen (1997) argue, cultural values, attitudes or beliefs are not fixed and within a culture new and old values are constantly in conflict. Moreover, cultures have an impact on each other, sometimes clashing, and sometimes absorbing each other's values, attitudes and beliefs. Authenticity, then, is a version of the culture that 'can be accommodated inside the range of values acceptable within that social group' (Mo and Shen, 1997, p. 160). In England, multiculturalism is represented as interaction between cultures within a multicultural social fabric, and this includes the majority Anglo culture. Janet and Allan Ahlberg's picturebooks, for example, depict a society of diverse races and classes as an aspect of everydayness. Multiculturalism in Australian children's literature is entirely based on ethnicity, whereas colour is at most incidental.

Multicultural children's literature has usually taken the form of advocacy politics, as in Susan Price's early, polemical *From Where I Stand* (1984), within which it has sought to affirm specific cultural practices against ideologically biased views and practices that assume universal validity. But now, in the early twenty-first century, societies in Europe, North America and Australia are becoming disinclined to maintain multiculturalist **ideologies**. The proliferation of citizenship tests for immigrants is but one indication of this tendency. A political response in children's literature has been the emergence of a literature about refugees, such as Armin Greder's *Die Insel* (2002; *The Island*, 2007), a picturebook which challenges the propensity of governments to pander to renewed social hostility towards **otherness**. Second, in the age of globalization, there is much space for forms of transculturalism, especially as a reciprocal sharing of understanding between two

cultures. The next agenda, in Janice Kulyk Keefer's terms, may be to produce literary texts with a looser structure, which, foregrounding the experience of 'minority' as opposed to 'dominant' groups, 'present themselves and are received as representative, even paradigmatic forms for an entire social formation, and not just for the ethnic or racial group with which the text's author is associated' (Keefer, 1993, p. 265). [JS]

See also Chapter 4.

Further reading

Cai (2002), Keefer (1993), Klein (1985), Mo and Shen (1997), Parekh (2006).

MYERS, MITZI (1939–2001) A **new historicist** and feminist critic whose work set new standards of scholarship in historical children's literature. Her work challenged the primacy of the **Romantic** construction of childhood that devalued the pioneering, late eighteenth-century women authors as dull, **didactic** oppressors of the imagination. Myers' masterful recontextualization of the works of Mary Wollstonecraft and Maria Edgeworth demonstrated their artistry, engagement with contemporary concerns and appeal to generations of young readers. Myers' intellectually rigorous writing was distinguished by its extensive research, command of British culture during the long eighteenth century, theoretical sophistication and exploration of the gendered politics of educational provision. One of the first children's literature critics to win wide recognition outside the field, she never advanced beyond the rank of lecturer because of her inability to produce a monograph. Her studies of Georgian women writers, of Maria Edgeworth, and her volumes for an Edgeworth edition, were left unfinished when she succumbed to health problems incurred when her house and enormous library burned to the ground in 2000. [ALI]

See also Chapter 1.

Further reading

Myers (1986, 1999b, 2000), Ruwe (2005).

MYTH By the end of the twentieth century, myth had developed two main senses in relation to children's literature. On the one hand, it denoted story elements or motifs within mythologies, primarily Graeco-Roman and Scandinavian ones, and by analogy, the myths and mythological systems of peoples throughout the world. Such stories employ supernatural beings to explain why the world is the way it is and are deemed to be applicable universally. Retellings of these myths use familiar story elements such as clearly defined beginnings and endings, coincidence, prophecy, and the recurrence of motifs and actions to present narrative form not only as an explanation but, beyond that, as a **teleology**. Because the process has its origins in the actions of supernatural beings, it is exemplary for all significant human activities, from birth, through the social life of people, to death, and imbues such incidents with the qualities and value of a religious or spiritual experience. As such, it guarantees that human experience of the world is not random and meaningless but repeatable and significant. Hence, a myth functions as a relational network with tangible links to a larger system or pattern of narratives and always has a significance over and above mere story outcome.

On the other hand, structural anthropologists argued that myth was not the expression of a concept but a system of communication – that is, a semiotic system. This position achieves fullest definition in the work of Roland **Barthes**, who proposes that the capacity for myth to make common social assumptions seem both natural and eternal conceals how myth naturalizes that which is political and historical. Barthes' ideas entered children's literature scholarship not only directly but were also notably mediated through the work of Jack **Zipes** (1994) on **fairy tales**.

How sense is made of these disparate approaches pivots on the kinds of significance attributed to myth and mythology. Apart from the basic function of filling gaps in children's literary knowledge, a myth may have five kinds of significance (**Stephens** and McCallum, 1998). First, its value as a *story* lies in its outworking of timeless and universal human **desires** and destinies. Meaning lies in the repeatability and structural similarity among otherwise apparently diverse stories. Second, retellings of myths conserve and promote cultural heritage and hence an understanding of the cultures and literatures of the past. There is certainly some truth in this, but the same retellings may also reproduce the individualism, imperialism, masculinism and misogyny which pervade some mythologies. Third, myths express spiritual insights in oblique narrative form because they derive from religious urges and aspirations. Fourth, they express psychic truth because they give narrative form to the stirrings of the human **unconscious**. Finally, they facilitate intercultural communication by bringing out the similarities between various world cultures and hence affirm the common humanity of people.

The Barthesian perspective would rather contend that such expressions of subjective wholeness are illusory, confusing a semiotic system with an inductive system that naturalizes 'commonsense' and formulaic ways of thinking about individuals and social relationships. Thus, though both conceptions of myth depend on a recognition of the **metanarratives** myths reflect and express, they also evaluate these metanarratives in mutually contradictory ways. [JS]

See also Chapters 2 and 7.

Further reading

Stephens and McCallum (1998), **Zipes** (1994).

NELSON, CLAUDIA (1960–) As a childhood studies researcher, Nelson has helped shape the discussion about how children's literature has constituted the notion of family. By focusing on individual family members and their roles, Nelson's work delineates the ways in which children's literature creates, reinforces and makes manifest cultural ideas about family and belonging, particularly in the Victorian period and early twentieth century. Of key interest

are Nelson's emphases on gender construction and sexuality in children's literature. Her research takes into account not just children's novels and periodicals, but legal documents, newspaper articles and information pamphlets, case studies and the testimonies of those who worked with and on behalf of children. In so doing, she is able to present in her work a wide-angle snapshot of how Victorians and Edwardians thought childhood ought to be. Nelson also indicates the changing fears about childhood and children. Her work on the Victorian period tracks the eclipse of fatherhood and the potential dangers of a self-involved or sexualized mother. Research into later periods tracks fears about race and class, often manifested in the dangerous sexuality of **adolescent** girls and the worrisome **otherness** of orphans. Her work on adoption, *Little Strangers* (2003), won the Children's Literature Association award for best scholarly book that year. [KSO]

Further reading

Nelson (2003, 2007), Nelson and **Vallone** (1994), **Zipes** (2001).

NEW CRITICISM This approach dominated literary criticism in the English-speaking world from the 1920s to the early 1970s, and is still widely, albeit implicitly, used in institutions whenever 'close reading' is encouraged. This, its grounding principle, involves a focused attention on literary texts and a rejection of practices based on any extrinsic, extra-textual sources, especially biography, history and sociology. Thus, the possible range of meanings of a particular text is always present within the text itself (i.e. meaning is intrinsic).

While this form of criticism derives its name from John Crowe Ransom's *The New Criticism* (1941), its origins are much earlier, and what in retrospect looks like a 'school' has two clear phases. Its beginnings were in England and can be attributed to key works by I. A. Richards and T. S. Eliot. The major impact of Richards' work lay in his attention to matters such as form, value, multiple meanings, metaphor, rhythm, tone and ambiguity, among others. His demonstration in *Practical Criticism* of how inept university students were in understanding poetry established a need for a more rigorous reading methodology. His removal of authorial and contextual information from the poems he asked students to comment on was later taken up as a central pedagogical practice wherever New Criticism was employed, on the understanding that it was a method that forced attention on the language and form of the text itself, and precluded the kind of stock response associated with contextual presupposition. Shortly afterwards, William Empson's *Seven Types of Ambiguity* (1930) made a pivotal contribution to critical practice. In placing ambiguity at the centre of literary meaning, this book articulated what became a key tenet of New Criticism and played a large part in originating its second phase, the rise of the 'school' in the United States in the 1940s and 1950s. Key ideas that began to shape criticism at this time involved rejection of two notable extra-textual assumptions: the 'intentional fallacy' (a naïve belief that the meaning of a

work is the same as its author's purported intention) and the 'affective fallacy' (the practice of interpreting texts according to the psychological or emotional responses of readers).

One of the most influential works of this period is Cleanth Brooks' *The Well-Wrought Urn* (1947), a collection of essays offering close readings of poems grounded in the position declared on the opening page, that 'paradox is the language appropriate and inevitable to poetry'. In one of these essays, 'The Heresy of Paraphrase', Brooks argues that a text's ideas and its form are inseparable, so that to attempt to paraphrase a poem's meaning is to disregard the effect of language and the poem's internal structure. Thus, an understanding of the literary work is reached by identifying the work's tensions – its paradoxes, ironies and ambiguities – and then identifying an idea or theme which resolves these into an organic unity. The process is carried out by careful focus on individual words, syntax and the ordering of sentences, imagery and figurative language, metre and rhythm, and other forms of sound patterning. Contrary to a widely held assumption, however, the method also allows considerable recourse to the historical context of literature.

While New Criticism was primarily concerned with poetry, its practices were extended to other literary forms, notably by Wayne C. Booth (1961), who made a crucial distinction between the author and the narrator in works of fiction and brought the notion of point of view into critical prominence. These distinctions had a deep, if not always obvious, influence on scholars in children's literature – for example, Barbara Wall's *The Narrator's Voice* (1991) is permeated by New Critical assumptions, even though its core terminology is drawn from structuralism.

Opponents of New Criticism argued that the 'text in itself' approach and its privileging of works of a particular quality masked its underlying **ideological** assumptions. Thus, feminists and **new historicists**, for example, argued that the supposedly 'universal' values celebrated by New Criticism were apt to be local, gendered and blind to issues of class and race. Such critique has tended to turn analysis back to content description and paraphrase, however, and to discourage discrimination between better and inferior writing. Whatever its actual or assumed failings, New Criticism played a formative role in the development of literary criticism, and close reading remains a fundamental practice, even if to a great extent replaced by more sophisticated approaches to textuality available through stylistics and discourse analysis. [JS]

See also Chapter 2.

Further reading

Booth (1961), Culler (1997), Eagleton (1996), Wellek (1995).

NEW HISTORICISM A literary movement that shows how a literary work is always embedded in its sociohistorical context, such that other texts, both literary and nonliterary, need to be studied alongside it. The usage of 'new' is there to make a statement and might be seen as similar to terms like **New Criticism**. It is, however, in complete contrast to New Criticism, in that this earlier movement sought to discuss the words on the page only, isolating a work from its context (as did later poststructuralist approaches, like deconstruction). There had, of course, been a long historically oriented tradition of criticism before new historicism, but the former tended to base its analyses on a presumed bedrock of historical fact, whereas the latter recognizes that most history exists only as 'text' of one sort or another. In this it is heavily influenced by the work of Michel **Foucault**. In Louis Montrose's memorable words, new historicism recognizes 'the historicity of texts and the textuality of history' (quoted in Colebrook, 1997, p. 209).

New historicism originated in the United States, initially associated with Stephen Greenblatt and Renaissance studies. However, there has also been work on the **Romantic** period (e.g. Jerome McGann and Alan Liu). Although the work of Foucault is central, new historicism is theoretically eclectic, drawing on concepts from Marxism, psychoanalysis and poststructuralism. Its approach is often linked to a more British variant, Cultural Materialism, chiefly associated with Alan Sinfield and Jonathan Dollimore. Cultural Materialism, though, has its roots more firmly in Marxism and is more interested in exposing potentially subversive 'faultlines' in a text. New historicism would seem to have much to offer children's literature studies, especially as it 'treats literary texts as a space where power relationships are made visible' (Brannigan, 1998, p. 6), and children are frequently found on the underside of history, marginalized and appropriated for their **signifying** potential. Studies that situate children's literature within this wider context (often under the name of 'Childhood Studies') are now more plentiful. 'Literary' texts (themselves subject to historical fashion) are examined alongside contemporary debates around education, religion, child development, representations of childhood in art and so on. In children's literature, Mitzi **Myers** was an early champion of such an approach, uncovering the lost female voices among traditional masculine conceptions of **Romanticism**. Lynne **Vallone** and Claudia **Nelson** have similarly made us aware of the wider social issues circulating around matters of gender, class and age in literature for and about children, especially in the nineteenth century. [DR]

See also Chapter 1.

Further reading

Brannigan (1998), Colebrook (1997), Vallone (1996).

NIKOLAJEVA, MARIA (1952–) An internationally renowned children's literature scholar; born in Russia, she emigrated to Sweden in 1981 where she taught children's literature and critical theory at Stockholm University from 1985 until 2008, when she became Professor of Education at the University of Cambridge. Nikolajeva is a prolific writer and reviewer and has also written fiction for a young audience. Publishing in three languages (English, Russian and Swedish), she is exceptional in her ability to give an international overview of the field, combining scholarship with an infectious enthusiasm to popularize the area.

With a background in structuralism, semiotics and narratology, Nikolajeva has taken a special interest in investigating the typical characteristics of children's literature in terms of form, content, structure and narrative pattern. She has written extensively on such varied subjects as fantasy literature, **folk** and **fairy tales**, picturebooks, literary characterization, translation and the historical development of a children's literature aesthetics. In working with a substantial number of literary texts from different languages and nationalities, Nikolajeva's comparative approach has prompted the criticism that she makes broad generalizations about children's literature. Yet her ability to draw attention to these general patterns has also been considered ground breaking, especially as she also seeks to apply contemporary literary theory to children's literature. In 2005 she received the International Brothers Grimm Award for a lifetime achievement in children's literature research. [MLS]

See also Chapter 9.

Further reading

Nikolajeva (1996, 2002, 2005), Nikolajeva and Scott (2001).

NODELMAN, PERRY (1942–) A Canadian critic and theorist of children's literature, best known for his influential argument that children's literature can 'usefully be considered a **genre** of literature in its own right' (Nodelman and Reimer, 2003, p. 187). Trained as a **New Critic** at Yale University in the 1960s, Nodelman builds his theory about texts for young readers by performing close readings from which he abstracts general patterns of meaning. His project to define children's literature as a genre first became visible in 'Interpretation and the Apparent Sameness of Children's Novels' (Nodelman, 1985) in which he observed that, despite the wide variation of surface details in a group of time-travel narratives, the act of interpretation reveals a shared core of meaning, expressed through a balancing of paradoxical ideas about the acceptance of what is and what ought not to be possible, a sameness that transcends any personal visions or significant uniqueness of the particular texts. This argument was extended in 1992, in *The Pleasures of Children's Literature* (2003), to a list of generic characteristics, including descriptions of the typical characters, conventional plots, distinctive styles and repeated thematic patterns found in children's literature. His theory can be summarized by his designation of the generic 'no-name story' as a home–away–home story, a label which neatly conflates the circular plots, domestic settings and binary themes characteristic of the form. In *The Hidden Adult* (2008), Nodelman returned to a proposition made in his earlier work – that the characteristics of children's literature emerge from enduring, ambivalent adult ideas about childhood – to develop the argument that children's literature simultaneously protects children from adult knowledge and works to teach it to them. Because children's literature addresses a child reader, it can be understood to invite those readers to share this ambivalence, 'to occupy or enact' a childlike view while also to recognize and repress the adult knowledge sublimated in its 'shadow texts'. Nodelman's account of the oppositional adult–child relationship that structures texts of children's literature began from his exploration of the explanatory power of Edward Said's claim that **Orientalism** is a 'style of thought' that produces the Orient as an object for domination (Nodelman, 1992). This use of Said's description as an analogy for adult discourse about childhood and children's literature has been seen by some critics as a false step in understanding the imbrication of children's literature and the British Empire. Clare **Bradford** (2001b), for example, notes that the comparison between child readers and colonized peoples breaks down when texts are produced by **colonial** writers for 'young colonizers'.

Nodelman's method of working from detailed observations about particular texts to general statements about kinds of texts is also observable in his first monograph, *Words about Pictures* (1988). His conclusion, that the relation of pictures and text in children's picturebooks is always an ironic one, has informed much subsequent sophisticated work on picturebooks, although his contribution to the theory of the form is not always acknowledged by later critics. Nodelman's study of picturebooks began from his work as a teacher in undergraduate classrooms at the University of Winnipeg, where he has spent 40 years of his career.

Pleasures was conceived specifically as a textbook and, now in its third edition, is a widely recognized key work. The provenance of his scholarship shows itself in the colloquial, conversational style he adopts in much of his writing, a style that encourages, and, indeed, often provokes, debate. He has also shaped the field of the study of children's literature through his editorial work, both for the *Children's Literature Association Quarterly* (1980–8) and *Canadian Children's Literature/Littérature canadienne pour la jeunesse* (2005–8). In 1993, he began a parallel career as a writer for young people, with the publication of the novel *The Same Place but Different*. To date, he has published ten novels and one picturebook, six of the novels in collaboration with Carol Matas. [MR]

Further reading

Nodelman (1985, 1988, 2008), Nodelman and Reimer (2003).

OEDIPUS COMPLEX Based on the experiences of the **mythical** character Oedipus, who unwittingly killed his father and married his mother, the Oedipus complex refers to the **unconscious desire** of the son to eliminate the father so as to possess the mother. **Freud** proclaimed this desire to be universal, inborn and crucial to the development of the psyche. Its resolution comes about when the child is able to identify with the father and accept substitutions for the mother. The concept has been denounced as inherently sexist and, certainly, attempts to articulate a similar structure pertaining to female development have not achieved the same level of critical acceptance. **Lacan**'s revision of Freud's idea turns the Oedipus complex into a structural feature of **subjectivity**. He claims that not only males but all children take their mothers as their first objects of desire and the imposition of the father as a force prohibiting or interfering with the relationship between mother and child is a constant threat to the child's well-being. Thus, the child as subject emerges out of the battle between his desire and the Law prohibiting that desire. Lacan also associates this tension with the castrating effect language has on our relationship to things: at stake in oedipalization is the acceptance of the representations of language and culture in place of the unmediated physical bliss associated with union with the mother. Another name for this Law is the Name-of-the-Father, and the child must both submit to and come to identify with it in order to function as a subject in the **Symbolic**. [KC]

See also Chapter 7.

Further reading

Coats (2004), Rollin and West (1999), Rustin and Rustin (1987).

ORIENTALISM Europe has a long tradition of discourses about what is loosely called 'the Orient', those parts of the world which include Arab cultures in North Africa and the whole of Asia. Because Orientalism has less to do with what such societies are actually like than with how Europeans have thought about and acted upon them, Edward Said (1978) has argued that Orientalism is a discourse designed to dominate, restructure and maintain authority over the Orient. More immediately pertinent to children's literature, where Orientalism is manifested not as a theoretical pre-occupation but as a textual artefact, Orientalism is a discourse about *otherness*, about that which is different from or opposite to the person whose per-spective determines a text's point of view. The identification of someone as 'Other' implies an unequal power rela-tionship, where the one being 'Othered' is perceived as inferior, or at best strangely exotic.

The exotic nature of the Oriental other is marked by contradictory terms such as sensuality and barbarism, mys-tery and charlatanism, opulence and decadence, all of which are indicative of once-great civilizations now in decline and in need of external guidance. A suc-cinct example of how the Orient is depicted as unable to see or speak for itself occurs towards the beginning of Rudyard Kipling's *Kim* (1901) through the figure of the white-bearded curator of the Wonder House, who mediates 'the labours of European scholars' for the quaint old Tibetan Lama, thereby explaining his own culture to him. The comic effect inherent in this situation remains a product of the otherness of Orientalism, as in Diana Wynne Jones's *Castle in the Air* (1990) or Robert Leeson's *The Last Genie* (1993).

Prior to, but reinforced by, the many translations of the *Arabian Nights* in the eighteenth and nineteenth centuries, a vogue for Oriental exoticism took strik-ing form in illustrations to Charles Perrault's *Bluebeard*, where, from eigh-teenth-century woodcuts through to the well-known illustrations of Edmund Dulac (1910) and Arthur Rackham (1919), the villainous husband was depicted as a turban-wearing, scimitar-wielding Oriental despot. Perhaps such marital tyranny seems more easily repre-sented in a character who is the Other, not like us. Similarly, it also appears in illustrations to 'Beauty and the Beast', that story about arranged marriage, by, for example, Dulac (1910) and Warwick Hutton (1985). Dulac's illustrations were later cited in passing in Disney's *Beauty and the Beast* (1991). Disney went further with *Aladdin* (1992) in which Orientalism functions to construct the forces of evil as the alien other, char-acterized by a totalitarian regime, whereas Aladdin and Princess Jasmine are represented as essentially Western in their behaviour and aspirations.

The perception of non-Western peoples as strange and different from how they perceive themselves has more recently been challenged by a perception that understands difference as operating from a different centre. The 'unknown' in the foreign culture is not something inherently mysterious and exotic but 'a condition of the nec-essarily limited understanding of the viewer' (Cuddy-Keane, 2003, p. 549). The best example to date in children's literature is Donna Jo Napoli's *Beast* (2000), which, narrated and **focalized** by the Beast, a transformed Persian prince, depicts how individuals from separate, complex cultures learn how to inhabit mutual space. [JS]

See also Chapter 4.

Further reading

Anon (2005), Cuddy-Keane (2003), Lowe (1991), Said (1978).

OTHER/OTHERNESS Generally, a term for that which has been neglected, marginalized. However, it has both social and psychoanalytical inflections. Socially, it is used to depict 'other' groups (women, non-whites, foreigners, children, workers, the disabled), though its overuse has tended to threaten its very alterity. This usage derived from feminism, originating in Simone de Beauvoir's work. It is also much used in **postcolonial** theorizing. Said (1978), for example, talks about the otherness of the Orient. The irony is that the West created this otherness (as exotic, peculiar, fearful), as something against which it could define its own identity (as normal). Without the other, the West lacked distinction; it thus depended on a process of 'othering'. In more philosophical terms, this relates to a notion that **Derrida** relentlessly pursued in that nothing can be self-definitional: no term ever has full meaning. Hence, words always need supplementing, conventionally with such phrases as 'in other words'.

Homi **Bhabha** (1994) brings these elements together in his use of the word 'other', adding a psychoanalytical inflection which he derives from **Lacan**, who argued that we are never fully present to ourselves and that we are, in fact, constituted by otherness. Lacan distinguishes the big Other (capitalized) from a little other. The former is society, with its laws and institutions, and its medium of communication, language (the **Symbolic**). Though we see these social institutions as distinct from us, they are what give us 'ID'. Thus, we describe ourselves as 'African' or 'Australian', and as speaking 'English', and we accordingly grow up imbibing a particular society's ways of behaving. Otherness inhabits us, then, from the outset. The little other, or *petit a* ('*a*' is for *autre*, 'other' in French), is more complicated, relating back to the roots of an individual's **desire**, which Lacan locates in the lost mother – the (m)other, as she is often represented. Lacan argues that, when we desire things, they are always in some way stand-ins for this primordial loss. Thus, we make **imaginary** identifications with people (lovers, pop stars) and with material goods (cars, clothes, gadgets), but they are never, finally, satisfactory: they are always other, despite our investment in them. Ironically, though, as noted earlier, our desires were never our own from the outset, as we are constituted by 'the desire of the Other'.

In a final usage, the philosopher Emmanuel Levinas argues that it is our encounter with otherness that makes possible our taking an ethical stance; that is, the other is someone we cannot assimilate to our way of thinking, which then provides us with the chance of redrawing our ethical co-ordinates. [DR]

See also Chapters 4 and 7.

Further reading

Eaglestone (1997), Paul (1998), Wilkie-Stibbs (2008).

PARATEXT A printed text does not stand alone but is accompanied by a number of textual, and even non-textual objects that are exterior to the text itself yet impact upon a reader's approach to the text. These objects constitute the paratext. Gérard Genette, who gave currency to the term, argued that it consisted of two components, the peritext and the epitext. The peritext includes all paraphernalia within the bound volume, that is, everything on and between the covers, which might include the author's name, the title, blurbs, cover illustrations, dust-jackets, end-papers, dedications, any preface or introduction, maps, epigraphs, authorial appendices and afterwords, footnotes or marginal notes, and glossaries. Thus, fantasy fiction frequently includes a map, and historical fiction, an afterword (and even a bibliography), as a contextualizing strategy. End-papers, especially in picturebooks, can anticipate theme, as when Shaun Tan uses them to evoke the notion of entropy in *The Lost Thing* (2000). The peritext also includes within-text illustrations, although this does not incorporate picturebook illustrations, which are part of the text proper. Margaret Higonnet, however, argues that the physical structure of many children's books belongs to the peritext: books that are an unusual shape, have moveable parts or pop-ups, fold-out pages, holes or cutouts. Lauren Child's *Who's Afraid of the Big Bad Book?* (2002) employs several such features.

The epitext includes elements outside the bound volume – interviews, reviews, diaries and so on. Nowadays the epitext also includes online study guides, often released simultaneously to accompany a novel, with a peritextual link included on the book's cover or dust-jacket. In some cases, actual places used for the settings of novels can have an epitextual function; for example, the White Horse of Uffington as a historical site used in Rosemary Sutcliff's *Sun Horse, Moon Horse* (1977), or the 'Oxford' of Philip Pullman's *Northern Lights* (1995), among innumerable others. Visits to such places endow them with an enhanced paratextual function.

Genette perceived the paratext as 'a threshold' where the transaction between reader and text begins and where an influence is exerted to shape the reception and understanding of the text. Peritextual elements, in particular, can engage readers through playfulness, as when the story seems to have got under way before the title page appears in Colin McNaughton's *Oops!* (1997), or through David Wyatt's mock-Victorian advertisements on the end pages of Philip Reeve's steampunk novel *Larklight* (2006). In all such cases, the paratext is an integral part of a reader's experience. As Higonnet (1990, p. 49) shrewdly observes, it leads readers both 'towards the materialization of the reading process as physical play, and towards the abstraction of narrative into a **metanarrative** projection'. [JS]

See also Chapter 9.

Further reading

Genette (1997), Higonnet (1990), McCallum (2004), Wilkie-Stibbs (2004b).

PARODY Because so much children's literature involves the retelling of already known stories, it is always apt to turn to parody, which, through humorous, satiric or ironic imitation, comments on or makes fun of an existing text or a recognizable cultural practice. Feminist writers, for example, frequently use the 'fractured fairy tale' to mock the perceived gender assumptions of classic **fairy tales**, and there are numerous parodic versions of '*Cinderella*', for instance. Extended isomorphic imitations of characters and plots enable a sustained play of ironic difference whereby three sisters, a ball, a prince and a fairy godmother become invested with new significance. In Ann Jungman and Russell Ayto's *Cinderella and the Hot Air Balloon* (1992), for example, Cinderella displays a forceful **agentic subjectivity**: she refuses to go to the ball, uses the godmother's power to improve the lives of the servants, disrupts the palace by running her own party and finally persuades a shy prince to elope with her in a balloon. This is a parody of the classic tale because it humorously inverts the meaning of familiar motifs in order to dismantle the version of helpless femininity associated with that tale.

Mikhail **Bakhtin** suggested that all **genres** eventually become parody. Thus, it seems inevitable that after the conventions of fairy tale film had been defined by Disney a parody stage would emerge, inverting audience expectations. The unexpected outcome of 'true love's kiss' in *Shrek* (2001) is a clear example, from a film that generally treats familiar conventions parodically. A comparable, although subtler, function is performed for young adult (YA) fiction by Stephen Chbosky's *The Perks of Being a Wallflower* (1999). Bakhtin (1981, p. 76) offers the constructive comment that 'in parody two languages are crossed with each other, as well as two styles, two linguistic points of view, and in the final analysis two speaking subjects'. A **dialogic** relationship between genres, registers and points of view is the core of a parodic narrative such as Jan Needle's *Wild Wood* (1981) as it engages with the politics and social assumptions of *The Wind in the Willows* (1908). The story of the capture of Toad Hall is retold from the perspective of a naive ferret, filtered through two further levels of fallible narration which parody stereotypes of working-class life and political struggle. As here, the substitution of a point of view different from the source text has strong parodic potential, especially when the juxtaposition of two incompatible perspectives destabilizes the assumptions of each.

The crossing of two languages is a strategy much evident in the work of Terry Pratchett, a master of parody. Young readers meet this in the 'Truckers' trilogy, where obvious parody in 'The Book of Nome' (Pratchett, 1989, p. 9) – 'And Arnold Bros (est. 1905) Moved upon the face of the Site, and Saw that it had Potential' – both imitates the discourse of its source text (the language of the King James Bible) in order to apply it incongruously, and alerts readers to the possibility of a more pervasive parody in the novel. The example also reminds us that parody is not necessarily satirical, but may function as a compliment or homage to an existing text, theme or cultural practice. [JS]

Further reading

Bakhtin (1981), Dentith (2000), Hutcheon (1985), Rose (1993).

PATRIARCHY A form of social organization based on male domination, in which the father assumes supremacy within the family unit. The term has broadly come to signify the widespread use of male power over women. Patriarchy is a particularly important concept for feminism, a movement which views patriarchy as responsible for the social and political oppression of women. Patriarchal **ideology**, which constructs masculinity and femininity as oppositional forces and privileges masculinity as superior, is evident in all **genres** of writing for children. However, it is perhaps most prevalent in fantasy. As a genre, fantasy has traditionally revolved around a masculine heroic paradigm based on patriarchal values which privilege action over inaction, aggression over submission and individualism over collectivism. Feminist retellings of traditional **fairy tales** by authors such as Tanith Lee, Robin McKinley, Donna Jo Napoli and Jane Yolen seek to correct this masculine bias by exposing the various ways in which patriarchal practices attempt to regulate women's bodies and behaviours. They do so by redressing the passivity conventionally associated with female characters in fairy tales: the equation of beauty with goodness, the limited and stereotypical representation of female roles (princess, evil stepmother or witch) and, finally, the paradigmatic fairy tale closure which establishes a young girl's happiness as wholly dependent upon her ability to secure a husband.

The widespread influence of feminism can also be seen in high fantasy, most notably in the manner that gender representation evolved in Ursula Le Guin's critically acclaimed 'Earthsea' series. Published between 1968 and 1972, the period in which second-wave feminism began to gain momentum, the first three novels closely conformed to classic fantasy conventions in their depiction of male heroism. However, *Tehanu: The Last Book of Earthsea* (1990) reflected the vast social changes which had occurred as a result of the feminist project by its departure from the conventional patriarchal fantasy model in its portrayal of a female protagonist in search of her own, independent identity. Mary Hoffman's *Women of Camelot: Queens and Enchantresses at the Court of King Arthur* (2000) is similar in that it revisits Arthurian **legends** from a feminist perspective.

A further example of changing attitudes to patriarchal values is the recent transformation and recuperation of the figure of the witch. Historically, witches were perceived as a threat to the patriarchal order of Christian society. This view was reinforced by writing for children, which up until the 1980s typically represented witches in a misogynistic fashion as the purveyors of evil. Since then, the figure of the witch has undergone a process of rehabilitation in children's books. Witches have come to be positively associated with nature as a result of both New Age philosophies and in opposition to postmodernity (**Stephens**, 2003); and, perhaps more obviously, their position as cultural outsiders has become an effective way of critiquing the general role of women in patriarchal societies. Novels such as Monica Furlong's *Wise Child* (1987) and Celia Rees' *Witch Child* (2002) reflect this paradigm shift. The representation of witch figures in young adult fiction by Diana Wynne Jones (*Howl's Moving Castle*, 1986) and Terry Pratchett (*Wyrd Sisters*, 1988; *Carpe Jugulum*, 1998) creates an **intertextual** and often very humorous dialogue between various conceptualizations of the witch.

The emergence of masculinity studies in the early 1990s has seen the term 'patriarchy' superseded to an extent by **hegemonic masculinity**. The two concepts overlap, but the variable nature of the latter makes it more useful to employ within a cultural context that, as a result of third-wave feminism, recognizes a diversity of masculine identities. [VF]

See also Chapter 3.

Further reading

Johnson (1997), Paul (2004), Stephens (2003), Walby (1990).

PERFORMANCE/PERFORMATIVITY These terms have become increasingly popular in postmodern times, where identity is seen not as something inherent and essential but, rather, as enacted. There are various overlapping roots to this concept, one being in the sociologist Erving Goffman's *The Presentation of Self in Everyday Life* (1959), where he uses the vocabulary of theatre to discuss our behavioural repertoires. However, this still presumes that we have more of a 'real' self, backstage. Another key root lies in J. L. Austin's 'speech act theory', where he described certain utterances as being 'performatives', by which he meant that the mere saying of them enacted their meaning – as, for example, in taking an oath, or in making a promise ('I give my word'). From here, later theorists have argued that all language is performative, and indeed, that our very identity is constructed through talk.

Judith **Butler** is most closely associated with this shift, introduced in *Gender Trouble*, where she describes gender as 'always a doing, though not a doing by a subject who might be said to preexist the deed' (Butler, 1990a, p. 25). All of us are, therefore, performing like drag artists, but we do it so often that we think this behaviour natural. 'Performativity', as she puts it, is 'the discursive mode by which ontological effects are installed' (Butler, 1993, p. 9) – which also opens the way for demonstrating how the heteronormativity of our performances can be disrupted or rewritten. However, Butler has been criticized for making this process seem too voluntaristic and neglecting the forces working against a rewriting. For such critics, Pierre **Bourdieu**'s related term 'habitus' (meaning our habituated ways of deporting ourselves) is sometimes preferred. Certainly, as gender is represented in children's books, it is aspects of the behavioural repertoire that are more often shown to be faulty. Famously, Huckleberry Finn's attempt to pass as a girl is undone because he still throws like a boy, and threads a needle wrongly. More recently, Anne Fine's drag-heroes in *Madame Doubtfire* (1987) and *Bill's New Frock* (1989) demonstrate their ineptness in passing.

Another shortcoming of Butler's position is one that she herself increasingly addresses (e.g. Butler, 2004):

how one develops a sense of cohesion in a world where one's identity is limited to performance (identity politics), and relatedly, the dangers of not doing so. In other words, in order to make choices, one must have a place from which to stand, and, arguably, it is those most aligned with society's hegemonic discourses that have the fewest problems with their performances.

Without trivializing the topic, the term 'performative' has also been productively used by Jerome McGann (1985) to show how books themselves are dressed up and made to perform in certain ways, dependent on their anticipated readerships (with both text and **paratext** contributing). Children's books, with their rapidly shifting packaging (especially of perennials like the **folk** and **fairy tale**, or the recent trend towards dually marketed **crossover** works), are especially worthy of attention in these terms. [DR]

See also Chapter 3.

Further reading

Butler (1990a, 2004), Loxley (2007), McGann (1985).

PHALLOCENTRISM/PHALLOGOCENTRISM
A system which privileges masculinity (i.e. the 'phallus') over femininity, producing and perpetuating hierarchical power relationships based on domination and subordination. Phallocentrism is commonly associated with Jacques **Lacan**, due to the significance he attributed to the phallus in the formation of **subjectivity**. Feminist criticism characterizes Lacan's theories as phallocentric because of his assertion that

children identify themselves as sexual subjects according to their possession or lack of the phallus, a fundamental **signifier**. Lacan understood the constitution of every subject in language as involving a negotiation between the phallus, the father and the rule of Law (an extension of the paternal metaphor) and he, therefore, viewed language as inherently masculine. (Phallocentrism thus has a broader application than **patriarchy**, although the two concepts are clearly related.)

Phallocentric assumptions are particularly relevant to **reader-response** theory, because of the ways in which women and girls are culturally conditioned to read as if they were men. Female readers are encouraged to align themselves with male characters and perspectives, as texts routinely privilege masculine viewpoints and experiences to the extent that women are forced to identify against themselves while reading. In fact, as Jonathan Culler (1982, p. 54) has suggested, 'to read as a woman is to avoid reading as a man, to identify the specific defenses and distortions of male readings and provide correctives'. The naturalization of masculine subject positions is widespread but is perhaps most explicit in narratives that contain male characters only, implying that masculine experience is universal. Howard Pyle's *The Merry Adventures of Robin Hood of Great Renown, in Nottinghamshire* (1968) is a good example. Jill P. May (1986, p. 200) applauds it, as 'there are no sex roles to suffer', but her assessment overlooks the phallocentric nature of the world that Pyle has constructed. What she perceives as 'no sex roles' (or stereotyped gender divisions) is actually achieved by eradicating femininity altogether. Aside from exhibiting conventionally masculine traits and behaviours, the male characters in this novel also perform domestic chores such as cooking and providing emotional support for each other. Women are unnecessary in this community, which is clearly depicted as a utopia.

Fantasy literature, in contrast, provides more of an opportunity for problematizing male heroism. Charles Keeping's illustrations for Kevin Crossley-Holland's retelling of the **legend** of Beowulf (1968) are thus deeply critical of the phallocentric nature of the heroic ideal, subverting Crossley-Holland's text by sympathetically representing Grendel and his mother as human-like, rather than evil or monstrous. John **Stephens** and Robyn McCallum (1998, pp. 116–17) note that Keeping's depiction of the open-mouthed, sinewy body of Grendel's mother in battle with Beowulf is an image in which 'the marginalized female is locked in an ambiguously sexual/agonistic embrace with a metonym of phallocentric patriarchy'. Beowulf's body 'becomes an optical illusion, a visual ambiguity that hesitates between a representation of a penile glans and a representation of a helmet', and this uncertainty makes it difficult to ascertain 'which figure is the hero, and which the monster'. Fantasy fiction that focuses on female heroism is generally more explicit in its critique of the phallocentrism associated with the male heroic paradigm. An instructive example is Tamora Pierce's 'Song of the Lioness' quartet (1983–8), a sword-and-sorcery series

about a young girl who disguises herself as a boy in order to enter the King's palace and commence training as a royal knight. Alanna's transgressive behaviour gives her unprecedented access to masculine spaces and privilege, and the story pivots on the ways in which she uses her feminine subjectivity to renegotiate phallocentric models of male heroism.

Young adult fiction provides an interesting counterpoint to this discussion, however, because it frequently constructs female sexuality as **abject** and, therefore, perpetuates rather than challenges phallocentrism. In her discussion of Margo Lanagan's *Touching Earth Lightly* (1996), Kathryn James argues that the character of Janey exemplifies 'monstrous femininity', a symbol of male castration anxiety 'that operates to reinforce the phallocentric notion that female sexuality is abject' (James, 2009, p. 78). James contends that the representation of feminine sexuality as monstrous is a common trope in YA fiction, demonstrating that phallocentric assumptions about women and sexuality remain highly visible in contemporary writing for **adolescents**. [VF]

See also Chapter 3.

Further reading

James (2009), May (1986), Stanger (1987), Stephens and McCallum (1998), Wilkie-Stibbs (2002).

PIAGET, JEAN (1896–1980) A Swiss researcher often described as a child psychologist, though he preferred the term 'genetic epistemologist', meaning that he was interested in the way the mind gained knowledge of different aspects of the world at different stages of development. Along with such diverse thinkers as the language theorist Noam Chomsky and the anthropologist Claude Lévi-Strauss, Piaget's approach was structuralist. That is, he argued that the mind went through several transformations in its developing interactions with the world, thus seeing the world in different ways. By the 1960s, these ideas had become hugely influential. In England, especially, the primary educational curriculum was designed with Piaget's conceptions in mind – which were also to have an impact on researchers into children's literature. Briefly, Piaget argued that the child moves from learning about the world through sensory experience (sucking and holding things) to a more 'concrete' manner, in which it tends to concentrate on single features; thus, a child might see a test tube of liquid magically reduce when it is poured into a wider, flatter dish (because the concrete thinker is only taking one dimension – height – into account). The child at this stage is also seen as very literal in its understanding of language, and as having an animistic conception of the universe. A. A. Milne's Pooh has been labelled a typical pre-operational thinker (Singer, 1972). After the age of 7, the child is seen as more capable of abstracting different aspects of experience, thus appreciating causality, multiple perspectives and so on. In turn, other thinkers followed Piaget's lead: Lawrence Kohlberg, for example, drew up a trajectory for moral development.

At the time, Piaget's work was praised for challenging Behaviourism, which saw the child as a **Lockean** 'blank slate', capable of learning anything if given the right reinforcement schedule. Piaget, though, always saw the child as involved in constructing its own version of the world (it is a constructive process). However, Piaget's findings were based on minimal empirical evidence; moreover, he always underestimated the role of language in constructing a child's reality, to the extent that he did not really seek to make his questions and experiments intelligible to the child. As subsequent studies have shown, if children are presented with Piagetian tasks in more accessible ways, their understanding seems to improve markedly (Donaldson, 1978). Finally, Piaget's work has been criticized for seeing masculine, scientific reasoning as the pinnacle of development, there being little attention to the emotions or intuition, or, indeed, to non-Western, alternative trajectories. In the world of children's literature, Nicholas **Tucker** has been a key proponent of Piagetian ideas. Poststructuralism has queried all such grand narratives, though, with some critical psychologists arguing that the whole notion of 'development' is a fabrication (Morss, 1996). [DR]

Further reading

Donaldson (1978), Morss (1996), Singer (1972), Tucker (1981).

POSTCOLONIALISM Refers to the effects of colonization upon cultures and societies. It does not refer to a period 'post' (i.e. after) **colonialism** and does not mean that colonialism is over and done with. In their seminal work, Bill

Ashcroft *et al.* (1989, p. 2) announce that they use the term 'postcolonial' to 'cover all the culture affected by the imperial process from the moment of colonization to the present day'. Although this definition has been contentious, it enables a wide-ranging examination of the processes whereby colonizers and their descendants, as well as later migrants, engage with indigenous cultures and with the effects of colonial discourses upon national **mythologies**. As a field of theory and critical practice, postcolonial studies bifurcates into contrasting modes of thought and interpretation. The first is an optimistic and even celebratory view of postcolonial societies emphasizing the transformative effects of **hybridity** and transculturation, as proposed by theorists such as Homi **Bhabha** and Mary Louise Pratt. The other direction taken by postcolonial studies is the more agonistic and sceptical line exemplified by Gayatri Chakravorty Spivak's famous essay 'Can the Subaltern Speak?', which argues that the voices of subaltern people are lost in the noise of Western theorists as they talk *about* the colonized. Ashcroft observes that 'postcolonial' is 'a *form of talk* rather than a *form of experience*' (2001, p. 13), enabling investigation into how texts represent colonialism in the past and its effects in the present and offering an array of concepts and critical strategies which inform analysis of individual texts as well as supporting comparisons across national literatures. In particular, postcolonial studies focuses on indigenous textuality, suggesting reading strategies which enhance understanding and appreciation of the cultural

and artistic practices that shape this important body of texts while acknowledging that non-indigenous readers are outsiders to indigenous cultures. [CB]

See also Chapter 4.

Further reading

Ashcroft (2001), Ashcroft *et al.* (1989).

POSTMAN, NEIL (1931–2003) A social commentator famous for seeing childhood as constructed by the printing press and the subsequent growth of literacy, only for it to be eroded more recently by television and other media. Postman moved from being a radical educational thinker who initially welcomed the new media, to a conservative who saw it destroying childhood, with TV the main culprit. It was not just 'the disappearance of childhood' (Postman, 1982), though, but the decline of a whole culture surrendering to technology, as his subsequent work, *Amusing Ourselves to Death* (1985), contends. His argument is often reduced to sound bites, but he himself was adept at coining them. Although he saw our modern conception of childhood as originating with the printing press, making reading competence a criterion for access to adult discourses, thus disempowering children, he also saw this construction as providential and worth fighting for. He could not accept a world where such a division no longer obtained – where, in fact, there was an 'adultified'/'childified' **hybridity**. Along with many other thinkers, the figure of the child proved too powerful a symbol of innocence to resist, although, as his argument elsewhere suggests, his thesis also concerns the disappearance of adulthood (as we know it). The technological determinism of his argument might detract, but Postman's general fears have certainly been taken up by others, fearful of education becoming 'edutainment', and of the increased penetration of market forces with the new media (Buckingham, 2000; Kenway and Bullen, 2001). [DR]

See also Chapters 1 and 8.

Further reading

Buckingham (2000), Hoikkala *et al.* (1987), Kenway and Bullen (2001), Postman (1982).

POSTMODERNISM A complex, yet paradoxically empty, term; in fact, to attempt a definition can be understood to be the antithesis of postmodernism. Fredric **Jameson** (1991) sees it as a response to high **modernism** and as the result of industrial mass production and late capitalism. According to him, postmodernism represents a crisis of boundaries, or of categorization, which manifests itself in a blending of **genres** and a drifting between different stylistic modes (Jameson, 1985, p. 112). Indeed, as a general cultural phenomenon, postmodernism tolerates and, in fact, celebrates ambiguity.

The term 'postmodernism' itself is ambiguous since it raises the inevitable question of periodization, suggesting that culturally we have moved beyond modernism. Yet the boundary between modernism and postmodernism remains a contentious issue. There is, for example, no critical consensus as to exactly when we became 'post'. Jean-François Lyotard (1984, p. 79), however, claims postmodernism is not modernism at its end, but modernism in 'the nascent state'. This suggests that the postmodern is not a new or alternative position, but represents a period of transition, which, without any fixed points of reference, manifests itself as doubt, or scepticism: what Lyotard describes as an 'incredulity towards **metanarratives**' (1984, p. xxiv); in other words, the *inability* to believe in the modernist (Cartesian) version of self and reality. Thus, all-encompassing grand narratives – the totalizing discourses of Religion, History, Marxism, Progress and Science that give cultural practices some form of authority – are considered inadequate or are exposed as narratives which, in their exclusivity, legitimize particular values while suppressing the 'little narratives' that inscribe or re-inscribe alternative or silenced 'voices'.

However, in the wake of consensus-oriented thought is an ontological uncertainty which manifests itself as indeterminacy, provisionality and fragmentation. Of course, it could be argued that the fragmented nature of self, meaning and reality were also concerns of modernist art. Although the modernists mourned what they perceived as the loss of unity and meaning, and attempted to uphold the idea that art can provide or restore, if not some kind of objective reality, at least an illusion of it ('These fragments I have shored against my ruins', as T. S. Eliot expresses it in *The Waste Land*, 1922), postmodern art does not lament what has apparently been lost; instead, it 'plays' with the fragments.

Both of the above attitudes are evident in Aidan **Chambers'** novels for **adolescents** ('Dance Sequence', 1978–2005). Chambers' texts represent an unrelenting series of attempts, via artistic expression, to find or recover some sense of meaning, as his **solipsistic**, angst-ridden protagonists consider the complexities of human experience. Yet Chambers' protean protagonists are also emblematic of the versatile postmodern self, constantly assuming new identities and experiencing themselves through various **performances**, for example through gender, in which the concept of unified sexuality is exchanged for the polymorphous (perhaps most explicitly depicted in *Postcards from No Man's Land*, 1999). The attempt to go beyond conventional cultural and social boundaries is characteristic of postmodernism; it is, as Lyotard (1984, p. 63) notes, 'working without rules in order to formulate the rules'.

Formally, Chambers' novels also include a commitment to and celebration of the key narrative and stylistic tropes of postmodernism. Written in a playful eclectic manner, and explicitly **intertextual**, they are a pastiche, no longer merely quoting texts, as Jameson claims that modernist writers did, but actually incorporating fragments of other works to the extent that the boundary between high art and popular culture is effaced (Jameson, 1985, p. 112). Indeed, Chambers' work investigates its own existence as a construct, thereby also rendering provisional the border between what is fiction and what is reality.

Another work that resists traditional narrative conventions, thereby drawing attention to the process of storytelling, is Philip Pullman's *Clockwork, or All Wound Up* (1996). This **metafictive** text consists of two narrative voices: the character Fritz, and the omniscient narrator who frames Fritz's story and comments on the characters in physical frames inserted periodically. Also, in line with Jameson's description of key postmodern characteristics, Pullman's text blends the genres of detective fiction and the **fairy tale**.

Contemporary picturebooks such as John Burningham's *Come Away from the Water, Shirley* (1977) and Anthony Browne's *Voices in the Park* (1998) also share a commitment to postmodern aesthetics, both formally and thematically. Neither text has a coherent or unified worldview. For example, in Burningham's book, there is no central or controlling authorial voice; no information is provided that might link the images of Shirley's parents on the beach with Shirley's wordless narrative. Similarly, in Browne's book, multiperspectivism takes the form of four different 'voices', each being represented by a different typeface. Thus, as is often evident in postmodern texts, indeterminacy rules, thereby allowing for alternative viewpoints and a plurality of response. [AMB]

See also Chapters 2, 6 and 9.

Further reading

Jameson (1985, 1991), Lyotard (1984), Sipe and Pantaleo (2008).

PROPP, VLADIMIR (1895–1970) A Russian formalist who contributed much to the development of structuralism and narratology and, more specifically, to the analysis of **folk** and **fairy tales** in his *Morphology of the Folktale* (1928). Taking a corpus of 'magical' Russian folktales, he identified 31 'functions', as he called them. These are particular moves or developments in the narrative. For example, a common, early one is for the hero to be forbidden from performing a certain action (an interdiction), such as going into a particular room in a castle, or talking to strangers on the way through the woods. Propp found that, although not all of the functions needed to be present, they always unfolded in the same sequence. He also argued that plots arose from one of two main functions, either villainy or lack (e.g. in 'Jack and the Beanstalk', the family lacks money). Apart from the form of the story, Propp also analysed the functions performed by the characters, who are not individuals but types, and any of them, whether animal or human, can fill the various 'spheres of action'; thus, there is a *villain*, who disrupts the initial equilibrium, often by threatening the *princess*, a victim; a *hero*, who tries to restore the status quo; a *dispatcher*, who sends the hero on a quest; a *helper*, who assists the hero; a *donor*, who provides the hero with something (e.g. information, an object); and lastly, a *false hero* – one that turns out not to be what she or he at first seems. As Propp noted, a character could perform more than one of these roles. His work is interesting in making us look more carefully at how narratives are structured, and it has been widely applied to other popular cultural forms, such as films and novels. However, its limitations are also often noted in that it divests itself of precisely what is special about narratives: the way that they *do* vary, so that we can be re-enchanted by very similar stories, finding one funny, another sad; also, different **ideological** inflections can make us react to stories in very different ways. Online there is a 'Proppian Fairy Tale Generator', which also demonstrates the shortcomings of the functions. [DR]

See also Chapter 5.

Further reading

Propp (1968), 'Proppian Fairy Tale Generator' (2001).

READER-RESPONSE CRITICISM A general term for those critics who think that readers have some legitimate influence over the way we make sense of texts. This said, the term covers a diverse range of approaches, some of which are at odds with one another. The German literary theorists Hans Robert Jauss and Wolfgang Iser are often said to be founders of this approach. In contrast to **New Criticism**, which argues that the meaning is within the text and that we should not be swayed by background knowledge or our emotional reactions (the 'affective fallacy'), reader-response criticism welcomes these dimensions. Indeed, it argues that they are unavoidable, reading a text being likened to how a musician might perform a score.

Iser (1974) used the term 'the implied reader', alluding to Wayne

Booth's concept of the 'implied author'. This organizing consciousness was seen to produce a meaningful and coherent reading from a text's codes, especially picking up on the gaps and indeterminacies therein. However, he saw this process as limited to works of literary quality, dismissing popular culture texts for tending to spell everything out. He details this process in *The Act of Reading* (1978), always emphasizing that, though readers may vary, they are bound to fulfil conditions specified by the text. He did not, therefore, encourage the more playful, liberated style of reading suggested by Roland **Barthes** in 'The Death of the Author'. Michael Benton (1992) follows Iser's lead in analysing the relationship between implied readers and authors in the openings of three children's novels. Despite its central importance to the very concept of children's literature (which, unusually, is defined by its readership), Iser's theory has had surprisingly little impact on children's literature criticism (see **Chambers**, 1985; Benton, 2004). John **Stephens** (1992a) is a notable exception; rightly challenging ahistorical accounts of the implied reader by previous critics, Stephens proceeds to demonstrate how **ideology** contributes to structuring the responses elicited by any given text.

In America, Stanley Fish developed a more open style of interpretation called 'affective stylistics', where he emphasized how a text unfolds over time, so that our understanding of it likewise changes through time. This 'slow' reading allows us to experience the text in a more dynamic manner. In Fish's model, the reader is given more latitude in realizing the text – although it still depends on a reader's background (it is not a completely subjective thing). He thus speaks of 'interpretive communities' to which readers belong, which help explain how psychoanalytical and New Critical interpretations, for instance, can coexist.

Beyond Fish, there are those that take a more individual approach still, such as in Norman Holland's (1975) and Michael Steig's (1989) accounts, the latter being unusual in refusing to distinguish children's from adults' books, all being seen as capable of giving some sort of pleasure; thus, he considers *Alice*, *Wind in the Willows* and Sendak's *Outside over There* alongside works by Austen, Dickens and others. Finally deserving mention here is Louise Rosenblatt's seminal *Literature as Exploration* (1938), which has probably had the most influence pedagogically on teachers of literature worldwide. Again, she emphasizes the **subjectivity** of transactions between reader and text, formulating a continuum from 'aesthetic' (for pleasure) to 'efferent' (for meaning) styles of reading.

While individual studies of reading continue to be influential (e.g. Wolf and Heath, 1992), reader-response criticism always needs to be aware of the different nature of children's literature, since the implied child reader is distinguishable from the community of actual adult readers (whether critics, reviewers or teachers) who still largely control the process of 'decoding' the text's possible meanings. Though the difficulties are still insufficiently acknowledged, children's literature critics have to contend not only with

234

textual gaps but also with the fissures separating child and adult reading consciousnesses. Children's authors usually circumvent this problem by claiming that they can still think like children, but for a literary critic this claim, whether true or not, is relevant only to the extent that it suggests a similar flexibility in the consciousness of an adult reader. The gap between implied child reader and actual adult critic has been filled in various, ingenious ways. At one end of the spectrum one finds the claim that the child reader is simply unknowable, and, therefore, should be excluded from hermeneutic enquiry altogether (Gupta, 2003, p. 11). At the other end, one finds the more appealing but equally impossible position that adult critics should read, think and write like children (**Hunt**'s notion of **childist criticism**, 1984a; 1984b; 1991, pp. 189–201).

Fortunately there are more pragmatic answers to hand: first, through young people participating in public discourse about children's literature as actual readers, critics and reviewers; we cannot then pretend that their responses are unknowable. Second, the new category of **crossover** literature has increased critical awareness of the many complex ways in which child and adult reading intersect. This, however, could eventually result in further complexity, for if the implied reader of a new generation of children's literature is radically unstable in terms of its 'address in time', then a whole new dimension of indeterminacy is opening before us. Not only is the text different each time it is read, so too are readers different each time they are played upon by a text. [RF/DR]

See also Chapter 2.

Further reading

Benton (1992, 2004), Iser (1974, 1978), Rosenblatt (1938), Steig (1989).

REAL In **Lacanian** psychoanalysis, the Real is one of the three orders or registers (the other two being the **Imaginary** and the **Symbolic**) through which the various dimensions of human experience may be understood. The Real is 'that which resists symbolization absolutely' (Lacan, 1988b, p. 66); as such, it can be imagined at one level as the brute materiality of things in the world. Once we put words to those things and thus give them qualities, we are no longer talking about the Real in itself, but our own mental perceptions and concepts. Thus, there is a distinction between the Real, which exists prior to and outside symbolization, and reality, which is composed of our impressions and the semiotic systems we use to designate and represent these impressions. Before infants begin to use and understand meaningful **sign** systems, they can be said to exist in the Real of bodies; after people begin to use signs, there is always the sense that there is something that cannot be fully expressed or contained in any semiotic system. An important feature of the Real is that it is undifferentiated; for instance, there are no categorical distinctions, such as those of gender, in the Real. The presence of the Real exerts pressure on our symbolic systems, causing us to make changes and rework our understandings of things, but it is not accessible in itself once we become users of language. [KC]

See also Chapter 7.

Further reading

Dean (2000), Fink (1995), Lacan (1988b).

REYNOLDS, KIMBERLEY (1955–) Professor of Children's Literature at Newcastle University, United Kingdom, Kimberley Reynolds has been an ambassador for the internationalization of children's literature studies. In a similar post at Roehampton University, she was founder of the National Centre for Research in Children's Literature (NCRCL), which, in association with the International Board on Books for Young People (IBBY), has mounted international summer schools and a long series of day conferences and associated papers. Through these and numerous other projects, Reynolds has helped bring children's literature studies into national and international focus.

Engaged both with literary and social theory, and the practical task of getting books to readers, she has challenged Jacqueline **Rose**'s view 'that children's literature is conservative and creatively dependent' by 'focusing on its demonstrable capacity for innovation' (Reynolds, 2007, pp. 8–9). Consequently, she has written extensively on such subjects as fear, sex, self-harming, death and textual technophobia – breaking the **myth** of childhood innocence (as constructed by writing adults) and placing children's literature in a multimedia context. She leads and epitomizes a distinctively pragmatic British school of children's literature studies that sees no conflict between historical bibliography and book distribution or literary theory and psychological response, as long as each contributing area of study is of the highest standard. [PH]

Further reading

Reynolds (1990, 1994, 2005, 2007).

ROMANTIC/ROMANTICISM A term central to childhood studies in that our modern conception of the child seems to originate in this period, roughly dated from the 1790s to the 1830s in England and Europe, though its influence is felt slightly later in America. The labelling of the period came later, however, drawing on the fascination the Romantics had with the Middle Ages and its art, including its romances and the **Gothic**. The word 'romance' initially connoted the language (and literature) of the commoner, as opposed to civilized Latin, so seemed particularly fitting for a movement that rejected the earlier Classicism. Instead, Romanticism celebrated a country's own literature, especially its older, oral forms (like the ballad and **folktale**); it also celebrated nature and the rural rather than the city and championed the individual over the State, hence the cry of 'Liberty, Equality and Fraternity' in the French Revolution of 1789, which is often seen as a key initiating event. Women's voices start to be heard in print, too, and they began to demand equal rights. Children, also, begin to feature more centrally in the arts, especially in the poetry of William Blake ('Songs of Innocence') in the 1790s. But with Romanticism's stress on the superiority of nature and all things natural, the child becomes not simply another being that has rights but a symbol for all that is good in the world: a being that possesses Edenic innocence, suffering the Fall only when growing up into adult society. Jean-Jacques Rousseau (1712–78) is the key philosophical exponent of this view, writing *Émile, or On Education* (1762), which imaginatively charts Rousseau's idea of an ideal development (which is a boy's; the girl, Sophie, who also features, is less fortunate).

It is of note that the *Bildungsroman* became popular at this time: a novel that charts an individual's development, showing that people do, in fact, develop and that childhood experiences are the bedrock of this process (Rousseau also wrote what is considered one of the first modern autobiographies, where he too dwells, uncharacteristic before this time, on his childhood). All this was very different from earlier views of children, which saw them as beings born into sin, thence to be redeemed. Now, with development so important (as John **Locke** had earlier averred), there was far more attention paid to education. The book was central in this enterprise (though not for Rousseau, who allows his Émile one work only: *Robinson Crusoe!*), with ever-increasing numbers of works for children being published.

Whereas earlier conceptions tended to celebrate the masculine side of Romanticism, more recently scholars have shown the huge impact of women writers and thinkers; in the area of children's books, Sarah Trimmer (1741–1810), Anna Barbauld (1743–1825), Hannah More (1745–1833) and Maria Edgeworth (1767–1849) deserve special mention. The difference between male and female views of English Romanticism is simplistically seen to turn on female writers' opposition to fantasy, despite the growing influence of the Gothic and the celebration of folk and **fairy tales**, which the Grimm Brothers were then researching in Germany. Moreover, fantasy works were appearing at this time, such as William Roscoe's incredibly popular narrative poem *The Butterfly's Ball* (1806–7). A woman's concerns, though, were more connected with her position as *Guardian of Education*, to borrow the title of Mrs Trimmer's periodical, the first to discuss children's literature (1802–6); and women (alongside others) were particularly concerned with possible lower-class discontent, rather than with fantasy *per se*, especially in the wake of the French Revolution.

It is only recently that the Romantic conception of the child has been challenged – although the Golden Age of Childhood was seen to end somewhat earlier (often dated *c.*1950) – with a number of writers demanding a more realistic and **agentic** conceptualization of young people. [DR]

See also Chapter 1.

Further reading

Day (1996), McGavran (1991, 1999), Plotz (2000).

ROSE, JACQUELINE (1949–) Known primarily as a psychoanalytically influenced cultural theorist, Rose has written widely on such topics as **Lacanian** theory, the biographical constructions of Sylvia Plath and, more recently, Zionism. However, although she wrote only one work in children's literature studies, it could be said to have revolutionized the discipline, disturbing a former cosiness about its object of study: the child. *The Case of Peter Pan, or the Impossibility of Children's Fiction* (1984) states its argument in its title, namely that the child represented in books for children is an adult construction: it represents what adults would like the child to be. Rose saw J. M. Barrie's *Peter Pan* as epitomizing the adult's **desire** for the figure of an eternal, innocent child. However, as Rose's book also demonstrates, Barrie's text is exemplary too in demonstrating the impossibility of such a figure's existence; hence, she argues, Barrie's inability to create a satisfying final version of his text. Bending the word 'case' in its psychoanalytical direction, Rose suggests that this **Romantic** child figure is a product of an adult need to create a space of innocence, beyond the divisions of society (of sex, gender, **ethnicity**, etc.), most keenly seen in Rousseau's ideal creation, Émile. Although such a child could never exist, fictional versions of this being have regularly been presented to children as role models. Though Rose keeps the theoretical basis of her argument in the background, its Lacanian roots are evident: the child being a creature of the **Imaginary**, representing a **mythical** state of wholeness, whereas the adult operates in the **Symbolic**, in the realm of language, that is, in a realm where words seem to have taken the place of a one-to-one relationship with things, and, most especially, with the mother.

Many commentaries on Rose's work, though, have not explored these intellectual roots. The constructionist basis of her argument has been most favoured, linking her to Philippe **Ariès**'s thesis. Controversial, and often misunderstood, as her book was on its first appearance, her views have now been assimilated and given differing inflections by later critics. [DR]

See also Chapters 1 and 2.

Further reading

Honeyman (2005), Kincaid (1992), **Lesnik-Oberstein** (2000), Rose (1984), Rudd (2007), Steedman (1995).

Sᴄʜᴏᴏʟ sᴛᴏʀʏ That many children's writers have been attracted to the school story **genre** probably results from its potential for creating a location largely insulated from the outside world, one in which young characters can have a considerable degree of initiative, while adults appear in a secondary role. The most memorable school stories seem to be those in which the school is almost a character in itself, something which probably explains both the lasting popularity of the boarding school as a setting and the consequent paucity of indigenous school stories from countries where this form of education has been less common. The fictional day school seldom provides the degree of intensification found in this almost claustrophobic type of location; stories which simply feature school as one of many possible settings where their characters may meet tend to become variants on the novel of social realism or the adventure tale. Consequently much of the history of the genre is inevitably that of stories set in boarding schools, though in some twentieth-century instances the setting within a day school is just as essential to the plot as in traditional examples.

Although more remote ancestors of the school story have been traced, the originator of the genre is usually judged to be Sarah Fielding's *The Governess, or The Little Female Academy* (1749), though its educational location provides little more than a framework for the sharing of tales. Thomas Hughes' *Tom Brown's Schooldays* (1857), although far from being the first story set in a boys' school, was undoubtedly the most influential, being followed swiftly by F. W. Farrar's *Eric, or Little by Little* (1858) and *St Winifred's, or The World of School* (1862). The popularity of these books encouraged a wide range of immediate successors of which probably the best known today is Talbot Baines Reed's *The Fifth Form at St Dominic's* (1887). Robert Kirkpatrick (2000, p. 3) suggests that Reed's success resulted from his combining 'the moralistic with the melodramatic', and in first being published in the flourishing *Boys' Own Paper* (*BOP*). A more subversive classic of the genre is Rudyard Kipling's *Stalky & Co* (1899), which provides a different 'take' on a theme found in many school stories both before and since: bullying. Periodicals featuring boys' school stories were particularly popular in the first half of the twentieth century, the heyday of the work of Charles Hamilton (alias Frank Richards, one of 28 pseudonyms), whose best-known character was Billy Bunter of Greyfriars School.

Many books set in educational establishments for girls were also written after *The Governess*, but as Sue Sims and Hilary Clare (2000) reveal, it was not until the 1870s that the girls' school story began to thrive, while the school as a world of its own scarcely comes to prominence until the work of L. T. Meade in the 1880s. The best known of her 200 or more books is the first, *A World of Girls* (1886), depicting, as do many of her novels, a small, home-like school. As was the case for boys' stories, periodicals became a major outlet for this type of fiction, but, like their male counterparts, these declined by the beginning of the Second World War.

Five authors were largely responsible for the considerable growth in girls' school stories during the first half of the twentieth century: Angela Brazil, Elsie Oxenham (Abbey School), Dorita Fairlie Bruce ('Dimsie' novels), Elinor Brent-Dyer (Chalet School) and Enid Blyton (Malory Towers and St Clare's). These stories share many features, notably the fact that the school itself, its continuity and values, can be seen as a character whose importance is comparable to that of the pupils and staff. Features which recur include the journey to school; the introduction of new pupils and their need to accept the school's code of honour; the significance to the plot of sporting, dramatic and musical events; and intense but completely asexual friendships. Many of these books are also notable for the caring attitude of the staff and a tolerance of difference, aspects less apparent in contemporaneous boys' books. The most notable later exponents of the genre have been the much acclaimed Antonia Forest (Kingscote School) and Anne Digby, whose recent books about Trebizon School, together with her continuations of Blyton's 'Naughtiest Girl' series, attest to the resilience of the girls' boarding school tradition.

The two most significant writers of boys' boarding school stories during this period, Anthony Buckeridge and William Mayne, were quite different from each other. Buckeridge's 'Jennings' series, spanning the second half of the twentieth century and featuring a lively and adventurous boy and his friends, is clearly within the tradition and formed the basis of a popular television series. Mayne, well known in other genres, wrote four novels based on his own education at the Canterbury Cathedral choir school; the complexity of his treatment of plot and relationships and the elegance of his style raise these books above more routine school stories.

As the twentieth century went on, there was an inevitable increase in books set in day schools, generally co-educational. Many of these, by authors such as E. W. Hildick, Geoffrey Trease, Robert Swindells and Gillian Cross, deal with social issues and portray a broad segment of society. In some instances the school setting is almost incidental, but often it allows a sharper focus, since the attitudes of both staff and fellow students serve to highlight those of society at large, as in the long-running *Grange Hill* series on British television, associated also with a number of novels by Robert Leeson. Race provides the agenda in Bernard Ashley's *Donovan Croft* (1974) and Jan Needle's *My Mate Shofiq* (1978) and gender in Gene Kemp's *The Turbulent Term of Tyke Tiler* (1977) and Anne Fine's *Bill's New Frock* (1989).

Despite the elegiac tone of critical studies by Frank Musgrave (1985) and Jeffrey Richards (1988), heralding the death of the school story, even the boarding school novel is still vigorous. Its most notable recent manifestations have been in the area of fantasy, especially Hogwarts School in J. K. Rowling's immensely popular 'Harry Potter' series (1997–2007). Prior to this, however, both Miss Cackle's Academy in Jill Murphy's 'Worst Witch' (1974–93) and Anthony Horowitz's 'Groosham Grange' (1988, 1999) had revealed the potential of linking traditional facets of the school location with the teaching of magic.

School stories seem to have always been a particularly British phenomenon, probably because boarding school education, at least in its public school form, was less common in other countries. Susan Coolidge's *What Katy Did at School* (1873), deriving from the author's own childhood experiences, is the best-known example from the nineteenth-century United States, but probably the most impressive American example is Robert Cormier's *The Chocolate War* (1974). The bullying and corruption at Trinity High School can be seen as an indictment of society as a whole. By contrast, series such as 'Sweet Valley High' and its associated television programmes may more accurately be described as teenage romance, and in a similar manner, Stephenie Meyer's very popular vampire romance saga (2005–8), subsequently filmed, treats Forks High School as little more than a convenient location for the characters to meet up. It could be argued that the school story is alive and healthy, particularly in America, with the many teen movies (*High School Musical*, etc.). However, in many of these films the school is merely a backdrop, rather than being a character in its own right.

Some novels at least partially set in school come from commonwealth authors, notably the Australian Louise Mack whose 'Teen' series (1897–1933) is original in its focus on the relationship between two teenage girls. Nevertheless, despite the popularity in many countries of translations of Blyton's books, and more recently of Rowling's, there are relatively few instances of school stories from non-English writers. Arja Peeter began a Dutch series using school as a setting, *De Olijke Tweeling* [The Roguish Twins; 1958], which has been continued by other writers. Other Dutch school stories by Jacques Vriens, especially *Die Rotschool met die Fijne Klas* [That nasty school with that fine class; 1976], have run into many editions. Similarly in Germany, 'Hanni and Nanni' (based on Blyton's 'St Clare's') and 'Tina and Tini' ('Malory Towers') have been popular.

It is difficult to foresee the future of school fiction, but the vigour shown by this genre in the past, and the number of classic texts of considerable originality that it has given rise to, suggest that any obituaries are premature. It may not be easy to find an alternative to the narrative opportunities of a setting such as school, where all the characters in a novel are constrained to be present, with consequent dramatic interactions which have the potential to reveal their personalities and develop the action. [PP]

See also Chapters 3 and 6.

Further reading

Auchmuty (1992), Cadogan and Craig (2003), Kirkpatrick (2000), Musgrave (1985), Richards (1988), Sims and Clare (2000), **Tucker** (2004).

SEDGWICK, EVE KOSOFSKY (1950–2009) An American critic generally considered to be one of the pioneers of both gay and lesbian studies and queer theory. Sedgwick's ground-breaking work on the concepts of homosociality, the homosexual–heterosexual binary and queer **desire** has helped to define the field of Gender Studies today.

Between Men: English Literature and Male Homosocial Desire (1985) introduced the concept of homosocial relationships and desire, arguing that **patriarchal** societies are structured according to the social bonds between men. Women are often used to legitimize such relationships (facilitating the transmission of status and property through marriage, for example), which is why Western societies define these male social bonds as being in opposition to homosexuality. However, Sedgwick suggests that the categories of 'homosociality' and 'homosexuality' are not separate at all but that they continually overlap. Homoerotic desire is thus potentially present in many socially sanctioned male-to-male relationships. Sedgwick's ideas about homosociality can be applied to children's texts that depict single-sex social spaces, as Roderick **McGillis** demonstrates in his analysis of American cowboy films. McGillis (2002b, pp. 185–6) claims that 'the homosocial world of the cowboy . . . is to a great extent a world in which women are unnecessary'. Though cowboy films are inherently conservative, they also reveal evidence of transgressive desire. The ideological construction of masculinity in these texts is often 'communal, parental, sensitive, self-assured' (p. 188) and is thus antithetical to **hegemonic masculine** ideals. Beverly Lyon Clark has also proposed that homosocial bonding is integral to *Jack Granger's Cousin* (1877), a novel by Julia A. Mathews, which reveals the contradictory nature of masculine discourses in late nineteenth-century American society. Clark analyses the narrative's 'homoerotic triangle', stating that 'nineteenth-century educated Englishmen, as Sedgwick and others have noted, accepted some homosexual activity in their schools but were expected to outgrow it – leading to associations of the homoerotic with childishness' (Clark, 2001, p. 216).

Epistemology of the Closet (1990), Sedgwick's most critically acclaimed and best-known work, is viewed as one of the key texts of queer theory. Analysing classic examples from American and European literature (including Henry James, Oscar Wilde and Marcel Proust), Sedgwick proposes that sexual identity is as important as gender in determining individual **subjectivity** and social organization. Her interest lies in disclosing the ambiguities

and incoherencies which plague the homosexual–heterosexual binary, in order to examine the nature of sexuality and deconstruct the 'naturalization' of identity categories such as 'gay' or 'straight'. *Tendencies* (1993) further develops these themes, interrogating the imposition of artificial identity categories on individuals according to their sexual preference. Queer, according to Sedgwick, is thus the 'open mesh of possibilities, gaps, overlaps, dissonances and resonances, lapses and excesses of meaning when the constituent elements of anyone's gender, of anyone's sexuality aren't made (or can't be made) to signify monolithically' (1993, p. 8). This volume also contains the essay 'How to Bring Your Kids Up Gay' (which has been included in several anthologies), a provocative indictment on Western society's marginalization and oppression of individuals who exhibit transgressive sexual desires: 'I've heard of many people who claim they'd as soon their children were dead as gay. What it took me a long time to believe is that these people are saying no more than the truth. They even speak for others too delicate to use the cruel words' (p. 2).

Children's literary criticism that engages with the concept of 'queer' is indebted to Sedgwick's work. Elizabeth A. Ford's analysis of Lesléa Newman's pro-gay narratives, such as the pioneering *Heather Has Two Mommies* (1989) and *Too Far Away to Touch* (1995), engage with Sedgwick's description of the experience of gay or gay-friendly children as a 'fraught' subject. Ford writes:

> books that present gay or lesbian themes to children may be seen

as opening up that 'fraught space' to their readers. Ultimately, it is the fear of what children might learn about their own sexual identities, not about the sexuality of adults around them, that makes these books controversial.

(Ford, 1998, p. 127)

Although she is not mentioned by name in Michael Cart and Christine Jenkins (2006), Sedgwick's legacy is discernible in this historical survey of gay, lesbian and queer themes in YA fiction that charts changing social attitudes towards homosexuality and the narrative strategies used to represent non-normative sexual desire. [VF]

Further reading

Ford (1998), Sedgwick (1985, 1990, 1993).

SIGNIFICATION – SIGN/SIGNIFIER/SIGNIFIED
The whole poststructuralist enterprise could be said to turn on a particular insight of the Swiss linguist Ferdinand de Saussure, namely that signs have two aspects, one sensory, the other conceptual, and that these are not of necessity conjoined. The sensory aspect (or signifier) is the medium in which the sign exists. In this book, it is visual: you are reading words. However, the book could also be read to you (through sound), or, indeed, the signs could be conveyed by touch, via a Braille edition. These sensory signifiers then seek to elicit mental or conceptual representations (signifieds). Thus, the word d-o-g (signifier) seeks to conjure up a four-legged creature that barks (signified). It seems

straightforward, and many alphabet books try to make it so, but each aspect of the sign has a certain arbitrariness, which is hidden only because of our continued, everyday iterations of such associations. Different cultures, however, conceive 'dogs' differently; in some they are seen more as working animals, in others as pets and, still others, as culinary dishes, and this is to leave aside derogatory associations, which can shift according to gender ('He's/She's a dog'). Here we are speaking about the signified, but signifiers also vary according to language (*hund*, *chien*), of course, and even within a language ('pooch', 'mutt'). It is on this discovery that the study of signs, semiotics, largely draws.

The power of this finding, though, lies in the fact that it gives us an insight into the workings of **ideology**, that is, the way that language not only shapes how we see things but also how 'things' might be seen otherwise. In terms of gender, then, there was once a stereotypical association of 'doctors' as male, 'nurses' as female. What about a more abstract category, like 'human being', though? How is one of this species conceptualized (signified), and how would we represent such a being visually (i.e. what signifiers would we use)? In children's books, certainly, the figure has been predominantly white and, if active, male, but this only scrapes the surface of possible signifiers – around colour, **ethnicity**, dress-style, weight, size, disability, nakedness – each with different ideological implications. Children's books, it is argued, are especially significant in either confirming or challenging everyday ways of signifying. Ursula

Le Guin, in making her Earthsea hero, Ged, dark-skinned, was certainly challenging stereotypes, but she herself did not think of having a female protagonist – not, at least, until the fourth book, *Tehanu* (1990), anyway.

This awareness of the arbitrary link between signifiers and signifieds is part of a general recognition of the relativity of our ways of thinking and being and is, therefore, a perspective that particularly appeals to those wanting to challenge the status quo: feminists, gay and lesbian activists, and those in race studies, disability studies and so on. Poststructuralism exhibits exactly this shift from the fixed structures of its predecessor, structuralism. In literature, Roland **Barthes**' proclamation of the 'Death of the Author' epitomized in wider terms the way that the sign had been freed from a controlling Authority figure. Readers were encouraged to approach texts in their own ways and, in the work of writers like Jacques **Lacan** and Jacques **Derrida** especially, the signifier was privileged over the signified, to open up the ways a text might signify.

However, such playfulness brought, in its wake, concerns about overinterpretation, which some see as connected to the subsequent debate about the 'end of theory' and a return to more grounded, ethical concerns (e.g. **multiculturalism** – especially in the wake of 9/11 – and **ecocriticism**). What this cultural shift cannot alter, though, is Saussure's insight into the fact that signs are only that: sensory indicators that are meant to evoke certain conceptual representations, neither of which can be mapped, neutrally, onto 'things' in themselves. [DR]

Further reading

Chandler (2006), Culler (1981), Simpkins (2001).

SOLIPSISM In philosophical discourse, solipsism refers to the view that only oneself exists, that it is impossible to distinguish between one's own self and the **otherness** of the world and of other people. Hence, the self is the only reality, and nothing is knowable outside the self. The solipsist thus relates to the outside world as if it were an aspect of the self. Children's literature has a particular concern with solipsism because it can describe what we presume to be an innate state of infancy (as opposed to a pseudo-philosophical account of self and the limits of language as communication). Hence, the trajectory of childhood is away from solipsism to an intersubjective form of social being, and it is perceived to be a failure of **subjectivity** if a person cannot perceive an other as another self, and hence denies that other a subject position independent of her or his self; or fails to perceive her or his self as independent of the world, finally to construct a sense of her or his self as **agentic**. The concept is enacted in Anthony Browne's picture book *Zoo* (1992), in which the three male members of the family visiting a zoo are incapable of thinking that other creatures (and this implicitly includes humans) have an inner life (thoughts, wants, feelings) of the kind which indicates separate personhood. Others, including the wife/mother of the family, hold little interest for them, and only their own needs (the egotism of the boys) or linguistic utterances (the stupid jokes of the father) are meaningful to them. The mother, in contrast, extends empathy to the captive animals. Robyn McCallum (after **Bakhtin**) extends the term to include 'cultural' or 'ethical' solipsism, whereby members of one culture or society are unable to perceive and comprehend the otherness of another culture or society. Thus, Armin Greder's picture book *Die Insel* (2002; *The Island*, 2007) links xenophobia and racism to solipsism. [JS]

Further reading

McCallum (1997), Rudrum (2005).

STEPHENS, JOHN (1944–) Emeritus Professor in English at Macquarie University, Australia, and one of the most internationally recognized critics working in the field of children's literature today. Stephens has made a significant contribution to the subject of narratology in children's fiction and film and has also published on subjects as diverse as schema theory, **intertextuality**, gender representation and retellings of traditional stories. *Language and Ideology in Children's Fiction* (1992a), a study of the narrative strategies that are used in writing for children to shape and inform the child reader's views of the world, brought Stephens international acclaim and remains one of the most highly cited works of children's literature criticism: a standard text for researchers in the area. *Retelling Stories, Framing Culture: Traditional Story and Metanarratives in Children's Literature* (1998), co-authored with Robyn McCallum, comprehensively

examines retellings for children across a variety of story categories, highlighting the strategies used to encode cultural values. Stephens edited and contributed two chapters to *Ways of Being Male: Representing Masculinities in Children's Literature and Film* (2002), one of the first collections of children's literature criticism to address the topic of masculinity. (Until this point, criticism of gender representation in children's books had focused almost exclusively on the construction of female characters.) In 2008 Stephens was awarded the prestigious International Brothers Grimm Award for his pioneering contribution to children's literature research. [VF]

See also Chapter 5.

Further reading

Bradford *et al.* (2008), Stephens (1992a, 2002b), Stephens and McCallum (1998), Stephens and Watson (1994).

SUBJECTIVITY What does the word 'I' refer to? In poststructuralist and postmodern cultural theory, ideas about 'the subject' and subjectivity have taken a central place, where they have been theorized in diverse and often conflicting ways. If an emerging direction is discernible, it is probably a trajectory progressing from theories which define the subject as constructed by social **ideology** to theories which delineate the possibility of a subject constituted intersubjectively, that is, a subject which participates actively in the discursive processes through which it comes into being. The concept, especially in the latter formulation, entered children's literature scholarship at the beginning of the 1990s and eventually became a common term, although 'subjectivity' is still often used as if it were interchangeable with 'identity' and 'selfhood'. The word 'subject', however, expresses a sense of social and cultural interaction which is not implicit in the word 'self': the subject is always related to something outside it, so that who we are and what constitutes what we think of as our interior lives is determined by our relationships. Subjectivity is thus not specific to the individual but arises intersubjectively, that is, within interrelationships with others.

Key terms in theories of subjectivity are subject and **agent**. In *Discerning the Subject* (1988) Paul Smith argues that the subject is best understood as an admixture of everchanging positions ('subject positions') which a person occupies in relation to the discourses of the surrounding society. Because such discourses are of different kinds (**ethnicity**, politics, gender, peer groups, advertising, etc.) and both momentary and intermittent in their operations, they are unlikely to coalesce into some kind of unified, overarching subject position. In opposition to some poststructuralist thinkers, such as Louis Althusser, Michel **Foucault** or Pierre **Bourdieu**, who argue that the subject is a social construction, subjected *to* the pressures of social discourses or ideologies, Smith (following Anthony Giddens) argues that the subject is also 'the agent of a certain discernment' (Smith, 1988, p. xxxiv). In other words, a person does not simply follow ideological scripts, but is also an *agent* who reads those scripts and determines whether or not to embrace them. In taking this position, Smith avoids both essentialist conceptions of the subject, which ground subjectivity in consciousness, unrestricted agency or essential selfhood – as **humanism** tends to do – and mechanistic social theories of subjectivity, which conceive of the subject as entirely socially constructed. In summary, subjectivity represents an individual's sense of always becoming a subject – in the sense of being subject to some measure of external constraint – and as an agent – that is, being capable of conscious and deliberate thought and action. And this identity is formed in dialogue with the social discourses, practices and ideologies constituting the culture which an individual inhabits, and with other people engaged in the same process.

The quest for intersubjective agency is a **metanarrative** that underlies and pervades most children's fiction. Conceptions of subjectivity are intrinsic to narratives of personal growth or maturation, to stories about relationships between the self and **others** and to explorations of relationships between individuals and the world, society or the past. The conflict between ideology and intersubjective agency can thus be seen to be splendidly encapsulated in Hester Shaw's words at the close of Philip Reeve's *Mortal Engines* (2001, p. 293): 'You aren't a hero, and I'm not beautiful, and we probably won't live happily ever after . . . But we're alive, and together, and we're going to be all right.' In such ways subjectivity is intrinsic to the major concerns of children's literature. [JS]

See also Chapter 7.

Further reading

Benjamin (1995), McCallum (1999), Magnus (2006), Smith (1988).

SUPEREGO One of the three **agencies** that structures the psyche in **Freudian** theory (the other two being the **id** and the **ego**), the superego is the internalized voice of external morals and prohibitions. It emerges during the **Oedipal** phase of development, where the father intervenes in the child's **desire** for the mother, prohibiting a sexual relationship between them. As a repressive agency aimed at regulating social relationships, it inspires guilt, shame and fear with regard to the child's instinctual orientation to his own desires, but the child responds to the threat by internalizing its prohibitions and developing what is commonly called a conscience. **Lacan** develops the tyrannical aspect of the superego even further than Freud, emphasizing not only its prohibiting function but also its imperative to enact and enjoy not its own will and desires but the desires of the **Other**. In this sense, it inspires a sense of duty and submission to culture that Lacan deems perverse. [KC]

See also Chapter 7.

Further reading

Freud (1961), Lacan (1988a), Žižek (1994).

SYMBOLIC The third register (the others being the **Real** and the **Imaginary**) in **Lacanian** psychoanalysis through which humans act and understand their experience, the Symbolic is the public realm of language and culture, the domain of interaction between subjects under the mediating force of the big **Other** (which must be understood in its multivalent dimensions). The latter represents a radical alterity that cannot be assimilated to the self through identification but which is also implicated in the political, linguistic and kinship structures through which the subject signifies herself. Lacan developed his notion of the way language functions in this order from the work of Saussure. The Symbolic is thus the realm of **signifiers** severed from any relationship they might have to the Real. Instead, the signifiers form relationships among themselves that constitute a Law that regulates **desire** and establishes the subject's position with respect to the Other. The realms of the Symbolic, Imaginary and the Real are heterogeneous, with symbolic signifiers taking absolute precedence over imaginary **signifieds**, and neither being determined in any way at all by the stuff of the Real. [KC]

See also Chapter 7.

Further reading

Fink (1995), Lacan (1988c).

TATAR, MARIA (1945–) An American scholar of **fairy tales** who brings psychoanalysis and cultural history to bear upon literary readings of a wide range of texts. Although an heir to the legacy of critics such as Bruno **Bettelheim**, Tatar's *oeuvre* provides an important corrective to his work;

she is as attuned to psychic realities as she is concerned with the history of psychoanalysis and **unconscious** biases that can inflect critical readings. Her work thus leavens the universalizing tendencies of psychoanalysis with incisive commentary about the material production of a given text, locating the story (or reader) in time and place. Mindful of the demarcations between folkloric and literary studies as well as of the significant issues surrounding translation, Tatar's critical contributions to the field acknowledge her debt to folklore, while providing her readers with an array of sturdy translations of the literary works themselves. Tatar's awareness of how '**ideological** fantasy' can distort the ways critics read fairy tales has produced self-reflective work that interrogates the history of childhood, as well as unarticulated assumptions readers have about adulthood (Tatar, 1993, 2003).

Tatar's career reflects an abiding interest in the stories that shape and captivate readers: from the fairy tales of childhood to the more 'adult' fascination with stories that often address the 'beastly' (e.g. serial murder). Best known for her work on the Grimm Brothers, her more recent scholarship reflects another fruitful intersection of the world of fairy tales and 'real life' – as her writings on Bluebeard, a fairy tale that combines an account of a serial murderer with a monitory (or celebratory) tale of a woman's curiosity, attest (Tatar, 2006). Her work on *Lustmord* (sexual murder) reflects her own intellectual history in the rich world of fairy tales – stories that often recount grisly acts of unthinkable violence – and, like her earlier work, these newer

publications return to uncover powerfully shaping stories about gender, **otherness** and contamination (Tatar, 1997). Her latest book, *Enchanted Hunters*, redeploys Nabokov's phrase to capture how children's literature affects and transforms readers.

This recent examination of the compelling hold childhood reading has on adults provides another example of how Tatar's work renders visible stories and histories that have been occluded or made invisible by other fictions, helping scholars see, in an almost **uncanny** way, how some of the most potent stories for adults and children contain familiar *and* unfamiliar histories – important narratives that live close to home and demand elucidation. [LAT]

Further reading

Tatar (1993, 1997, 2003, 2006, 2009).

TELEOLOGY In philosophy, teleology refers to explanations which attempt to account for things or phenomena by considering their contribution to optimal states, wholes or systems. When applied to literary works, especially fiction, teleology refers to an interpretation of a work or its structure (or a work's interpretation of its own events and participants) which apparently discloses evidence of design or purpose in nature, society or the universe, so that the meaning of the parts inheres in the outcome towards which those parts move. Teleology thus depends on the assumption that causality in a text is determinable, and hence the final meaning perceived may be viewed as the inevitable consequence to which the parts – the network of textual perspectives and relationships, events, character interactions – have been leading. A key example of teleological explanation, common throughout the history of the novel, has been the coincidence plot, which implies not a failure in realism or a simplistic plot device but some providential force at work. For example, Erich Kästner's *Das doppelte Lottchen* (1949; in English, *Lottie and Lisa*) pivots on the **uncanny** coincidental meeting and bonding of twin sisters separated soon after birth and their scheme to change places and reunite their divorced parents. In realizing a **metanarrative** about the optimal version of the family unit, the novel is overtly teleological. The appeal of this teleology is attested to by the large number of the book's film adaptations, in six languages, including two in English (*The Parent Trap*, 1961, 1998). As this example suggests, the remarkable conjunctions of space and time that cause the pivotal coincidence provoke a reader's **desire** for explanation, and when considered from the novel's close the coincidence plot is endowed by the reader with teleological force, implying a causality more significant than mere coincidence. In more recent, self-reflective novels such as Gregory Maguire's *What-the-Dickens* (2007), the almost outrageous frequency of coincidence may serve to subvert causal explanatory systems and linear patterns of origin, so that readers become aware of the constructedness of teleology. [JS]

See also Chapter 5.

Further reading

Dannenberg (2004), Sternberg (1992).

TOWNSEND, JOHN ROWE (1922–) A pioneering critic of children's literature, and an award-winning author. He was a journalist and children's book editor of *The Guardian* until 1978. He wrote his first children's books *Gumble's Yard* (1961) and *Hell's Edge* (1963) because he felt that 'books dealing with the rougher side of real life, and with the problems and joys of growing up in contemporary society, were far too scarce in Britain' (Chevalier, 1989, p. 971). Because his novels (more than 20 of them) were often linked to specific contemporary themes (such as *Goodnight, Prof Love* [1970], about class and sex in the 1960s), they have dated *The Intruder* (1970), however, which won the Mystery Writers of America Edgar Allan Poe Award in 1971 for the Best Juvenile Mystery, is a notable exception, retaining its ability to disturb.

His major contribution to children's literature studies was *Written for Children: An Outline of English Children's Literature*, which was the first comprehensive popular history of the area and was for many years the standard work. In the introduction to the first edition, Townsend (1965, p. 9) wrote: 'I believe that children's books must be judged by much the same standards as adult literature. A good children's book must not only be pleasing to children: it must be a good book in its own right.' 'In 1968 he coined the distinction between 'book people' and 'child people', which he refined in his most influential essay, 'Standards of Criticism for Children's Literature' (1971). Despite being challenged by some critics (e.g. **Lesnik-Oberstein**, 1994), it remains a standard categorization in children's literature studies. He also produced a survey of contemporary writers, *A Sense of Story* (1971), updated as *A Sounding of Storytellers* (1979).

More recently Townsend has produced a book on the publisher John Newbery (Townsend, 1994) and, with the novelist Jill Paton Walsh, set up Green Bay Publications, which published Ursula K. Le Guin's seminal *Earthsea Revisioned* (1993) and Paton Walsh's novel *Knowledge of Angels*, shortlisted for the Booker Prize in 1994. [PH]

See also Chapters 1 and 6.

Further reading

Townsend (1979, 1990, 1994).

TRITES, ROBERTA SEELINGER (1962–) A professor of English at Illinois State University, Trites first attracted international attention with the publication of *Waking Sleeping Beauty: Feminist Voices in Children's Novels* (1997), in which she analyses the representation of feminine subject positions across a range of children's books. Trites' focus in this book is on the way that authors can resist gender stereotyping and create **agentic subjectivities** for female characters – although she also proposes that a feminist children's novel is actually any 'novel in which the main character is empowered regardless of gender' (Trites, 1997, p. 4). In addition to feminist literary criticism, Trites has also published widely on the subjects of **adolescence** and adolescent fiction. *Disturbing the Universe: Power and Repression in*

Adolescent Literature (2000) was one of the first comprehensive studies of the **genre** of adolescent or young adult fiction and won the Children's Literature Association Book Award in 2002. Using a theoretical framework that draws primarily on Michel **Foucault** (with references to **Bakhtin**, **Barthes** and **Lacan**), Trites explores the operation of power in literature for teenagers, contending that such texts simultaneously seek to empower and repress adolescent readers. In her most recent book, *Twain, Alcott and the Birth of the Adolescent Reform Novel* (2007), Trites draws parallels between the work of well-loved authors Mark Twain and Louisa May Alcott, suggesting that each used adolescent characters as vehicles for social change in their novels. [VF]

See also Chapter 3.

Further reading

Trites (1997, 2000, 2007).

TUCKER, NICHOLAS (1926–) An educational psychologist, now honorary senior lecturer in cultural studies at the University of Sussex, Tucker has been a prolific reviewer and broadcaster, contributing thousands of articles and reviews to UK national newspapers such as *The Independent* and *The Times*. Perhaps his most important book was *The Child and the Book: A Psychological and Literary Exploration* (1981); based on the work of Jean **Piaget**, this is a 'pre-theory' guide centred on helping parents and teachers to choose appropriate books for their children. It is, however, acutely aware of the dangers of constructing and manipulating 'the child', and Tucker described the book as 'literary and psychological detective work, and not a little honest speculation'. More recently, his pragmatic and accessible approach has been put to good use in three 'Rough Guides' to children's literature, reviewing over 400 books and linking them to the main stages of a child's development. Tucker has always tackled the wider issues of what children are and what children's culture is, and has recognized and celebrated the appeal of lullabies, nursery rhymes and oral bedtime stories, besides the often denigrated popular writers, such as Enid Blyton. He has been particularly concerned about what might disturb a child and the dangers of children's books that are **depressive** rather than optimistic (Tucker, 1976, 2006). [PH]

Further reading

Tucker (1976, 1981, 2002a, 2002b), Tucker and Eccleshare (2002).

UNCANNY A term meaning strange or disturbing, which was given more specific resonance by psychoanalytical critics in the wake of Sigmund **Freud**'s essay on the topic, but has subsequently broadened its range considerably, into what has been termed 'uncanny studies' (Collins and Jervis, 2008, p. 1). Freud traces the etymology of the word which, in German, is *unheimlich*, or 'unhomely'. But Freud notes that the word *heimlich* ('homely') itself has a seemingly opposite sense, meaning 'hidden', or 'out of sight'. The word thus effectively slides into its opposite, containing instability at its root. It has, therefore, come to designate that which disturbs because of its very familiarity – as family secrets often do. The uncanny, as Freud states, is 'the name for everything that ought to have remained secret and hidden but has come to light' (quoting Schelling, Freud, 1955, p. 224).

Freud's essay itself seems to demonstrate an uneasiness around the term in that he misses certain key factors that might induce it (e.g. a sense of *déjà vu*); however, he does mention doubles (repetition of characters or situations, including coincidences), the inanimate becoming animate (and vice versa) and cases where imaginary or psychic occurrences seem to displace reality (as in wish-fulfilment). He sees these as disturbing because they remind us of what we have repressed, namely a fear of castration, which Freud says accounts for other elements of the uncanny, that is, dismembered limbs, especially when they show signs of life, female genitals and being buried alive. The last two elements are seen as unhomely precisely because they point to what was once home to us all (the womb); they thus point not only to a state of castration but also towards what **Kristeva** would later term **abjection**.

Freud uses E. T. A. Hoffmann's fantastic story 'The Sandman' to illustrate his case. While the concept of the uncanny would, therefore, seem to have much mileage in the discussion of children's texts (e.g. Rudd, 2008), Freud specifically excludes such areas as **fairy tales**, precisely because supernatural events are too commonplace (or homely) in this **genre** (a moot point). As others have noted, though, Freud seems particularly evasive about certain aspects of the uncanny, a key one being a fear of death.

Subsequent theorists have broadened the use of the term, pointing to the uncanniness of such tropes as metaphor, where the known is invaded by something different yet familiar; moreover, key poststructuralist notions such as presence and absence, of meanings sliding away under **signs**, of the **Real** breaking through the **Symbolic**, also capture a sense of uncanniness; indeed, Jacques **Derrida**'s notion of *différance* seems to point exactly to the continual insecurity of language, where words seem haunted by traces of **otherness**, as captured in his term 'hauntology', which puns disturbingly on 'ontology'. In a related vein, Julia Kristeva has suggested that we are 'strangers to ourselves'; and other writers, such as Homi **Bhabha**, have used the uncanny to explore the **postcolonial** situation, where notions of home become inflected with otherness – especially for diasporic communities.

Finally, there have been attempts to delimit the term historically, suggesting that the uncanny is specific to modernity, a dark underside to the Enlightenment project (the **Gothic** being a key facet), with developments like photography, film and sound recording, let alone virtual reality, demonstrating an absence that lies at the heart of our experiences of presence (Collins and Jervis, 2008). While the term sometimes seems in danger of losing all specificity, there is no doubt that it captures something that resonates with contemporary society. This might explain why it is the 'canny' – what seems perfectly clear and homely – that we now approach with more trepidation. [DR]

See also Chapter 7.

Further reading

Collins and Jervis (2008), Freud (1955), Royle (2003b), Rudd (2008).

UNCONSCIOUS Usually referred to as **Freud**'s most significant discovery, the term functions as both adjective and noun. As an adjective, it describes mental functioning that is not perceptible as such, like a background program that is constantly running on a computer; basic body functions are performed unconsciously, as are procedural and associative memory formations and linguistic systems that enable us to act and understand automatically, as it were. As a noun, the unconscious takes on more distinctive features. For Freud, it is a repository of representations of instinctual drives that have been repressed: the **id** is thus unconscious. For **Lacan**, the repression is more broadly conceived: the unconscious is an effect of the process of signification itself. That is, for Lacan, language ineradicably separates the realm of things from the subject. **Signifiers** operate independently of their **signifieds** in that they form relationships among themselves and continually defer any fixity of meaning. This radical disconnection of language constitutes the unconscious as a discourse of free-floating signifiers that exert pressure on conscious, cognitive functions in ways that can be creative and sometimes irrational.

Crucial to Lacan's formulation of the unconscious is its linguistic quality, which links it to the **Symbolic**, and denies any notion that it is internal to the subject; that is, our unconscious is not populated with our own instincts and **desires**, but with the desires and discourse of the **Other**. Thus, our most profound expression of self is always implicated in the Other through a shared vocabulary of signifiers set adrift in the unconscious. [KC]

See also Chapter 7.

Further reading

Freud (1957), Lacan (2006).

VALLONE, LYNNE (1962–) Children's literature scholar noted for feminist, **new historicist** and interdisciplinary work, primarily on American and British girlhood. Trained as an eighteenth-century literature scholar, in *Becoming Victoria* (2001) Vallone developed the approach to children's literary culture that she had first shown in *Disciplines of Virtue* (1995). Both books exemplify historically grounded research, reflecting extensive archival work and considering children's texts and institutions in the context of mainstream 'adult' literature and culture. In *Disciplines of Virtue*, Vallone 'reads' classic children's texts alongside *Pamela*, conduct manuals, marriage settlement papers and the practices of both the English Magdalen Hospitals for former prostitutes and the American Florence Crittenden Homes for 'fallen' girls. In *Becoming Victoria*, she traces the future queen's personality development by examining her unexcised childhood diaries in tandem with diaries of other girls of the period, her copybooks and educational programme, contemporary children's literature, and Victoria's juvenilia. Her new historicist approach shows itself most plainly in the range of texts she examines and through her exploration of the power relationships in which unmarried daughters, former prostitutes and the young Victoria herself find themselves embedded.

Vallone's historical method has attracted reviewers in history journals and broadened the prestige of the academic study of children's literature beyond its usual disciplinary confines (Vallone contributed a piece on 'The Young Victoria' to the BBC History website). In keeping with her interdisciplinary work, she now chairs the recently formed Department of Childhood Studies at Rutgers University, Camden. With Claudia **Nelson**, Vallone edited *The Girls' Own: Cultural Histories of the Anglo-American Girl, 1830–1915* (1994), which examines the literary, visual and institutional representation of girls in England and the United States. Finally, she has been instrumental in the production of two notable textbooks in the field: *The Norton Anthology of Children's Literature* (2005) and *The Oxford Handbook of Children's Literature* (2010). [LT]

Further reading

Mickenberg and Vallone (2010), Vallone (1995, 1998, 2001), Vallone and Nelson (1994).

WARNER, MARINA (1946–) A highly esteemed British author of adult fiction and non-fiction, whose ground-breaking study of **fairy tales**, *From the Beast to the Blonde* (1994a), made a significant contribution to the field of children's literature. In this book, Warner critically analyses the role of women in traditional fairy tales, as well as turning her eye to the female capacity for storytelling and assessing the ways in which acts of retelling can affect a story's meaning and significance. *No Go the Bogeyman: Scaring, Lulling and Making Mock* (1998) is a cultural exploration of fear. Changing her focus to male characters, Warner examines the role of fear in texts produced for child audiences, such as **folk** and fairy tales, classic **myths** and nursery rhymes.

In addition to her cultural criticism, Warner has written several highly acclaimed novels and two children's books, as well as editing *Wonder Tales: Six Stories of Enchantment* (1994c), a collection of subversive, seventeenth-century French fairy tales by authors such as Marie-Jeanne L'Heritier, Charles Perrault and the Abbé of Choisy.

Warner delivered the BBC's prestigious Reith Lectures in 1994 – only the second woman to be invited to do so. Her lectures explored the relationship between modern social issues and mythology and were published as *Managing Monsters: Six Myths of Our Time* (1994b). Both this work and her 2001 Clarendon Lectures, entitled 'Fantastic Metamorphoses and Other Worlds: Ways of Telling the Self', contain much of relevance to children's literature studies. Warner was made a

CBE in 2008 for her services to literature. [VF]

Further reading

Warner (1994a, 1994b, 1994c, 1998).

WHITENESS A term which refers to the ways in which whiteness is accorded the status of normalcy in contemporary multi-ethnic societies. 'Whiteness' refers not so much to the colour of a person's skin as to a 'normative structure, a discourse of power, and a form of [racialized] identity' (Ware and Back, 2002, p. 13). The field of whiteness studies critically examines how whiteness claims and maintains its power through representation and systemic practices. It is a fundamental aspect of whiteness that it operates by being invisible; for instance, whiteness is rarely regarded as an **ethnicity**, but simply exists as the normal way for people to be. As Richard Dyer (1997, p. 3) says, 'whites are not of a certain race, they're just the human race'. The historical and symbolic processes which have privileged whiteness are specific to time and place, taking on a variety of forms. In Australia, for instance, traditional forms of whiteness are those which figure European (and most often, British) cultures, bodies and practices as superior to those of indigenous people, so that the history of whiteness in Australia derives from the nation's **colonial** origins and is sustained in contemporary Australia through discrimination against non-white **others**. In the United Kingdom, national identification focuses on the superiority of the British character – forged through imperialism, the Second World War and especially the Blitz – over those from countries formerly under Britain's imperial yoke, and contemporary racism is bound up with resentment towards non-white immigrants. While racism in the United States proceeds from colonization and the assault on Native American cultures and peoples, it is shaped in a particular way by the discourses and politics of slavery and its consequences. Whiteness is a highly unstable category, changing over time and constantly redefining itself. Nevertheless, it is commonly promoted as the stable, orderly centre upon which national identity is formed. [CB]

See also Chapter 4.

Further reading

Dyer (1997), Ware and Back (2002).

WINNICOTT, D. W. (1896–1971) A British object–relations psychoanalyst whose ideas have been particularly influential in children's literature. In contrast to the '**ego** psychologists', led by Anna Freud, the object-relations psychoanalysts gave more attention to **unconscious** processes. Winnicott, especially, lays particular stress on the 'good-enough mother', who acts in an almost symbiotic relationship with the young child, mirroring the child's behaviour so that the infant comes to see itself as omnipotent, as capable of being a creative force in the world. Over time, the mother gradually helps the child separate a subjective reality from the objective world, there being a transitional space between the two in which creative play (and later art and literature) takes place. What he called 'transitional objects' are also crucial in assisting the child's development as a separate being. As Winnicott (1971, p. xi) expressed it, 'one must recognize the central position of Winnie the Pooh'. Books themselves could be important in this way, too, perhaps especially those read at bedtime, before the child is separated from its primary caregiver. Margery Wise Brown's *Good Night Moon* has been seen as particularly 'Winnicottian' in this way, 'assuring [the child] of the "me" before the lights go out at bedtime' (Bosmajian, 2004, p. 135). Relatedly, Winnicott published his own account of a child being treated for night terrors, called *The Piggle* (1977).

Winnicott's *Playing and Reality* was particularly popular in the 1970s in education courses, when notions of child-centred education were in the ascendant. However, in his neglect of the pre-existing context within which the mother–child dyad operates (of **patriarchy**, of language) – let alone the huge stress he lays on a mother to ensure a child's proper development – Winnicott's work has fallen from grace in favour of Jacques **Lacan**, Julia **Kristeva** and others. [DR]

See also Chapter 7.

Further reading

Bosmajian (2004), Rustin and Rustin (1987), Winnicott (1971, 1977).

ZIPES, JACK (DAVID) (1937–) A leading authority on **folk** and **fairy tales**, whose work has redefined children's literary criticism in this area. Zipes is primarily concerned with the sociohistorical context of these tales in Western culture and is responsible for introducing the area to the critical approaches of the Frankfurt school, a group of German scholars that includes Herbert Marcuse, Theodor Adorno, Max Horkheimer and Jürgen Habermas. *Breaking the Magic Spell* (1979) uses a Marxist critical perspective (for which Zipes is renowned) to trace the historical evolution of the tales, suggesting that such stories have an inherently utopian social function. *Fairy Tales and the Art of Subversion* (1983) examines how fairy tales are used to socialize young readers by focusing on the ways in which retellings are reshaped over time in order to reflect dominant cultural values. *Don't Bet on the Prince: Contemporary Feminist Fairy Tales in North America and England* (1986) combines revisions of traditional fairy tales by notable authors such as Margaret Atwood, Jane Yolen, Angela Carter and Tanith Lee, with commentary from Zipes about how these retellings seek to redress the gender imbalance of conventional fairy tales: by depicting heroines with **agentic subjectivities**, contesting the association of female beauty with good character and interrogating stereotypical feminine roles such as witch, evil stepmother and princess. In his various critical discussions of literary fairy tales, Zipes adapts the methods associated with the sociohistorical analysis of folktales. However, rather than asserting that such tales reflect the **ideology** of a particular society at a particular time, Zipes prefers to view the tales as preserving 'traces' of historical cultures that no longer exist, despite their constant

and progressive ideological modification as they are retold over time.

Zipes was also one of the first critics to link written fairy tales with oral culture, arguing that the tales were originally passed down by people unable to read or write, before they were collected and written down in a process that involved both alteration and stylization. Since there is no way of definitively ascertaining the origins of fairy tales (Ruth **Bottigheimer** [2007] asserts that connections between fairy tales and oral culture are both 'untested' and 'untestable'), the matter must always, to some extent, be speculative. For Bottigheimer, who makes a clear distinction between folk and fairy tale, the latter did not originate until the sixteenth century.

More recently, Zipes (1997) has turned his focus to the relationship between fairy tales and modern culture, discussing the impact of film and television on traditional fairy tales. Zipes directly criticizes companies like Disney, arguing that the implicit capitalist ideology which informs their **animated** versions of classic fairy tales has resulted in the commodification (or **Disneyfication**) of these stories. Zipes (2001) similarly analyses the influence of capitalist market conditions on other texts produced for children, suggesting that such forces act to homogenize children's literature and stifle creativity. *Why Fairy Tales Stick* (2006) takes Zipes' previous work on fairy and folktale in a new direction. Drawing on Richard Dawkins' work on memetics, which suggests that the principles of evolution can be applied to the cultural transmission of ideas, Zipes claims that the continued popularity of particular fairy tales is the result of evolutionary forces. While critical reactions to this book have been varied, Zipes' extensive knowledge of fairy tales makes this unusual theoretical approach interesting if not entirely persuasive.

From 1990 to 2001, Zipes was editor of *The Lion and the Unicorn*, a journal dedicated to the criticism of children's culture, literature and film. He also edited *The Oxford Companion to Fairy Tales* (2000) and was editor-in-chief of *The Oxford Encyclopaedia of Children's Literature* (2006), a comprehensive reference work on the area. In addition to his extensive array of critical publications, Zipes – who is Professor Emeritus of German at the University of Minnesota – has translated the works of the Brothers Grimm (among others) into English. He received the International Brothers Grimm Award in 1999 for his significant and pioneering contribution to children's literature criticism. [VF]

Further reading

Bottigheimer (2007), Zipes (1979, 1983, 1997, 2006a).

ŽIŽEK, SLAVOJ (1949–) A Slovenian cultural theorist whose ideas are profoundly informed by Jacques **Lacan**'s version of **Freudian** psychoanalysis, though he also draws extensively on Marx, Hegel and an array of other thinkers. Since his first book in English, *The Sublime Object of Ideology* (1989), he has been a prolific commentator on popular culture, cinema, literature, jokes, politics, philosophy, 9/11, religion, ecology – among many other topics. Recognizing his influence, since 2007 there has been an *International Journal of Žižek Studies*.

Reading his work is always an invigorating experience, but can be frustrating for anyone seeking a linear argument, formally introduced and summarized. Instead Žižek darts from topic to topic, examining jokes, popular science fiction films, and indeed Shakespeare and opera, making provocative and arresting claims. One could justify this by suggesting that he is deliberately challenging and puncturing what Lacan called 'master discourses', while avoiding the trap of forging his own. His strength lies in the way he puts other thinkers to work, demonstrating their contemporary relevance. Žižek is, therefore, someone who makes us think, whether we are for or against him.

In his first work he famously takes issue with those who would see **ideology** as a form of false consciousness that can be overcome; rather, as Žižek (1989, p. 21) puts it, it is 'this reality itself which is already to be conceived as "ideological"'. He is thus critical of those cynical **postmodernists** who think that they now see through the hype of capitalism. Their cynicism, he argues, is simply a feature of late capitalism, shown by the fact that they continue to invest their money and consume society's goods. Postmodernity's cynicism about such grand narratives as a belief in God is also hypocritical in that such beliefs are usually replaced with substitutes in the form of cults, conspiracy theories and the like. We might be cynical about the **Other** (society), but – as he notes – we still often have faith in some 'Other of the Other'.

We must, therefore, recognize that we cannot live without some form of ideology, for it screens us from the void of the **Real** – that which lies outside our symbolized world. However, although we exist within this **symbolic** realm, we are not simply its functionaries. The symbolic is always incomplete, never capable of ridding itself of a surplus of the Real. Hence, we continually fantasize to try to cover up this mismatch, to make up for what we seem to lack. Feeling somewhat hollow or lacking, then, our whole existence revolves around our struggle for wholeness – for what Žižek terms our answer to the Real. We stage this in our lives, and in our stories, too, trying to determine the coordinates of our **desire**. *Peter Pan* (1904) can productively be read in these terms, with Peter Pan himself representing the fantasy of a complete being, experiencing utter enjoyment (*jouissance* or bliss); however, the book also demonstrates how impossible it is for such a figure to exist; that is, to organize or 'quilt' a stable symbolic world (Rudd, 2006a).

Fantasy is, therefore, crucial (it is not mere escapism) in maintaining our sense of reality, however destructive it might sometimes be. It is, therefore, also implicated in such social pathologies as racism, where a particular 'other' seems to be enjoying life more than we are. It is reasoned that if this 'other' (e.g. rich Jewish bankers,

Blacks with their physical prowess, the decadent West, etc.), who is seen to be stealing our *jouissance*, could be eliminated, then we ourselves would experience complete harmony and fulfilment. Malorie Blackman's *Noughts & Crosses* is a clever fictional representation of this, where it is **whiteness** that is seen to count for 'nought'.

Productive as Žižek's work has been, he has been criticized for appropriating other philosophers for his own devices; thus, his Hegel is not the familiar one of the dialectic; even his Lacan, although it builds on the later work of this thinker, is still regarded as deviant, especially in Žižek's theorization of the Real, which he interprets as a void, whereas others have argued that the Real is only 'an emptiness *at the level of the* **signifier**' (Belsey, 2005, p. 54). In other words, it is our symbolic world of language that empties out the Real, but it still exists, in all its unfathomable richness. Despite these criticisms, though, Žižek still has much of relevance to inform current cultural criticism, and in many ways it is his very assertiveness that makes him so engaging as a thinker. [DR]

See also Chapter 7.

Further reading

Belsey (2005), Myers (2003), Rudd (2006a), Žižek (1989, 1991).

Part III

TIMELINE

INTRODUCTION

Where does a timeline begin? Children's literature could arguably go back to Sumeria, 4,000 years ago, according to Gillian Adams (2004). But Steven Mithen (2006) has tacitly pushed back this date a couple of million years earlier, arguing that lullabies originated with humankind's upright stance, allowing mothers to soothe their children at a distance. This timeline, you might be pleased to hear, is far less extensive, beginning with the printing press in the Middle Ages (bar one, suspect entry). It is also deliberately selective, avoiding endless lists of titles, where trends and a sense of rationale are sometimes lost. Selectivity, of course, has its own problems: why some works at the expense of others? A timeline can, therefore, play up notions of **canon**icity, or it can query them. When timelines extend beyond national boundaries, they become even more difficult, as individual countries' narratives tend to compete and conflict. When a timeline then seeks to add parallel developments (in other arts, in politics and science) things become more complicated still. And in setting these events alongside each other, we raise the question: is there some influence going on and, if so, what influenced what? Here I have mentioned a few contiguous events but leave it to the reader to discern whatever patterns (or their lack) they might descry.

While the timeline aims to be accurate, I would hope that it also engenders a healthy scepticism about the construction of such chronologies – an awareness, that is, of the problems of the 'grand narrative' (see Chapter 1). So, lists will inevitably tend towards the canonical, celebrating a unified national voice and giving less space to more marginal groups and their literatures. Here, certainly, a white Western perspective prevails, one in which many nineteenth-century adventure books are seen to emerge from the 'Dark Continent' (i.e. Africa), which – it was once thought – was in the process of becoming civilized, forgetting the West's actual plundering of that continent, which included a long-term complicity in the slave trade, let alone an ignorance of the great civilizations that had existed there far earlier (as at Great Zimbabwe, Benin and Timbuktu, for instance). So, many nations are absent entirely from this timeline, and anything not in English is immediately at a disadvantage. Furthermore, like so many other works on children's literature, this timeline follows the common prejudice of privileging fiction: far less poetry is featured, less drama still and next to no non-fictional works (see Chapter 11; Duh, 2007).

Even what is here, though, should be considered circumspectly. While dates of publication are significant, they are also problematic. Not that it affects this list much, but dating systems have themselves changed with the switch from the Julian to the Gregorian calendar, which occurred in different countries at very different periods. Furthermore, to alight on a specific year of publication is itself sometimes arbitrary in that, for instance, many works appeared first in serial format, before their debut as books (Thomas Hardy's one children's work, *Our Exploits in West Poley* [1952], took some 60 years to make this transition). Even when books appear, though, there are sometimes significantly different editions as, for instance, with Alcott's *Little Women* (1868/1880) and Swift's *Gulliver's Travels*. With the latter, for example, it is the 1735 edition that is most frequently used, which is several down the line from the 1726 original. Publication isn't the same thing as composition, either – the latter being even more complex. Thus, scholars of *Pilgrim's Progress* are divided as to whether Bunyan started it in 1675, during his second imprisonment, or during his first term in gaol (1660–72). The first edition of 1678 was then itself expanded the following year, before a second part appeared in 1684. A third part, which was published alongside the other two till the middle of the nineteenth century, was not in fact by Bunyan at all! And yet, regardless of the latter's inauthenticity, it was still influential – perhaps even having an impact on *Little Women*!

In short, *caveat lector* (reader beware)! Timelines have no extra-textual existence: they are constructions, albeit with a view to being useful heuristically, giving us our bearings. But among the useful, informative material herein, you might also detect more light-hearted comments to keep you on your toes (and amused). In fact, the opening entry is certainly apocryphal.

TIMELINE

1300s
1386 'On the Twenty-second of July', to be exact, rats invaded Hamelin – at least, according to Robert Browning's 'The Pied Piper' (1842) – resulting in the eventual disappearance of the town's children (bar one) and, consequently, leaving little need for a children's literature there.

1400s
1484 William Caxton's *Aesop's Fables* – one of the first books printed from the first printing press in England. The Fables were not specifically for children but later came to be seen as most suitable for them.

1500s
1512 *The Friar and the Boy* – a celebration of farting, some centuries ahead of Dahl's whizzpopping.

1600s

1658 Comenius' *Orbis Sensualium Pictus* – one of earliest picturebooks for children – written by a Czech with the idealistic view that such works might ultimately lead to a better-educated society.

1663 John Milton's *Paradise Lost* – exploring the extent to which man could revolt against divine authority, something to which Pullman would respond over 300 years later, with *His Dark Materials* (1995–2000).

1671 James Janeway's *A Token for Children* – though celebrating 'joyful deaths' isn't everyone's idea of a good read, this work had immense popularity over a long period. A 1795 American edition is available online at http://www.book-academy.co.uk/commentaries/puritans.php#jamesjaneway.

1678 John Bunyan's *The Pilgrim's Progress* – 'from this world to that which is to come', as the title continues. It exists in countless versions and as an **intertext** (e.g. to Alcott's *Little Women*). Available online at http://www.gutenberg.org/etext/131.

1688–90 *The New England Primer* – the first primer specifically for the American colonies, heavily influenced by Puritan thinking (1777 ed, available online at http://www.sacred-texts.com/chr/nep/1777/index.htm). More recently, those advocating religious education in public schools in the United States have used the primer as a precedent, arguing that it was not then seen as unconstitutional. A new edition accordingly appeared in 1996. Available online at http://neprimer.com.

1690 John **Locke**'s *An Essay Concerning Human Understanding* – an incredibly influential volume, establishing 'the self' in modern terms and arguing that the child starts life as a 'blank slate'.

1692 Roger L'Estrange's *Fables of Æsop*, updating Caxton's 1484 version. George Fyler Townsend's 1860s version, though, later became the standard, emphasizing the moral endings. Available online at http://www.gutenberg.org/etext/21. Also, Countess d'Aulnoy's *Les contes des fées*, **fairy tales** addressed to a far more adult audience than Perrault's. Available online at http://www.gutenberg.org/etext/18367.

1693 John **Locke**'s *Some Thoughts Concerning Education* – ideas on child development articulated, seeing the early years as crucial in determining the resulting adult. The work had a huge impact on writers for children. Available online at http://books.google.com/books.

1697 Charles Perrault's *Histoires ou contes du temps passé* – subtitled 'Tales of Mother Goose', this work made old **folktales** hugely popular, though the epithet 'fairy' was new.

1700s

1700 Cotton Mather's *A Token for Children of New England* – an American version of Janeway (discussed earlier).

1704 Arabic *Book of the Thousand and One Nights* first appears in Europe, in a French translation. However, two of its most famous tales are not there: 'Aladdin's Lamp' and 'Ali Baba and the Forty Thieves'. Richard Burton's more faithful, unexpurgated version appeared in the 1880s, and a new English translation has recently appeared. Many tales are available online at http://www.al-hakawati.net/english/Stories_Tales/lailaindex.asp.

1715 Isaac Watts' *Divine Songs for Children* – contains the famous verse 'Against idleness and mischief', which Lewis Carroll made more famous in his **parody** 'How doth the little crocodile'. Available online at http://www.gutenberg.org/etext/13439.

1719 Daniel Defoe's *Robinson Crusoe* – one of the most adapted books in English, leading to a whole new sub**genre**: the 'Robinsonade' (e.g. *The Swiss Family Robinson, The Coral Island*).

1726 Jonathan Swift's *Gulliver's Travels* – retold numerous times, and often used as an **intertext**, as in T. H. White's *Mistress Masham's Repose* (1946).

1744 John Newbery's *Little Pretty Pocket-Book*. Available online at http://lcweb2.loc.gov/cgi-bin/ampage?collId=rbc3&fileName=rbc0001_2003juv05880page.db. Also, Mary Cooper's *Tommy Thumb's Song Book, Vol. 2*, the first extant collection of nursery rhymes. Available online at http://www.archive.org/details/tommythumbssongb00loveiala.

1749 Sarah Fielding's *The Governess* – regarded as the first **school story**.

1762 Rousseau's *Émile, or On Education* – celebrating the natural, **Romantic** child, continuing in Kipling's 'man cub', *man* being indicative.

1765 John Newbery's *Little Goody Two-Shoes*.

1786 Sarah Trimmer's *Fabulous Histories [The History of the Robins]* – early **ecocritical** plea for kindness to animals.

1789 William Blake's *Songs of Innocence* – children take centre stage in his poems.

1792–6 John Aikin and Anna Laetitia Barbauld's *Evenings at Home* – compilation of stories and verse, with the emphasis on the **didactic**.

1795 Hannah More's *Cheap Repository Tracts* – attempts to win hearts and minds against cheap chapbook material.

1800s

1802 Sarah Trimmer's *The Guardian of Education* – first journal to consider children's literature.

1804 Jane and Ann Taylor's *Original Poems for Infant Minds* – verses that 'awoke the nurseries of England' according to **Darton**.

1806–7 William Roscoe's *The Butterfly's Ball* – incredibly popular English nonsense poem, preparing the way for later fantasies.

1812 Grimms' *Kinder- und Hausmärchen*. Grimms' **fairy tales** are probably the best-known versions in the Western world.

1818 Mary Martha Sherwood's *The History of the Fairchild Family* – famous for its severe, uncompromising views on educating children on how to be good (or else!).

1823 Clement Clarke Moore's 'A Visit from St Nicholas' – also known as 'The Night before Christmas' – key work in establishing modern notions of Santa Claus, versions of which still thrive today in works like Allsburg's *The Polar Express*.

1824 *The Children's Friend* (–1882) – a penny magazine, and a fine 'friend', repeatedly foregrounding death and hellfire.

1842 James Orchard Halliwell's *The Nursery Rhymes of England* – one of the first scholarly investigations of the form. Also, Robert Browning's 'The Pied Piper of Hamelin' – the rats' version had to await Terry Pratchett's *The Amazing Maurice and His Educated Rodents* (2001).

1843 Start of the pseudonymous 'Felix Summerly', popular fantasy books, by a writer who also helped define the West's Christmas celebrations, inventing the family Christmas card (1846).

1844 Charles Dickens' *A Christmas Carol* – first of a number of Christmas tie-in books; F. E. Paget's *The Hope of the Katzekopfs* – the first full-length fantasy celebrating nonsense; J. O. Halliwell's *The Nursery Rhymes of England*. Also, Alexandre Dumas' *The Count of Monte-Cristo* – Dumas was a French writer, celebrated not only for his writing but for his ancestry, having a slave grand-mother from Martinique (as noted in Mildred Taylor's *Roll of Thunder*).

1845 Heinrich Hoffmann's *Struwwelpeter* (trans. to English, 1848) – **didactic** verses or, more likely, a **parody** thereof.

1846 Hans Christian Andersen's **fairy tales** appear in English.

1852 Catharine Parr Traill's *The Canadian Crusoes* – one of Canada's first children's novels. Also, Harriet Beecher Stowe's *Uncle Tom's Cabin* published – one of the few books, arguably, to have changed attitudes on a large scale; in this case, against slavery.

1857 Thomas Hughes' *Tom Brown's Schooldays* – reputedly written 'by an Old Boy'; it was the bully 'Flashman', though, who later became more celebrated in fictional spin-offs.

1858 F. W. Farrar's *Eric, or, Little by Little* – famously described by **Darton** as a 'moral jelly-fish left behind by the tide'. Also, R. M. Ballantyne's *The Coral Island*, of which *The Lord of the Flies* is a dark **intertext**.

1859 Darwin's *On the Origin of Species* – life before upright humans (with their lullabies).

1863 Charles Kingsley's *The Water-Babies* – one of the earliest children's books to show a negative reaction to Darwinism.

1864 Jules Verne's *Journey to the Centre of the Earth* – science fiction pioneer.

1865 Lewis Carroll's *Alice's Adventures in Wonderland* – an alternative, and more scary, view of life underground (than Verne); Mary Mapes Dodge's *Hans Brinker* – novel where the children effectively become the parents; Wilhelm Busch's *Max and Moritz* – Busch was a pioneering German writer, influential in development of comic art, influencing American *Katzenjammer Kids*. Finally, *Boys of England* – well-known penny dreadful, best known for serial about Jack Harkaway.

1867 Hesba Stretton's *Jessica's First Prayer* – immensely popular street Arab story about a poor Victorian waif.

1868 Alcott's *Little Women* – first of four novels about the March sisters; also, Horatio Alger's *Ragged Dick, or, Street Life in New York* – get your American Dreams here! A rags-to-riches classic. Available online at http://etext.virginia. edu/toc/modeng/public/AlgRagg.html.

1869 Matthew Arnold's *Culture and Anarchy* – lays down the gauntlet for 'culture' in the United Kingdom (just over 100 years later, The Sex Pistols reversed the argument, as celebrated by the protagonists of Melvin Burgess' *Junk*, 1996).

1871 Edward Lear's *Nonsense Songs* – appeared Christmas 1870, containing extended fantasies like 'The Jumblies'. Also, George MacDonald's *At the Back of the North Wind* – a fantasy drawing on Christian themes, which had a big impact on both Tolkien and Lewis.

1872 Susan Coolidge's *What Katy Did* – incredibly popular novel showing girls, in particular, how to deport themselves.

1873 *St. Nicholas Magazine* (–1943) – very successful American children's magazine.

1876 Mark Twain's *Tom Sawyer* – a more realistic portrayal of an American boy's life (than, say, Raggedy Dick, above).

1877 Anna Sewell's *Black Beauty* – one of the most popular animal stories ever, originally subtitled 'the autobiography of a horse' – although the horse denies it.

1878 Kate Greenaway's *Under the Window* – key publication by seminal illustrator who also influenced girls' dress, and was championed by John Ruskin. Also, Randolph Caldecott's *John Gilpin* – one of the first works to be illustrated by this prolific artist.

1879 *The Boy's Own Paper* (–1967), or *BOP*, founded by the Religious Tract Society with an eye on curbing the spread of penny dreadfuls, the 'video nasties' of their day.

1880 Joel Chandler Harris' *Uncle Remus* – first written versions of the Brer Rabbit stories, told in 'quaint dialect', causing controversy ever since, especially as the stories are narrated to a white child. Also, *The Girl's Own Paper* (–1965) – another RTS publication, 'for girls of all classes' and, as Humphrey Carpenter notes, for girls up to 25, given its competition age-limit.

1881 Johanna Spyri's *Heidi* – a Swiss classic, still in print.

1882 Richard Jefferies' *Bevis: The Story of a Boy* – sequel to his *Wood Magic*; a British equivalent to Twain, and an influence on Arthur Ransome. Also, F. Anstey's *Vice Versa* – very influential novel of adult–child reversal, filmed several times; Mark Twain's *The Prince and the Pauper* – a similar reversal, this time of rich and poor; Emilia Marryat's *Jack Stanley, or, The Young Adventurers* – a novel about English engagements with the Maori.

1883 Robert Louis Stevenson's *Treasure Island* – a novel that grew out of a map drawn by Stevenson; *Silver's Revenge* (1979) by Robert Leeson provides an interesting counterpoint. Also, Carlo Collodi's *Pinocchio* – for many, the only known Italian children's book, though too often attributed to the less-than-Italian **Disney**.

1884 Mark Twain's *The Adventures of Huckleberry Finn*. Also, *Ally Sloper's Half Holiday* – first regular British comic, featuring a disreputable, gin-drinking young layabout; that is, lad-lit ahead of its time.

1885 Stevenson's *A Child's Garden of Verses* – incredibly influential collection of verse exploring the lost world of childhood; *Kidnapped* published, too. Also, L. T. Meade's *A World of Girls* – one of the first successful girls' **school stories**.

1886 Coca-Cola invented, prominently using Santa Claus in its advertising.

1887 Talbot Baines Reed's *The Fifth Form at St. Dominic's* – a trendsetter (serialized in *BOP*, 1881–2).

1888 Oscar Wilde's *The Happy Prince* – first of two plangent collections of **fairy tales**.

1889 Andrew Lang (ed.) *The Blue Fairy Book* – first of 12, colour-coded **fairy tale** collections.

1890 Joseph Jacobs' *English Fairy Tales* – classic collection. Also, Harmsworth's *Comic Cuts and Chips* (–1953) launched.

1892 Mrs Field's *The Child and His Work* – the only extensive work to consider English children's literature prior to **Darton**.

1894 Kipling's *Jungle Book* – a second volume appeared in 1895; immensely popular to this day (see Neil Gaiman's *The Graveyard Book*, 2008). Also, Ethel Turner's *Seven Little Australians* – known as the antipodean *Little Women*.

1895 Bertha and Florence Upton's *The Adventures of Two Dutch Dolls – and a Golliwogg* – start of hugely popular and, later, highly controversial series.

1897 *The Katzenjammer Kids* – America's oldest comic strip. Also, Ernest Thompson Seton's *Wild Animals I Have Known* – naturalistic animal tales; J. Meade Falkner's *Moonfleet* – classic adventure story, still in print.

1899 E. Nesbit's *The Story of the Treasure Seekers* – the birth of a new, modern voice in children's writing. Also, Helen Bannerman's *The Story of Little Black Sambo* – controversial but immensely popular story; Ethel C. Pedley's *Dot and the Kangaroo* – a perennially popular Australian fantasy, in the manner of Carroll.

1900s

1900 L. Frank Baum's *The Wonderful Wizard of Oz* – first of the numerous books about this alternative world, even better known from the 1939 film.

1901 Kipling's *Kim* – richly **hybrid colonial** tale of Anglo-Indian cultures.

1902 Beatrix Potter's *Tale of Peter Rabbit* – launch of illustrious career of early picturebook author/artist. Also, Kipling's *Just So Stories*; E. Nesbit's *Five Children and It*.

1903 Kate Douglas Wiggin's *Rebecca of Sunnybrook Farm* – famous girl's story, often filmed.

1904 J. M. Barrie's *Peter Pan* – the original 'case' of children's fiction's impossibility. Also, Laura Lee Hope's *The Bobbsey Twins* (–1992) – 'Hope' being one of a number of pseudonyms for Stratemeyer's series writers.

1906 Angela Brazil's *The Fortunes of Philippa* – inventive slang and fun characters helped reinvigorate the **school story**. Also, Hilaire Belloc's *Cautionary Verses* – one of his several volumes of comic verse, **parodying** the earlier, more **didactic** variety; A. A. Watts' *The Child's Socialist Reader*, illustrated by Walter Crane – proof that children's literature wasn't always conservative.

1907 'Teddy Bear' invented after American President 'Teddy' Roosevelt saved a bear cub from his gun; Winnie-the-Pooh, note, only carries a cork-shooting one.

1908 Kenneth Grahame's *The Wind in the Willows* – Toad, Ratty and Mole, universally known. Also, L. M. Montgomery's *Anne of Green Gables* – first of popular series about the feisty redhead; *The Magnet* (–1940) – best known for Frank Richards' original 'Famous Five', and the indolent, greedy 'Billy Bunter'.

1909 Gene Stratton Porter's *A Girl of the Limberlost* – more famous than *Freckles* (1904), her story about a boy from the swamp, who sank – metaphorically – without trace. Also, Kewpie dolls invented – supposedly for getting people out of the trouble that Cupids got them into.

1910 Mary Grant Bruce's *A Little Bush Maid* – first of 15-novel, Australian 'Billabong' series (–1942).

1911 Frances Hodgson Burnett's *The Secret Garden* – incredibly popular book, and films thereof.

1912 Jean Webster's *Daddy-Long-Legs* – empowering girls' story, turned into a play and several film versions.

1913 Eleanor H. Porter's *Pollyanna* – renowned for her 'glad game'. Also, Walter de la Mare's *Peacock Pie* – poetry collection that established the author.

1914 Edgar Burroughs' *Tarzan of the Apes* – serialized from 1912 with the first film in 1918, and numerous sequels. Also, *Rainbow* – first British comic explicitly for children.

1915 Charlie Chaplin's *The Tramp* – a character popular across the age range.

1918 May Gibbs' *Snugglepot and Cuddlepie* – eccentric but engaging Australian stories about two babies. Also, Norman Lindsay's *The Magic Pudding* – rollicking Australian fantasy tale in verse; Rose Fyleman's *Fairies and Chimneys* – first collection of an amazingly popular British poet, whose fairy-based verse caught the *zeitgeist*.

1920 Hugh Lofting's *The Story of Doctor Dolittle* – first in the series. Also, Elsie J. Oxenham's *The Abbey Girls* – the second, and establishing, story of the series; Rupert Bear in the *Daily Express*, the bear most commonly associated with Alfred Bestall, subsequently a popular TV series.

1922 Margery Williams Bianco's *The Velveteen Rabbit* – picturebook celebrating animism. Also, Richmal Crompton's *Just William* – first of more than 40 titles about this mischief maker; Carl Sandburg's *The Rootabaga Stories* – first of four volumes of homespun, American **folktales**; BBC's *The Children's Hour* (–1964) – key programme in bringing children's works to young people, including classics like *Tales of Toytown* and *Worzel Gummidge*; Enid Blyton's *Child Whispers* – her first book (of around 700).

1923 Felix Salten's *Bambi* – a far harder-hitting story than that retold by Disney in 1942.

1924 'Little Orphan Annie' – birth of hugely popular American comic strip, eventually becoming the musical and film *Annie*.

1925 Elinor Brent-Dyer's *The School at the Chalet* – first in a long series set at an international **school** in the Tyrol (–1970).

1926 Milne's *Winnie-the-Pooh* – the most famous teddy ever.

1927 F. W. Dixon's *The Tower Treasure* – first of Hardy Boys series. Also, John Masefield's *The Midnight Folk* – magical fantasy; *Rin-Tin-Tin* (–1950s) – German Shepherd dog who, with successors, starred in Hollywood films and later a TV series.

1928 Wanda Gág's *Millions of Cats* – early, classic picturebook. Also, *Steamboat Willie* – Disney cartoon that established Mickey Mouse, though his more rat-like early appearance would be revised; the cartoon was named after the Buster Keaton classic of the same year. Finally, bubble-gum was invented, to many teachers' and parents' chagrin!

1929 Hergé's *Tintin in the Land of the Soviets* – first of 23 adventures. Also, Eric Kästner's *Emil and the Detectives* – first story to show gang of children overcoming a crook; *Popeye* debuts as a comic strip, later to be a cartoon, TV series and film.

1930 Carolyn Keene's *The Secret of the Old Clock* – first Nancy Drew. Also, Arthur Ransome's *Swallows and Amazons* – first of 12 highly successful novels.

1931 Jean de Brunhoff's *The Story of Babar* (in English, 1934) – first of series sometimes read as allegory of **colonialism**.

1932 Captain W. E. Johns' 'The White Fokker' – first story about Biggles the pilot, appearing in *Popular Flying*. Also, Laura Ingalls Wilder's *Little House in* *the Big Woods* – first of her very successful, but controversial, series about pioneering life in nineteenth-century America, made into popular TV serial; Harvey **Darton**'s *Children's Books in England* – a key history.

1934 Mary Travers' *Mary Poppins* – first of series (–1988). Also, Geoffrey Trease's *Bows against the Barons* – a socialist take on Robin Hood; Patricia Lynch's *The Turf-Cutter's Donkey* – Irish classic, full of magic and **mythology**.

1936 Edward Ardizzone's *Little Tim and the Brave Sea Captain* – picturebook debut by the renowned artist. Also, Munro Leaf's *The Story of Ferdinand* – delightful picturebook about a pacifist bull; Barbara Euphan Todd's *Worzel Gummidge* – first of many books about the scarecrow, later a TV series; Noel Streatfeild's *Ballet Shoes* – career girls 'r' them.

1937 Tolkien's *The Hobbit* – marking exam scripts, the sentence 'In a hole in the ground there lived a hobbit' reputedly came to Tolkien. The rest, as they say, isn't history – though it sounds like it might have been. Also, Eve Garnett's *The Family from One End Street* – one of the first children's novels in Britain to feature a working-class family; J. B. S. Haldane's *My Friend Mr. Leakey* – series of short stories combining fantasy with science, written by a communist geneticist; Dr Seuss' *And to Think That I Saw It on Mulberry Street* – his first children's book, the famous anapaestic tetrameter supposedly inspired by the throb of a ship's engines; *Snow White and the Seven Dwarfs* – Disney's first feature-length **animation**; Marjorie Kinnan Rawlings' *The Yearling* – a still powerful coming-of-age novel; Kathleen Hale's *Orlando the Marmalade Cat* – a series seen as a breakthrough in the development of the picturebook.

1938 T. H. White's *The Sword in the Stone* – beginning of his Arthurian saga, later brought together as *The Once and Future King* (1958).

1939 Ludwig Bemelmans' *Madeline* – first in successful series of picturebooks. Also, Virginia Lee Burton's *Mike Mulligan and His Steam Shovel* – about an unusually feminine-gendered shovel, though she does end up domesticated, heating a Town Hall.

1940 Maud Hart Lovelace's *Betsy-Tacy* – first of series that (unusually) follows the protagonist into adulthood. Also, Eric Knight's *Lassie Come-Home* – better known in TV and film versions, but the novel is far superior; *Tom and Jerry* cartoon shorts begin.

1941 Elizabeth Enright's *The Saturdays* – first of series about the talented Melendy family. Also, the Reys' *Curious George* – a book that was smuggled into America from Nazi Germany, becoming a huge success; Mary Treadgold's *We Couldn't Leave Dinah* – powerful war novel, set in Channel Islands; André Maurois' *Fattypuffs and Thinifers* – delightful fantasy about two different countries beneath Earth's surface; Pamela Brown's *The Swish of the Curtain* – influenced by *Ballet Shoes* and, in turn, influencing British comic Victoria Wood.

1942 Maureen Daly's *Seventeenth Summer* – a daring early novel about teenage love. Also, BB's (pseudonym for Denys-Watkins Pitchford) *The Little Grey*

Men – delightful story of three gnomes, set in a vanishing rural England; Blyton's *Five on a Treasure Island* – first of her longest running series (–1963).

1943 Saint-Exupéry's *Le Petit Prince* – a hugely popular parable of **Romantic** childhood. Also, Esther Forbes' *Johnny Tremain* – story of an apprentice, set during the American Revolution; the slinky invented, later to feature in *Toy Story*.

1944 Astrid Lindgren's *Pippi Longstocking* (trans. 1950) – launch of the series about a perennially anarchic girl.

1945 Revd W. Awdry's *The Three Railway Engines* – first of the famous railway series, better known through the second, *Thomas the Tank Engine*; also popular as a TV series. Also, George Orwell's *Animal Farm* – a work that he denied was for children, although some critics treat it as such.

1946 Grahame Greene's *The Little Train* – first of four children's books by an author keenly fascinated with childhood and notions of innocence.

1947 Margaret Wise Brown's *Goodnight Moon* – seminal picturebook written by an admirer of **modernism**, who managed to have Gertrude Stein's *The World Is Round* (1939) published. Also, *The Diary of Anne Frank* – original publication of the heart-rending story of the German Jewish family hiding in Amsterdam (rev. edn, *The Diary of a Young Girl* [1995]).

1948 C. Day Lewis' *The Otterbury Incident* – based on a French film, about children playing on a bombsite. Also, the Wurlitzer jukebox invented, just in time for the new 'teenager'.

1949 Blyton's *Noddy in Toyland* – first book about her bestselling creation, not beloved by all.

1950 C. S. Lewis' *The Lion, the Witch and the Wardrobe* – launch of Narnia series, also loved and reviled. Also, *Eagle* (–1969) – well-known English comic, famous for Dan Dare, Pilot of the Future; BBC's *Watch with Mother* (–1973) – 15-minute series of programmes, with favourites like 'Andy Pandy' and 'The Flowerpot Men'; Schultz's 'Peanuts' begins, featuring Snoopy.

1951 J. D. Salinger's *Catcher in the Rye* – first teenage, angst-ridden, first-person anti-hero, Holden Caulfield.

1952 E. B. White's *Charlotte's Web* – tempting to link this with Eleanor Fenn's *Cobwebs to Catch Flies* (*c*.1783), where children are gently brought within language through a gradual lengthening of words and sentences; Charlotte, though, does it more entertainingly. Also, Opies' *The Oxford Dictionary of Nursery Rhymes* – authoritative collection on rhymes and their history; Ben Lucien Burman's *High Water at Catfish Bend* – successful series about animal inhabitants in Louisiana; Mary Norton's *The Borrowers* – first of five rich novels exploring the perspective of a literal 'underclass'; Dorothy Edwards' *My Naughty Little Sister* – amusing depiction of everyday events from superior view (–1974); Mr Potato Head patented, again featuring in *Toy Story*.

1954 Lucy M. Boston's *The Children of Green Knowe* – mysterious and atmospheric series set in Cambridgeshire (–1976). Also, Rosemary Sutcliff's *The Eagle of the Ninth* – first of innovative novel series about the Romans in Britain; Tolkien's *The Fellowship of the Ring* – first of the trilogy set in Middle Earth (–1956), since given filmic justice in Jackson's adaptations; Ray Kroc founds 'McDonalds'.

1955 Crockett Johnson's *Harold and the Purple Crayon* – first of successful series about a boy who draws himself into his adventures (crayons themselves being invented in 1903). Also, Natalie Babbitt's *Tuck Everlasting* – a brilliant exploration of the downside of immortality; Nicholas Ray's film *Rebel without a Cause* gives teenage angst a more attractive face than Holden Caulfield, thanks to iconic star James Dean.

1956 Ian Serraillier's *The Silver Sword* (*Escape from Warsaw* in the United States) – brilliant story about family reuniting after the Second World War. Also, Beverly Cleary's *Fifteen* – another early example of 'teenage' fiction; Duvoisin and Fatio's *The Happy Lion* – Swiss work, winner of first West German children's fiction award.

1957 Dr Seuss' *The Cat in the Hat* – written, using just 223 words, to show that school readers could be entertaining.

1958 Philippa Pearce's *Tom's Midnight Garden* – classic time-shift fantasy, disturbing in shifting us from childhood to old age. Also, Catherine Storr's *Marianne Dreams* – another disturbing fantasy about two ailing children; William Mayne's *A Grass Rope* – another enduring fantasy classic, from a versatile and prolific author; the Hula-Hoop invented (not the cylindrical potato snack, which came later, in 1973).

1959 Opies' *The Lore and Language of Schoolchildren* – breakthrough work showing the existence of a relatively independent children's culture, mimicking adults'. Also, Barbie Doll invented (famously appearing not in the first *Toy Story*, but its sequel).

1960 Harper Lee's *To Kill a Mocking Bird* – sole book by the author, filmed in 1962. Also, Scott O'Dell's *Island of the Blue Dolphins* – classic survival tale about a native girl stranded off Californian coast; Adamsons' 'Topsy and Tim' series begins (relaunched in 2003); **Townsend**'s *Gumble's Yard* – hard-hitting family story, reflecting the social realism of early 1960s Britain.

1962 Madeleine L'Engle's *A Wrinkle in Time* – Christian science fiction in C. S. Lewis tradition. Also, Ivan Southall's *Hills End* – first of his Australian novels about **adolescents** facing crises, told in breath-taking prose; Ezra Jack Keats' *The Snowy Day* – award-winning picturebook unusual for featuring an African American character; *Growing Point* – Margery Fisher launches her incredibly influential English review of children's books (–1992); *Spacewar* – the first computer video game.

1963 Maurice Sendak's *Where the Wild Things Are* – surely the most discussed picturebook ever, filmed and turned into an opera. Also, Joan Aiken's *The Wolves* *of Willoughby Chase* – first in series set in alternative nineteenth-century England, where the Stuarts' rule continued; Ted Hughes' *How the Whale Became* – series of **mythical** stories, in Kipling vein, written for his two children by Sylvia Plath.

1964 Louise Fitzhugh's *Harriet the Spy* – a child's slightly jaundiced view of adult society, with which some adult readers were uncomfortable. Also, Lloyd Alexander's *The Book of Three* – first of five *Chronicles of Prydain*; Dahl's *Charlie and the Chocolate Factory* – one of Dahl's most well-known children's books, with trademark zaniness, filmed twice; Leon Garfield's *Jack Holborn* – Garfield's first novel, told in rollicking, exuberant prose, set loosely in the eighteenth century.

1965 Susan Cooper's *Over Sea, Under Stone* – first novel of the 'Dark Is Rising' series. Also, BBC's *Jackanory* begins on TV, bringing stories to children in 15-minute programmes, five days a week; Anne Holm's *I Am David* (orig. Danish, 1963) – boy's journey home from a concentration camp.

1967 Alan Garner's *The Owl Service* – elemental mix of fantasy and reality, told in limpid prose. Also, Russell Hoban's *The Mouse and His Child* – brilliant, uncategorizable quest narrative; K. M. Peyton's *Flambards* – first of trilogy, since extended, showing the breakdown of rigid class divisions in early twentieth century; S. A. Wakefield's *Bottersnikes and Gumbles* – first of series about two antagonistic fantasy species living in the Australian bush; George Clutesi's *Son of Raven, Son of Deer* – book of aboriginal literature from British Columbia: the Tse-shaht people in particular (in 1973 Clutesi published *Tales from the Longhouse*, stories especially for children); Ursula K. Le Guin's *A Wizard of Earthsea* – first in series of works about a realized fantasy world, which powerfully changed ideological direction with *Tehanu* (1990); S. E. Hinton's *The Outsiders* – regarded as one of the first, realistic, young adult novels, written by an 'actual' teenager; Beverly Cleary's *Ramona the Pest* – Ramona had featured earlier in 'Henry Huggins', but popular demand resulted in her own series; Paul Zindel's *The Pigman* – Zindel's first novel of **adolescent** life and strife; Barry Hines' *A Kestrel for a Knave* – about a modern-day waif, filmed as *Kes*.

1968 Ted Hughes' *The Iron Man* (*The Iron Giant*, United States) – story rooted in Hughes' mythopoeic imagination, which might explain why *The Iron Woman* (1993) was less well realized. Also, Leila Berg's British 'Nippers' reading scheme (1976), revolutionary in depicting working-class life.

1969 William H. Armstrong's *Sounder* – powerful coming-of-age novel, set in American South. Also, Margaret Mahy's *A Lion in the Meadow* – picturebook from the perfervid imagination of New Zealand writer later known for her **adolescent** fiction; Penelope Farmer's *Charlotte Sometimes* – powerful and disturbing time-slip fantasy; John Donovan's *I'll Get There. It Better Be Worth the Trip* – recognized as the first adolescent novel to address gayness; Judy Blume's *Are You There, God? It's Me, Margaret* – launched Blume as a novelist dealing with the problems of adolescence; Charles Causley's *Figgie Hobbin* – Causley's first collection of poems for children, overbubbling with energy and rhythm; Judith Kerr's *Mog, the Forgetful Cat* – first book about this endearing cat, who eventually dies in *Goodbye*

Mog (2002); Maya Angelou's *I Know Why the Caged Bird Sings* – powerful autobiography featuring child abuse.

1971 Judith Kerr's *When Hitler Stole Pink Rabbit* – first of trilogy of autobiographical works about a Jewish family, fleeing Nazi Germany. Also, Robert C. O'Brien's *Mrs Frisby and the Rats of NIMH* – prescient tale about animal experimentation; *Go Ask Alice* – controversial work about a teenage casualty of sex and drugs, initially marketed as a true story.

1972 Richard Adams' *Watership Down* – epic story set in rabbit society. Also, Norma Klein's *Mom, the Wolf Man, and Me* – daring novel for its time, depicting life in a non-traditional family; Jean Craighead George's *Julie of the Wolves* – powerful survival story set in Alaskan 'Eskimo' community.

1973 Paula Fox's *The Slave Dancer* – gripping novel about slavery, albeit criticized for racism. Also, Raymond Briggs' *Father Christmas* – famous for its comic-strip format, and for depicting a more human, working-class, Father Christmas; Nina Bawden's *Carrie's War* – outstanding novel about the inner turmoil of **adolescence**; Children's Literature Association founded.

1974 Shel Silverstein's *Where the Sidewalk Ends* – brilliant, eccentric, illustrated verses by a controversial writer. Also, Virginia Hamilton's *M.C. Higgins the Great* – Hamilton was a prolific African-American writer, something of a Toni Morrison for the young, of which this coming-of-age novel is representative; Robert Cormier's *The Chocolate War* – a seminal novel that realistically challenged the default happy ending; Blake and Hoban's *How Tom Beat Captain Najork and His Hired Sportsmen* – a madcap fantasy, displaying both creators' inventiveness at full throttle; start of 'Dungeons and Dragons', one of the earliest, and most successful, role-playing games.

1975 Judy Blume's *Forever* – her most infamous work, renowned for its detailed, technical guide to 'sex': a first in children's books and still controversial. Also, Robert Westall's *The Machine Gunners* – gritty novel about children in the Second World War; Robert Leeson's *The Third-Class Genie* – fantasy in a realistic context.

1976 Mildred Taylor's *Roll of Thunder, Hear My Cry* – gripping and painful insight into oppressed African Americans in the South in the 1930s. Also, Alan Garner's *The Stone Book* – first of what would eventually become a quartet of books: a beautifully crafted, autobiographically based account of one family's historical and geographical rootedness; Jan Mark's *Thunder and Lightnings* – outstanding debut, a sympathetic portrayal of character with learning difficulties; Bruno **Bettelheim**'s *The Uses of Enchantment* – bestselling exploration of **fairy tales**.

1977 Katherine Paterson's *Bridge to Terabithia* – novel dealing with spiritual needs of an **adolescent** in the face of death. Also, Gene Kemp's *Turbulent Term of Tyke Tiler* – witty and evocative **school story**, challenging gender stereotypes; Jenny Wagner's *John Brown, Rose and the Midnight Cat*, illustrated by Ron

Brooks – rich, award-winning, classic picturebook; *Star Wars*, George Lucas – first of sequence of films, imaginatively pitting light against dark, good against evil; Diana Wynne Jones' *Charmed Life* – first of her Chrestomanci series, showing fantasy at its most inventive.

1978 Aidan **Chambers**' *Breaktime* – first of his 'Dance Sequence', experimental novels about **adolescence**. Also, Sandra Scoppetone's *Happy Endings Are All Alike* – early exploration of adolescent lesbian identity; Shirley Hughes' *Up and Up* – this work captures Hughes' technical and storytelling abilities in full flight.

1979 Peter Dickinson's *Tulku* – one of his many outstanding novels, this one set in Tibet.

1980 Robert Munsch's *The Paper Bag Princess*, illustrated by Michael Martchenko – clever and witty challenging of **fairy tale** gender stereotypes. Also, David McKee's *Not Now, Bernard* – witty parable about child–parent relations; William Horwood's *Duncton Wood* – first of very successful series of novels detailing the epic struggles of moles in tales that resonate with real-world conflicts everywhere.

1981 *Postman Pat* – very popular stop-frame British TV **animation**, celebrating a **mythical** English country village.

1983 Anthony Browne's *Gorilla* – though Browne has earlier, groundbreaking books, this consolidated his reputation as a unique voice, using surreal visual metaphor to tell stories. Also, Mem Fox's *Possum Magic*, illustrated by Julie Vivas – incredibly popular picturebook originating in Australian **folktale** (and interesting to juxtapose with *Not Now, Bernard*); Cynthia Voigt's *Homecoming* – first of 'Dicey's Song' series, in which children come to terms with adult world; Susanne Bösche's *Jenny Lives with Eric and Martin* – infamous picturebook addressing gay parenting (orig. Danish, 1981); Cabbage Patch dolls marketed.

1984 John Burningham's *Granpa* – an outstanding exploration of ageing, communication, memory and more. Also, Dahl's *Boy* – the first of his two, popular autobiographical works (*Going Solo*, 1986); Ian Strachan's *The Boy in the Bubble* – sensitive, serious but also funny story about a character screened from the world.

1985 Janni Howker's *The Nature of the Beast* – an individual voice in British children's literature, voicing the grim impact of Thatcherism. Also, Van Allsburg's *The Polar Express* – one of his many picturebooks taking readers on a beautiful but disconcerting journey into fantastic realms.

1986 Fiona French's *Snow White in New York* – imaginative contemporary retelling of the **fairy tale**. Also, Janet and Allan Ahlberg's *The Jolly Postman* – an innovative work that brilliantly exploits **intertextuality**, both literary and non-fictional; Babette Cole's *Princess Smartypants* – an empowered princess rewrites the fairy tale; Roberto Innocenti's *Rose Blanche* – daring picturebook about life (and death) under the Nazis.

1987 Martin Handford's *Where's Wally?* – incredibly successful series of picturebooks.

1988 Grace Nichols' *Come on into My Tropical Garden* – Guyanan folklore and Amerindian **legend** mix in these inventive tales. Also, digital cellphones appear.

1989 Mette Newth's *The Abduction* – Inuit girl survives assault by Europeans and is taken to Norway. Also, Anne Fine's *Bill's New Frock* – much-cited book about boy who wakes as a girl; Lesléa Newman's *Heather Has Two Mommies* – picturebook featuring lesbian mothering (equivalent of Bösche's work [1983], and Willhoite [1990] below).

1990 David Macaulay's *Black and White* – inventive and challenging picture-book. Also, Gillian Cross' *Wolf* – imaginative reworking of 'Little Red Riding Hood'; Salman Rushdie's *Haroun and the Sea of Stories* – a verbal *tour de force*, drawing on Rushdie's own experiences as a censored storyteller; Michael Willhoite's *Daddy's Roommate* (see Bösche, 1983) – a work regularly featuring in the American Library Association's Most Challenged Books lists; arrival of www, http and html, and *The Simpsons* as an independent show.

1991 Berlie Doherty's *Dear Nobody* – sensitive novel told by a pregnant teenager in a series of letters to her unborn child. Also, Gary Crew's *Strange Objects* – addresses the confrontation of European settlers and Australian Aboriginals; Malorie Blackman's *Noughts & Crosses* – first of incredibly pop-ular and challenging series about a world where Black people hold power and Whites are nothing.

1992 R. L. Stine's *Welcome to Dead House* – first of the amazingly successful 'Goosebumps' series, opening up the horror fiction **genre**. Also, John Scieszka and Lane Smith's *The Stinky Cheese Man*, featuring frame-breaking, **metafic-tional** versions of **fairy tales**.

1993 Lois Lowry's *The Giver* – powerful dystopian novel set in an emotionally repressed future.

1994 Marion Dane Bauer (ed.) *Am I Blue? Coming out from the Silence* – early anthology dealing with lesbian, gay, bisexual, transgender (LGBT) issues. Also, Shyam Selvadurai's *Funny Boy* – Sri Lankan work celebrating the queering of gender.

1995 Pullman's *Northern Lights* (*The Golden Compass*, United States) – first of his classic trilogy *His Dark Materials* (2000) which, with its promise of a 'Republic of Heaven', seemed a fitting way to begin the new millennium. Also, Christopher Paul Curtis' *The Watsons Go to Birmingham – 1963*, powerful novel exploring racial segregation in the United States; Jenkins and LaHaye, *Left Behind* – first of immensely popular Christian series of books (11 million copies sold by 2008); *Toy Story* – first feature **animated** film shot entirely on location in Virtual Reality (i.e. fully computer-generated imagery [CGI]).

1996 Melvin Burgess' *Junk* (*Smack* in the United States) – highly controversial novel about teenagers' involvement with heroin.

1997 Rowling's *Harry Potter and the Philosopher's Stone* – the one book that everyone on the planet knows, whether the seven-book series or the film versions now rolling out. Also, *Buffy the Vampire Slayer* (–2003) – Joss Whedon's incredibly successful, teen vampire TV series; Peter Wells' *Boy Overboard* – another **adolescent** novel celebrating queerness; *Princess Mononoke* – Studio Ghibli masterpiece exploring female power and ecological awareness.

1998 Louis Sachar's *Holes* – ingeniously plotted novel that both excavates and fills in some lacunae in history, now filmed. Also, Karen Hesse's *Out of the Dust* – innovative novel about 'dust bowl' Depression, written in free verse, organized as a diary.

1999 Louise Erdrich's *The Birchbark House* – worthy counterpoint to 'Little House' books, showing Native American view of European settlers. Also, Lemony Snicket's *The Bad Beginning* – first publication of cult series (13 long) 'A Series of Unfortunate Events', subsequently filmed.

2000s

2000 Lauren Child's *Clarice Bean, That's Me* – first in series of witty, scrapbook-style picturebooks about a young girl's life and times.

2001 Julius Lester's *When Dad Killed Mom* – unrelenting exploration of family tensions, related through the children. Also, Alex Sanchez's *Rainbow Boys* – first of celebrated series about three gay teenagers; David Wiesner's *The Three Little Pigs* – a **metafictional** reworking of the traditional tale; Terry Pratchett's *The Amazing Maurice and His Educated Rodents* – prolific fantasy author's reworking of Pied Piper story; Philip Reeve's *Mortal Engines* – first of Reeve's wildly inventive series; Sharon Creech's *Love That Dog* – one of the most popular and successful verse novels; *Fellowship of the Ring* – first of Peter Jackson's majestic movies of Tolkien's trilogy; iPods launched.

2002 Neil Gaiman's *Coraline* – the prolific author's first children's novel, effectively scary and compulsive, now a stop-motion **animation**. Also, M. T. Anderson's *Feed* – dystopian novel exploring plugged-in consumerism.

2003 Mark Haddon's *The Curious Incident of the Dog in the Night-Time* – bestselling **crossover** novel featuring a 'defamiliarizing' protagonist.

2004 Julie Ann Peters' *Luna* – much praised young adult (YA) novel about a transsexual.

2005 Marilyn Nelson's *A Wreath for Emmett Till* – explores the case of a 1950s teenage African American boy killed for whistling at a white woman. Also, Scott Westerfeld's *Uglies* – first of trilogy about a future where 'looks' are everything – and compulsory; YouTube invented.

2006 Geraldine McCaughrean's *Peter Pan in Scarlet* – the 'official' sequel by prolific, award-winning novelist. Also, Stephenie Meyer's *Twilight* – first of cult series giving the vampire an image makeover, now filmed; John Boyne's *The*

Boy in the Striped Pyjamas – controversial story approaching the Holocaust from a 9-year-old's perspective.

2007 Sherman Alexie's *The Absolutely True Diary of a Part-Time Indian* – moving and humorous account of teenager living between two worlds. Also, Jacqueline Wilson's *Jackie Daydream* – first of her autobiographical works.

2008 David Almond's *The Savage* – powerful tale given extra bite through Dave McKean's gritty illustration. Also, Gaiman's *The Graveyard Book* – cleverly plotted novel about a boy growing up amongst the dead.

2009 Welcome to what *was* the present, at the time of writing: a time when the barometer of cultural significance loses some accuracy. But these works, currently, appear outstanding and innovative: Emily Gravett's *The Rabbit Problem* – the most recent picturebook by this gifted artist/writer; Rebecca Stead's *When You Reach Me*, a brilliant and mysterious tale; Jacqueline Kelly's *The Evolution of Calpurnia Tate*, a historical novel using Charles Darwin's work as **intertext**; and Frances Hardinge's *Gullstruck Island*, a powerful and original fantasy.

Part IV

Resources

New Review of Children's Literature and Librarianship http://www.tandf.co.uk/ journals/titles/13614541.asp

Papers: Explorations into Children's Literature http://search.informit.com.au/ browseJournalTitle;res=E-LIBRARY;issn=1034-9243

Sankofa: A Journal of African Children's and Young Adult Literature meenakh@aol.com

School Librarian, The http://www.sla.org.uk

School Library Journal http://www.schoollibraryjournal.com

Signal [ceased publication in 2003, but back issues available at http://www. thimble press.biz/backissues.htm]

Viewpoint: On Books for Young Adults http://extranet.edfac.unimelb.edu.au/ LLAE/viewpoint

ORGANIZATIONS FOR CHILDREN'S LITERATURE CRITICISM

ACLAR – Australian Children's Literature Association for Research http://www.aclar.org.au

CBHS – Children's Books History Society cbhs@abcgarrett.demon.co.uk

ChLA – Children's Literature Association http://www.childlitassn

IBBY – International Board on Books for Young People http://www.ibby.org

IRSCL – International Research Society for Children's Literature http://www.irscl.ac.uk

ISSCL – Irish Society for the Study of Children's Literature http:// www.isscl.com

Seven Stories: The Centre for Children's Books http://www.sevenstories. org.uk/home/index.php

Online discussion lists

Child_Lit – American-based list hosted by Michael Joseph of Rutgers University (USA): http://www.rci.rutgers.edu/ ~mjoseph/childlit/about.html

children-literature-uk – UK list for academic discussion of children's litera- ture: https://www.jiscmail.ac.uk/lists/CHILDREN- LITERATURE-UK.html

BIBLIOGRAPHY

Aarseth, Espen (1997) *Cybertext: Perspectives on Ergodic Literature*, Baltimore: Johns Hopkins University Press.

Abbott, H. Porter (2002) *The Cambridge Introduction to Narrative*, Cambridge: Cambridge University Press.

Adams, Gillian (2004) 'Ancient and Medieval Children's Texts', in Peter Hunt (ed.) *International Companion Encyclopedia of Children's Literature*, 2nd edn, Vol. 12, London: Routledge, 223–38.

Adams, Stephen (2008) 'Fiction for Teenagers is Becoming More Violent', *Daily Telegraph*, 19 November: 4.

Alderson, Brian (1995) 'A Widish, Widish World', *Children's Books History Society Newsletter*, 51: 14–17.

Alderson, Brian (1999) 'New Playthings and Gigantick Histories', *Princeton University Chronicle*, 60.2: 178–95.

Alderson, Brian and Oyens, Felix de Marez (2006) *Be Merry and Wise: Origins of Children's Book Publishing in England, 1650–1850*, London: British Library; New Castle: Oak Knoll Press.

Alderson, Brian W. (1969) 'The Irrelevance of Children to the Children's Book Reviewer', *Children's Book News*, 4.1: 10.

Alexander, Joy (2005) 'The Verse-Novel: A New Genre', *Children's Literature in Education*, 36.3: 269–83.

Alexie, Sherman (2007) *The Absolutely True Diary of a Part-Time Indian*, London: Andersen Press.

Almond, David (2003) *The Fire-Eaters*, London: Hodder.

Althusser, Louis (2001) 'Ideology and Ideological State Apparatuses', in *Lenin and Philosophy and Other Essays*, trans. Ben Brewster, New York: Monthly Review Press, 121–73 [orig. 1971].

Andersen, Hans Christian and Drewsen, Adolph (1984) *Christine's Picture Book*, ed. E. Dal, trans., intro. and postscript, Brian Alderson, London: Kingfisher.

Anderson, Graham (2000) *Fairytale in the Ancient World*, London: Routledge.

Anon (2005) 'Before and After Orientalism: Orientalism and the Legacy of Edward Said', *Amerasia Journal*, 31.1, special issue.

Anon (2008) 'Philip Pullman's His Dark Materials Film Trilogy in Doubt after Golden Compass Sequel in Limbo', 18 July, *Telegraph.co.uk*, http://www.telegraph.co.uk/arts/main.jhtml?xml=/arts/2008/07/18/npullman118.xml [26.08.08].

Archard, David (1993) *Children: Rights and Childhood*, London: Routledge.

Ariès, Philippe (1973) *Centuries of Childhood*, trans. Robert Baldick, Harmondsworth: Penguin [orig. 1960].

Arizpe, Evelyn and Styles, Morag (2003) *Children Reading Pictures: Interpreting Visual Texts*, London: RoutledgeFalmer.

Arizpe, Evelyn and Styles, Morag (2009) 'Bringing "Wisdom into the Hearts of Young Persons": Aesop, Watts and Newbery as Sources for Jane Johnson's Fables and Maxims', in Morag Styles and Evelyn Arizpe (eds) *Acts of Reading: Teachers, Texts and Childhood*, London: Trentham, 29–42.

Arizpe, Evelyn and Styles, Morag, with Heath, Shirley Brice (2006) *Reading Lessons from the Eighteenth Century*, Lichfield: Pied Piper Press.

Armitt, Lucie (2005) *Fantasy Fiction: An Introduction*, New York: Continuum.

Ashcroft, Bill (2001) *Post-Colonial Transformation*, London: Routledge.

Ashcroft, Bill, Griffiths, Gareth and Tiffin, Helen (1989) *The Empire Writes Back: Theory and Practice in Post-Colonial Literatures*, London: Routledge.

Ashcroft, Bill, Griffiths, Gareth and Tiffin, Helen (2000) *Post-Colonial Studies: The Key Concepts*, London: Routledge.

Ashford, Daisy (1966) *The Young Visiters*, London: Chatto & Windus [orig. 1919].

Ashliman, D. L. (1987) *A Guide to Folktales in the English Language: Based on the Aarne-Thompson Classification System*, Westport, CT: Greenwood.

ASSITEJ (2009) 'Constitution', http://www.assitej-international.org/english/documents/constitution.aspx [6.03.09].

Atkins, Barry (2006) 'What Are We Really Looking At? The Future-Orientation of Video Game Play', *Games and Culture*, 1.2: 127–40.

Atwood, Margaret (2008) *Payback: Debt and the Shadow Side of Wealth*, Toronto: Anansi.

Auchmuty, Rosemary (1992) *A World of Girls: The Appeal of the Girls' School Story*, London: Women's Press.

Auden, W. H. and Garrett, John (1935) *The Poet's Tongue: An Anthology*, London: G. Bell.

Auerbach, Eric (2003) *Mimesis: The Representation of Reality in Western Literature*, trans. Willard Trask, Princeton: Princeton University Press [orig. German, 1946].

Auerbach, Nina and Knoepflmacher, U. C. (eds) (1992) *Forbidden Journeys: Fairy Tales and Fantasies by Victorian Women Writers*, Chicago, IL: University of Chicago Press.

Ayres, Brenda (ed.) (2003) *The Emperor's Old Groove: Decolonizing Disney's Magic Kingdom*, New York: Peter Lang.

Bacchilega, Cristina (1997) *Postmodern Fairy Tales: Gender and Narrative Strategies*, Philadelphia: University of Pennsylvania Press.

Baghban, Marcia (1984) *Our Daughter Learns to Read and Write*, Newark, NJ: International Reading Association.

Bakhtin, M. M. (1981) *The Dialogic Imagination*, ed. Michael Holquist, trans. Caryl Emerson and Michael Holquist, Austin, TX: University of Texas Press.

Bakhtin, M. M. (1984a) *Problems of Dostoevsky's Poetics*, ed. and trans. Caryl Emerson, London: University of Minnesota Press [orig. 1929].

Bakhtin, M. M. (1984b) *Rabelais and His World*, trans. Hélène Iswolsky, Bloomington, IN: Indiana University Press.

Bal, Mieke (1985) *Narratology: Introduction to the Theory of Narrative*, Toronto: University of Toronto Press.

Bal, Mieke (1987) *Lethal Love: Feminist Literary Readings of Biblical Love Stories*, Bloomington: Indiana University Press.

Balibar, Etienne (1991) 'Is there a "Neo-Racism"?', in Etienne Balibar and Immanuel Wallerstein (eds) *Race, Nation, Class: Ambiguous Identities*, London: Verso, 17–28.

Barfield, Steven (2005) 'Of Young Magicians and Growing Up: J.K. Rowling, Her Critics, and the "Cultural Infantilism" Debate', in Cynthia Hallett (ed.) *Scholarly Studies in Harry Potter*, Lampeter: Edwin Mellen, 175–98.

Barker, Martin (1984) *A Haunt of Fears: The Strange History of the British Horror Comics Campaign*, London: Pluto Press.

Barker, Martin (1989) *Comics: Ideology, Power and the Critics*, Manchester: Manchester University Press.

Barrs, Myra (2004) 'The Reader in the Writer', in Teresa Grainger (ed.) *The RoutledgeFalmer Reader in Language and Literacy*, London: RoutledgeFalmer, 267–76.

Barthes, Roland (1975) *The Pleasure of the Text*, trans. Richard Miller, Oxford: Blackwell.

Barthes, Roland (1977) 'The Death of the Author', in *Image, Music, Text*, trans. Stephen Heath, London: Fontana, 142–8.

Barthes, Roland (1990) *S/Z*, trans. Richard Miller, Oxford: Blackwell.

Barthes, Roland (1993) *Mythologies*, trans. Annette Lavers, London: Verso.

Bazalgette, Cary and Buckingham, David (eds) (1995) *In Front of the Children: Screen Entertainment and Young Audiences*, London: British Film Institute.

Beckett, Sandra (ed.) (1999) *Transcending Boundaries: Writing for a Dual Audience of Children and Adults*, New York: Garland.

Beckett, Sandra (2008) *Crossover Fiction: Its Historical Antecedents and International Dimensions*, New York: Routledge.

Bell, Elizabeth, Haas, Lynda and Sells, Laura (eds) (1995) *From Mouse to Mermaid: The Politics of Film, Gender, and Culture*, Bloomington, IN: Indiana University Press.

Belsey, Catherine (1980) *Critical Practice*, London: Methuen.

Belsey, Catherine (2005) *Culture and the Real*, London: Routledge.

Benjamin, Jessica (1995) *Like Subjects, Love Objects: Essays on Recognition and Sexual Difference*, New Haven, CT: Yale University Press.

Bennett, David (1998) 'Introduction', in David Bennett (ed.) *Multicultural States: Rethinking Difference and Identity*, London: Routledge, 1–26.

Bennett, Gillian, Smith, Paul and Widdowson, J. D. A. (eds) (1987) *Perspectives on Contemporary Legend*, Sheffield: Sheffield Academic Press.

Benson, Stephen (2003) *Cycles of Influence: Fiction, Folktale, Theory*, Detroit, MI: Wayne State University Press.

Benton, Michael (1992) *Secondary Worlds: Literature Teaching and the Visual Arts*, Open University Press: Milton Keynes.

Benton, Michael (2004) 'Reader-Response Criticism', in Peter Hunt (ed.) *International Companion Encyclopedia of Children's Literature*, 2nd edn, Vol. 1, New York: Routledge, 112–28.

Berryman, Charles (1999) 'Critical Mirrors: Theories of Autobiography', *Mosaic*, 32: 71–84.

Bettelheim, Bruno (1976) *The Uses of Enchantment: The Meaning and Importance of Fairy Tales*, London: Thames & Hudson.

Bettelheim, Bruno and Zelan, Karen (1982) *On Learning to Read: The Child's Fascination with Meaning*, New York: Knopf.

Bhabha, Homi K. (1994) *The Location of Culture*, London: Routledge.

Bird, Anne-Marie (2005) 'Circumventing the Grand Narrative: Dust as an Alternative Theological Vision in Pullman's *His Dark Materials*', in Millicent Lenz and Carole Scott (eds) *His Dark Materials Illuminated*, Detroit: Wayne State University Press, 188–98.

Bissex, Glena L. (1980) *Gnys at Work: A Child Learns to Read and Write*, Cambridge, MA: Harvard University Press.

Bloome, David and Egan-Robertson, Ann (1993) 'The Social Construction of Intertextuality in Classroom Reading and Writing Lessons', *Reading Research Quarterly*, 28.4: 304–23.

Blyton, Enid (1951) *Noddy and His Car*, London: Sampson Low.

Blyton, Enid (1952) *The Story of My Life*, London: Pitkin.

Boethius, Ulf (ed.) (1998) *Modernity, Modernism and Children's Literature*, Stockholm: Stockholm University.

Bolter, Jay David and Grusin, Richard (1999) *Remediation: Understanding New Media*, Cambridge, MA: MIT Press.

Booth, Wayne C. (1961) *The Rhetoric of Fiction*, Chicago: University of Chicago Press.

Booth, Wayne C. (1988) *The Company We Keep: An Ethics of Fiction*, Berkeley, CA: University of California Press.

Bosmajian, Hamida (1979) *Metaphors of Evil: Contemporary German Literature and the Shadow of Nazism*, Iowa City: University of Iowa Press.

Bosmajian, Hamida (2004) 'Psychoanalytical Criticism', in Peter Hunt (ed.) *International Companion Encyclopedia of Children's Literature*, 2nd edn, Vol. 1, New York: Routledge, 129–39.

Bottigheimer, Ruth B. (1987) *Grimms' Bad Girls and Bold Boys: The Moral and Social Vision of the Tales*, New Haven, CT: Yale University Press.

Bottigheimer, Ruth B. (1996) *The Bible for Children from the Age of Gutenberg to the Present*, New Haven, CT: Yale University Press.

Bottigheimer, Ruth B. (2002) *Fairy Godfather: Straparola, Venice, and the Fairy Tale Tradition*, Philadelphia, PA: University of Pennsylvania Press.

Bottigheimer, Ruth B. (2004) 'Catechistical, Devotional and Biblical Writing', in Peter Hunt (ed.) *International Companion Encyclopedia of Children's Literature*, 2nd edn, Vol. 1, New York: Routledge, 299–305.

Bottigheimer, Ruth B. (2007) 'Reply', *Marvels & Tales*, 20.2: 280–4.

Bottigheimer, Ruth B. (2008) *Bibliography of British Books for Children and Adolescents, 1470–1770*, Stony Brook, New York: Stony Brook University Libraries, http://dspace.sunyconnect.suny.edu/handle/1951/43009 [6.02.2009].

Botting, Fred (1996) *Gothic*, London: Routledge.

Bourdieu, Pierre (1984) *Distinction: A Social Critique of the Judgement of Taste*, trans. Richard Nice, London: Routledge.

Bourdieu, Pierre (1993) *The Field of Cultural Production: Essay on Art and Literature*, ed. and intro. Randal Johnson, New York: Columbia University Press.

Bowers, Maggie Ann (2004) *Magic(al) Realism*, London: Routledge.

Bowler, Tim (2008) *Bloodchild*, Oxford: Oxford University Press.

Boyce, Frank Cottrell (2008) *Cosmic*, London: Macmillan.

Boyd, Brian (2006) 'Theory Is Dead – Like a Zombie', *Philosophy and Literature*, 30: 289–98.

Bracher, Mark (2002) 'Identity and Desire in the Classroom', in Jan Jagodzinski (ed.) *Pedagogical Desire: Authority, Seduction, Transference, and the Question of Ethics*, Westport, CT: Bergin & Garvey, 93–121.

Bradford, Clare (ed.) (1996) *Writing the Australian Child*, Nedlands, WA: University of Western Australia Press.

Bradford, Clare (2001a) 'The End of Empire: Colonial and Postcolonial Journeys in Children's Books', *Children's Literature*, 29: 196–218.

Bradford, Clare (2001b) *Reading Race: Aboriginality in Australian Children's Literature*, Melbourne: Melbourne University Press.

Bradford, Clare (2007) 'Representing Islam: Female Subjects in Suzanne Fisher Staples's Novels', *Children's Literature Association Quarterly*, 32.1: 47–61.

Bradford, Clare (2008) *Unsettling Narratives: Postcolonial Readings of Children's Literature*, Waterloo, ON: Wilfrid Laurier University Press.

Bradford, Clare, Mallan, Kerry, Stephens, John and McCallum, Robyn (2008) *New World Orders in Contemporary Children's Literature: Utopian Transformations*, Basingstoke: Palgrave Macmillan.

Brah, Avtar and Combes, Annie E. (eds) (2000) *Hybridity and Its Discontents: Politics, Science, Culture*, London: Routledge.

Branch, Michael P. and Slovic, Scott (eds) (2003) *The ISLE Reader: Ecocriticism, 1993–2003*, Athens, GA: University of Georgia Press.

Brannigan, John (1998) *New Historicism and Cultural Materialism*, London: Macmillan.

Briggs, Julia (1997) *A Woman of Passion: The Life of E. Nesbit 1858–1924*, London: Hutchinson [orig. 1987].

Briggs, Raymond (1998) *Ethel & Ernest*, London: Cape.

Brooks, Cleanth (1947) *The Well-Wrought Urn: Studies in the Structure of Poetry*, New York: Reynal and Hitchcock.

Brooks, Peter (1984) *Reading for the Plot: Design and Intention in Narrative*, Oxford: Clarendon.

Brown, David (1997) 'The Children's Literature Web Guide', http://www.ucalgary.ca/~dkbrown/writings.html [10.11.08].

Bruner, Jerome (1991) 'The Narrative Construction of Reality', *Critical Inquiry*, 18.1: 1–22.

Brunhoff, Jean de (1953) *Babar the King*, London: Methuen Children's Books [orig. 1936].

Brunhoff, Jean de (1955) *The Story of Babar the Little Elephant*, London: Methuen [orig. French, 1931, trans. 1934].

Buchbinder, David (1994) *Masculinities and Identities*, Melbourne: Melbourne University Press.

Buckingham, David (1993) *Children Talking Television: The Making of Television Literacy*, London: Falmer Press.

Buckingham, David (2000) *After the Death of Childhood: Growing Up in the Age of Electronic Media*, Cambridge: Polity Press.

Bueno, Fernando (2007) *The Golden Compass: Prima Official Game Guide*, Roseville, CA: Prima Games.

Burger, Patrick R. (2001) *The Political Unconscious of the Fantasy Sub-Genre of Romance*, Lewiston, NY: Edwin Mellen Press.

Burgess, Melvin (2004) 'Sympathy for the Devil', *Children's Literature in Education*, 35.4: 289–300.

Burkitt, Ian (1999) *Bodies of Thought: Embodiment, Identity and Modernity*, Thousand Oaks, CA: Sage.

Butler, Judith (1990a) *Gender Trouble: Feminism and the Subversion of Identity*, New York: Routledge.

Butler, Judith (1990b) 'Performative Acts and Gender Constitution: An Essay in Phenomenology and Feminist Theory', in Sue-Ellen Case (ed.) *Performing Feminisms: Feminist Critical Theory and Theatre*, Baltimore, MA: Johns Hopkins University Press, 270–82.

Butler, Judith (1993) *Bodies that Matter: On the Discursive Limits of 'Sex'*, New York: Routledge.

Butler, Judith (2004) *Undoing Gender*, New York: Routledge.

Butler, Judith, Guillory, John and Thomas, Kendall (eds) (2000) *What's Left of Theory? New Work on the Politics of Literary Theory: Essays from the English Institute*, New York: Routledge.

Cadnum, Michael (1998) *In a Dark Wood*, London: Scholastic.

Cadogan, Mary and Craig, Patricia (2003) *You're a Brick, Angela: The Girl's School Story, 1839–1985*, rev. edn, Bath: Girls Gone By [orig. 1986].

Cai, Mingshui (2002) *Multicultural Literature for Children and Young Adults: Reflections on Critical Issues*, Westport, CT: Greenwood.

Carpenter, Humphrey (1985) *Secret Gardens: A Study of the Golden Age of Children's Literature*, London: Allen & Unwin.

Carroll, Joseph (1995) *Evolution and Literary Theory*, Columbia: University of Missouri Press.

Carroll, Joseph (1999) 'The Deep Structure of Literary Representations', *Evolution and Human Behavior*, 20: 159–73.

Cart, Michael (1996) *From Romance to Realism: 50 Years of Growth and Change in Young Adult Literature*, New York: HarperCollins.

Cart, Michael and Jenkins, Christine A. (2006) *The Heart Has Its Reasons: Young Adult Literature with Gay/Lesbian/Queer Content 1969–2004*, Lanham, MD: Scarecrow Press.

Cavallaro, Dani (2002) *The Gothic Vision: Three Centuries of Horror, Terror and Fear*, New York: Continuum.

CBHS (1992) 'Annual General Meeting', *Children's Books History Newsletter*, 44.

Chambers, Aidan (1985) 'The Reader in the Book', in *Booktalk: Occasional Writing on Literature and Children*, Stroud: The Thimble Press, 34–58.

Chandler, Daniel (2006) *Semiotics: The Basics*, London: Routledge.

Chatman, Seymour (1978) *Story and Discourse: Narrative Structure in Fiction and Film*, Ithaca: Cornell University Press.

Cherland, Meredith Rogers (1994) *Private Practices: Girls Reading Fiction and Constructing Identity*, London: Taylor & Francis.

Chevalier, Tracy (ed.) (1989) *Twentieth-Century Children's Writers*, 3rd edn, London: St James Press.

Chukovsky, Kornei (1963) *From Two to Five*, trans. M. Morton, Berkeley, CA: University of California Press [orig. 1925].

CILIP (2008) 'Kate Greenaway Medal Criteria', http://www.carnegiegreenaway.org.uk/greenaway/award_criteria.php [21.11.08].

Cixous, Hélène (1976) 'The Laugh of the Medusa', trans. Keith Cohen and Paula Cohen, *Signs*, 1.4: 875–93.

Clark, Beverly Lyon (2001) *Regendering the School Story*, New York: Routledge.

Clark, Beverly Lyon and Higonnet, Margaret R. (1999) *Girls, Boys, Books, Toys: Gender in Children's Literature and Culture*, Baltimore, MA: Johns Hopkins University Press.

Clarke, Norma (1997) '"The Cursed Barbauld Crew": Women Writers and Writing for Children in the Late Eighteenth Century', in Mary Hilton, Morag Styles and Victor Watson (eds) *Opening the Nursery Door: Reading, Writing, and Childhood, 1600–1900*, London: Routledge, 91–103.

Clendinnen, Inga (1999) *True Stories*, Sydney: ABC Books.

Coats, Karen (2004) *Looking Glasses and Neverlands: Lacan, Desire, and Subjectivity in Children's Literature*, Iowa City: University of Iowa Press.

Coats, Karen (2008) 'Between Horror, Humour, and Hope: Neil Gaiman and the Psychic Work of the Gothic', in Anna Jackson, Karen Coats and Roderik McGillis (eds) *The Gothic in Children's Literature: Haunting the Boundaries*, New York: Routledge, 77–92.

Coats, Karen S. (2001) 'Keepin' It Plural: Children's Studies in the Academy', *Children's Literature Association Quarterly*, 26.3: 140–50.

Cocks, Neil (2004) 'The Implied Reader. Responses and Responsibility: Theories of the Implied Reader in Children's Literature Criticism', in Karín Lesnik-Oberstein (ed.) *Children's Literature: New Approaches*, Basingstoke: Palgrave Macmillan, 93–117.

Colebrook, Claire (1997) *New Literary Histories: New Historicism and Contemporary Criticism*, Manchester: Manchester University Press.

Colebrook, Claire (2006) *Deleuze: A Guide for the Perplexed*, London: Continuum.

Collett-White, Mike (2007) 'Pullman Fantasy Film "Promotes Atheism to Kids"', *Mail&Guardian Online*, 28 November, http://www.mg.co.za/article/2007-11-28-pullman-fantasy-film-promotes-atheism-to-kids [31.10.08].

Collins, Christopher (1991) *The Poetics of the Mind's Eye: Literature and the Psychology of Imagination*, Philadelphia, PA: University of Pennsylvania Press.

Collins, Jo and Jervis, John (eds) (2008) *Uncanny Modernity: Cultural Theories, Modern Anxieties*, Basingstoke: Palgrave Macmillan.

Connell, R. W. (1995) *Masculinities*, St Leonards: Allen and Unwin.

Cosslett, Tess (2002) '"History from Below": Time-Slip Narratives and National Identity', *The Lion and the Unicorn*, 26.2: 243–53.

Costea, Bogdan, Crump, Norman and Holm, John (2005) 'Dionysus at Work? The Ethos of Play and the Ethos of Management', *Culture and Organization*, 11.2: 139–51.

Crago, Maureen and Crago, Hugh (1983) *Prelude to Literacy: A Preschool Child's Encounter with Picture and Story*, Carbondale: Southern Illinois University Press.

Creed, Barbara (1999) 'Horror and the Monstrous-Feminine: An Imaginary Abjection', in Sue Thornham (ed.) *Feminist Film Theory: A Reader*, Edinburgh: Edinburgh University Press, 251–66.

Cremin, Teresa, Bearne, Eve, Mottram, Marilyn and Goodwin, Prue (2008) 'Primary Teachers as Readers', *English in Education*, 42.1: 9–23.

Crews, Frederick C. (1964) *The Pooh Perplex: A Student Casebook*, London: Barker.

Crews, Frederick C. (1995) *The Memory Wars: Freud's Legacy in Dispute*, New York: New York Review of Books.

Crossley-Holland, Kevin (1987) *British Folk Tales*, London: Orchard Books.

Cuddy-Keane, Melba (2003) 'Modernism, Geopolitics, Globalization', *MODERNISM/modernity*, 10.3: 539–58.

Culler, Jonathan (1981) *The Pursuit of Signs: Semiotics, Literature, Deconstruction*, London: Routledge and Kegan Paul.

Culler, Jonathan (1982) *On Deconstruction*, Ithaca, NY: Cornell University Press.

Culler, Jonathan (1997) *Literary Theory: A Very Short Introduction*, Oxford: Oxford University Press.

Cunningham, Hugh (1995) *Children and Childhood in Western Society since 1500*, London: Longman.

Cunningham, Hugh (2006) *The Invention of Childhood*, London: BBC Books.

Currie, Mark (ed.) (1995) *Metafiction*, London: Longman.

Curtis, Christopher Paul (1995) *The Watsons Go to Birmingham – 1963: A Novel*, New York: Delacorte.

Cutt, Margaret Nancy (1979) *Ministering Angels: A Study of Nineteenth-Century Evangelical Writing for Children*, Wormley: Five Owls Press.

Daniels, Steven V. (1990) '*The Velveteen Rabbit*: A Kleinian Perspective', *Children's Literature*, 18: 17–30.

Dannenberg, Hilary P. (2004) 'A Poetics of Coincidence in Narrative Fiction', *Poetics Today*, 2.3: 399–436.

Danow, David K. (1995) *The Spirit of Carnival: Magical Realism and the Grotesque*, Lexington: University Press of Kentucky.

Darton, F. J. Harvey (1982) *Children's Books in England: Five Centuries of Social Life*, 3rd edn, rev. Brian Alderson, Cambridge: Cambridge University Press [orig. 1932].

Davies, Tony (1996) *Humanism*, London: Routledge.

Davis, Lennard J. (1995) *Enforcing Normalcy: Disability, Deafness and the Body*, London: Verso.

Day, Aidan (1996) *Romanticism*, London: Routledge.

De Berg, Henk (2003) *Freud's Theory and Its Uses in Literary and Cultural Studies: An Introduction*, Rochester, NY: Camden House.

Dean, Tim (2000) *Beyond Sexuality*, Chicago: University of Chicago Press.

Dégh, Linda (2001) *Legend and Belief: Dialectics of a Genre*, Bloomington, IN: Indiana University of Press.

Delamar, Gloria T. (1987) *Mother Goose from Nursery to Literature*, Jefferson, NC: McFarland.

Deleuze, Gilles (1995) *Negotiations: 1972–1990*, trans. Martin Joughin, New York: Columbia University Press.

Deleuze, Gilles and Guattari, Félix (1984) *Anti-Oedipus: Capitalism and Schizophrenia*, trans. Robert Hurley, Mark Seem and Helen R. Lane, Minneapolis: University of Minnesota Press.

Deleuze, Gilles and Guattari, Félix (2004) *A Thousand Plateaus*, trans. Brian Massumi, London: Continuum [orig. 1980].

Demers, Patricia (ed.) (2009) *From Instruction to Delight: An Anthology of Children's Literature to 1850*, 3rd edn, Ontario: Oxford University Press [orig. 1982].

Dentith, Simon (2000) *Parody*, London: Routledge.

Derrida, Jacques (1979) 'Living On. Border Lines', in Harold Bloom, Paul de Man, Jacques Derrida, Geoffrey Hartman and J. Hillis Miller (eds) *Deconstruction and Criticism*, New York: Seabury Press, 75–176.

Derrida, Jacques (1981) 'The Law of Genre', in W. J. T. Mitchell (ed.) *On Narrative*, Chicago, IL: University of Chicago Press, 51–77.

Derrida, Jacques (1992) *Acts of Literature*, ed. Derek Attridge, London: Routledge.

Dickinson, Peter (1982) *Tulku*, London: Puffin Books.

Dobrin, Sidney I. and Kidd, Kenneth B. (eds) (2004) *Wild Things: Children's Culture and Ecocriticism*, Detroit: Wayne State University Press.

Donaldson, Margaret (1978) *Children's Minds*, Glasgow: Fontana.

Doonan, Jane (1986) '*Outside Over There*: A Journey in Style', parts 1 and 2, *Signal*, 50: 92–103; 51: 172–87.

Duff, David (ed.) (2000) *Modern Genre Theory*, London: Longman.

Duh, Ming Cherng (2007) 'The Hegemony of Western Categorisation and the Underdevelopment of Children's Literature in "Other" Worlds', *Papers: Explorations into Children's Literature*, 17.2: 7–15.

Dundes, Alan (1991) 'Bruno Bettelheim's Uses of Enchantment and Abuses of Scholarship', *Journal of American Folklore*, 104: 74–83.

During, Simon (1992) *Foucault and Literature: Towards a Genealogy of Writing*, London: Routledge.

Dusinberre, Juliet (1987) *Alice to the Lighthouse: Children's Books and Radical Experiments in Art*, New York: St Martin's.

Dutton, Dennis (2004) 'The Pleasures of Fiction', *Philosophy and Literature*, 28: 453–66.

Dyer, Richard (1997) *White*, New York: Routledge.

Dyson, Anne Haas (1997) *Writing Superheroes: Contemporary Childhood, Popular Culture, and Classroom Literacy*, New York: Teachers College Press.

Eaglestone, Robert (1997) *Ethical Criticism: Reading after Levinas*, Edinburgh: Edinburgh University Press.

Eagleton, Terry (1996) *Literary Theory: An Introduction*, 2nd edn, Oxford: Blackwell.

Eagleton, Terry (2003) *After Theory*, London: Allen Lane.

Eccleshare, Julia (2004) 'The Differences between Adult and Child Fiction', in Pat Pinsent (ed.) *Books and Boundaries: Writers and Their Audiences*, Lichfield, Staffs: Pied Piper, 213–15.

Eliot, T. S. (1991) *Collected Poems, 1909–1962*, New York: Harcourt Brace Jovanovich.

Empson, William (1930) *Seven Types of Ambiguity*, London: Chatto & Windus.

Engel, Susan (1995) *The Stories Children Tell: Making Sense of the Narratives of Childhood*, New York: W. H. Freeman.

Engelhardt, Tom (1991) 'Reading May Be Harmful to Your Kids: In the Nadirland of Today's Children's Books', *Harper's Magazine*, June: 55–62.

Erikson, Erik (1968) *Identity: Youth and Crisis*, New York: Norton.

Falconer, Rachel (2004) 'Crossover Literature', in Peter Hunt (ed.) *International Companion Encyclopedia of Children's Literature*, 2nd edn, Vol. 1, New York: Routledge, 556–75.

Falconer, Rachel (2009) *The Crossover Novel: Contemporary Children's Literature and Its Adult Readership*, New York: Routledge.

Faris, Wendy B. (2004) *Ordinary Enchantments: Magical Realism and the Remystification of Narrative*, Nashville, TN: Vanderbilt University Press.

Fink, Bruce (1995) *The Lacanian Subject: Between Language and Jouissance*, Princeton, NJ: Princeton University Press.

Fisher, David James (2008) *Bettelheim: Living and Dying*, Amsterdam: Rodopi.

Flanagan, Victoria (2007) *Into the Closet: Cross-Dressing and the Gendered Body in Children's Literature and Film*, New York: Routledge.

Fletcher, John and Benjamin, Andrew (eds) (1990) *Abjection, Melancholia and Love: The Work of Julia Kristeva*, New York: Routledge.

Fludernik, Monika (1993) *The Fictions of Language and the Languages of Fiction*, London: Routledge.

Fludernik, Monika (1996) *Towards a 'Natural' Narratology*, London: Routledge.

Ford, Elizabeth A. (1998) 'H/Z: Why Lesléa Newman Makes Heather into Zoe', *Children's Literature Association Quarterly*, 23.3: 128–33.

Foucault, Michel (1977) 'What is an Author?', in Donald F. Bouchard (ed.) *Language, Counter-Memory, Practice*, Ithaca, NY: Cornell University Press, 113–38.

Foucault, Michel (1980) *Power/Knowledge: Selected Interviews and Other Writings, 1972–1977*, Brighton: Harvester Wheatsheaf.

Foucault, Michel (1998) 'Theatrum Philosophicum', in Victor E. Taylor and Charles E. Winquist (eds) *Postmodernism*, trans. Donald F. Bouchard and Sherry Simon, London: Routledge, 295–316 [orig. 1977].

Fox, Carol (1993) *At the Very Edge of the Forest: The Influence of Literature on Storytelling by Children*, London: Cassell.

Freeman, Thomas (1977) 'Heinrich Hoffmann's Struwwelpeter: An Inquiry into the Effects of Violence in Children's Literature', *Journal of Popular Culture*, 10: 808–20.

French, Philip (2007) Review of *The Golden Compass*, *The Observer*, 9 December, http://film.guardian.co.uk/News_Story/Critic_Review/Observer_Film_of_the_week/0,,22 24482,00.html [10.06.08].

Freud, Sigmund (1955) 'The Uncanny', in *The Standard Edition of the Complete Psychological Works of Sigmund Freud*, Vol. 17, ed. and trans. James Strachey, London: Hogarth, 217–56 [orig. 1919].

Freud, Sigmund (1957) 'The Unconscious', in *The Standard Edition of the Complete Psychological Works of Sigmund Freud*, Vol. 14, ed. and trans. James Strachey, New York: Hogarth, 166–216.

Freud, Sigmund (1958) 'Remembering, Repeating, and Working Through', in *The Standard Edition of the Complete Psychological Works of Sigmund Freud*, Vol. 12, ed. and trans. James Strachey, London: Hogarth, 147–56.

Freud, Sigmund (1959) 'Creative Writers and Daydreaming', in *The Standard Edition of the Complete Psychological Works of Sigmund Freud*, Vol. 9, ed. and trans. James Strachey, London: Hogarth, 143–53 [orig.1908].

Freud, Sigmund (1961) 'The Ego and the Id', in *The Standard Edition of the Complete Psychological Works of Sigmund Freud*, Vol. 19, ed. and trans. James Strachey, New York: Hogarth.

Freud, Sigmund (1966) 'New Introductory Lectures on Psychoanalysis', in *The Standard Edition of the Complete Psychological Works of Sigmund Freud*, Vol. 23, ed. and trans. James Strachey, New York: Hogarth.

Frow, John (2005) *Genre*, London: Routledge.

Frye, Northrop (1963) *The Educated Imagination*, Toronto: Canadian Broadcasting Corporation.

Frye, Northrop (1966) *Anatomy of Criticism: Four Essays*, New York: Atheneum.

Frye, Northrop (1973) *The Critical Path*, Bloomington: Indiana University Press.

Frye, Northrop (1976) *The Secular Scripture: A Study of the Structure of Romance*, Cambridge, MA: Harvard University Press.

Frye, Northrop (1988) *On Education*, Markham, Ont.: Fitzhenry & Whiteside.

Gaiman, Neil (2008) *The Graveyard Book*, London: Bloomsbury.

Gannon, Susan R. (2001) 'Hunt for a Discipline: Charting the Children's Literature Scene', *Signal*, 96: 155–73.

Gavin, Jamila (2008) *The Robber Baron's Daughter*, London: Egmont.

Gay, Peter (ed.) (1995) *The Freud Reader*, New York: Vintage.

Geertz, Clifford (1973) 'Thick Description: Toward an Interpretive Theory of Culture', *The Interpretation of Cultures: Selected Essays*, New York: Basic Books, 3–30.

Genette, Gérard (1997) *Paratexts: Thresholds of Interpretation*, trans. Jane E. Lewin, Cambridge: Cambridge University Press.

Gibson, Mel (2000) 'On British Comics for Girls and Their Readers', in Nickianne Moody (ed.) *Consuming for Pleasure*, Liverpool: University of Liverpool John Moores Press, 210–27.

Gibson, Mel (2008a) 'The Powerful World of Graphic Texts', in Prue Goodwin (ed.) *Understanding Children's Books: A Guide for Education Professionals*, London: Sage, 109–18.

Gibson, Mel (2008b) 'What You Read and Where You Read It, How You Get It, How You Keep It: Children, Comics and Historical Cultural Practice', *Popular Narrative Media*, 2: 153–67.

Gibson, Mel (2009) *Comics Scholarship on the Net: A Brief Annotated Bibliography*, http://www.dr-mel-comics.co.uk/sources/academic.html.

Gittins, Diane (1998) *The Child in Question*, Basingstoke: Macmillan.

Glotfelty, Cheryll and Fromm, Harold (eds) (1996) *The Ecocriticism Reader*, Athens, GA: University of Georgia Press.

Goldthwaite, John (1996) *The Natural History of Make-Believe: A Guide to the Principal Works of Britain, Europe, and America*, New York: Oxford University Press.

Gooderham, David (1995) 'Children's Fantasy Literature: Toward an Anatomy', *Children's Literature in Education*, 26.3: 171–83.

Gorak, Jan (1991) *The Making of the Modern Canon: Genesis and Crisis of a Literary Idea*, London: Athlone Press.

Graham, Tony (2005) 'Unicorn – The Pioneer Children's Theatre', in Stuart Bennett (ed.) *Theatre for Children and Young People*, Twickenham: Aurora Metro Press, 76–86.

Greenfield, Susan (2008) *The Quest for Identity in the Twenty-First Century*, London: Hodder and Stoughton.

Greimas, A. J. (1983) *Structural Semantics: An Attempt at a Method*, trans. D. McDowell, R. Schleifer and A. Velie, Lincoln, NE: University of Nebraska Press [orig. 1966].

Grenby, Matthew (2004) 'Bibliography', in Peter Hunt (ed.) *International Companion Encyclopedia of Children's Literature*, 2nd edn, Vol.1, New York: Routledge, 203–21.

Grinstein, Alexander (1995) *The Remarkable Beatrix Potter*, Madison, CT: International Universities Press.

Groensteen, Thierry (2007) *The System of Comics*, trans. Bart Beaty and Nick Nguyen, Jackson: University of Mississippi Press.

Gupta, Suman (2003) *Re-Reading Harry Potter*, Basingstoke: Palgrave Macmillan.

Hacking, Ian (1999) *The Social Construction of What?*, Cambridge, MA: Harvard University Press.

Hade, Daniel (2002) 'Storyselling: Are Publishers Changing the Way Children Read?', *Horn Book Magazine*, Sept–Oct: 509–17.

Hall, Stuart (1997) 'The Local and the Global: Globalization and Ethnicity', in Anne McClintock, Aamir Mufti and Ella Shohat (eds) *Dangerous Liaisons: Gender, Nation and Postcolonial Perspectives*, Minneapolis: University of Minnesota Press, 173–87.

Hall, Stuart and du Gay, Paul (eds) (1996) *Questions of Cultural Identity*, London: Sage.

Halliwell, Martin and Mousley, Andy (2003) *Critical Humanisms: Humanist/Anti-Humanist Dialogues*, Edinburgh: Edinburgh University Press.

Harding, D. W. (1977) 'Psychological Processes in the Reading of Fiction' [orig. 1961], in Margaret Meek, Aidan Warlow and Griselda Barton (eds) *The Cool Web: The Pattern of Children's Reading*, London: Random House, 59–72.

Harman, Paul (2005) 'Window on the World – ASSITEJ', in Stuart Bennett (ed.) *Theatre for Children and Young People*, Twickenham: Aurora Metro Press, 53–8.

Harpham, Geoffrey Galt (1982) *On the Grotesque: Strategies of Contradiction in Art and Literature*, Princeton, NJ: Princeton University Press.

Harries, Elizabeth Wanning (2001) *Twice Upon a Time: Women Writers and the History of the Fairy Tale*, Princeton: Princeton University Press.

Harris, Mark (ed.) (2007) *Ways of Knowing: New Approaches in the Anthropology of Knowledge and Learning*, Oxford: Berghahn.

Harrison, Paul (2007) *The Golden Compass: The Story of the Movie*, New York: Scholastic.

Hart, Jonathan (1994) *Northrop Frye: The Theoretical Imagination*, London: Routledge.

Hayles, N. Katherine (1999) *How We Became Posthuman: Virtual Bodies in Cybernetics, Literature, and Informatics*, Chicago: University of Chicago Press.

Hazard, Paul (1944) *Books, Children and Men*, trans. M. Mitchell, Boston: The Horn Book [orig. Paris, 1932].

Heath, Shirley Brice (1983) *Ways with Words: Language, Life and Work in Communities and Classrooms*, Cambridge: Cambridge University Press.

Heer, Jeet and Worcester, Kent (eds) (2009) *A Comic Studies Reader*, Jackson: University of Mississippi Press.

Heins, Marjorie (2007) *Not in Front of the Children: Indecency, Censorship, and the Innocence of Youth*, 2nd edn, New Brunswick, NJ: Rutgers University Press.

Herman, David (2002) *Story Logic: Problems and Possibilities of Narrative*, Lincoln: University of Nebraska Press.

Herman, David (ed.) (2003) *Narrative Theory and the Cognitive Sciences*, Stanford, CA: CSLI Publications.

Higonnet, Anne (1998) *Pictures of Innocence: The History and Crisis of Ideal Childhood*, London: Thames & Hudson.

Higonnet, Margaret R. (1990) 'The Playground of the Peritext', *Children's Literature Association Quarterly*, 15.2: 47–9.

Hilton, Mary (ed.) (1996) *Potent Fictions: Children's Literacy and the Challenge of Popular Culture*, London: Routledge.

Hilton, Mary, Styles, Morag and Watson, Victor (eds) (1997) *Opening the Nursery Door: Reading, Writing and Childhood 1600–1900*, London: Routledge.

Hirsch, Eric D. (1967) *Validity in Interpretation*, New Haven, CT: Yale University Press.

HMI (2007) *Poetry in Schools: A Survey 2006–2007*, London: HMSO.

Hoikkala, Tommi, Rahkonen, Ossi, Tigerstedt, Christoffer and Tuormaa, Jussi (1987) 'Wait a Minute Mr Postman! Some Critical Remarks on Neil Postman's Childhood Theory', *Acta Sociologica*, 30.1: 87–99.

Holifield, Chris (2008) 'Where Have All the Children's Poetry Books Gone?', *English, 4–11*, Autumn: 14–16.

Holland, Norman N. (1968) *The Dynamics of Literary Response*, New York: Oxford University Press.

Holland, Norman N. (1975) *5 Readers Reading*, New Haven, CT: Yale University Press.

Hollindale, Peter (1988) *Ideology and the Children's Book*, Stroud: Thimble Press.

Hollindale, Peter (1991) *Peter Pan in Kensington Gardens; and Peter and Wendy*, Oxford: Oxford University Press.

Hollindale, Peter (1996) 'Drama', in Peter Hunt (ed.) *International Companion Encyclopedia of Children's Literature*, New York: Routledge, 206–19.

Hollindale, Peter (1997) *Signs of Childness in Children's Books*, Stroud: Thimble Press.

Homer, Sean (2005) *Jacques Lacan*, London: Routledge.

Honeyman, Susan (2005) *Elusive Childhood: Impossible Representations in Modern Fiction*, Columbus: Ohio State University Press.

Huddart, David (2006) *Homi K. Bhabha*, London: Routledge.

Huggan, Graham (2007) *Australian Literature: Postcolonialism, Racism, Transnationalism*, Oxford: Oxford University Press.

Hunt, Peter (1984a) 'Childist Criticism: The Subculture of the Child, the Book and the Critic', *Signal*, 43: 42–59.

Hunt, Peter (1984b) 'Questions of Method and Methods of Questioning: Childist Criticism in Action', *Signal*, 45: 180–200.

Hunt, Peter (1991) *Criticism, Theory and Children's Literature*, Oxford: Blackwell.

Hunt, Peter (1994) *An Introduction to Children's Literature*, Oxford: Oxford University Press.

Hunt, Peter (1995) 'Scholars, Critics and Standards: Reflections on a Sentence by Brian Alderson', *Children's Books History Society Newsletter*, 52: 18–22.

Hunt, Peter (ed.) (1996) *International Companion Encyclopedia of Children's Literature*, London: Routledge.

Hunt, Peter (ed.) (2004) *International Companion Encyclopedia of Children's Literature*, 2nd edn, London: Routledge.

Hunt, Peter (2006) *Children's Literature: Critical Concepts in Literary and Cultural Studies*, 4 vols, London: Routledge.

Hürlimann, Bettina (1967) *Three Centuries of Children's Books in Europe*, trans. Brian W. Alderson, London: Oxford University Press.

Husain, Shahrukh (1995) *Women Who Wear the Breeches: Delicious and Dangerous Tales*, London: Virago.

Hutcheon, Linda (1985) *A Theory of Parody: The Teachings of Twentieth-Century Art Forms*, New York: Methuen.

Hutcheon, Linda (2006) *A Theory of Adaptation*, New York: Routledge.

Hutton, Patrick H. (2004) *Philippe Ariès and the Politics of French Cultural History*, Amherst, MA: University of Massachusetts Press.

Hyde, Mary (1977) *The Thrales of Streatham Park*, Cambridge, MA: Harvard University Press.

IndigoNight and RayneStorm (2007) 'Alternate Ending to the Golden Compass', http://www.fanfiction.net/s/3941878/1/Friendship [18.12.07].

Inglis, Fred (1981) *The Promise of Happiness: Value and Meaning in Children's Fiction*, Cambridge: Cambridge University Press.

Irigaray, Luce (1985) 'This Sex Which Is Not One', in *This Sex Which Is Not One*, Ithaca, NY: Cornell University Press, 23–33 [orig. 1977].

Iser, Wolfgang (1974) *The Implied Reader: Patterns of Communication in Prose Fiction from Bunyan to Beckett*, Baltimore, MD: Johns Hopkins University Press.

Iser, Wolfgang (1978) *The Act of Reading: A Theory of Aesthetic Response,* London: Routledge.

Ishiguro, Kazuo (2005) *Never Let Me Go,* London: Faber and Faber.

Islamic Bookstore (2009) http://islamicbookstore.com/children.html [8.4.09].

Jackson, Anna, Coats, Karen and McGillis, Roderick (eds) (2008) *The Gothic in Children's Literature: Haunting the Borders*, New York: Routledge.

Jackson, Luke (2002) *Freaks, Geeks and Asperger Syndrome: A User Guide to Adolescence*, London: Jessica Kingsley.

Jackson, Rosemary (1981) *Fantasy: The Literature of Subversion*, London: Methuen.

Jacobs, Joseph (1992) 'Jack and the Beanstalk', in Neil Philip (ed.) *English Folktales*, London: Penguin, 1–10.

Jagose, Annamarie (1996a) *Queer Theory: An Introduction*, Carlton, Victoria: Melbourne University Press.

Jagose, Annamarie (1996b) 'Queer Theory', *Australian Humanities Review*, 4, http://www. australianhumanitiesreview.org/archive/Issue-Dec-1996/jagose.html [10.12.08].

James, Allison and Prout, Alan (eds) (1990) *Constructing and Reconstructing Childhood: Contemporary Issues in the Sociological Study of Childhood*, London: Falmer Press.

James, Allison, Jenks, Chris and Prout, Alan (1998) *Theorizing Childhood*, Cambridge: Polity Press.

James, Kathryn (2009) *Death, Gender and Sexuality in Contemporary Adolescent Literature*, New York: Routledge.

Jameson, Fredric (1975) 'Magical Narrative: Romance as Genre', *New Literary History*, 7.1: 135–64.

Jameson, Fredric (1981) *The Political Unconscious: Narrative as a Socially Symbolic Act*, Ithaca, NY: Cornell University Press.

Jameson, Fredric (1985) 'Postmodernism and Consumer Society', in Hal Foster (ed.) *Postmodern Culture*, London: Pluto Press, 111–25.

Jameson, Fredric (1991) *Postmodernism, or, The Cultural Logic of Late Capitalism*, London: Verso.

Jameson, Fredric (2000) *The Jameson Reader*, ed. Michael Hardt and Kathi Weeks, Oxford: Blackwell.

Jenkins, Henry (1992) *Textual Poachers: Television Fans and Participatory Culture*, New York: Routledge.

Jenkins, Henry (2004) 'Game Design as Narrative Architecture', in Noah Wardrip-Fruin and Pat Harrigan (eds) *First Person: New Media as Story, Performance, and Game*, Cambridge, MA: MIT Press, 118–30.

Jenkins, Henry (2008) *Convergence Culture: Where Old and New Media Collide*, rev. edn, New York: New York University Press.

Jenkins, Jerry B. and LaHaye, Tim (1995) *Left Behind: A Novel of the Earth's Last Days*, Wheaton, IL: Tyndale.

Johnson, Allan G. (1997) *The Gender Knot: Unraveling Our Patriarchal Legacy*, Philadelphia, PA: Temple University Press.

Johnson, Barbara (1981) *The Critical Difference: Essays in the Contemporary Rhetoric of Reading*, Baltimore, MD: Johns Hopkins University Press.

Johnson, Jane (2001) *A Very Pretty Story*, ed. Gillian Avery, Oxford: Bodleian Library [orig. ms 1744].

Johnson, Jane (2009) 'Guide to the Jane Johnson Manuscript Nursery Library . . .', Lilly Library, University of Indiana, Bloomington, http://www.dlib.indiana.edu/collections/jane-johnson [6.04.09].

Johnston, Ollie and Thomas, Frank (1995) *The Illusion of Life: Disney Animation*, rev. edn, New York: Disney Editions.

Jones, Ann Rosalind (1981) 'Writing the Body: Toward an Understanding of L'Ecriture Feminine', Feminist Studies, 7.2: 247–263.

Jung, Carl Gustav (1978) Man and His Symbols, London: Picador.

Kaczorowski, Craig (2004) 'Gay and Lesbian Studies', in Claude J. Summers (ed.) An Encyclopedia of Gay, Lesbian, Bisexual, Chicago, IL: West Adams.

Karner, Christian (2007) Ethnicity and Everyday Life, London: Routledge.

Kayser, Wolfgang (1981) The Grotesque in Art and Literature, trans. Ulrich Weisstein, New York: Columbia University Press.

Keefer, Janice Kulyk (1993) 'On Being a Canadian Writer Today', in Hans Bak (ed.) Multiculturalism and the Canon of American Culture, Amsterdam: Vu University Press, 261–71.

Keenan, Celia (2007) 'Divisions in the World of Irish Publishing for Children: Re-Colonization or Globalization?', in Mary Shine Thompson and Valerie Coghlan (eds) Divided Worlds: Studies in Children's Literature, Dublin: Four Courts Press, 196–208.

Keith, Lois (2001) Take Up Thy Bed and Walk: Death, Disability and Cure in Classic Fiction for Girls, New York: Routledge.

Kenway, Jane and Bullen, Elizabeth (2001) Consuming Children: Education–Entertainment–Advertising, Buckingham: Open University Press.

Kermode, Frank (1967) The Sense of an Ending, Oxford: Oxford University Press.

Kertzer, Adrienne (2001) My Mother's Voice: Children, Literature and the Holocaust, Peterborough, Ont.: Broadview Press.

Kidd, Kenneth B. (2004) Making American Boys: Boyology and the Feral Tale, Minneapolis: University of Minnesota Press.

Kiley, Dan (1983) The Peter Pan Syndrome: Men Who Have Never Grown Up, New York: Dodd, Mead.

Kimball, Roger (1990) Tenured Radicals, Chicago: Ivan R. Dee.

Kincaid, James R. (1992) Child-Loving: The Erotic Child and Victorian Culture, London: Routledge.

King, Margaret L. (2007) 'Concepts of Childhood: What We Know and Where We might Go', Renaissance Quarterly, 60.2: 371–407.

Kirkpatrick, Robert (2000) The Encyclopedia of Boys' School Stories, Aldershot: Ashgate.

Klein, Gillian (1985) Reading into Racism: Bias in Children's Literature and Learning Materials, London: Routledge.

Klein, Kerwin Lee (1995) 'In Search of Narrative Mastery: Postmodernism and the People without History', History and Theory, 34: 275–98.

Klein, Melanie (1986) The Selected Melanie Klein, ed. Juliet Mitchell, Harmondsworth: Penguin.

Kress, Gunther (1988) Communication and Culture: An Introduction, Kensington, NSW: New South Wales University Press.

Kristeva, Julia (1982) Powers of Horror: An Essay on Abjection, trans. Léon S. Roudiez, New York: Columbia University Press.

Kristeva, Julia (1986) The Kristeva Reader, ed. Toril Moi, Oxford: Blackwell.

Kristeva, Julia (1990) 'The Adolescent Novel', in John Fletcher and Andrew Benjamin (eds) Abjection, Melancholia, and Love, London: Routledge, 8–23.

Kümmerling-Meibauer, Bettina (1999) 'Metalinguistic Awareness and the Child's Developing Concept of Irony: The Relationship between Pictures and Text in Ironic Picture Books', The Lion and the Unicorn, 23.2: 157–83.

Kutzer, M. Daphne (2000) Empire's Children: Empire and Imperialism in Classic British Children's Books, New York: Routledge.

Lacan, Jacques (1988a) 'The Family Complexes' [orig. 1938], Critical Texts, 5.3: 12–29.

Lacan, Jacques (1988b) *The Seminar of Jacques Lacan Book I: Freud's Papers on Technique, 1953–1954*, trans. John Forrester, New York: Norton.

Lacan, Jacques (1988c) *The Seminar of Jacques Lacan Book II: The Ego in Freud's Theory and in the Technique of Psychoanalysis, 1954–1955*, trans. Sylvana Tomaselli, New York: Norton.

Lacan, Jacques (1993) *The Seminar of Jacques Lacan Book III: The Psychoses, 1955–1956*, trans. Russell Grigg, New York: Norton.

Lacan, Jacques (2006) *Écrits: The First Complete Edition in English*, trans. Bruce Fink, New York: Norton.

Lang, Andrew (1996) *The Red Fairy Book*, New York: Courier Dover Publications [orig. 1890].

Lanser, Susan (1986) 'Toward a Feminist Narratology', *Style*, 20: 341–63.

Latham, Rob (2002) *Consuming Youth: Vampires, Cyborgs, and the Culture of Consumption*, Chicago: University of Chicago Press.

Lawson, Jon Arno (2008) *Inside Out: Children's Poets Discuss Their Work*, London: Walker.

Leavis, F. R. (1948) *The Great Tradition*, London: Chatto & Windus.

Leeson, Robert (1985) *Reading and Righting: The Past, Present and Future of Fiction for the Young*, London: Collins.

Lehman, David (1991) *Signs of the Times: Deconstruction and the Fall of Paul de Man*, New York: Poseidon.

Lenz, Millicent and Scott, Carole (eds) (2005) *His Dark Materials Illuminated: Critical Essays on Philip Pullman's Trilogy*, Detroit: Wayne State University Press.

Lesnik-Oberstein, Karín (1994) *Children's Literature: Criticism and the Fictional Child*, Oxford: Clarendon Press.

Lesnik-Oberstein, Karín (2000) 'The Psychopathology of Everyday Children's Literature Criticism', *Cultural Critique*, 45: 222–42.

Lesnik-Oberstein, Karín (ed.) (2004) *Children's Literature: New Approaches*, Basingstoke: Palgrave Macmillan.

Lévi-Strauss, Claude (1966) *The Savage Mind*, Chicago: University of Chicago Press.

Lewis, David (1996) 'Pop-Ups and Fingle-Fangles: The History of the Picturebook', in Victor Watson and Morag Styles (eds) *Talking Pictures: Pictorial Texts and Young Readers*, London: Hodder & Stroughton, 5–22.

Lewis, David (2001) *Reading Contemporary Picturebooks: Picturing Text*, London: RoutledgeFalmer.

Lodge, David (2002) *Consciousness and the Novel: Connected Essays*, Cambridge, MA: Harvard University Press.

Lofting, Hugh (1920) *The Story of Doctor Dolittle*, London: Jonathan Cape.

Lofting, Hugh (1998) *The Story of Doctor Dolittle*, New York: Dell Publishing [rev. 1988].

Lowe, Lisa (1991) *Critical Terrains: French and British Orientalism*, Ithaca, NY: Cornell University Press.

Lowe, Virginia (2007) *Stories, Pictures and Reality: Two Children Tell*, London: Routledge.

Loxley, James (2007) *Performativity*, London: Routledge.

Lukens, Rebecca J. (2006) *A Critical Handbook of Children's Literature*, 8th edn, Boston: Allyn and Bacon [orig. 1976].

Lundin, Anne (2004) *Constructing the Canon of Children's Literature: Beyond Library Walls and Ivory Towers*, New York: Routledge.

Lyotard, Jean-François (1984) *The Postmodern Condition: A Report on Knowledge*, trans. Geoff Bennington and Brian Massumi, Manchester: Manchester University Press [orig. 1979].

McCallum, Robyn (1997) 'Cultural Solipsism, National Identities and the Discourse of Multiculturalism in Australian Picture Books', *Ariel: A Review of International English Literature*, 28.1: 101–16.

McCallum, Robyn (1999) *Ideologies of Identity in Adolescent Fiction: The Dialogic Construction of Subjectivity*, New York: Garland.

McCallum, Robyn (2004) 'Metafictions and Experimental Work', in Peter Hunt (ed.) *International Companion Encyclopedia of Children's Literature*, 2nd edn, Vol. 1, New York: Routledge, 587–98.

McCloud, Scott (1993) *Understanding Comics: The Invisible Art*, New York: HarperCollins.

McFarlane, Brian (1996) *Novel to Film: An Introduction to the Theory of Adaptation*, Oxford: Clarendon.

McGann, Jerome (1985) *The Beauty of Inflections: Literary Investigations in Historical Method and Theory*, Oxford: Clarendon Press.

McGavran, James Holt (ed.) (1991) *Romanticism and Children's Literature in 19th Century England*, Athens, GA: University of Georgia Press.

McGavran, James Holt (ed.) (1999) *Literature and the Child: Romantic Continuations, Postmodern Contestations*, Iowa: University of Iowa Press.

McGillis, Roderick (1985) 'The Child is Critic: Using Children's Responses in the University Classroom', *Children's Literature Association Quarterly*, 10.1: 4–6.

McGillis, Roderick (1996) *The Nimble Reader: Literary Theory and Children's Literature*, New York: Twayne.

McGillis, Roderick (2002a) '"Captain Underpants is My Hero": Things Have Changed – Or Have They?', *Children's Literature Association Quarterly*, 27.2: 62–70.

McGillis, Roderick (2002b) 'Trigger Pals: A Case History', in John Stephens (ed.) *Ways of Being Male: Representing Masculinities in Children's Literature and Film*, New York: Routledge, 185–99.

McGillis, Roderick (2003a) '"A Fairytale Is Just a Fairytale": George MacDonald and the Queering of Fairy', *Marvels & Tales*, 17.1: 86–99.

McGillis, Roderick (2003b) 'What Literature Was: The Canon Becomes Ploughshare', in Angel G. Cano Vela and Cristina Perez Valverde (eds) *Canon, Literatura Y Juvenil Y Otras Literaturas*, Cuenca: Ediciones de la Universidad de Castilla-La Mancha, 31–42.

McInally, Kate (2010) *Desiring Girls in Young Adult Fiction*, Basingstoke: Palgrave Macmillan.

Mackey, Margaret (2002) 'The Mediation and Multiplication of *Peter Rabbit*', in Margaret Mackey (ed.) *Beatrix Potter's Peter Rabbit: A Children's Classic at 100*, Lanham, MD: Children's Literature Association and Scarecrow Press, 173–88.

Mackey, Margaret (2005) '*Northern Lights* and Northern Readers: Background Knowledge, Affect Linking, and Literary Understanding', in Millicent Lenz and Carole Scott (eds) *His Dark Materials Illuminated: Critical Essays on Philip Pullman's Trilogy*, Detroit, MI: Wayne State University Press, 57–67.

McKinley, Robin (1997) *Rose Daughter*, New York: Greenwillow.

McLeod, Anne Scott (1998) 'Writing Backward: Modern Models in Historical Fiction', *The Horn Book Magazine*, 74: 26–33.

McLynn, Frank (1994) *Robert Louis Stevenson: A Biography*, London: Pimlico.

McNay, Lois (2000) *Gender and Agency: Reconfiguring the Subject in Feminist and Social Theory*, Oxford: Polity Press.

Magnus, Kathy Dow (2006) 'The Unaccountable Subject: Judith Butler and the Social Conditions of Intersubjective Agency', *Hypatia*, 21.2: 81–103.

Males, Mike A. (1998) *Framing Youth: Ten Myths About the Next Generation*, Monroe, ME: Common Courage Press.

Marryat, Emilia (1882) *Jack Stanley; or, The Young Adventurers*, London: Frederick Warne.

Marsh, Jackie and Millard, Elaine (2000) *Literacy and Popular Culture: Using Children's Culture in the Classroom*, London: Paul Chapman.

Martin, Peter (1985) 'Coming Soon: TV's New Boy Network', *The New York Times*, 11 August.

Martin, Wallace (1986) *Recent Theories of Narrative*, Ithaca, NY: Cornell University Press.

Masson, Jeffrey (1984) *The Assault on Truth: Freud's Suppression of the Seduction Theory*, New York: Farrar, Strauss & Giroux.

Mathijs, Ernest (2006) '*The Lord of the Rings* and Family: A View on Text and Reception', in Ernest Mathijs and Murray Pomerance (eds) *From Hobbits to Hollywood: Essays on Peter Jackson's* Lord of the Rings, Amsterdam: Rodopi, 41–63.

May, Jill P. (1986) 'The Hero's Woods: Pyle's *Robin Hood* and the Female Reader', *Children's Literature Association Quarterly*, 11.4: 197–200.

Mayne, William (1957) *A Grass Rope*, Oxford: Oxford University Press.

Meek, Margaret (1987) *How Texts Teach What Readers Learn*, Stroud: Thimble Press.

Meek, Margaret (1992) 'Literacy: Redescribing Reading', in Keith Kimberley, Margaret Meek and Jane Miller (eds) *New Readings: Contributions to an Understanding of Literacy*, London: A & C Black, 224–34.

Meek, Margaret (ed.) (2001) *Children's Literature and National Identity*, Stoke on Trent: Trentham.

Meek, Margaret and Watson, Victor (2005) *Coming of Age in Children's Literature*, London: Continuum.

Meek, Margaret, Warlow, Aidan and Barton, Griselda (eds) (1977) *The Cool Web: The Pattern of Children's Reading*, London: Random House.

Meletinsky, E., Nekludov, S., Novik, E. and Segal, D. (1974) 'Problems of the Structural Analysis of Fairytales', in Pierre Maranda (ed.) *Soviet Structural Folkloristics*, The Hague: Mouton, 73–139.

Mendlesohn, Farah (2009) *The Inter-Galactic Playground: A Critical Study of Children's and Teens' Science Fiction*, London: McFarland.

Metcalf, Eva-Maria (1996) 'Civilizing Manners and Mocking Mortality: Dr. Heinrich Hoffmann's *Struwwelpeter*', *The Lion and the Unicorn*, 20: 201–16.

Meyer, Stephenie (2006) *Twilight*, London: Atom.

Mickenberg, Julia L. (2006) *Learning from the Left: Children's Literature, the Cold War, and Radical Politics in the United States*, Oxford: Oxford University Press.

Mickenberg, Julia and Vallone, Lynne (eds) (2010) *The Oxford Handbook of Children's Literature*, New York: Oxford University Press.

Milburn, Colin (2002) 'Nanotechnology in the Age of Posthuman Engineering: Science Fiction as Science', *Configurations*, 10: 261–95.

Mills, C. Wright (1959) *The Sociological Imagination*, New York: Oxford University Press.

Mithen, Steven (2006) *The Singing Neanderthals: The Origins of Music, Language, Mind and Body*, Cambridge, MA: Harvard University Press.

Mo, Weimin and Shen, Wenju (1997) 'Reexamining the Issue of Authenticity in Picture Books', *Children's Literature in Education*, 28.2: 85–93.

Moore-Gilbert, Bart (1996) 'The Bhabhal of Tongues: Reading Kipling, Reading Bhabha', in Bart Moore-Gilbert (ed.) *Writing India, 1757–1990*, Manchester: Manchester University Press, 111–38.

Morris, David (1985) 'Gothic Sublimity', *New Literary History*, 16.2: 299–319.

Morrison, Toni (1992) *Playing in the Dark: Whiteness and the Literary Imagination*, Cambridge, MA: Harvard University Press.

Morson, Gary Saul and Emerson, Caryl (1990) *Mikhail Bakhtin: Creation of a Prosaics*, Stanford, CA: Stanford University Press.

Morss, John R. (1996) *Growing Critical: Alternatives to Developmental Psychology*, London: Routledge.

Moss, Anita and Stott, Jon (1986) *The Family of Stories: An Anthology of Children's Literature*, New York: Holt, Rinehart and Winston.

Mulvey, Laura (1975) 'Visual Pleasure and Narrative Cinema', *Screen*, 16.3: 6–18.

Murray, Simone (2008) 'Materializing Adaptation Theory: The Adaptation Industry', *Literature Film Quarterly*, 36.1: 4–20.

Musgrave, P. W. (1985) *From Brown to Bunter: The Life and Death of the School Story*, London: Routledge.

Myers, Mitzi (1986) 'Impeccable Governesses, Rational Dames, and Moral Mothers: Mary Wollstonecraft and the Female Tradition in Georgian Children's Books', *Children's Literature*, 14: 31–58.

Myers, Mitzi (1992) 'Little Girls Lost: Rewriting Romantic Childhood, Righting Gender and Genre', in Glenn Edward Sadler (ed.) *Teaching Children's Literature: Issues, Pedagogy, Resources*, New York: MLA, 131–42.

Myers, Mitzi (1999a) 'Child's Play as Women's Peace Work: Maria Edgeworth's "The Cherry Orchard", Historical Rebellion Narratives and Contemporary Cultural Studies', in Beverly Lyon Clark and Margaret Higgonet (eds) *Girls, Boys, Books, Toys: Gender in Children's Literature and Culture*, Baltimore, MA: Johns Hopkins University Press, 25–39.

Myers, Mitzi (1999b) 'Reading Children and Homeopathic Romanticism: Paradigm Lost, Revisionary Gleam, or "plus ça change, plus c'est la même chose"?', in James Holt McGavran (ed.) *Literature and the Child: Romantic Continuations, Postmodern Contestations*, Iowa: University of Iowa Press, 44–84.

Myers, Mitzi (2000) 'Literature for Children', *Encyclopedia Americana*, International edn, 561–79.

Myers, Mitzi and Knoepflmacher, U. C. (1997) '"Cross-Writing" and the Reconceptualizing of Children's Literary Studies', *Children's Literature*, 25.

Myers, Tony (2003) *Slavoj Žižek*, London: Routledge.

Napier, Susan J. (2005) *Anime from Akira to Howl's Moving Castle: Experiencing Contemporary Japanese Animation*, rev. edn, Basingstoke: Palgrave Macmillan.

Neale, Stephen (1995) 'Questions of Genre', in Oliver Boyd-Barrett and Chris Newbold (eds.) *Approaches to Media: A Reader*, London: Arnold, 460–72.

Nelson, Claudia (2003) *Little Strangers: Portrayals of Adoption and Foster Care in America, 1850–1929*, Bloomington, IN: Indiana University Press.

Nelson, Claudia (2007) *Family Ties in Victorian England*, New York: Praeger.

Nelson, Claudia and Vallone, Lynne (1994) *The Girl's Own: Cultural Histories of the Anglo-American Girl, 1830–1915*, Athens, GA: University of Georgia Press.

Nightingale, Andrea (2006) 'Mimesis: Ancient Greek Literary Theory', in Patricia Waugh (ed.) *Literary Theory and Criticism*, Oxford: Oxford University Press, 37–47.

Nikolajeva, Maria (1996) *Children's Literature Comes of Age: Toward a New Aesthetic*, New York: Garland.

Nikolajeva, Maria (1998) 'Exit Children's Literature?', *The Lion and the Unicorn*, 22.2: 221–36.

Nikolajeva, Maria (1999) *From Mythic to Linear: Time in Children's Literature*, Lanham, MD: Scarecrow Press.

Nikolajeva, Maria (2002) *The Rhetoric of Character in Children's Literature*, Lanham, MD: Scarecrow Press.

Nikolajeva, Maria (2005) *Aesthetic Approaches to Children's Literature: An Introduction*, Lanham, MD: Scarecrow Press.

Nikolajeva, Maria (2006) 'Fantasy', in Jack Zipes (ed.) *The Oxford Encyclopedia of Children's Literature*, Vol. 2, Oxford: Oxford University Press, 58–63.

Nikolajeva, Maria and Scott, Carole (2000) 'The Dynamics of Picturebook Communication', *Children's Literature in Education*, 31.4: 225–39.

Nikolajeva, Maria and Scott, Carole (2001) *How Picturebooks Work*, New York: Garland.

Nilsen, Alleen Pace and Bosmajian, Hamida (eds) (1996) 'Censorship in Children's Literature', *Para*Doxa: Studies in World Literature*, 2: 3–4.

Nobus, Danny (ed.) (1998) *Key Concepts in Lacanian Psychoanalysis*, New York: Other Press.

Nodelman, Perry (1985) 'Interpretation and the Apparent Sameness of Children's Novels', *Studies in the Literary Imagination*, 18.2: 285–96.

Nodelman, Perry (ed.) (1985–9) *Touchstones: Reflections on the Best in Children's Literature*, 3 vols, West-Lafayette, IN: Children's Literature Association.

Nodelman, Perry (1988) *Words about Pictures: The Narrative Art of Children's Picture Books*, Athens, GA: University of Georgia Press.

Nodelman, Perry (1992) 'The Other: Orientalism, Colonialism, and Children's Literature', *Children's Literature Association Quarterly*, 17.1: 29–35.

Nodelman, Perry (2007) 'The Precarious Life of Children's Literature Criticism', *Canadian Children's Literature*, 32.2: 1–16.

Nodelman, Perry (2008) *The Hidden Adult: Defining Children's Literature*, Baltimore, MA: Johns Hopkins University Press.

Nodelman, Perry and Reimer, Mavis (2003) *The Pleasures of Children's Literature*, 3rd edn, Boston: Allyn and Bacon [orig. 1992].

Ofsted (2007) *Poetry in Schools: Survey of Practice 2006/7*, London: Ofsted.

O'Malley, Andrew (2003) *The Making of the Modern Child: Children's Literature and Childhood in the Late Eighteenth Century*, London: Routledge.

Onega, Susana and Landa, José Ángel García (1996) *Narratology*, London: Longman.

Opie, Iona (1996) 'Playground Rhymes and the Oral Tradition', in Peter Hunt (ed.) *International Companion Encyclopedia of Children's Literature*, New York: Routledge, 177–89.

Opie, Iona and Opie, Peter (1973) *The Oxford Dictionary of Nursery Rhymes*, Oxford: Clarendon Press.

Opie, Iona and Opie, Peter (eds) (1992) *I Saw Esau: The Schoolchild's Pocket Book*, illus. Maurice Sendak, rev. edn, Cambridge, MA: Candlewick.

Pantaleo, Sylvia (2007) 'Scieszka's *The Stinky Cheese Man*: A Tossed Salad of Parodic Re-versions', *Children's Literature in Education*, 38.4: 277–95.

Papamichael, Stella (2007) Review of *The Golden Compass*, BBC Movies, 7 December, http://www.bbc.co.uk/films/2007/12/03/the_golden_compass_2007_review.shtml [10.06.08].

Parekh, Bikhu (2006) *Rethinking Multiculturalism: Cultural Diversity and Political Theory*, Basingstoke: Palgrave Macmillan.

Parry, Benita (1994) *Postcolonial Studies: A Materialist Critique*, London: Routledge.

Paul, Lissa (1998) *Reading Otherways*, Stroud: Thimble Press.

Paul, Lissa (2004) 'Feminism Revisited', in Peter Hunt (ed.) *International Companion Encyclopedia of Children's Literature*, 2nd edn, Vol.1, New York: Routledge, 140–53.

Payne, Michael and Schad, John (eds) (2003) *Life After Theory*, New York: Continuum.

Pearce, Philippa (1976) *Tom's Midnight Garden*, Harmondsworth: Puffin [orig. 1958].

Pennell, Beverley and Stephens, John (2002) 'Queering Heterotopic Spaces: Shyam Selvadurai's *Funny Boy* and Peter Wells *Boy Overboard*, in John Stephens (ed.) *Ways of Being Male: Representing Masculinities in Children's Literature and Film*, New York: Routledge, 164–84.

Petzold, Dieter (2006) 'Grotesque', in Jack Zipes (ed.) *The Oxford Encyclopedia of Children's Literature*, Vol. 2, Oxford: Oxford University Press, 182–3.

Philip, Neil (1981) *A Fine Anger: A Critical Introduction to the Work of Alan Garner*, London: Collins.

Phillips, Adam (1994) *On Kissing, Tickling, and Being Bored: Psychoanalytic Essays on the Unexamined Life*, Cambridge, MA: Harvard University Press.

Pickering, Samuel F. (1982) *John Locke and Children's Books in Eighteenth Century England*, Knoxville, TN: University of Tennessee Press.

Pickstone, John (2001) *Ways of Knowing: A New History of Science, Technology, and Medicine*, Chicago: University of Chicago Press.

Pierce, Bea (2006) 'The Girl with a Head Full of Words', http://www.20-20.org/blog/index.php?m=01&y=06 [10.11.08].

Pileggi, Mary S. and Patton, Cindy (eds) (2003) 'Bourdieu and Cultural Studies', *Cultural Studies*, 17: 3–4.

Plaistow, Jenny (ed.) (2006) *Owners of the Means of Instruction? Children's Literature: Some Marxist Perspectives*, Hatfield: University of Hertfordshire.

Plotz, Judith (2000) *Romanticism and the Vocation of Childhood*, Basingstoke: Macmillan.

Postman, Neil (1982) *The Disappearance of Childhood*, New York: Delacorte Press.

Potolsky, Matthew (2006) *Mimesis*, London: Routledge.

Potter, Troy (2007) '(Re)constructing Masculinity: Representations of Men and Masculinity in Australian Young Adult Literature', *Papers: Explorations into Children's Literature*, 17.1: 28–35.

Pouliot, Suzanne (2004) 'Children's Literature in Quebec and French-Speaking Canada', in Peter Hunt (ed.) *International Companion Encyclopedia of Children's Literature*, 2nd edn, Vol. 2, New York: Routledge, 1019–24.

Prasad, Leela, Bottigheimer, Ruth B. and Handoo, Lalita (eds) (2007) *Gender and Story in South India*, Albany, NY: SUNY Press.

Pratchett, Terry (1989) *Truckers*, New York: Doubleday.

Pratt, Mary Louise (1992) *Imperial Eyes: Travel Writing and Transculturation*, London: Routledge.

Prince, Gerald (1982) *Narratology: The Form and Functioning of Narrative*, Berlin: Mouton.

Prince, Gerald (2005) 'On a Postcolonial Narratology', in James Phelan and Peter J. Rabinowitz (eds) *Companion to Narrative Theory*, Oxford: Wiley-Blackwell, 372–81.

Propp, Vladimir (1968) *Morphology of the Folktale*, 2nd edn, trans. Laurence Scott, Austin: University of Texas Press [orig. 1928].

'Proppian Fairy Tale Generator' (2001) http://www.brown.edu/Courses/FR0133/Fairytale_Generator/gen.html [6.04.09].

Prout, Alan (ed.) (2005) *The Future of Childhood: Towards the Interdisciplinary Study of Children*, London: Routledge Falmer, 7–34.

Pullman, Philip (1995) *The Golden Compass*, New York: Knopf.

Pullman, Philip (1998) '"Let's Write It in Red": The Patrick Hardy Lecture', *Signal*, 85: 44–62.

Pullman, Philip (1999) *The Golden Compass*, unabridged audiobook, Listening Library/Random House.

Pullman, Philip (2007) 'My Golden Compass Sets a True Course', *Times Online*, 2 December, http://entertainment.timesonline.co.uk/tol/arts_and_entertainment/film/article2982762.ece [31.10.08].

Punter, David (ed.) (2001) *A Companion to the Gothic*, Oxford: Wiley-Blackwell.

Rabinow, Paul (ed.) (1984) *The Foucault Reader*, Harmondsworth: Penguin.

Randall, Don (2000) *Kipling's Imperial Boy: Adolescence and Cultural Hybridity*, Basingstoke: Palgrave.

Realebooks.com (2009) http://www.realebooks.com [10.11.08].

Reeve, Philip (2001) *Mortal Engines*, London: Scholastic.

Reimer, Mavis (2004) 'Canadian Children's Literature in English', in Peter Hunt (ed.) *International Companion Encyclopedia of Children's Literature*, Vol. 2, 2nd edn, London: Routledge, 1011–19.

Reynolds, Kimberley (1990) *Girls Only: Gender and Popular Children's Fiction in Britain 1880–1910*, Hemel Hempstead: Harvester Wheatsheaf.

Reynolds, Kimberley (1994) *Children's Literature in the 1890s and the 1990s*, Plymouth: Northcote House/British Council.

Reynolds, Kimberley (ed.) (2005) *Modern Children's Literature: An Introduction*, Basingstoke: Palgrave Macmillan.

Reynolds, Kimberley (2007) *Radical Children's Literature: Future Visions and Aesthetic Transformations in Juvenile Fiction*, Basingstoke: Palgrave Macmillan.

Reynolds, Kimberley (2009) 'Modernism', in Philip Nel and Lissa Paul (eds) *Keywords for Children's Literature*, New York: New York University Press.

Richards, Jeffrey (1988) *Happiest Days: The Public Schools in English Fiction*, Manchester: Manchester University Press.

Rimmon-Kenan, Shlomith (1983) *Narrative Fiction: Contemporary Poetics*, London: Methuen.

Roberts, Adam (2000) *Fredric Jameson*, London: Routledge.

Rollin, Lucy and West, Mark I. (1999) *Psychoanalytic Responses to Children's Literature*, Jefferson, NC: McFarland.

Roman, Leslie G., Christian-Smith, Linda K. and Ellsworth, Elizabeth (eds) (1988) *Becoming Feminine: The Politics of Popular Culture*, London: Falmer Press.

Rorty, Richard (2006) 'Looking Back at "Literary Theory"', in Haun Saussy (ed.) *Comparative Literature in an Age of Globalization*, Baltimore: Johns Hopkins University Press, 63–7.

Rose, Jacqueline (1984) *The Case of Peter Pan, or the Impossibility of Children's Fiction*, Basingstoke: Macmillan.

Rose, Margaret (1993) *Parody: Ancient, Modern and Post-Modern*, Cambridge: Cambridge University Press.

Rosenblatt, Louise (1938) *Literature as Exploration*, New York: Appleton-Century.

Rosenblatt, Louise (1978) *The Reader, the Text, the Poem: The Transactional Theory of the Literary Work*, Carbondale: Southern Illinois University Press.

Rosoff, Meg (2007) *What I Was*, London: Penguin.

Rowland, Susan (ed.) (2008) *Psyche and the Arts: Jungian Approaches to Music, Architecture, Literature, Painting and Film*, London: Routledge.

Rowling, J. K. (1997) *Harry Potter and the Philosopher's Stone*, London: Bloomsbury.

Royle, Nicholas (2003a) *Jacques Derrida*, London: Routledge.

Royle, Nicholas (2003b) *The Uncanny*, Manchester: Manchester University Press.

Rudd, David (1994) 'Shirley, the Bathwater, and Definitions of Children's Literature', *Papers: Explorations into Children's Literature*, 5.2–3: 88–103.

Rudd, David (2004a) 'Border Crossings: *Carrie's War*, Children's Literature, and Hybridity', in Sebastien Chapleau (ed.) *New Voices in Children's Literature Criticism*, Lichfield: Pied Piper, 63–70.

Rudd, David (2004b) 'Theorizing and Theories: The Conditions of Possibility of Children's Literature', in Peter Hunt (ed.) *International Companion Encyclopedia of Children's Literature*, 2nd edn, Vol.1, London: Routledge, 29–43.

Rudd, David (2006a) 'The Blot of Peter Pan', in C. Anita Tarr and Donna R. White (eds) *J. M. Barrie's Peter Pan In and Out of Time: A Children's Classic at 100*, Lanham, MD: Scarecrow Press, 263–78.

Rudd, David (2006b) 'Where It Was, There Shall Five Children Be: Staging Desire in *Five Children and It*', in Raymond E. Jones (ed.) *E. Nesbit's Psammead Books: Children's Classics at 100*, Lanham, MD: Scarecrow Press, 135–49.

Rudd, David (2007) 'Children's Literature and the Return to Rose', *Working Papers on the Web*, Sheffield Hallam University, http://extra.shu.ac.uk/wpw/childrens/Rudd.html [6.04.09].

Rudd, David (2008) 'An Eye for an "I": Neil Gaiman's *Coraline* and the Question of Identity', *Children's Literature and Education*, 39.3: 159–68.

Rudrum, David (2005) 'Living Alone: Solipsism in *Heart of Darkness*', *Philosophy and Literature*, 29.2: 409–27.

Russell, David (1988) 'The Common Experience of Adolescence: A Requisite for the Development of Young Adult Fiction', *Journal of Youth Services and Libraries*, 2.1: 58–63.

Rustin, Margaret and Rustin, Michael (1987) *Narratives of Love and Loss: Studies in Modern Children's Fiction*, London: Verso.

Ruwe, Donelle (ed.) (2005) *Culturing the Child 1690–1914: Essays in Memory of Mitzi Myers*, Lanham, MD: Children's Literature Association/Scarecrow Press.

Said, Edward (1978) *Orientalism*, London: Routledge and Kegan Paul.

Said, Edward (1993) *Culture and Imperialism*, London: Chatto & Windus.

Said, Edward (2004) *Humanism and Democratic Criticism*, New York: Columbia University Press.

Salih, Sarah (2004) *The Judith Butler Reader*, Oxford: Blackwell.

Scholastic (2008) *2008 Kids & Family Reading Report. Reading in the 21st Century: Turning the Page with Technology*, New York: Scholastic/Yankelovich, http://www.scholastic.com/readingreport [2.07.08].

Sedgwick, Eve Kosofsky (1985) *Between Men: English Literature and Male Homosocial Desire*, New York: Columbia University Press.

Sedgwick, Eve Kosofsky (1990) *Epistemology of the Closet*, Berkeley and Los Angeles, CA: University of California Press.

Sedgwick, Eve Kosofsky (1993) *Tendencies*, Durham, NC: Duke University Press.

Shavit, Zohar (1986) *Poetics of Children's Literature*, Athens, GA: University of Georgia Press.

Shen, Dan (2005) 'Why Contextual and Formal Narratologies Need Each Other', *JNT: Journal of Narrative Theory*, 35.2: 141–71.

Showalter, Elaine (1986) 'Feminist Criticism in the Wilderness', in Elaine Showalter (ed.) *The New Feminist Criticism: Essays on Women, Literature, and Theory*, London: Virago.

Simpkins, Scott (2001) *Literary Semiotics: A Critical Approach*, Lanham, MD: Lexington.

Sims, Sue and Clare, Hilary (eds) (2000) *The Encyclopedia of Girls' School Stories*, Aldershot: Ashgate.

Sinfield, Alan (1992) *Faultlines: Cultural Materialism and the Politics of Dissident Reading*, Oxford: Clarendon Press.

Singer, Dorothy G. (1972) 'Piglet, Pooh, and Piaget', *Psychology Today*, 6: 70–4.

Sipe, Lawrence R. and Pantaleo, Sylvia (2008) *Postmodern Picturebooks: Play, Parody, and Self-Referentiality*, New York: Routledge.

Sloan, Glenna Davis (1991) *The Child as Critic: Teaching Literature in Elementary, Middle Schools*, 3rd edn, New York: Teachers College Press [orig. 1984].

Smith, Bridget (1994) *Through Writing to Reading: Classroom Strategies for Supporting Literacy*, London: Routledge.

Smith, Paul (1988) *Discerning the Subject*, Minneapolis: University of Minnesota Press.

Smoodin, Eric (ed.) (1994) *Disney Discourse: Producing the Magic Kingdom*, London: Routledge.

Sony (2007) *The Golden Compass*, Sony PSP game: Sega.

Soper, Kate (1986) *Humanism and Anti-Humanism*, LaSalle, IL: Open Court.

Soper, Kate (1995) *What is Nature? Culture, Politics and the Non-Human*, Oxford: Blackwell.

South Bank Show (2003) *Philip Pullman*, Episode 13, Season 26, 9 March.

Spiegel, Lynn and Olsson, Jan (eds) (2004) *Television after TV: Essays on a Medium in Transition*, Durham, NC: Duke University Press.

Squier, Susan (2004) *Liminal Lives: Imagining the Human at the Frontiers of Biomedicine*, Durham, NC: Duke University Press.

Stainton Rogers, Rex and Stainton Rogers, Wendy (1992) *Stories of Childhood: Shifting Agendas of Child Concern*, London: Simon & Schuster.

Stallybrass, Peter and White, Allon (1986) *The Politics and Poetics of Transgression*, Ithaca, NY: Cornell University Press.

Stanger, Carol A. (1987) '*Winnie the Pooh* through a Feminist Lens', *The Lion and the Unicorn*, 11.2: 34–50.

Steedman, Carolyn (1995) *Strange Dislocations: Childhood and the Idea of Human Interiority, 1780–1930*, London: Virago Press.

Steig, Michael (1989) *Stories of Reading: Subjectivity and Literary Understanding*, Baltimore, MA: Johns Hopkins University Press.

Stein, Murray and Corbett, Lionel (eds) (1991) *Psyche's Stories: Modern Jungian Interpretations of Fairy Tales*, Wilmotte, IL: Chiron.

Steinberg, Shirley R. and Kincheloe, Joe L. (eds) (1998) *Kinder-Culture: The Corporate Construction of Childhood*, Boulder, CO: Westview Press.

Stephens, John (1992a) *Language and Ideology in Children's Fiction*, London: Longman.

Stephens, John (1992b) 'Modernism to Postmodernism, or The Line from Insk to Onsk: William Mayne's *Tiger's Railway*', *Paper: Explorations into Children's Literatures*, 3.2: 51–9.

Stephens, John (1996) 'Gender, Genre and Children's Literature', *Signal*, 79: 17–30.

Stephens, John (2002a) '"I'll Never Be the Same After that Summer": From Abjection to Subjective Agency in Teen Films', in Kerry Mallan and Sharyn Pearce (eds) *Youth Cultures: Texts, Images and Identities*, Westport, CT: Greenwood Press, 123–38.

Stephens, John (ed.) (2002b) *Ways of Being Male: Representing Masculinities in Children's Literature and Film*, New York: Routledge.

Stephens, John (2003) 'Witch-Figures in Recent Children's Fiction: The Subaltern and the Subversive', in Ann Lawson Lucas (ed.) *The Presence of the Past in Children's Literature*, Westport, CT: Praeger, 195–202.

Stephens, John and McCallum, Robyn (1998) *Retelling Stories, Framing Culture: Traditional Story and Metanarratives in Children's Literature*, New York: Garland.

Stephens, John and Watson, Ken (eds) (1994) *From Picture Book to Literary Theory*, Sydney: St Clair Press.

Sternberg, Meir (1992) 'Telling in Time (II): Chronology, Teleology, Narrativity', *Poetics Today*, 13.3: 463–541.

Stevenson, Deborah (2006) 'Biography', in Jack Zipes (ed.) *The Oxford Encyclopedia of Children's Literature*, Oxford: Oxford University Press, Vol. 1, 163.

Street, Douglas (1983) *Children's Novels and the Movies*, New York: Ungar.

Stryker, Susan (2005) 'Transgender', in Claude J. Summers (ed.) *glbtq: An Encyclopedia of Gay, Lesbian, Bisexual, Transgender and Queer Culture*, http://www/glbtq.com/social-sciences/gay-lesbian-queer-studies.html [10.12.08].

Styles, Morag (1998) *From the Garden to the Street: An Introduction to 300 Years of Poetry for Children*, London: Cassell.

Sugg, Richard (ed.) (1993) *Jungian Literary Criticism*, Evanston, IL: Northwestern University Press.

Sullivan III, C. W. (1996) 'High Fantasy', in Peter Hunt (2004) *International Companion Encyclopedia of Children's Literature*, London: Routledge, 436–46.

Summers, Claude J. (ed.) (2005) *glbtq: An Encyclopedia of Gay, Lesbian, Bisexual, Transgender, and Queer Culture*, http://www.glbtq.com/social-sciences/gay_lesbian_queer_studies. html [10.12.08].

Sutton-Smith, Brian (1981) 'Early Stories as Poetry', *Children's Literature*, 9: 137–50.

Tatar, Maria (1993) *Off with Their Heads! Fairy Tales and the Culture of Childhood*, Princeton: Princeton University Press.

Tatar, Maria (1997) *Lustmord: Sexual Murder in Weimar Germany*, Princeton, NJ: Princeton University Press.

Tatar, Maria (2003) *The Hard Facts of the Grimms' Fairy Tales*, 2nd edn, Princeton, NJ: Princeton University Press [orig. 1987].

Tatar, Maria (2006) *Secrets beyond the Door: The Story of Bluebeard and His Wives*, Princeton, NJ: Princeton University Press.

Tatar, Maria (2009) *Enchanted Hunters: The Power of Stories in Childhood*, New York: Norton.

Thacker, Deborah Cogan (2001) 'Feminine Language and the Politics of Children's Literature', *The Lion and the Unicorn*, 25.1: 3–16.

Thompson, Kirsten (2003) *Storytelling in Film and Television*, Cambridge, MA: Harvard University Press.

Thompson, Stith (1977) *The Folktale*, Berkeley: University of California Press [orig. 1946].

Thorpe, David (2006) *Hybrids*, London: HarperCollins.

Thurschwell, Pamela (2000) *Sigmund Freud*, London: Routledge.

Thwaite, Ann (1974) *Waiting for the Party: The Life of Frances Hodgson Burnett, 1849–1924*, London: Secker & Warburg.

Thwaite, Ann (1990) *A.A. Milne: His Life*, London: Faber and Faber.

Thwaite, Mary F. (1972) *From Primer to Pleasure in Reading: An Introduction to the History of Children's Books in England from the Invention of Printing to 1914 . . .* , 2nd edn, London: Library Association.

Thwaites, Tony, Davis, Lloyd and Mules, Warwick (1994) *Tools for Cultural Studies: An Introduction*, South Melbourne: Macmillan.

Tolkien, J. R. R. (1964) 'On Fairy-Stories', in *Tree and Leaf*, London: Allen & Unwin, 11–70 [orig. 1947].

Tonkin, Boyd (2005) 'A Week in Books', *The Independent*, 2 September.

Townsend, John Rowe (1965) *An Outline of English Chidlren's Literature*, London: Garnett Miller.

Townsend, John Rowe (1979) *A Sounding of Storytellers*, Harmondsworth: Kestrel.

Townsend, John Rowe (1990) *Written for Children: An Outline of English-Language Children's Literature*, 5th edn, London: Bodley Head [orig. 1965].

Townsend, John Rowe (1994) *Trade & Plumb-Cake Forever, Huzza! The Life and Work of John Newbery 1713–1767*, Cambridge: Colt Books.

Townshend, Dale (2008) 'The Haunted Nursery: 1764–1830', in Anna Jackson *et al.* (eds) *The Gothic in Children's Literature: Haunting the Boundries*, New York: Routledge, 15–38.

Trites, Roberta Seelinger (1997) *Waking Sleeping Beauty: Feminist Voices in Children's Novels*, Iowa City: University of Iowa Press.

Trites, Roberta Seelinger (2000) *Disturbing the Universe: Power and Repression in Adolescent Literature*, Iowa City: University of Iowa Press.

Trites, Roberta, Seelinger (2007) *Twain, Alcott and the Birth of the Adolescent Reform Novel*, Iowa City: University of Iowa Press.

Tuastad, Dag (2003) 'Neo-Orientalism and the New Barbarian Thesis: Aspects of Symbolic Violence in the Middle East Conflict(s)', *Third World Quarterly*, 24.4: 591–9.

Tucker, Nicholas (1972) 'How Children Respond to Fiction', *Children's Literature in Education*, 3.3: 48–56.

Tucker, Nicholas (1976) *Suitable for Children? Controversies in Children's Literature*, London: Chatto & Windus, for Sussex University Press.

Tucker, Nicholas (1981) *The Child and the Book: A Psychological and Literary Exploration*, Cambridge: Cambridge University Press.

Tucker, Nicholas (2002a) *The Rough Guide to Children's Books 0–5 Years*, London: Rough Guides.

Tucker, Nicholas (2002b) *The Rough Guide to Children's Books 5–11 Years*, London: Rough Guides.

Tucker, Nicholas (ed.) (2004) *School Stories: From Bunter to Buckeridge*, 2nd edn, Lichfield: Pied Piper.

Tucker, Nicholas (2006) 'Depressive Stories for Children', *Children's Literature in Education*, 37.3: 199–210.

Tucker, Nicholas and Eccleshare, Julia (2002) *The Rough Guide to Books for Teenagers*, London: Rough Guides.

TYA (2009) 'Events', http://www.tya-uk.org/events.asp [6.03.09].

Vallone, Lynne (1995) *Disciplines of Virtue: Girls' Culture in the Eighteenth and Nineteenth Centuries*, New Haven, CT: Yale University Press.

Vallone, Lynne (ed.) (1996) 'Children's Literature and New Historicism', *Children's Literature Association Quarterly*, 21.3: 102–32, special issue.

Vallone, Lynne (1998) 'Children's Literature within and without the Profession', *College Literature*, 25.2: 137–45.

Vallone, Lynne (2001) *Becoming Victoria*, New Haven, CT: Yale University Press.

Vallone, Lynne and Nelson, Claudia (eds) (1994) *The Girls' Own: Cultural Histories of the Anglo-American Girl, 1830–1915*, Athens, GA: University of Georgia Press.

Van Haute, Phillipe (2001) *Against Adaptation: Lacan's 'Subversion of the Subject'*, New York: Other Press.

Vanden Bossche, Chris (2005) 'What Did Jane Eyre Do? Ideology, Agency, Class and the Novel', *Narrative*, 13.1: 46–66.

Virilio, Paul (2003) *Art and Fear*, trans. Julie Rose, New York: Continuum.

Waetjen, Jarrod and Gibson, Timothy A. (2007) 'Harry Potter and the Commodity Fetish: Activating Corporate Readings in the Journey from Text to Commercial Intertext', *Communication and Critical/Cultural Studies*, 4.1: 3–26.

Walby, Sylvia (1990) *Theorizing Patriarchy*, Oxford: Blackwell.

Wall, Barbara (1991) *The Narrator's Voice: The Dilemma of Children's Fiction*, Basingstoke: Macmillan.

Waller, Alison (2008) *Constructing Adolescence in Fantastic Realism*, London: Routledge.

Ware, Vron and Back, Les (2002) *Out of Whiteness: Color, Politics, and Culture*, Chicago: University of Chicago Press.

Warhol, Robyn (1989) *Gendered Interventions: Narrative Discourse in the Victorian Novel*, New Brunswick, NY: Rutgers University Press.

Warlow, Aidan (1977) 'Alternative Worlds Available', in Margaret Meek, Aidan Warlow and Griselda Barton (eds) *The Cool Web: The Pattern of Children's Reading*, London: Random House, 97–102.

Warner, Marina (1994a) *From the Beast to the Blonde: On Fairy Tales and Their Tellers*, London: Chatto & Windus.

Warner, Marina (1994b) *Managing Monsters: Six Myths of Our Time*, London: Vintage.

Warner, Marina (ed.) (1994c) *Wonder Tales: Six Stories of Enchantment*, London: Chatto & Windus.

Warner, Marina (1998) *No Go the Bogeyman: Scaring, Lulling and Making Mock*, London: Chatto & Windus.

Watson, Victor (ed.) (2001) *The Cambridge Guide to Children's Books in English*, Cambridge: Cambridge University Press.

Waugh, Patricia (1984) *Metafiction: The Theory and Practice of Self-Conscious Fiction*, London: Routledge.

Weinreich, Torben (2000) *Chidlren's Literature: Art or Pedagogy?* Trans. Don Bartlett, Frederiksberg: Roskilde University Press.

Weitz, Chris (2008) *The Golden Compass*, DVD, NewLine Home Entertainment [orig. 2007].

Wellek, René (1995) 'The New Criticism: Pro And Contra', in William Spurlin and Michael Fischer (eds) *The New Criticism and Contemporary Literary Theory: Connections and Continuities*, New York: Garland, 55–72.

Wellek, René and Warren, Austin (1956) *Theory of Literature*, New York: Harcourt, Brace [orig. 1942].

Wells, Paul (2002) *Animation: Genre and Authorship*, London: Wallflower Press.

Wertham, Fredric (1954) *Seduction of the Innocent*, New York: Rinehart.

West, Mark I. (1988) *Trust Your Children: Voices against Censorship in Children's Literature*, 2nd edn, New York: Neal-Schuman.

Westall, Robert (1979) 'How Real Do You Want Your Realism?', *Signal*, 28: 34–46.

Westman, Karen (2007) 'Children's Literature and Modernism: The Space Between', *Children's Literature Association Quarterly*, 32.4: 283–6.

Westwater, Martha (2000) *Giant Despair Meets Hopeful: Kristevan Readings in Adolescent Fiction*, Edmonton, Alberta: University of Alberta Press.

Wilkie-Stibbs, Christine (2002) *The Feminine Subject in Children's Literature*, New York: Routledge.

Wilkie-Stibbs, Christine (2004a) 'Childhood, Didacticism and the Gendering of British Children's Literature', in Peter Hunt (ed.) *International Companion Encyclopedia of Children's Literature*, New York: Routledge, 352–61.

Wilkie-Stibbs, Christine (2004b) 'Intertextuality and the Child Reader', in Peter Hunt (ed.) *International Companion Encyclopedia of Children's Literature*, 2nd edn, Vol.1, New York: Routledge, 179–90.

Wilkie-Stibbs, Christine (2006) 'Borderland Children: Reflection on Narratives of Abjection', *The Lion and the Unicorn*, 30.3: 316–36.

Wilkie-Stibbs, Christine (2008) *The Outside Child: In and Out of the Book*, London: Routledge.

Williams, Jay (1978) *The Practical Princess, and Other Liberating Fairy Tales*, New York: Parent's Magazine Press.

Wilson, Budge (1990) *My Cousin Clarette and Other Stories*, St Lucia: University of Queensland Press.

Wilson, Michael (1998) 'Legend and Life: "The Boyfriend's Death" and "The Mad Axeman"', *Folklore*, 109: 89–95.

Wimsatt, W. K. (1970) *The Verbal Icon: Studies in the Meaning of Poetry*, London: Methuen [orig. 1954].

Winnicott, D. W. (1971) *Playing and Reality*, Harmondsworth: Penguin.

Winnicott, D. W. (1977) *The Piggle: An Account of the Psychoanalytic Treatment of a Little Girl*, Harmondsworth: Penguin.

Wittig, Monique (1992) 'One Is Not Born a Woman', in *The Straight Mind and Other Essays*, Boston: Beacon Press, 9–20.

Wojcik-Andrews, Ian (2000) *Children's Films: History, Ideology, Pedagogy, Theory*, New York: Garland.

Wolf, Shelby Anne and Heath, Shirley Brice (1992) *The Braid of Literature: Children's Worlds of Reading*, London: Harvard University Press.

Wood, David (2009) 'Theatre: Writing for Children', in *The Children's Writers' & Artists' Yearbook*, London: A & C Black.

Woodward, Kay (2007) *The Golden Compass: Lyra's World*, New York: Scholastic.

Wright, Nicholas (2003) *Philip Pullman's His Dark Materials*, London: Nick Hern Books.

Young, Robert (ed.) (1981) *Untying the Text: A Post-Structuralist Reader*, London: Routledge & Kegan Paul.

Young, Robert J. C. (1995) *Colonial Desire: Hybridity in Theory, Culture and Race*, London: Routledge.

Zacharek, Stephanie (2007) Review of *The Golden Compass*, *Salon*, 7 December, http://www.salon.com/ent/movies/review/2007/12/07/compass/index.html?CP=IMD [10.06.08].

Zipes, Jack (1979) *Breaking the Magic Spell: Radical Theories of Folk and Fairy Tales*, London: Heinemann.

Zipes, Jack (1983) *Fairy Tales and the Art of Subversion: The Classical Genre for Children and the Process of Civilization*, London: Heinemann.

Zipes, Jack (ed.) (1986) *Don't Bet on the Prince: Contemporary Feminist Fairy Tales in North America and England*, Aldershot: Gower.

Zipes, Jack (1993) *The Trials and Tribulations of Little Red Riding Hood: Versions of the Tale in Sociocultural Context*, 2nd edn, London: Routledge.

Zipes, Jack (1994) *Fairy Tale as Myth, Myth as Fairy Tale*, Lexington: University of Kentucky Press.

Zipes, Jack (1995) *Fairy Tales and the Art of Subversion: The Classical Genre for Children and the Process of Civilization*, London: Routledge.

Zipes, Jack (1997) *Happily Ever After: Fairy Tales, Children, and the Culture Industry*, New York: Routledge.

Zipes, Jack (2001) *Sticks and Stones: The Troublesome Success of Children's Literature from Slovenly Peter to Harry Potter*, New York: Routledge.

Zipes, Jack (2006a) *Why Fairy Tales Stick: The Evolution and Relevance of a Genre*, New York: Routledge.

Zipes, Jack (ed.) (2006b) *The Oxford Encyclopedia of Children's Literature*, Oxford: Oxford University Press.

Žižek, Slavoj (1989) *The Sublime Object of Ideology*, London: Verso.

Žižek, Slavoj (1991) *Looking Awry: An Introduction to Lacan through Popular Culture*, Cambridge, MA: MIT Press.

Žižek, Slavoj (1994) *The Metastases of Enjoyment*, New York: Verso.

Žižek, Slavoj (1998) 'The Seven Veils of Fantasy', in Dany Nobus (ed.) *Key Concepts of Lacanian Psychoanalysis*, New York: Other Press, 190–218.

Zornado, Joseph L. (2001) *Inventing the Child: Culture, Ideology, and the Story of Childhood*, New York: Garland.

Zunshine, Lisa (2006) *Why We Read Fiction: Theory of Mind and the Novel*, Columbus: Ohio State University Press.

INDEX

Note: page numbers in **_bold italic_** refer to an entry in Part II, Names and terms; page numbers in _italic_ refer to a detailed discussion of the entry.